Stephen Vincent Benét

By the Same Author

The Apprenticeship of Ernest Hemingway

Editor

The Best Short Stories of World War II

Stephen Vincent Benét

The Life and Times of an
American Man of Letters
1898-1943

by Charles A. Fenton

New Haven, Yale University Press
1958

To My Wife

Acknowledgments

THE practice of biography has received prodigal comment and ample edict from literary critics and historians. The biographers themselves have also been garrulous on the subject of their trade. Mindful that it is not traditionally included among the sanctified triumverate of poetry, drama, and fiction, the biographers have nevertheless insisted that theirs too is an art. If it is an art, however, biography is as much the art of unscrupulous theft as of narrative and portrait.

For no biography was ever composed without the theft of material and wisdom and time which belonged to others. This is doubly true of contemporary biography, and I have thieved the hours and memories of innumerable friends and kin and associates of my subject. I have made poor acknowledgment of many of my obligations in the notes. Some from whom I stole, however, were particularly vulnerable and notably generous.

For their assistance and their patience I am greatly indebted to Mrs. Philip Barry, Bernice Baumgarten, Alfred Bellinger, Laura Benét, the late Carl Brandt, Henry S. Canby, Henry Carter, John F. Carter, Jr., Basil Davenport, Mrs. Benjamin Abbott Dickson, Effingham Evarts, John and Margaret Farrar, Mrs. Valentine Mitchell Gammell, Mrs. John M. Harlan, Thomas P. Hazard, C. D. Jackson, Andrew D. T. Jones, Mrs. Matthew Josephson, the late Christopher LaFarge, Florence Locke, Fred W. Lorch, Henry Luce, Archibald MacLeish, Robert E. McClure, Douglas Moore, Mr. and Mrs. Richard E. Myers, Robert Nathan, Mrs. Neill Phillips, Norman Rosten, Muriel Rukeyser, and Culbreth Sudler.

The biographer also loots the shelves of libraries and the files of business houses. I was greatly assisted by the knowledge and labor of Charles Abbott, the Lockwood Memorial Library, University of Buffalo; Elliott E. Andrews, Librarian, Providence *Journal;* Rodney Armstrong, Librarian, Davis Library, the Phillips Exeter Academy; Mrs. Lillian C. Bezanson, University Archives, State University of Iowa; William H. Bond, Curator of Manuscripts, the Houghton Library, Harvard University; Alice H. Bonnell, assistant Librarian, Special Collections, Columbia University Libraries; John W. Bonner, Jr., Special Collections Librarian, the University Libraries, the University of Georgia; Jean D. Cochran, Director, Augusta Regional Library; Frederic S. Cushing, Assistant Director, College Department, Rinehart and Co.; Kent R. Greenfield, Chief Historian, Office of the Chief of Military History; Hermann Hagedorn, Theodore Roosevelt House; Mildred D. Johnson, Secretary to the President, Gettysburg College; Herman Kahn, Director, Franklin D. Roosevelt Library; Ken McCormick, Doubleday and Co.; David C. Mearns, Chief, Manuscripts Division, the Library of Congress; May Morris, Librarian, Dickinson College Library; Wade H. Nichols, Jr., Editor-in-chief, *Redbook;* John R. Russell, Director of Libraries, the University of Rochester; Ellen Shaffer, Rare Book Librarian, the Free Library of Philadelphia; Edward Weeks, the *Atlantic;* John H. Washburn, Chairman, Executive Council, Alpha Delta Phi; Neda M. Westlake,

Assistant Curator, Rare Book Collection, University of Pennsylvania; Katherine S. White, the *New Yorker;* and Roberta Yerkes, Yale University Press.

I owe particular debts to Donald C. Gallup, Curator, Yale Collection of American Literature; Chester Kerr, Secretary, the Yale University Press; Norman Holmes Pearson, of Yale; Ronald Sohigian, Class of 1958; and Dorothy W. Bridgwater, Jane W. Hill, Barbara D. Simison, and Jean Chandler Smith, Assistant Reference Librarians, Yale University Library. For the generous use of their own Benét research, both published and unpublished, I am grateful to Dearing Lewis, Gladys Maddocks, Lois Milani, and Eleanor M. Sickels.

This biography could not have been written, quite literally, without the support and encouragement of Mrs. Stephen Vincent Benét. She not only tolerated but encouraged its invasions. I am more indebted to her than I can properly say.

The biographer, if he is fortunate, is the beneficiary of those who subsidize the assignment which he would perform less thoroughly without their bounty. I owe much to both the John Simon Guggenheim Memorial Foundation and to Yale University. The latter gave me not only the leisure of a Morse Fellowship but also, even more valuable, the professional and personal support unique to the atmosphere of a university. Biography is less an art than a collaboration. All these were my collaborators.

CHARLES A. FENTON

New Haven, Conn.
December 29, 1957

Contents

Acknowledgments   vii

1. The Colonel's House   1
2. Georgia   21
3. Bright College Years   45
4. War   65
5. The Beginning of Wisdom   92
6. Ballads In Grub Street   119
7. The Literary Life   143
8. Goodly Fellowship   164
9. John Brown's Body: One   180
10. John Brown's Body: Two   205
11. The Wages of Cinema   231
12. Younger Poets And Other Americans   253
13. Angry Poet   274
14. Man of Letters   297
15. Academician   314
16. Western Star   333
17. Casualty   354

Notes   375

Index   411

Illustrations

Frontispiece. Benét in his study at Stonington.

A drawing by William Rose Benét of his father and his younger brother appears opposite page 6. Illustrations 1–12 are grouped in a section following page 230.

1a. Brigadier General Stephen Vincent Benét (1827–1895). The poet's grandfather, later Chief of Ordnance, United States Army, as a young lieutenant shortly after graduation from West Point.

b. Colonel James Walker Benét (1857–1928). The poet's father, a career officer in the United States Army from his graduation from West Point in 1880 until his retirement in 1921.

c. Colonel Benét's "Only" Children. Laura, Stephen Vincent, and William Rose, in 1900.

d. Mrs. James Walker Benét (d. 1940). The poet's mother, photographed in 1915 when the Benéts were stationed at Augusta.

2. Colonel James W. Benét, U.S.A. (Ret.). In 1927, the year before his death.

3a. Stephen Vincent Benét, at the age of four, sitting in the breech of a 16-inch gun at the Watervliet (N.Y.) Arsenal, where his father was stationed from 1899 to 1904.

b. Two years later, on the lawn in front of Officers Row at the Watervliet Arsenal.

c. In 1907, aged nine.

4*a.* Stephen Vincent Benét and his brother, William Rose Benét, stand together on the Yale campus in the fall of 1915, the younger Benét a freshman, his older brother, a member of the Class of 1907, already a well-known poet and an assistant editor of *Century Magazine.*

b. *Yale Literary Magazine* Board, 1919. Robert M. Coates, managing editor; J. J. Schieffelin, memorabilia; Thornton Wilder, book reviews; Donald M. Campbell, editor's table; Stephen Vincent Benét, chairman; Frank P. Heffelfinger, business manager.

5. Benét in 1921, just before his marriage to Rosemary Carr.

6*a.* Benét's uncle, Laurence V. Benét, managing director of Hotchkiss et Cie.

b. Carl Brandt, Benét's literary agent and close friend from 1922 until the poet's death in 1943.

c. Benét and his wife Rosemary, in Paris in 1928, just after *John Brown's Body* had been finished.

7*a.* The stone studio on Henry Canby's country property in Killingworth, Conn., where Benét wrote most of *Western Star.*

b. Benét reads to his two oldest children, Tommy and Stephanie Jane.

8*a.* Rosemary and Stephen Benét in 1934, a few months after their collaboration on *A Book of Americans.*

b. Benét and his publishers, John Farrar and Stanley Rinehart, posed for a publicity photograph, rejoicing over the great success of "The Devil and Daniel Webster."

9a–b. The Benét family at their summer home in Stonington, Conn., during the summers of 1941 and 1942.

10. Benét and Raymond Massey, who acted in and read several of the poet's wartime radio scripts, stand obediently for an NBC photographer in June 1942.

11. *Life's* photograph of Benét, taken in 1942 in connection with the magazine's publication of his Fourth of July radio script, *Listen to the People.*

12a. Benét's son at the exhibition of his father's books and manuscripts in the Yale Library in 1944.

b. The Liberty ship *Stephen Vincent Benét* after its launching in San Francisco in 1944.

This flesh was seeded from no foreign grain

But Pennsylvania and Kentucky wheat,

And it has soaked in California rain

And five years tempered in New England sleet.

JOHN BROWN'S BODY

1. The Colonel's House

I cannot agree with those who say that the military mind is narrow and insensitive.[1]

THE new Colonel and his family, in 1907, were not an easy household to define. They should have presented no difficulties to the practiced assessments of junior officers and their watchful wives. The Colonel, after all, appeared to be supremely recognizable; he was old army. His father, the Brigadier—for whom the youngest grandson, Stephen Vincent Benét was named—had been Chief of Ordnance for seventeen years, from 1874 until his retirement in 1891. The son—the Colonel, that is—had himself been Ordnance almost continuously since he, too, finished at the Point, Class of 1880. The Colonel had the reputation, and certainly the appearance, of being a first-class officer. He had lingered in grade as lieutenant and captain less tiresomely long than many of his classmates. . . . but if you were a good officer *and* your father was the Brigadier, well, that was the army and only to be expected.

And as a young officer, to be sure, in the 1880's and 1890's, Colonel Benét had had his quota of abrupt transfers and separations from his family and the provincial backwaters of Ordnance. He'd done his share, and more,

1

of the long tours of subordinate duty at Frankford Arsenal, at Watervliet, at Rock Island, and at the Bethlehem Iron Works where young Stephen had been born, nine years before, on July 22, 1898. Colonel James Walker Benét had earned the new assignment to Benicia Arsenal, on California's Suisan Bay.

His fellow officers in Ordnance, on the other hand, regarded his present duty as less desirable than the earlier posts. It was characteristic of the Colonel, however, that he responded with enthusiasm to those very characteristics of Benicia which most dismayed his comrades. They were distressed by its remoteness, two hours inland by train and ferryboat from San Francisco; the Colonel was delighted by the isolation. The vast distance from Washington made Benicia seem a professional banishment to the average officer; the Colonel could never be sufficiently separated from the red tape and bureaucracy of the capital. He was enchanted by his new command. He set to work improving the grounds and extending the natural charm of the locale.

"It wasn't like an arsenal," one of their week-end visitors remembered years later. "It was like the back-drop of a romantic play, all pepper trees and acacias, and fountains, and pillared porches." [2]

It was pleasant to have the Commandant's quarters occupied again by an attractive family, with young people and parties and a gracious hostess. The Colonel's predecessor had been a hard-drinking bachelor who used to wangle exasperating extensions of his Benicia command, often at the very moment his juniors anticipated his departure; he gave neither tone nor dignity to the spacious, broad-verandahed house. Certainly the Benét family brought both warmth and distinction to the Post. The Colonel was competent and just; clearly he was a gentle-

2

man, and army to the fingertips. His lady was charming and hospitable.

The three Benét children, Laura, William Rose, and Stephen Vincent, were delightful—odd, yet nice, of course, that they should be so scattered in age, Laura an undergraduate at Vassar, William twenty in 1907, Stephen only eight—but there had never been a Commandant's house so overflowing with books and magazines, and the callers and guests were likely to be young instructors from the university at Berkeley, and poets, and a red-headed Yale classmate of the oldest Benét boy who was said to be a socialist. His name was Lewis, Sinclair Lewis . . . no doubt he was very intelligent, and the Benét children themselves were all very intelligent, and delightful, but . . . it was a difficult household for the junior officers and their watchful wives to assess.

Colonel Benét was thoroughly conscious of the gently puzzling contradictions of his family. Like most of what he observed in life, the contradictions amused and interested him, but they did not trouble him. His wife was an unfailing richness, and he possessed precisely the kind of children he would have chosen, had so rational an arrangement been possible; indeed, in his quiet way he had contributed rather more than most American fathers of the period to the essential shaping of his household.

He himself was articulate, civilized, and widely read. Since he adored his children, quietly, and was a father to be both revered and respected, it was not unnatural that all three of their children should themselves aspire, in their individual ways, to be similarly articulate, civilized, and widely read. His wife was talented and lovely; the fluency of their three children was foreshadowed in her immense correspondence and occasional verse. The pleasures of domesticity were consolidated by an excellent Chinese cook and a diligent Irish maid, and there was an enlisted man assigned to the Colonel's family as driver.

It was a wonderfully pleasant life, the old army, if you had a vein of irony to shield you from the disappointments and stupidities, and a deep love of poetry to protect you from becoming a barbarian or an alcoholic, and a charming wife and children for garrison companionship. The Colonel was entertained by the incongruity of an intellectual career officer with an artistic family. He liked to refer to himself, in civilian company, as a member of the brutal and licentious soldiery, "with," his youngest son remembered many years later, "that sidewise glance that hesitated for just one instant to see if you understood, and, if you didn't, passed on." [3]

Despite his irony the Colonel was a proud man; or, more likely, the irony was merely to provide decent reticences for his emotions. He was proud of his ancestry, with its long heritage of Minorcan vitality and New World leadership, and proud, too, of his profession. His father, the Brigadier, had held the first appointment to West Point from the new state of Florida, in 1845, and was graduated third in his class. During his subsequent forty-two years of active service General Stephen Vincent Benét had shaped the Ordnance Department into an effective technological unit, and had made it a haven of research, publication, and practical application in the long decades after the Civil War, when Congress penny-pinched the army into little more than a frontier police. He had been nimble in the politics of Washington, able to restrain in himself, at least in his official role, the lively sense of the ridiculous which seemed to flower in all the Benét males.

4

Each of the Brigadier's two sons, James and Laurence, born respectively in 1857 and 1863, had this same contempt for pretense. It was to prevent the elder—James, the Colonel—from becoming Chief of Ordnance, but in Laurence the quality was more restrained. Laurence Benét had chosen the civilian side of Ordnance as his career. He was now an official of La Société Hotchkiss et Cie, the international munitions makers. In this year 1907, of course, both he and the Company were making a great deal of money. Laurence Benét, being a shrewd analyst of European politics and continental nationalism, could look forward to making a good deal more money in the near future. The Colonel nevertheless preferred the army, though it would be pleasant, perhaps, if one of his own boys should join their childless Uncle Larry in the more profitable field of commercial firearms.

The eldest of the Colonel's two sons, William Rose, had been intended from the beginning for the army. Thus, as part of the strategy which it was hoped would lead to a West Point appointment, he had enrolled in the Sheffield Scientific School at Yale rather than in Yale College, where his natural abilities would have been better placed. The appointment never materialized, however; the family always felt that the dispatch with which Theodore Roosevelt filled all the places had cost William a just opportunity. It was apparent, however, that William's talents and aspirations were really in the direction of literature, evidently for some contemporary Grub Street where the Benét sagacity would nevertheless permit him to prosper.

William was already getting his professional bearings, even though he had only just graduated from Yale. He wrote delightful verse and in fact had a real facility for every literary genre and a genuine taste and enthusiasm for all things artistic. The Colonel was proud of his oldest son, and amused by the adoration with which his wife and daughter engulfed Billy. He hoped it would prepare the boy for dealing intelligently with those inevitable successors who were certain to give him less selfless adoration. He doubted that it would.

It was too early to visualize a career for his youngest boy, Stephen. The eight-year-old's truly insatiable appetite for the printed word indicated no real affinity for Laurence's guns and cosmopolitan salesmanship. The family legend that at the age of five Stephen had read a translation of Dante—which he discovered, magnificently illustrated, among the Colonel's books, and subsequently referred to as Dant—was an exaggeration in degree only. It was wholly true, on the other hand, that he had also found Shakespeare on the same shelves and read the rich lines with zest if without total understanding.

"I like that man's writing," he had said at dinner that night, parroting the idiom he heard from all his elders. "Has he written anything else?"

The little boy worshiped his older brother and sister, and had already begun to imitate them by writing verse. He was a delightful child, uncomplaining under frequent illnesses, serious without being solemn, and precocious without the repellent disunities of the prodigy. "I have had my hair cut," he wrote his mother in 1909, just before his eleventh birthday, "and much resemble a convict. Prince is a little sick and sends love. Is everything all right with you? The radishes are half dead and one tomato is dying. Raffles has been caught by a young artist. God bless you all." The Colonel, however, had no favorites among his three children.

"I've been very lucky," he told people who inquired

Father

Drawn by
WRB at
Benicia,
California

Steve

A contemporary drawing by William Rose Benét of his
father and brother at Benicia

about the parental problems of raising three children so separated in age. "You see, I've really had three 'only' children."

It was apparent to others, however, both then and later, that the resemblance between the Colonel and Stephen was substantial. The children shared certain common traits—particularly their rich responsiveness to literature in general and to poetry in particular. They all possessed deep courtesy, profound family pride, and a sense of comfortable security. These characteristics and values were a tightly-woven blend of the inherited and the acquired. They came in equal measure from each parent.

Laura's grace and William's romantic good looks, on the other hand, were more directly the gift of Mrs. Benét. Stephen seemed rather to have inherited his physical qualities from the Colonel. He not only had, in greater measure than his brother or sister, their father's slight reserve, but he even displayed in an uncanny way an identical physical symptom of this shyness; like the Colonel, he had the curious mannerism, already apparent to the family and their friends, of seeming to slide crab-like into a room rather than entering it directly. He also had—certainly in larger proportion than his brother, and very early in life—the same calm poise and self-discipline.

Above all, Stephen responded most fully to his father's profession and the atmosphere in which it was practiced. "I was born and brought up in the Army—and in an intelligent branch of the army, the ordnance," he said with pride in the late 1930's, when it was more fashionable to belittle the military than to speak of a family association with them. "My grandfather developed the rim-fire cartridge, my father was in charge of the first

7

16-inch gun ever made in this country, my uncle helped invent one of the earliest light machine guns, the Benét-Mercier." Stephen was never either bored or offended by army life. "It was an intensely interesting world for a child to grow up in," he wrote much later, in one of his short stories, "a world with a code and a flavor all its own." [4]

Stephen never doubted, during his maturity, that he would happily have gone to West Point at eighteen had not scarlet fever weakened his eyes when he was three. He studied his father's junior officers with interest, noting their various professional qualities, and his own collection of toy soldiers—over four hundred of them—were all carefully catalogued. During the 1930's, when an important part of his income came from the public lecturing for which he generally had such distaste, he always looked forward to the annual talks he gave to the cadets at West Point on *John Brown's Body* and Civil War history.

"I lectured at West Point two days last week," he told a friend in 1934, "and as an old Army boy was filled with nostalgia." [5]

His hosts on that occasion showed him the oil portrait of his grandfather, hanging with the pictures of the other distinguished graduates of the Academy, and in the museum he saw an early model of the Benét-Mercier machine gun. His children were baptized in the West Point chapel; the committal service at his own funeral in 1943 was conducted by a former chaplain of the United States Military Academy.

Like his father, to be sure, Stephen had no illusions about the Regular Army. "That life produces, at its best," he said many years later, speaking explicitly of the Colonel, "a remarkably fine type of human being. At its best, I know—I have seen the worst of it also." [6]

Stephen was proud of his father's skill in handling men. Acute as he was, he noticed that the Colonel was without the petty jealousies of command, and that he quietly insisted his young officers learn responsibility. "Well, Jones," the Colonel would say to a subordinate who should have solved an unimportant problem himself rather than bringing it to the commanding officer, "what would you do if I were dead? Consider me dead."

"But, Colonel, I—"

"Consider me dead." [7]

Stephen cherished the family story of how the Colonel refused to delegate authority when a batch of shells was condemned, himself withdrawing the defective charges by hand. The boy delighted in the ritual of unhooking the Colonel's sword after dress parade. He digested instinctively and thoroughly the rigorous creed of the regular army officer, with its multiple pillars of duty, integrity, patriotism, and honor. All during his mature life, detesting war and violence as his father had done, Stephen maintained this very real kinship with the fundamental code that flowers in the best of each successive generation of each successive old army. The stereotype of filial rebellion simply couldn't exist in such a relationship, between such partners as the ironic Colonel and the inquisitive little boy.

They took long walks together, and played wonderful sets of tennis on the Post court. Sometimes the boy frantically matched his young speed in singles against the Colonel's sly, underhand serve; sometimes they united against all comers. "We play tennis nearly every day now," Stephen wrote his mother in the fall of 1909, telling her of the routine which occupied them at the Arsenal while she was visiting her relatives in Carlisle, Pennsylvania. "Father and I beat Billy and Capt. Platt. I am teaching Laura and Mrs. Platt to play. They're very good pupils."

Inevitably the Colonel had more time for this young son than he'd had as a junior officer for either of the two older children. The Colonel had the great gift of treating a boy seriously without boring him with adult absurdities. From the beginning the Colonel always conversed with his children with the same grave wit that he employed with his contemporaries. "This is your birthday," he wrote Stephen in 1903, "and it is only meet that you should receive some acknowledgement from your fond father. There is a dress cap, a pair of shoulder boats, a belt etc. awaiting your return so that I think you will have material for a full uniform." The Colonel enveloped the five-year-old in the masculine conspiracy which so delights a boy. "Say to your Mother that I haven't heard from her for two days. Everyone at the Post says, 'Have you heard from your wife today?' Then I say, 'No,' and they say 'Oh!' Have your wife better trained, my son."

As Stephen grew older, during the years at Benicia, the Colonel talked endlessly to him of the strategies and personalities of soldiering, and of the Civil War in which both the boy's grandfathers—in opposing armies—had served. The Colonel always encouraged the talk to become a discussion. He read poetry to the boy, as he had read it to Laura and William, until poetry, too, became another element in the rocklike creed of durable verities. It was the Colonel who called the family's attention to the first poems by E. A. Robinson when they began to appear occasionally in *Scribner's*. He showed them with appreciation those early verses of Stephen Crane, which the Colonel had read when they were first published in the 1890's; they were splendidly different from most of the magazine poetry of the 1900's. Together they made additions to the Colonel's celebrated collection of what he called Minus-Poetry, the scrapbook where he preserved the gross and ridiculous samples of poetry at its worst.

"He knew more about English poetry than most poets and all professors," Leonard Bacon once wrote of the Colonel, "and he had the Elizabethan lyrics by heart." [8]

In 1933, when he was himself the father of two children, Stephen Benét was asked to write an article on poetry for *Compton's Pictured Encyclopedia*. He called it "The Magic of Poetry and the Poet's Art." In his clear exposition on origins and functions and technique he invoked and renewed the lessons first heard from his father at Benicia. "If [the first poet] had merely wanted to tell his friends that he was hungry," Benét explained to his youthful audience, "or that he had seen a fine herd of deer in the forest, he would not have needed the drum or the cry or that chant. He would have said what he had to say in prose, as we do when we write an ordinary letter about ordinary things. But he wanted to do more than that. He wanted his friends to remember what he said and to think about it. He wanted to excite and stir them as he was excited and stirred. So he made a song, in words." [9] This was the kind of eloquent tutorial Stephen attended daily under the Colonel.

"[My father] was interested in everything from the Byzantine Emperors to the development of heavy ordnance," the son wrote in 1940, "and was the finest critic of poetry I have ever known." "He taught me," Stephen remembered on another occasion, "many things about the writing of English verse, and tolerance, and independence and curiosity of mind." [10]

It was as rich a heritage as a father could bequeath a young American who might some day want to write about his native land and its people. "For I was lucky enough," the Colonel's youngest boy wrote simply and proudly in a memoir about his father, "to be the son of an officer in the Ordnance Department of the United States Army." [11]

There didn't appear to be a single missing ingredient of idyllic youth. Less adaptable boys might have yearned for more playmates their own age. Stephen had them through his family. The roles which the five Benéts played in their joint and individual relationships meant that Stephen never needed to be without a companion. There were books to read, evening games in the broad living-room, horses to ride, and the limitless excitements of the Post itself. "Merely to enjoy the hospitality of that family in such a place," Leonard Bacon remembered, "was more than one deserved, and to know the Colonel, for a man of my tastes, was like a delightful electric shock." [12] Stephen Vincent Benét was having a boyhood which was the precise image of what American writers of his generation often attempted to create imaginatively for themselves; they could rarely achieve it in the business-oriented families within which the majority of them originated.

The closest equivalent American experience would have been an academic home. In the Benét household, however, there was during this period no genteel poverty, and none of the aching compulsion for upward mobility which frequently possesses the professorial child. Nor were there the patronizing snobberies that often compensate academic families in their resentment of the more opulent layers of middle-class America. A soldier, after all, existed for the service and welfare of the whole American people; he would never either condescend to them or permit it in his children.

Here there was serenity, tolerance, literacy without affectation. One's anxiety to write poetry—or bloody pirate adventure—was encouraged in a matter-of-fact way, and received sympathetically. Years later, discussing the aptitude of one of his contemporaries for literature, Benét discovered the root in his friend's ancestry. "But there was writing in the family," Benét wrote of John Marquand in 1939, "and, once that has happened, it is apt to crop up again." It was a truism among the Colonel's friends that, good soldier though he was, he would have made an even better editor. During his retirement he forewent the gardening and golf of most of his military peers; instead he wrote his autobiography.[13]

To be surrounded by the act of composition was as natural to Stephen as the games of baseball he played with Captain Bellinger's sons. "William writes in the summerhouse in the garden," the boy explained casually to his mother in a letter of 1909. "He has fixed it up with books and a chair—there are also wasps who have built a nest there." Even at the age of ten, influenced by the early movies as much as by his reading, he was beginning to translate his favorite literary situations into new melodramas. "I would have liked to have been in the tower with a .22 caliber revolver," he wrote his friend Philip Bellinger in 1908, describing the Calvert correspondence school assignment he had just finished in Robin Hood, "when the nun was bleeding him to death. Face at the window! Collapse of nun! bandages for Robin! See!"

In a domestic circle of poets and critics, however, there was healthy skepticism as well as generous sympathy. The professionalism of the military atmosphere was reproduced in the family attitude toward writing. You wrote to be read, or at least to be heard. Neither the casual dilettante nor the misunderstood artist could flourish in such a climate. It was the attitude Benét himself expressed years later, when one of his own children earned fifty cents for a book review in a scholastic magazine. "Good. That's fine," he told his wife, who had wondered if the little girl should be encouraged by such mercenary means. "I don't want any of my kids to be amateurs."

Although Benét was the most reticent of men in most of his adult relationships, and never a consistently autobiographical writer in his fiction, he nevertheless made an intensely personal record of these boyhood years in some of his early verse. The rich happiness of the Benicia period is movingly clear in a poem he published ten years later as an undergraduate, in a 1917 issue of the *Yale Literary Magazine*. He imagined himself "back in the great room,"

Curled in a chair with all of them beside
And the whole world a rush of happy voices,
With laughter beating in a clamorous tide . . .
Once more knew eves of perfume, days ablaze
With clear, dry heat on the brown, rolling fields;
Shuddered with fearful ecstasy in bed
Over a book of knights and bloody shields [14]

These, however, were the poem's central lines. The opening ones had seemed to promise no more than a description of an exciting ferry trip across San Francisco

Bay. A reader might have wondered, indeed, why the young poet had chosen to set his verse in the somber late afternoon, with the sky lit only by "the dead sun's last glimmer." Then the scenes of buoyant retrospection, as the boy watches dusk fall across the water. Suddenly the ferryboat jars into its berth. The boy is shocked out of reverie and into reality. Now the full meaning of the poem's title—"Going Back to School"—is poignantly apparent. The appropriateness of dusk is explicit. "There, straight ahead,"

Were dock and fellows. Stumbling, he was whirled
Out and away to meet them—and his back
Slumped to the old half-cringe, his hands fell slack;
A big boy's arm went round him—and a twist
Sent shattering pain along his tortured wrist,
As a voice cried, a bloated voice and fat,
"Why it's Miss Nancy! Come along, you rat!"

Benét was recalling at nineteen the absolute horror of the eight months he had spent at twelve, in 1910 and 1911, at the Hitchcock Military Academy, twenty miles north of San Francisco at Jacinto. This was in real measure a dark moment of his life. Now he encountered an initial testing of the endurance he later displayed so conspicuously in the face of adult pain and disappointment. His year at Hitchcock was an agonizing caricature of what every sensitive, overcherished Anglo-Saxon boy endures in the first terms at boarding school, and of which so many have purged themselves in their first novel.

Benét had encountered discipline at home. The Colonel knew too much of the world—and was too devoted a father—to have failed his children through that kind of parental self-indulgence. The punishment, however, had

15

always been swift, just, and understandable. Benét described such an episode in another of his undergraduate poems:

> After the whipping he crawled into bed,
> Accepting the whipping with no great weeping.
> How funny uncle's hat had looked striped red!
> He chuckled silently. . .[15]

At Hitchcock, however, Benét was the victim of the conventional brutalizing of any boy who, as he later wryly described himself in a letter to his fiancée, was "timid, fattish, and very spectacled." He had read, with his generation, the heroic school tales of Ralph Henry Barbour. These alone were sufficiently distorted to account for his appalled misery when he met the reality of boarding school. He had also previously cherished all things military. Now he was thrust into a burlesque of the soldier's code; the creed he had honored was soon recognized to be at Hitchcock no more than a mean justification for ugliness.

"Ten years of teaching at Kitchell Military Academy," says the hero of Benét's first novel, *The Beginning of Wisdom,* published in 1921, describing one of his instructors, "have left him with the restraint of a hanging judge and the ingenuity in small cruelties of a Jesuit Inquisitor."

Hitchcock was neither better nor worse than other contemporary institutions of the species. Like most of them, it represented the educational slum of private education, administered on the whole by a commonplace faculty without professional standards or training, and attracting to its harassed student body an unwholesome percentage of the neurotic, the miserable, or the merely sluggish. A worse school for such a boy as Benét could not have been found.

16

The decision had been made hastily and unhappily by his parents, under the urgent insistence of a physician who argued persuasively that the boy required companionship and competition. These were expected to serve as counter agents both to the lingering effects of an attack of scarlet fever and to the fact that perhaps Stephen was outgrowing the Calvert correspondence system in which he'd been studying, his father supervising the work in arithmetic, and Laura the other subjects. The boy reacted commendably to such academic competition as existed at Hitchcock. He was awarded Excellent in each of his eight subjects. He scored 100 on the final exams in spelling, arithmetic, grammar, history, and geography, and, ironically, 95 in composition and literature.

The doctor's illusion that Hitchcock would provide companions and friends, however, was a bitter one for Benét. The school's major esprit was a traditionally brutal one. The savage bullying was a confusing ugliness for a boy trained in fair play. Benét's memories of Hitchcock were to become the most vivid episodes in *The Beginning of Wisdom*. "Star takes the other wrist and experiments with it. In that thick, choking moment Philip knows, as only a boy who lives always by present seconds can know it, despair, utterly bleak and sardonic and final. They have got him and they are going to hurt him all they want. That is all. There is to be no escape, any more than for a worm stuck on a fish-hook."

The twelve-year-old Benét, however, gave no hint to his parents of his misery. The stability of his class work indicated Stephen's rigid self-control under circumstances whose more conventional result should have been the disintegration of his studies and his morale. His letters home, read with hindsight, are pathetic attempts to conceal unhappiness beneath the buoyant idiom of a Barbour hero. Occasional lines in his letters were poignant with implication of petty tyranny and small barbarisms. "About two weeks ago," Benét wrote his mother in the fall of 1910, "I asked you to send me an extension for my light. You said that you had written Dr. Hitchcock about it and he had said he would see. I have not got it yet so if you would either get one or ask Dr. Hitchcock if I can have an order to go down to San Rafael and get one."

By the spring of 1911 he had learned to grasp whatever evasions were available. "I had a fine time in the city," he wrote home in April, in a letter that contained only this one sentence, "going to *Wildfire* instead of the other Confirmation class today so I have to hurry." Not until the year was over, and his father's impending transfer ensured that he need not return to Hitchcock, did the boy disclose even a fraction of the real story to his family. They did not fully grasp the nature of his experience until they read his poems nearly a decade later. Their distress and self-reproach, as the boy had suspected when he concealed his unhappiness, was overwhelming.

The boy himself buried the wound speedily. He resurrected it briefly in the undergraduate poetry, and in the early chapters of *The Beginning of Wisdom,* and spoke of it rarely in adult life. When he did mention the period, it was with uncharacteristic bitterness. Once, watching with his wife the schoolroom brutality of a Dickens movie, he abruptly whispered to her that he thought he'd go outside; he'd meet her later, he said, in the theater lobby. Once, too, at a time when the financial aid would have been a welcome rescue, he refused with an abrupt and horrified finality Laurence Benét's offer to underwrite his own son's education at Culver, where the munitions magnate was a trustee. Later, when he could no longer

18

postpone the parental dilemma, Stephen insisted on carefully inspecting, in the company of his boy, a number of
schools. Having finally decided with hope and misgivings
on Exeter, he bleakly wrote his mother about the decision. "Well," he conceded, perhaps in final absolution
of her part in his own ancient scar, "what can a parent
tell by just looking around a school?"

The Hitchcock experience, scrutinized with the com-
placent objectivity of the detached observer, was nevertheless a healthy one for Benét in 1910. It would not be
fanciful to argue that it introduced the boy to ugliness
if not to evil. Benét himself always encouraged young
writers to confront reality rather than to withdraw, for
example, into such available sanctuaries as university
jobs. He tended to add, dryly, that the cure was almost
as bad as the disease. Yet his horizon had been extended.
He had survived an episode which has frequently damaged characters seemingly more resilient than his. His
perspective had matured. His calm poise, inherited from
his father and strengthened by observation of him, was
toughened; in later years, in moments of stress, he drew
upon the boyhood pain. "I haven't been homesick," he
told his fiancée in 1921, during an exceedingly difficult
period of separation, "since boarding school."

The year 1911 ended for him, however, on the healing
note of a shift across the continent to the Augusta Arsenal
in Georgia. Benét's next four years would be spent ac-
cumulating an additional stock of material for his national background. Born in Pennsylvania, he had spent
his early childhood in upper New York and his boyhood
in California. He had known a rewarding summer in the
Sierras, and a number of vacations at the home of his
mother's family in Carlisle. "I am as much a Pennsyl-
vanian as anything at all," Benét once said, in 1938, but

19

this was the tactful remark of a celebrity who happened to be lecturing at the time in Chambersburg.[16] He might as justly have described himself as a New Yorker or a Californian or a Georgian.

He had known the new America of the west coast as thoroughly as the older one of the middle states. Carlisle was at the northern end of the Civil War country; he had visited the battlefields and shrines many times, as he had visited the Spanish culture of lower California. Now he would encounter, and by no means at the fringe, a very special region which had accompanying implications for the whole of America. Augusta, after all, was the frozen residuum of what still remained, in 1911, of the antebellum South. The trials of Hitchcock were admirable seasoning for the ambiguities of Dixie.

2. Georgia

Hasn't anybody on the Post *ever seen a Southern possum hunt or a Southern mob? What a lot they've missed.*[1]

NONE of the Benéts responded to the Georgia transfer with more than stoic resignation. They were too much an army family, on the other hand, to remain depressed for very long by the prospect of moving from even so pleasant a post as Benicia. Mrs. Benét had married into the army in the days when junior officers were turned out of their quarters without notice to make room for seniors, even if the seniority was no more than date of promotion to the identical rank; as a young bride she had watched in horror as her first home was emptied onto a dusty Post street. Laura was as much an army daughter as her mother was an army wife. Billy was the least affected by the shift. He was in New York beginning an editorial job with the *Century Magazine* after four productive but insecure years as a free-lance poet and essayist.

They had all been extremely happy at Benicia, however, and certainly this particular move was more of a wrench than usual. The Colonel had enjoyed the faculty visitors from Berkeley. It had been a rare treat to have week ends of conversation and argument with young poets like Leonard Bacon and Billy's other friends from the university and from San Francisco. He was near retirement age; it would be an anticlimax to spend his last command in a Georgia backwater. The intellectual company in Augusta would be equally anticlimactic. Even the thirteen-year-old Stephen, for all his realistic sense of army procedure and necessity, seemed none too pleased with the transfer.

Stephen, indeed, though he welcomed the permanent reprieve from Hitchcock, made up his mind that he would detest everything about Georgia. On the family machine he pecked out, in the summer of 1911 while they were still at Benicia, a very inexpert typescript of a poem he had just written. His frame of mind, judging by "Ku Klux," was not a promising one:

> A black cross is set against his name.
> They came to his house in the night.
> The door opens, a rifle shot,
> And the house lies under a blight.

Even the defiant signature and place of residence of the author, typed firmly beneath the verse, were a challenging declaration of war by a militant abolitionist from a free state. "Stephen V. Benét," he announced. "Benicia Arsenal, Benicia Cal."

Like the rest of the family, however, the boy was too much army to remain overtroubled by the dislocation. Years later he used such episodes to explain the necessity for clarification of atmosphere and situation in the short story. "I spent my childhood," he told a young writer who was attempting some difficult sketches of her own early life, "on a series of Regular Army posts. If I were writing stories about that, I would have to explain a few things about the Army. . . . I'd have to give you a sense of being in a world of your own that children

22

have—I'd have to show you that it is quite as natural for an Army child to move to a different Post every few years as for a civilian child to grow up in one town." [2]

Earlier, in 1928, Benét put some of this same mood of the Augusta transfer into the only direct use he ever made of his army childhood, in a short story called "The Giant's House."

> The move hardly upset me at all—I was used to moving, being an army child. Wherever we went there was always a post and a striker and a big flag sinking down at evening from a white flagpole . . . Sometimes there were many children, sometimes only a few—but there was always the same big doherty with the army mules to carry them off to school—and the same line of cleavage between us and the civilian rest of the world. [3]

In this particular case, however, the Klan outburst was a more accurate index to the boy's immediate response. Adaptable as he was, it nevertheless took him a little while to adjust to the new atmosphere. "I hated it at first," he told Margaret Mitchell many years later, discussing her own record of the area in *Gone with the Wind*. "I came from California and had been very happy there—and then [I] grew very fond of it indeed." [4] He had been impressed by Miss Mitchell's reproduction of the red clay land around Augusta. "I can still shut my eyes," he went on in 1936, "and remember the particular look of that country."

To continue to hate the new environment, in fact, would have required a perverse act of will in so imaginative a boy as Benét. Here, after all, there was spread out for him a vivid dramatization of the long talks he'd already had with the Colonel, and continued to have, about the Civil War. Here, too, was documentation of what he was now beginning to read in the Colonel's copies of *Battles and Leaders of the Civil War* and in *The Rebellion Record*. Once again there had occurred a happy meeting at an appropriate time between his responsive mind and a fertile American object.

The painful maturation required of him at Hitchcock could now be extended a little further. A contradictory mosaic—plantations, slums, barbarism, grace, cultivation, illiteracy—not only surrounded the Arsenal, a seemingly chaste Federal oasis entombed within the unreconstructed South, but was also to an exceptional degree apparent in the Post itself. In 1911 the Arsenal—though its military complement was but a single company of the 79th Ordnance—was an important assignment. It was the principal depot in the southeastern command, as it had been for more than one hundred and fifty years. The permanent buildings had an extraordinary beauty. The architecture was a pure and successful southern adaptation of the Greek revival style of the very early nineteenth century. Even the history of the Colonel's new command was a romantic one.

The original military post from which the Augusta Arsenal derived had been established on the banks of the Savannah River in 1735. Its primary responsibility had been to provide protection from Indian insurrection for the Georgia settlers. In 1826 almost the entire garrison of the low-lying installation had been wiped out by swamp fever. One of the few survivors was the Commanding Officer; he happened to have been visiting on the plantation—seventy-two acres—of a local magnate. Having thus been spared the fever through the immunity of high ground, the resourceful officer persuaded his host to sell the entire acreage to the federal government as a new, healthy site for the arsenal. Its construction accelerated by the abundant supply of local slave labor, the new Arsenal was ready for occupancy the next year. This same four-walled compound remained the center of the post when Colonel Benét assumed its command in 1911.

The central building of the fortlike heart of the Arsenal —the crossed cannon of Ordnance carved above the great entrance—was still used as a storehouse, repair shop, and wheelwright section. To the south, separated only by a paved walk, was the imposing, pillared residence of the commanding officer. To the north, a precise facsimile save for a slight, appropriate reduction in scale, were the quarters of the assistant officer—in 1911 a captain. These three buildings, a flowing, gold-brick façade, formed the east wall. The south and north sides of the compound were loopholed walls of the same gold brick. The rear, west wall was the two-story enlisted men's barracks.

Throughout its first hundred years the Arsenal served the entire region as a manufacturing center for cartridges and powder and as a maintenance base for military equipment. In 1860 the Secretary of War ordered 22,000 muskets and rifles sent to this strategically located base. They arrived just in time to be surrendered by the Federal commander in early January 1861, to a Confederate colonel who had been his West Point classmate twenty-four years earlier. These small, important dramas and melodramas of national epic were now being displayed for the boy. He could not hate such an atmosphere for long.

He lived in the cool, high-ceilinged rooms of what might have been a plantation house but was equally the principal structure of a compound that had once housed

Indian fighters, scouts, settlers waiting for safe convoy, captive Seminoles, beleaguered federal troops, triumphant confederates. A few hundred yards to the north was the conventional military cemetery of every post he had known. Here, however, there rested unidentified rebels, Northern casualties, and three graves which were merely labeled "Colored."

Here, too, were the ancient tombstones of two of the eighteenth-century commanding officers of the Arsenal. In front of the headquarters building, twenty yards from the boy's front porch, were four brass cannon made from Southern churchbells and presented to Semple's Battery in 1861 for the defense of the Confederacy. Not far from his window stood the wrought iron salute gun which, as it had been for more than a century, was fired each day at sunrise and sunset. At his mother's teas he observed and listened to elderly ladies who discussed the griefs and losses of the War Between the States as if the final battle had been fought the previous month, ladies who, when necessity compelled them to use a postage stamp with Sherman's portrait on it, always pasted it on the envelope upside down.

The boy began to know the various other Souths too, the crossroad hamlets of the back country as well as the plantations that fringed the Arsenal. Years later, when he was reading new fiction each week for the *Herald Tribune* and the *Saturday Review of Literature*, Benét was one of the first of the widely read reviewers to endorse and value Faulkner. "And all this material," he wrote, "the violence and the laziness, the nightmare and the tropic warmth of the deep South, is brought together and orchestrated . . . like listening to the gossip of a country store, with its cruelty." [5]

Now, too, the boy became accustomed to an additional

annual holiday. Each year the schools were closed on June 4 throughout Georgia—and also, it was pointed out to him, throughout Florida, Alabama, Mississippi, Texas, Arkansas, and South Carolina—to celebrate the birthday of the President of the Confederate States of America. General Sherman himself, it was still imagined locally, personally spared the Arsenal in 1864. He deliberately swung around Augusta, it was asserted, because as a young officer he had lost his heart to a neighborhood belle. These were translatable documents of American history, from frontier to national crisis.

His summers were spent in Highlands, a North Carolina mountain village which was not only a refuge from the Georgia sun but also an additional extension of his involvement with a variety of Americas. Imaginative and well-read, gently tutored by the most recent in the long line of officers who had commanded the Augusta Arsenal, the boy would never be able to disassociate American history from the various American individuals who made it. The entire scene and experience were natural fodder for the principle Benét always enunciated in connection with any fictional use of the past. "The thing, of course," he told a friend in 1932, at a time when he was just beginning his series of notable American folk tales, "is to make the people come alive. They do, if you can dig them out of the dust." [6] For him, thanks to an observant father and to such boyhood worlds as Augusta, the dust never really had a chance to settle.

The Hitchcock Military Academy, despite the three-thousand-mile interval, made one final intrusion into the boy's life in the autumn of 1911. As a result of his own excellent scholastic record there, as well as the headmaster's effusive recommendation—"8th grade work will be child's play to him"—young Benét now skipped the last year of grammar school altogether. He began high school immediately, enrolling that fall in the Summerville Academy.

Summerville was as different an institution from Hitchcock as—the cliché applied accurately—day from night. Only a few minutes' walk from the Arsenal, the coeducational Academy was an endowed school without boarders. It served the handful of large landowners in the immediate neighborhood and the relatively small Augusta middle class of the period. Summerville had a faculty of five—a male principal and four maiden ladies. "*Two* of them," a classmate of Benét remembered forty years later, "were Yankees." [7]

The principal himself, John W. Dow, was a young and energetic alien from Indiana. In 1915, the year Benét graduated from Summerville, Dow became head of the department of general science in the Springfield, Massachusetts, public schools, then as later one of the nation's best systems. A good teacher and well-trained, Dow was trying diligently to make Summerville a school of higher standards than most such provincial academies. Benét did well in his work there from the beginning, primarily, one suspects—judging by his subsequent difficulty with the college entrance exams in 1915—because of his enormous reading, his articulate tongue, and the sound memory he had inherited from the Colonel.

His classmates at Summerville, many of them not a little impressed to have as companion the son of the commanding officer at the Arsenal, where some of their fathers were employed as civilian technicians, were simultaneously struck by Benét's extraordinary poetic facility and his shy willingness to join awkwardly in their never-ending ball games. Augusta, after all, was the home of the fabulous Ty Cobb. The Georgia Peach, who owned a house only a few hundred yards from the Academy, was almost as luminous a local figure as those Augustans who had figured in the War Between the States and in the great days when the town had been first the colonial and then, for a time, the state capital.

As for his poetry, Benét's schoolmates, one of them wrote many years later, "loved to read [it]. Many a time," the classmate continued, "we would see him stroke his bushy dark hair with his hands, trying to concentrate on what he was about to say or do. His hair was thick and therefore appeared to be mussed up most of the time. This hair covered a head full of knowledge I often thought." [8]

It was during these next four years in Augusta, in fact —and in particular the last two—that Benét emerged as a genuine prodigy. Up until then one might have speculated that his impulse was merely a perishable, boyish emulation of his brother and sister. The adolescent productivity, however, no matter how important the factor of imitation had originally been, was thoroughly sustained. He wrote constantly from 1913 on—poems for *St. Nicholas*, blank verse tragedies, a violent poetic monologue within the story of Noah.

"God!" the latter began. "How the rain roars down upon this rock!" It had surely been inspired—Benét called it "The Twelfth Day"—by the torrential Georgia weather. "I can still remember," Benét said in 1936, "reading Conrad's *Typhoon* at night, in the middle of a typical Georgia thunderstorm." [9] He wrote a Renaissance tragedy which had one act and four characters—a Duke, his Duchess, her lover, and an off-stage tiger in a cage. The curtain, Benét explained once, finally fell upon a completely empty stage and a full tiger. He also wrote, his brother recalled, "a short, crisp, and startling" story called "The Butcher's Bill," and a grim ballad which began:

> I have been on the old tramp steamer
> When heads were quickly bashed,
> When dead men rolled in the scuppers
> And revolvers spat and flashed [10]

Now too, at the age of thirteen, his "The Regret of Dives" won a cash award of three dollars from the St. Nicholas League. He later confessed that his Latin pronunciation was more confident than accurate; he had conceived "dives" as a rhyme for "hives." Fortunately the noun occurred only in the title. "Of course they were terrible poems," Benét recalled, "but I was fortunate enough not to know it. There is a time when words like 'golden,' 'glorious,' 'splendid' seem neither inexact nor well-known but golden, glorious, splendid new-minted discoveries, shining with their own light." [11]

In another poem of the period the boy attacked what he termed "The Proud Man." His theme was a denunciation of any withdrawal from human affairs. Already his professional and personal creed was beginning to define itself, even in the rhetoric of these inflated melodramas. All his life Benét credited his father and his brother with the major role in the formation of these attitudes. From them, he wrote later, he learned that poetry "was not a dead thing or an alien thing or a dry game of words. I knew there were rules and that you could break the rules but that you must never break them unintentionally. I knew [poetry] was always written by the living, even though the date-line said that the man was dead." [12]

Neither the Colonel nor his library were merely bookish, nor was the study an adult sanctuary where the parent went to escape his family. The boy was always welcome there, though like the other members of the household he learned to enter on his intellectual guard. "My father," William Rose Benét said once, "could tease more expertly than anyone I have ever known. He could be merciless if he thought he perceived a joint in your armor. This went along with a great companionableness and kindness. But it was always there, and kept one upon the alert." [13]

Books were scattered throughout the Augusta quarters, as they had been in Benicia and would be in the apartments and houses of Benét's own adulthood. There were review copies sent on or left by Billy, presentation copies from his and Laura's writer friends, Ordnance handbooks, government directives—"I cut my teeth on Congressional appropriations [and] War Department red-tape" [14]—Thackeray, new novels by Conrad and old ones by Marryat, Kipling, historical fiction by Mary Johnston and Winston Churchill. The Colonel, his youngest son remembered, "was apt to find the genuine before most people found it, and he would have been the fortune of a publisher. . . . he told us about [his discoveries] before they were known." [15]

The Colonel enjoyed debate, and his youngest son now became his favorite opponent. The family enjoyed the running warfare. The boy, his brother recalled, would slip down "upon the back of his neck in a certain large familiar leather armchair, drawing his 'Maybe so, but —' to some argument of my father's who sat across from him beyond the book-laden table. What was being argued about was . . . either Socialism or sundry campaigns of Grant or Lee." [16]

Stephen quickly learned that he had better avoid flagrant improvisation. He discovered a fresh lode of Amer-

31

ican history—factual ammunition of a sort his father would honor—in the Colonel's four volumes of Hart's *American History Told by Contemporaries*. Benét recommended the volumes years later to an expatriate friend in search of Americana for her French-bred son. He couldn't remember the editor, but even in 1932 he recalled the precise bindings and contents. "The buff-and-blue source books I speak of were to me fascinating. . . . They had things like the Pope's Bull dividing the New World up—some of Smith, Bradford, Raleigh, early voyagers, etc." [17]

Creatively speaking—the kind of phrase Benét's detested—creatively speaking, the American material was settling for the moment into layers of his subconscious on which he wouldn't draw for another twenty years. His adolescent poetry was mainly a precocious, discordant patchwork of influences: his roaring zest for classical tragedy and bombast, the lushness of late Victorian rococo, Browning monologues, the ballads of Alfred Noyes and Masefield and Kipling, and, above all, the poetry of Morris. It soon became impossible to identify the literary derivation; there was too much from too many sources. The whirlpool of influence was an aspect of literary criticism that always amused and sometimes exasperated Benét.

"I once made a list of all the people reviewers said had influenced me," he wrote in 1935 to Paul Engle, the Iowa poet who was troubled by the charge that his poetry grew so transparently from Benét's. "I think there were something like seventeen of them. Yet none of them caught the derivation from William Morris, whom I read and reread in my youth. It doesn't matter very much." [18]

From the time he was five until his death at forty-four

there was rarely a day on which Benét did not finish one book or begin another. "I am now reduced to the lesser known works of Margaret Deland," he wrote a friend one summer from Rhode Island, "having read all the Wilkie Collins available in the Peace Dale Library. I do not mind Margaret Deland but I can't say that I do so with burning enthusiasm. However, it is better to read a dull book than none at all." [19]

He read with critical discrimination, to be sure, even as a boy. "So far as literary taste was concerned," his brother remembered of him at ten, "he had already perceived the difference between a work like "The Haystack in the Floods" and such tripe as *The Helmet of Navarre*." [20] Like the Colonel, however, he was a connoisseur of the false and the pretentious; both of them could find some profit in all printed matter. It was the mutual characteristic which sent him and the Colonel to the movies each week in Augusta, where they sat grandly together in the most expensive seats (ten cents).

Stephen inherited William's old books, and now, in the manner of younger brothers, he carefully wrote his name underneath Billy's on the first page of each one. Like Billy, too, he devotedly numbered and catalogued each volume in the growing library. By the enlisted men and civilian workers at the Arsenal he was always remembered as a rangy, friendly boy steering a large bicycle dangerously with his right hand because in his left he held an open book. He would pedal a few feet and halt; still astride the bike, he would read several pages and then move on again. He listened to the barrack-room tales of Indian campaigns and the conquest of a frontier. Thirty years later he still remembered "the queer reality that old soldiers can sometimes give, even when they ramble." [21]

33

His pocket money went for additional books and money. "Raffles has been caught by the artist," he had written his mother in 1909, bringing her up to date on the latest installment in the adventures of the celebrated English cricketer-cracksman. One of the solaces of Hitchcock had been the second-hand bookstalls in San Francisco. He had prowled them on Saturday afternoons, searching for Algernon Blackwood and E. Nesbit. "I got *The Phoenix and the Carpet*," he remembered as a young writer in 1922, "for a quarter. It was dirty but priceless—I can feel it yet in my hand." [22]

He read and reread *Henry Esmond,* as he would continue to do all his life; it was his favorite novel, by his favorite author. He read H. G. Wells; *Trilby;* all the Dumas novels, with the electrifying illustrations by Maurice Leloir; *The Cloister and the Hearth;* even the whole of the Barchester series. When he reread Trollope, twenty years afterward, he still felt as he had at fourteen "[He] is long drawn out," Benét declared, "and often subservient to the ideals of the pig and full of pettiness, and yet, within its limits, human life and character, so well done, so not at all smartly, with a great quality of survival. The vitality is there, for all the muslin." [23]

Already, as a high school student, he had a literary stability that not only was reflected in its hearty appetite and in his own work but was even apparent in his manner and diction. In 1912 he received from Sinclair Lewis a copy of the latter's recently published juvenile, *Hike and the Aeroplane.* The boy wrote back promptly, and with confidence. "It's swell," he told Lewis, in a different idiom but with all the aplomb of his elders, "one of the best boys books this year, indeed the best. Are you going to write a sequel? I guess you are for you let the villain escape! Miss Granicle who has been visiting us says she will present a copy to the Benicia library. So you see how famous you are!" [24]

Benét had assurance of a vocation at an age when for most boys the act of composition is a torment. In 1913, when Leonard Bacon and his bride spent a part of their honeymoon at the Arsenal, the Benéts characteristically sat up late the first night in order to greet the couple at breakfast with a long, joint wedding ode. Stephen's section, Mrs. Bacon remembered years later, was astonishing in its deft humor and lack of conventional solemnities.

Already Benét had demonstrated in other ways the craftsmanlike facility which during his maturity enabled him, with distaste but competence, to write Christmas stories on order—in mid-August—for the big circulation magazines. In May 1912 he read with interest the announcement of a new *St. Nicholas* competition. The prospectus didn't give the young competitors much to go on. "To contain not more than twenty-four lines. Subject, 'A Song of the Woods.'" The fourteen-year-old went to work promptly, utilizing as always a blend of his reading—in this case Howard Pyle's version of Robin Hood—and his imagination. *St. Nicholas* published his poem with the other winning entries in the September issue. His charming stanzas had in genuine measure the quality of song that the title required; one would not have expected this to survive so fully the troublesome mechanical rigors of exposition, theme, and prosody.

> *There's many a forest in the world,*
> *In many lands leaves fall;*
> *But Sherwood, merry Sherwood,*
> *Is the fairest wood of all.*

35

They say that on midsummer night,
If mortal eyes could see aright,
    Or mortal ears could hear,
A wanderer on Sherwood's grass
Would see the band of Robin pass,
    Still hunting of the deer.

And sometimes to his ears might come
The beating of an elfin drum,
    Where Puck, the tricksy sprite,
Would dance around a fairy ring,
With others of his gathering,
    All on midsummer night.

Queen Guinevere would ride again
With all her glittering, courtly train,
    Through Sherwood's lovely glades;
'Till dawn begins to glow near by,
And from the kingdom of the sky,
    The magic darkness fades.

There's many a forest in the world,
    In many lands leaves fall;
But Sherwood, merry Sherwood,
    Is the fairest wood of all.

Thus, by inclination and temperament and encouragement from his family, Stephen Benét served all through his boyhood and adolescence a kind of perennial internship to letters. From New York his brother mailed the new poetry magazines and his own favorites among the older poets. Early in 1915 William sent him a volume of Vachel Lindsay; the boy rejoiced in the beat of "The Congo" and the lush mysticism of the Moon Poems.

"Lindsay is a great poet," Stephen wrote William, who entirely agreed. All morning long, the boy said, there ran through his head the thumping line "the big black bucks in the wine-barrel room."

Lindsay's war verse, Stephen felt—as became a fervent supporter of the Allies who signed his letters "For France!"—was "not so good," but in Chesterton's *Magic,* he told William, the episode where the red lights turned blue was "a great moment, great, GREAT." William sent him some Rossetti, too—"a splendid edition," the boy said gratefully—and a volume of nineteenth-century poets. "How many great men lie buried in the Victorian Anthology!" the sixteen-year-old declared precociously. "Men like Mangan and Sir Samuel Ferguson and John Davidson."

William now began to encourage him to look beyond *St. Nicholas* for his market. In May 1915, two months before his seventeenth birthday, the boy was able to tell his brother triumphantly of his first thoroughly professional sale. "The *New Republic* paid me fifteen (Count 'em, FIFTEEN) luscious dollars for Icarus. I feel terribly cocky. I put on my hat with a boot-jack." The verse was published in early August, the lead poem in a two-page selection that included a blend of such established and youthful talent as Max Eastman, Witter Bynner, Amy Lowell, and Max Bodenheim. At the age of seventeen young Benét thus assumed a modest but official place in the new poetry and the renaissance it inaugurated in American literature.

"Winged Man," as Benét entitled the *New Republic* poem, was a respectable performance by a high school senior. It contained some monumentally sour lines— "Icarus, Icarus, though the end is piteous"—but there was a nice sense of man's compulsion toward flight, and

37

there was the rich palette of color which was his primary strength at this time. The verse as a whole, however, was probably as ominous for his future development as it was temporarily a confirmation of his brilliance. It was thinned and stretched by repetition and easy emotion; its rhymes were often more facile than firm. The stanzas were a medley of the imaginative and the merely poetic:

Floating downward, very clear, still the echoes reach the ear
Of a little tune he whistles and a little song he sings,
Mounting, mounting still, triumphant, on his torn and broken wings! [25]

A high school student with this kind of sensibility could easily have become a tiresome young prig. Despite the sly deflation of the Colonel, and the towering presence of an older brother and sister almost as precocious as himself, the danger was always present. Benét was spared not only by his family's sane acceptance of his talent—"They did not appear to be awestruck over my inimitable gifts nor did they laugh at my folly" [26]—but also by a salutary blow he received early in July 1915. He flunked his entrance examinations for Yale in Latin prose and mathematics.

He had taken the exams in Augusta in June—twelve in less than a week—and his letters during the period were game but a little desperate. "Nothing much has happened this week," he wrote his mother, who was visiting in Carlisle, "except study. Twelve examinations! which I probably will not pass. Well, maybe not quite that—but if I passed in Geometry, Algebra or Physics—well, I would be surprised!" The time was too brief, however, and the comfortable standards of Summerville Academy too deep-rooted; he failed in areas where he had won prizes at commencement a few weeks earlier.

It was a healthy catastrophe for a seventeen-year-old whose life, save for the year at Hitchcock, had been a series of victories. Yale had been a fixed object on his horizon ever since he conceded he could not go to West Point and listened instead to William's tales of New Haven literary splendor. He was the brother and nephew of Yale men; now his own place in the sequence was doubtful. The fixed object was suddenly remote. The Colonel, a calm man accustomed to crisis, took charge. Letters were exchanged with the Admissions Office. Soon there appeared at the Commandant's quarters Mr. Donald S. Bridgman, Yale 1913.

"I have a tutor here," the Colonel informed a fellow officer in late July, "tutoring him at vast expense for September. If he passes then, the family will have to go barefoot for the rest of the year to support him in luxury." [27]

Mister Stephen, as the boy was now addressed by both the fond housekeeper and the ironic Colonel—the one out of affectionate respect, the other in sardonic adaptation of the method of address for a lowly second lieutenant—Mister Stephen would not go north this summer as during previous Georgia holidays. Instead he was to endure the indignity of a tutor during the baking remainder of July and all of August. Bridgman, however, turned out to be anything but an indignity. He was much more than a competent tutor. He had made an excellent academic record at Yale, to be sure, and had already taught briefly in a small private school. More important, he spoke for a different Yale than the one Stephen had seen through the eyes of William and William's friends.

39

Bridgman had held good scholarships and earned Phi Beta Kappa, but he had also been the type of extra-curricular man whom the College especially honored, extravagantly in many cases, and of whom Stephen had hitherto encountered no genuine representative. Bridgman had played hockey and baseball, belonged to a fraternity, served on the Freshman Flag Committee, done Boys Club work, led a mission study group. He was a classic illustration of the well-rounded man of civic virtue and literate maturity whom Yale prided itself on producing in large numbers. Bridgman had not been one of the half-dozen big men of his collegiate generation, on the other hand, and this was just as well. Both Stephen and the Colonel would have had difficulty in restraining their mirth if confronted for six weeks by such a version of greatness. Bridgman—himself the grandson, son, and nephew of Yale graduates—communicated his enthusiasm to Stephen. It was a nice balance for the exclusively literary image in which the boy had previously conceived an undergraduate experience. They had an active, hard-working summer.

"I shall always feel very grateful to Donald Bridgman for two things," Benét said in 1933. "He tutored me so efficiently I was able to enter Yale that fall and he did not work me on Sundays. So every Sunday, during that summer, I wrote a poem." [28] What he in fact produced during July and August of 1915 was *Five Men and Pompey*, his first book of verse.

The poems Benét wrote during those six successive Sundays in 1915 were by far the most remarkable he had yet done. Gone, for the moment, was the rather wordy fluency of "Winged Man," where a single insight had not really been sufficient to support an entire episode. These new half-dozen poems, all of them portraits by monologue, marked the apparent end of precocity and the beginning of professional adulthood. Benét himself always dated his literary career from *Five Men and Pompey*. In retrospect he saw it as an achievement which dwarfed a good deal of the work he subsequently did in the early 1920's. He linked *Five Men and Pompey* instead to his major epic poem, *John Brown's Body*, the first sustained work of his maturity—published in 1928 —with which he was even partially satisfied.

"The method of *John Brown's Body*," Benét said emphatically in 1939, "is an expansion of the method used in *Five Men and Pompey*." [29]

As he would do thirteen years later in *John Brown's Body*, Benét presented a series of sketches of actual and fictional characters through which was narrated, in this case, not the rise of the American republic but the fall of the Roman. *Five Men and Pompey* also displayed, as would *John Brown's Body* in greater skill and extension, a variety of poetic techniques with particular emphasis upon blank verse narrative and dialogue, broken by brief, colloquial songs. A characteristic one was the stanza which Benét gave to Lucullus:

> I thought of love as mixed with earth,
> One with the bloom of the sods.
> My love is air and wine and fire,
> Breaker of metes and rods,
> A slender javelin tipped with light,
> Hurled at the gods.

The portraits themselves were vivid and dramatic, remarkable for their shrewd analysis of character by a seventeen-year-old. The verse was both lean and swift, the proficiency bolstered now by thematic substance.

41

Even the Colonel was impressed. He told the boy that the songs were rather pretty, though he faulted the blank verse as betraying too plainly the influence of Browning. "As far as writing goes," the father told a brother colonel, allowing himself more parental pride than he cared to show his son, "[Stephen] has had unusual success for a boy 17." [30]

William arranged with a Boston firm, The Four Seas Company, for the subsidized publication of *Five Men and Pompey*. An edition of three hundred copies was printed in the early winter of 1915, the sixth volume in a uniform series of poems and verse plays by Gordon Bottomley, Richard Aldington, Lewis Worthington Smith, Robert Alden Sanborn, and Gilbert Moyle. The Four Seas was a reputable house, whose ventures also included the important *Poetry Journal* in which so much of the new poetry was appearing. In the issue of October 1915, just before book publication, the magazine printed in its entirety "After Pharsalia," the final monologue from *Five Men and Pompey*. *Poetry Journal* tended to represent the conservative wing of the poetic renaissance; its regular contributors included Conrad Aiken, Untermeyer, William Rose Benét, Bynner, and Arthur Davison Ficke. Stephen Benét was thus allied at the start of his career with the more traditional elements of the poetic revolt.

In one important respect, however, *Five Men and Pompey* differed radically from most of the new poetry. It showed a concern for political theory and philosophy that was essentially alien to much of the poetic renaissance. Years later one of Benét's disciples went so far as to identify its tone as specifically anti-Fascist. This was no more than pietistic hindsight, but there was certainly a concern for political liberty and the democratic freedoms which was rarely characteristic of the vaguely aristocratic position of the new poetry. "Though both of us have failed," Pompey reminds Caesar, "your cause yet rules, / Your Empire."

> Any fool can govern fools.
> To make fools rule themselves and do it well,
> That is the task. If you could rule forever,
> Caesar . . . but little men will seize your work,
> Your great machine. That's where the paths dissever!
> And Rome roars blindly down amid the murk
> To swift destruction. . . .

This, too, was an additional link between *John Brown's Body* and *Five Men and Pompey*. It was a natural product of the Benét heritage in general and the Colonel's private creed in particular. In the fall of 1915 Stephen Benét thus seemed plainly destined for a collegiate career, at Yale or elsewhere, that would combine political and poetic ferment. The Colonel gave his youngest son a generous check, and strict instructions as to his responsibility for accounting for its expenditure, and placed the last of his three "only" children on the train for New Haven. Boyhood was sternly over. If he passed the make-up exams, as Bridgman assured him he would, Benét would enter at Yale a world as fiercely competitive as any that then existed for a young middle-class American.

His brother had enjoyed that world immensely. Other young writers—aspirant or arrived—had detested it. Sinclair Lewis, the boy knew, had been bitterly mutinous at times. Undergraduate life as Lewis sometimes described it sounded a little like an urbane version of Hitchcock. Benét arrived in New Haven knowing not a single contemporary, the only one of his class at Summerville to come this far north to college. He lacked even a dormitory room, since he had not yet been officially admitted. For all his emotional maturity, and despite the adult quality of many of his responses, Benét confronted an unpredictable four years.

3. Bright College Years

This book is dedicated to Stephen Vincent Benét,
our most distinguished classmate for whom we all . . .[1]

IT was called a university. Its graduate schools bestowed a number of advanced degrees each spring. It had a substantial library, though the librarian discouraged the withdrawal of books by either teachers or students. A minority of its faculty were indeed the scholars whom they all imagined themselves to be, but in 1915 it was really still a college. "Here [at Harvard] we have thought but no school," William James had said recently, adding, "at Yale a school, but no thought."[2] It was undeniable that Yale College, in terms of power, autonomy, and prestige, thoroughly dominated Yale University.

These were the years when the national image of Yale was created. Quite naturally the image was a collegiate one. From the outside it seemed an institution of fierce loyalties, ritualistic organizations, social and economic privilege, powerful athletes, and aggressive, upwardly mobile undergraduates. Few of Yale's sons were disturbed then or later by such an image: it was the one they themselves preferred. These were the years when the great Yale songs were written, to be memorized eagerly, chanted fervently, remembered forever. Only its vast, still untapped wealth separated it from the provincial New England colleges—Williams, Amherst, Bowdoin, Dartmouth—to whom it condescended. It appeared to be a most unlikely spot for a literary renaissance.

To a degree, nevertheless, this renaissance was in process when Benét arrived in September 1915, and it reached a modest peak during his years as an upperclassman. In a small way the renaissance even became a part of the national image of Yale. In a much larger way it became a part of Yale's conception of itself. Like most images, it depended for its magnitude on the angle from which it was viewed.

Benét, who in the folklore of the image has been consistently cited as a major illustration of the Yale literary revival, was always skeptical of its reality. "You cannot force writers like early peas," he said in 1935, in reply to a question about the value of undergraduate writing courses. "And then—writing is about life. And all life can't be in a college." [3] His scrupulous accuracy would not permit him to distort the nature of his obligation, despite his abundant regard for the college and for the experience.

"Individual members of the English Department," he said on that same occasion in 1935, "did encourage me when I was in college. And [they] helped to get a scholarship or two afterwards. They didn't aid me in the sense of criticizing or pointing out merits or demerits in my verse. But then I never asked them to do so." All his life, as a consequence of the professionalism he acquired early from his family, Benét mistrusted any short cut to writing.

"The whole thing," he continued, "is in the man. You cannot devise any course to teach people to write. If you have the right sort of man, however, he can teach something about writing to most people. Even he, in my mind, cannot teach an original creator of the first or second rank although he might help him to avoid certain mistakes."

There were several such men on the Yale faculty during this period—John Berdan, Chauncy Tinker, Lawrence Mason, Charlton Lewis, perhaps Phelps, certainly Henry Canby—and Benét profited variously from an association with all of them. On the whole, however, the literary renaissance was little more than an atmosphere. In certain respects it was made possible at Yale by no more than negative aspects of that atmosphere; the mere suspension of active hostility to literary endeavor was an important factor. In reality, too, it was a national phenomenon as much as a local flowering. Much the same eruption of collegiate literary talent was occurring almost simultaneously at other American universities, at Harvard in particular, at Princeton, at the Universities of Pennsylvania and California, at Ohio State.

At Harvard there was a major literary tradition which extended back through a dozen generations. "I went to Harvard," Van Wyck Brooks remembered, "just as students in the twelfth century went to Paris . . . for I knew I was a writer born . . . and I supposed that Harvard was the college for writers." [4] At Yale, on the other hand, the partial acceptance of literary facility within the intricate local value system was a recent and significant change. It brought with it encouragement and sponsorship for undergraduates who had formerly sublimated these gifts in debating and theatricals.

The fundamental tone of the Yale renaissance was therefore hearty and gregarious. It was a literary milieu not unlike that which many of its members would also

47

create in New York in the 1920's. It was a literature of clubs and dinners and mild snobberies and appreciation. There was little awareness of literature as an art, though there was considerable declaration of beauty as truth. There was no visible recognition of any discrepancy between literary values and the values of the college as a whole.

Writing was simply an additional accomplishment which no longer invalidated manliness. It was another facet of competition, and some of the writing fellows were damn good sports. Archibald MacLeish was a varsity football player, captain of water polo, and member of Skull and Bones; Briton Hadden, soon to be a cofounder of *Time,* was one of the big men of his college generation. A few of the writers, to be sure, very definitely weren't good sports at all, but these took no part in the shared glories and rewards of the renaissance. They lived on the top floors of ancient and awkwardly situated dormitories. Their companions were apt to be the Chinese and Indians who represented the unassimilated fringe of a student body that was unhealthily homogeneous.

Benét himself, without distress, and content as always with the arrangements of fate and the pleasures of his imagination and a new scene, very nearly slipped painlessly into this collegiate no-man's land. The make-up exams safely behind him, he patiently submitted to bureaucratic misadventures. He purchased forty-one dollars worth of furniture for Pierson Hall quarters on which he'd assumed squatter's rights, and then was ejected when a prior claimant appeared. He moved, leaving his furniture behind, into a remote rooming-house. "Somewhat off the center," he wrote the Colonel dryly.

The boy sent his father a precise accounting of his expenses that first hectic week, including a dollar and sixty-five cents' worth of magazines—"A monstrous heap!" he conceded—and a twenty-five-cent item which he listed as "short changed (unfortunate)." His attempt to balance the filial account became increasingly complicated as the bookkeeping progressed, and ended on an ironically desperate note.

"I deposited the check with the New Haven Bank," he told the Colonel with a confident flourish, "and promptly drew a check for $14.00 and sent it to William as it's his. I will therefore account for this with the $100.00 as if I had subtracted it from the remains of the 80.00 it would leave me with a minus 4.00—at which the brain reels!" He also forwarded the Colonel a gift for the Minus-Poetry scrapbook. "I send you a poem I am sure you will appreciate—it's from *The Trimmed Lamp*, a nutty Chicago paper."

The younger brother of Bill Benét, 1907S—nephew as well of Laurence V. Benét, 1884S—couldn't be left long unattended either in an off-campus boarding house or on the top floor of Pierson Hall, to which he was soon recalled by the college authorities. Bill's friends on the faculty had been alerted by now to the presence of his young brother. They had been told of the astonishing reality that he was already the author of a volume of verse. He was in fact already known on the campus, without sarcasm and with the same deference that was paid, say, to a promising athlete in a minor sport, as the Freshman Poet. *Five Men and Pompey* was tangible if unread testimony; there it was, on sale at the Yale Co-op. The wheels of an elaborate in-group began to turn.

Henry Canby, still a restless assistant professor of English poised for flight to New York, mentioned young Benét to Dean Frederick S. Jones. The Dean, in a ges-

49

ture wholly characteristic of this collegiate atmosphere of artistic teamsmanship, summoned several prominent literary sophomores. He told them of the prodigy and dispatched them to Pierson Hall to inspect and, if appropriate, to sign him up. The sophomores found their poet; they observed that he needed a haircut, was using language coarse beyond the limits of Yale's currently muscular Christianity, and was pitching pennies on the stone floor with unsuitable companions. He was taken in hand.

It was the first in an unbroken sequence of rehabilitation programs by Benét's contemporaries. For the next twenty-eight years they fastened unsuccessfully upon him, a succession of prominent sophomores sent by a succession of worldly deans. At Yale they hoped to contain his talent within a form that would permit him not only to remain a poet but also to become an eligible candidate for Skull and Bones; his wayward humor forced them to settle for the less impressive Wolf's Head. In the 20's they scolded him for remaining unmoved by the expatriate glories which had now replaced Bones in their value system; he persisted in his charming but naive Americanism. "Seine and Piave," he wrote in 1927 in France, "are silver spoons,"

> But the spoonbowl metal is thin and worn,
> There are English counties like hunting-tunes
> Played on the keys of a postboy's horn,
> But I will remember where I was born.[5]

In their middle age, when he had become a national literary figure in the late 1930's and early 1940's, they were distressed by his clothes as they had once been troubled by his long hair; he bought his suits at Brooks, as he should, but he distorted the well-cut pockets with papers and letters and packages. He would not commit himself to Hollywood in accordance with the wishes of some; he would not abandon the rewards of magazine fiction that dismayed others. The intensity with which they tried to reclaim Benét to their various images of him was touching proof of their affection and aspiration; it was also related, of course, to the infinite variety of his friendships. From the beginning he had devoted friends in almost every literary camp. Only the extremists, all his life, could resent his sweet tolerance, serene purpose, and inflexible core of just principle.

"The single outstanding trait I have repeatedly remembered," said one of his classmates, who became a headmaster and spent his life in the observation of young men, "[was] his ability to be . . . congenial with all sorts of people, whatever their interests. He was distinctly a literary person, of course, but Steve would have been perfectly at home dining with the football team. He was genuinely interested in people and people as individuals." [6]

Thus it was characteristic that Benét retained throughout his four years at Yale the friendship of the group with whom he was first intimate and from whom his undergraduate successes separated him. The friends of his Pierson Hall obscurity never resented his removal from their orbit. They found him as warmly interested in them in 1918—after he had become chairman of the literary magazine, an editor of the *Record,* fraternity man and stagline fixture, senior society demigod—as he had been on the top floor of Pierson in 1915, when they printed a ribald newspaper parody of Yale.

His poetry was the principal agent of his fame. Like the hero of his 1921 novel, *The Beginning of Wisdom,* he arrived in New Haven with a summer's harvest of poems behind him, "which he fed cautiously, three or four a month, through the letter-slit in the door of the *Lit.* office." From the first he overwhelmed an organization traditionally indifferent to freshmen. Each of the eight issues of the redoubtable *Yale Literary Magazine* contained at least one of his poems that first year. He had two in the February number; in April, in addition to another pair of poems, he published his first short story.[7]

There had been nothing like it in the memory of current historians of the eighty-year-old magazine, even though its recent contributors and editors included undergraduates as mature as Leonard Bacon, as prolific as his own brother, as well-rounded as Archibald MacLeish, as belligerent as Waldo Frank. Benét quickly became a deviant celebrity in this world whose legends were more normally made by the lineman, rake, or purposeful Dwight Hall deacon. "He was reputed," one of his friends remembered of this freshman period, "to spend his time in a sort of garret, often with a bottle beside him, scribbling furiously." [8]

His isolation was probably in part deliberate. The Hitchcock wounds were still painful, even after four years; he had no desire to expose himself to further savagery, even of a collegiate kind. More particularly, he was having a splendid time, despite the absolute, momentary anonymity which later puzzled the friends of his upperclassman years. They wondered why they hadn't known Steve during the early weeks of that first year. The explanation lay not only in the nature of the Pierson Hall ghetto, but also in their own origins.

Almost without exception the companions of his final three years at Yale were graduates of the Eastern preparatory schools. In frozen blocs they had come to Yale, as to their rightful preserve; during most of Freshman Year they mingled only with their own kind. But, the hero of *The Beginning of Wisdom* observes, "a Yale class, like most real and historic democracies, begins with a hereditary aristocracy, grows tired of it and knocks out its underpinnings so that its members slide gently back into the general mass."

By the spring of 1916, and emphatically by the fall of that year, a tentative cross-breeding could begin. Benét passed, probably with less calculated design than any previous entrant, into more gilded company. The companions whom his talents acquired for him had come to Yale from Hotchkiss, Taft, St. Paul's, Groton, Hill, and St. Mark's. Of his genuine intimates, only John Farrar and Philip Barry had entered Yale from the obscurity of schools as unknown as his own Summerville.

Like Benét, Farrar was catapulted into a favored category by his poetic talent. Unlike Benét, he also possessed considerable local ambition and an acute political sense. Farrar had been one of the original sophomore delegation sent by Dean Jones to verify the Pierson Hall poet. Until he graduated in 1918, Farrar satisfied a part of his compelling drives by supervising Benét's Yale career, as he would later serve his friend's talents in New York as editor and then publisher.

Farrar, whose true gifts were as literary impressario and editor, during this period thought of himself primarily as a poet. Such a conception revealed a good deal about the Yale renaissance. Much of its momentum came from young men whose mature careers were to be in advertising, journalism, education, and publishing. Their talents were expository and promotional. Like some of their English professors, they suffered all their lives from a mild susceptibility to literature.

For one group the *Lit* and the *Record*, the one for

belles-lettres, the other for humor, were little more than powder charges that would detonate them into a Senior Society. For others the act of composition provided the temporary therapy characteristic of undergraduate composition. For a handful—MacLeish, Benét, Wilder, Philip Barry, Phelps Putnam, Robert Coates—there was some sense of commitment to an arduous undertaking. Even for these, however, it was at this time no more complex than Fitzgerald's Princeton exuberance or Dos Passos' Harvard aestheticism.

Benét, while never the most solemn or the most dedicated, was in a very real sense their talisman and their hostage. It was apparent to the others that he had in abundance the talent about which most of them were still seeking assurance. He also had an adult and professional charity toward literary clumsiness of which they were often still incapable; they wrote savage rejections on contributors' manuscripts and scratched each other bitterly.

"Without exerting any leadership, or ever being acknowledged as the leader," said a contemporary who knew them all, with the objectivity of friendship without intimacy, "Steve was the center and hub of this group. Without him all the same fellows would have been there —but each one of them had his 'separating' trait. Steve was not merely a poet, he was poetry. We did not think of him as a great man. He was not forbidding. He was just everybody's favorite companion." [9]

The resemblance to a nineteenth-century academy, which it had so recently been, survived at Yale in the paternalistic role of the faculty. Many of them cultivated for themselves personalities appropriate in various ways to such a function. The nature of much of the instruction—drill, lecture, examination—perpetuated adolescence and bestowed gianthood on teachers who were merely adults. Some played a lively and unwholesome part in the senior societies and fraternities. Each of the more luminous had his creatures and his abominations. Faculty feuds were occasionally inherited by and even delegated to suitable undergraduates.

Benét walked this hothouse atmosphere with immunity and innocence. He owned and maintained an excellent relationship with the Colonel; he was not in need of a father-substitute. Nor was the cultural indoctrination a revelation to a young man raised and tutored by poets and critics. Years later Archibald MacLeish, discussing a dynamic teacher of the period whom he himself had found extremely stimulating and to whom he dedicated his first book, speculated that for Benét the experience of being Professor Mason's student would have necessarily been far less significant. "Before he ever got to Yale," said MacLeish, "Benét had read all those exotic, obscure poets whom Larry Mason got us so excited about. Things like that, which were absolutely new to us, were old stuff to Steve." [10]

Benét had a kind of emotional and professional jump on his Yale contemporaries, particularly those who were interested in writing. "As I see it now," said one of the most thoughtful of his acquaintances ten years after Benét's death, "Steve was a very realized person, even at that young age, and therefore more or less simple. He was pretty much of an achievement himself, regardless of his work." [11] In certain important respects this jump lasted all Benét's life.

The poems he published freshman year in the *Lit* had been written before he got to Yale; he was finished with Shelleyesque mysticism by the time his classmates discovered it. As a sophomore he was avidly reading "The Conning Tower" every morning in the *Tribune,* and bombarding F.P.A. with contributions; he was eyeing New York while they were reacting to Tinker's Dr. Johnson and Phelps' Browning. By the winter of 1917 he'd had poems published not only in the *New Republic* but also in the *Century, Chimaera,* and the *Seven Arts.*[12]

In the very winter of his freshman year the *Century*—of which Bill was now literary editor—published his robust pirate ballad "The Hemp," in a lavish four-page spread in the Christmas issue, complete with four illustrations by John Wolcott Adams. Written in Augusta the previous summer, "The Hemp" was sleek and proficient, without the exciting verse and characterization of *Five Men and Pompey* but extraordinary in its deft use of standard material and hackneyed situations. It seemed the work of a seasoned pro, its stanzas rolling with chantey and menace.

> But down by the marsh where the fever breeds,
> Only the water chuckles and pleads;
> For the hemp clings fast to a dead man's throat,
> And blind Fate gathers back her seeds.[13]

Here again, as in the case of the undeniable evidence of *Five Men and Pompey,* was another concrete testimonial to Benét's special status. "We were all very much impressed," a classmate remembered thirty-five years later. "Even our callow 'rough-housers' realized that we had an accredited poet in our midst." [14]

His achievement was further consolidated in 1917, when "The Drug Shop" won the important Albert Stanburrough Cook Prize, awarded annually for the best unpublished poem or group of poems by any regularly enrolled student in the University, and was then printed in hard cover by the Brick Row Book Shop. At the age of nineteen Benét had published two books and appeared in a stately monthly, a liberal weekly, and the avant-garde little magazines. "The Drug Shop," its rather contrived situation overwhelmed by the homage to Keats, was in no way the poetic equal of *Five Men and Pompey* —or, allowing for the differences in genre, of "The Hemp"—but the lack of development went unnoticed in the general awe and admiration.

Now his fame extended beyond Yale. "Young Benét at New Haven," F. Scott Fitzgerald wrote Edmund Wilson from Princeton, "is getting out a book of verse before Xmas that I fear will obscure John Peale [Bishop]'s. His subjects are less precieuse & decadent." Malcolm Cowley remembered that as editor of the Harvard *Advocate* he had been similarly conscious of their Yale contemporary. "Benét," said Cowley in 1957, "was the bright star not only of Yale but of all the Eastern colleges." [15]

When Benét and his classmates became seniors, anxiously eligible for Yale's single undergraduate writing course, the celebrated "Daily Themes," Professor Berdan told him he would not accept him. He was too far along. It would be a waste of time. Like most undergraduates —but unlike the typical aspirant poet—Benét profited far more from his friendships with a variety of classmates than from the sponsorship of his instructors. He never denied the claims they later tried to fix on him, but he was entertained by the assurance of their memories.

"You must not be annoyed with Billy [Phelps]'s autobiography," he wrote an angry classmate in 1943, a few weeks before his death, "because I am quite sure that he now thinks Red Lewis, Phil [Barry], Thornton [Wilder] and I were all in the same class." [16]

Benét felt that the faculty points of view he valued most came from two of his history instructors. The first debt, to Sidney K. Mitchell, he described explicitly in 1921 in *The Beginning of Wisdom,* remembering Mitchell as "one of the few, rare, lucently-forceful intellects that can vivisect the smallest nerve or joint of a subject without ever losing its place and importance in the general anatomical scheme." Such a man—and his general utility to a writer who would eventually want to dramatize American legend—had a greater appeal than those who pressed belles-lettres upon him or read appreciatively aloud the English lyricists he had known since childhood.

From the second historian Benét acquired a basis for specific historical principle. The professional position of Charles M. Andrews, Farnam Professor of American History at Yale from 1910 until 1931, was that the United States could be properly understood only in terms of the English and European institutions from which it derived. Benét's undergraduate years occurred at the beginning of Andrews' most productive years. In books, articles, and lectures the distinguished colonial historian was clarifying his declaration that America represented first a transference and then a revision of English values.

American aspirations and institutions, Andrews insisted in the course which Benét took under him as a senior, had to be defined in terms not only of mother-country origins but also of ocean-passage refinement. It was persuasive doctrine for Benét, thoroughly logical to a young man whose own family history verified the New World mutation of an Old World heritage. "Steve," said his friend Archibald MacLeish in 1954, "was more conscious of being an American than any other man I ever knew."

58

Benét spoke often of the insights he received from Andrews. One of the tangible pleasures of his prominent role in the American Academy of Arts and Letters in the late 1930's arose from the opportunity it afforded to press successfully the award of a Gold Medal to Andrews. Benét offered an even more specific acknowledgment in his own work. As early as 1926, in magazine fiction that was still awkward and experimental, he made a blunt overstatement of it. Later, when he had mastered the American material, his translation of Andrews became more subtle and more thoroughly his own. The birth of the American temperament was a fundamental theme of his posthumous *Western Star*.

And those who came were resolved to be Englishmen,
Gone to the world's end, but English every one,
And they ate the white corn-kernels, parched in the sun,
And they knew it not, but they'd not be English again.

The avenue between Benét and Andrews, above all, was of a special kind. It was made natural and informal because of the close friendship between young John Andrews and Benét. The professor's son was a class behind Benét; he succeeded him as chairman of the *Yale Literary Magazine* and became a member of most of the less formal organizations in which Benét was active. Andrews was one of the first in an endless belt of writers —contemporaries as well as younger men and women— who became Benét's literary dependents during the next twenty-five years.

The Andrews home on St. Ronan Street was not unlike the Colonel's various quarters. It was hospitable and literate, and though the professor was in his study rather more than the Colonel, young Benét saw a good deal of him between 1916 and 1920. He enjoyed without seeking it deliberately—which he could not have done either temperamentally or properly—a portion of the kind of discipleship that produced for Andrews a distinguished group of scholar-protégés. From Benét's point of view this was a healthier relationship, as a crony of the professor's son and daughter, than the intense faculty-student relationships more characteristic of the renaissance.

The presence of Ethel Andrews, in fact, attractive and intelligent, a year or so younger than her brother, meant that the house was a center of undergraduate gaiety. Her friends from music school made it their New Haven headquarters. The range of Benét's Yale life was never the literary stereotype of sullen and misunderstood withdrawal. Very shortly his light verse for the *Record* began to reflect both his ironic frustrations with proms and their beauties, and the beginnings of the graceful songs that would culminate, in 1925, in *Tiger Joy.* "Some men prefer," he wrote in an April 1916 issue of the *Record,*

> Glad girls and free;
> Others aver
> Solemnity
> Is best to see;
> Some love the small—
> But, as for me,
> I like them all! [17]

Perhaps, in fact, the great contribution of the Yale renaissance was its lack of solemnity. During these four years Benét was required to write for an audience which was in large part a miniature of the one he would have to entertain from 1920 till 1943 as a popular writer. The *Yale Literary Magazine* was subscribed to by a majority of his contemporaries and read at least casually by some of them; the entire junior class still voted in the election of each year's chairman. The *Record*, frivolous and frequently vulgar, was subscribed to by almost every undergraduate and read devotedly by the majority.

Benét, writing prolifically for both magazines, was thus provided with two very different audiences. As a consequence his more serious work gradually acquired a neat coating of wit and satire; his light verse became less coltish. He preserved a stable perspective about both aspects of his work. His fluency was to a degree a constant prescription of purges. Unlike some of his less productive classmates, he was cleansed of the worst of what otherwise would have remained no more than adolescent fertility.

There were also real hazards in such a seemingly beneficent atmosphere. Benét's technical virtuosity was encouraged as the principal ingredient of much of his verse. His mature work would be similarly damaged for some years by this well-rewarded reliance on skills as a versifier. He became overaccustomed to writing under pressure for a never-ending sequence of deadlines. His contemporaries were vastly impressed by the rapidity with which he wrote his verse, frequently in the late evening after a movie or a rowdy excursion to Savin Rock. Unlike Farrar, who rented a room in which he composed poetry for two hours each day, Benét dashed off his work in class, in rooms full of noisy friends, or on the tavern tables.

The Elizabethan Club, beloved and abused by generations of Yale men, symbolized the ambivalence of the renaissance and its effects. The club was very genuinely their Mermaid Tavern; it was also their Rotary and Kiwanis. It was a fruitful center for comradeship and education; it was also another ludicrous gambit in the boosterism that led to the promised land of the Senior Societies. Here they could talk profitably among themselves. They could talk with—or at least listen to— Phelps and Berdan, and to such exciting younger teachers as Merrill Clement and Larry Mason. Here, on memorable occasions, they met Masefield and Drinkwater and Yeats; here, too, however, there gathered the promoter and the huckster and the effetely precious. Benét, as one consequence of all this, would never be pompous about himself or his trade, but there would be a kind of vocational hangover from which he would not fully recover until the mid-1920's.

In the meantime, however, he wrote prodigiously and enjoyed himself immensely. There were those who felt he enjoyed himself too much. One of his acquaintances later speculated solemnly that Benét's life was shortened by excessive drinking as an undergraduate. Another was certain that at the very least he damaged his constitution. This was the voice of the deacons and the heavies whom Benét was satirizing in his *Record* verse; here were the gullible adornments of his undergraduate legend. It was a provincial, gossipy world. When he collapsed in a snowbank outside Mory's, overcome as much by hilarity and limericks as by the celebrated green cup, there were those to say he had lain there till carried senseless from drink to his room.

It was in reality, as for most American undergraduates, a period of extremely modest dissipation. The major refutation of the myth, as one of Benét's closest friends later pointed out, was their unanimous lack of money.[18] In the company of several cronies he imagined himself deeply in love with a notable prom girl of their generation; they haunted the debutante parties that year and became briefly cynical. He flunked freshman physics and thumbed his poetical nose at the august Senior Societies.

> Who shivers a shudder effete
> On walking along High Street?
> > Who the posture assumes,
> > At the College Street Tombs,
> Of a sheep that is going to bleat?
> These verses will calm all your fears.
> Your chances will soon disappear
> > If you take vain delight
> > In the things that we write
> And you'll mourn for the rest of the year.[19]

In the tradition of the Societies, of course, Benét and his fellow blasphemers were among the first to be tapped. In this way, according to the skeptical, detractors were annually gagged. Their elevation did not occur, however, until May 1918. Meanwhile Benét wrote and then edited the *Lit*. He manufactured gay lampoons of every aspect of the local scene, for the *Record* and for the singing and drinking groups. For one of them, the Vorpal Blades, he wrote the major share of a series of satires called "The Songs of Dear Old Yale." The father of one of the Blades—himself a Yale man—agreed to underwrite their publication; having read them, however, he withdrew in alumnus dudgeon.

Benét read constantly, "the only man in our class," according to one contemporary, "who used the Library as an undergraduate." [20] He did the modest studying necessary to stay out of difficulty with the Dean's Office. He was never so harsh as some of his contemporaries in subsequent denunciations of what they cited as their intellectual betrayal by the College. He was too realistic to ignore the fact that he could have acquired a much better formal education had he been so minded. He was always conscious of the emotional immaturity and essential monasticism of prewar Yale, though he cherished its friendships and memories; in the 1930's he marveled at the poise of that decade's undergraduates. His gifts were encouraged and honored, and the range of his relationships brought new depth to an instinctive understanding of people.

The momentum of the intellectual vigor he had brought with him from home, on the other hand, was temporarily delayed by the insularity and complacence of the particular Yale which he and his friends inhabited. His interest in fresh ideas was not truly stimulated, nor was the political awareness of his adolescence encouraged to further development. He acquired no real awareness of economics or of contemporary historical reality. Like most of his generation, he would have to educate himself on his own time.

For the moment he and his friends were as indifferent to world affairs as to the complexity of those American institutions which would be so severely questioned and tested during their maturity. Few of the faculty encouraged them to examine their ignorance. Like the nation itself, they were astonished to find themselves participants in a world war in April 1917. The college campuses exploded with a kind of football rally excitement. There was a glorious orgy of indiscriminate idealism, subscription to solemn codes of duty, and romantic visions of self-destruction. It was an abrupt demarcation point for a son of the regular army.

4. War

Friendly fools speak an excessively bitter truth when they say that the task of us, the stay-behinds, the unwilling laggers, is the harder task.[1]

So quickly did the war overtake the undergraduates that it was some time before they tuned their public voices to the shift. The *Record* required several issues to use up the copy on hand concerning girlies, proms, and the Dean's Office. It was an awkward adjustment. The *He–She* jokes were revised hastily; *He* became a second lieutenant, *She* a nurse. Majors and colonels were substituted for the freshmen and professors who were the traditional butts of the *Record's* wit. Satiric verse about calisthenics and artillery problems began to filter in by mid-May. Throughout the spring of 1917, however, the *Record* was as giddy as the campus itself, a mirror of the gay parties which each night launched another group of friends to martial glory. "*Everyone* falls for the blonde!" Benét wrote in an April issue, improvising the verse just before press time to accompany a tardy, captionless drawing by his friend Don Campbell:

The giggling, the golden, the fond!
The dimpling, dumb maid of marshmallowy kisses!

Poor simpering slaves! *I* salute you with hisses!
Away with such pink-and-white, chocolate-cream blisses!
And give me the eyes black as jet,
The passionate wave of the dusk dear tresses,
The lips red as poppies, the smile that is Tess's,
The ling'ring embrace and the long sweet caresses!
The darling, entrancing brunette! [2]

Benét filled the pages of the *Record* with his light verse and satire that spring, but it was composed automatically and with as heavy a burden of inner depression as he had yet experienced. It was written between fruitless trips to each recruiting office in the area. He was rejected monotonously by every conceivable kind of military and volunteer unit. His eyesight made him absolutely unacceptable. Each alcoholic send-off at Mory's deepened his sense of frustration and self-reproach.

In Augusta the Colonel was already engulfed by the war, his single company of regulars swollen to a command of almost twenty thousand men, whom he trained with calm dispatch for Ordnance commissions. His brother Bill had been accepted in the Signal Corps and was waiting to be called. Soon came word of the deaths of several of his acquaintances, in training accidents, from the flu, one or two in combat. It was a grim, unhappy period, made no easier by the College's solemn and urgent insistence that the civilian undergraduates redouble their academic labors as their contribution to the war effort. Benét mocked the absurdity:

"For God, for country, for Yale!" is the cry
Of men who have left us, to conquer or die;
They'll do more for old Eli than ever before—
But study your English—you'll help win the war! [3]

66

Nevertheless the days had to be got through in one way or another. There were no more recruiting offices to besiege; it would be months before any doors would be opened by the strings he and Johnny Carter and Phil Barry were clumsily pulling in the State Department. The thought of a summer in Augusta, the Arsenal filled with the Colonel's thousands of officer candidates, was not endurable. He was rescued by the fears of a mother for her attractive daughter, and by the daughter's distaste for Red Cross ladies.

Along with half a dozen of his classmates, Benét had been squiring the beautiful Grace Hendrick at proms and beach parties and fraternity dances. He had read his poetry aloud to her; it was she who inspired the love poems with which he was beginning to vary his ballads. Mrs. Hendrick, a decisive matriarch, now felt that Grace had been exposed sufficiently to fashionable and uniformed gaiety. She would surely profit from a summer at correct but staid North Haven, Maine. Grace herself, who had disliked a brief stint with a Red Cross unit following a year or two at Bryn Mawr, was glad of a respite from the rigors of service.

Mrs. Hendrick, however, was not naive enough to deprive her daughter abruptly of all male companionship. She invited Ethel Andrews, Benét, John Andrews, and John Carter—the latter, like Benét, one of Grace's steady beaus—to spend the summer at North Haven. Mindful of the war, Mrs. Hendrick included the proviso that the young men must find suitable employment on the neighboring farms, thus combining in one stroke her duty to her country and to her daughter.

The summer was a great success. When the farm work did not materialize, Mrs. Hendrick resourcefully found them jobs in one of North Haven's two grocery stores; she suggested to the rival proprietors that she would give her considerable business to whichever employed her house guests. The hours were not arduous; the trio was hired as a single unit, dividing the day's work between them.

Removed from the tormenting sight of uniforms which could not be theirs, their abundant leisure occupied by two attractive girls, the three Yale men passed the time pleasantly. Carter, busily liberating himself from a ministerial home and four years at St. Mark's, had a lively, sardonic wit and the intellectual fluency that would later bring him celebrity in Washington during the 1930's as the New Deal columnist Jay Franklin. John Andrews, an admirable foil for Benét and Carter and full of regard for Benét in particular, had a sweet and engaging disposition. Grace Hendrick provided in full measure the stimulating but elusive object which Benét's romanticism required at this time.

He used a little of the North Haven scene in one of his magazine short stories in 1922, building the plot of "Canned Salmon," published in *Everybody's,* around a grocery store in a summer colony.[4] A more immediate and durable product of the summer was a touching and evocative poem, "Flood-Tide," which he later subtitled "Maine Coast—1917." It was printed in the *Yale Review,* the new national quarterly which Wilbur Cross was editing. Benét always exempted "Flood-Tide" from the severe pruning he exercised when collecting his verse in hard covers; it was reprinted in *Heavens and Earth* in 1920 and in *Ballads and Poems* in 1931. Even in the remote idyll of a boat ride under a full moon, "like a spilling of milky sap from the sky," the war was implicitly present in the tender sense of youth, and then savagely an intruder in the final emphatic stanza.

Quiet, quiet and quiet, said the march of the wave beneath.
Oh, immaculate shone the mind while the lotos of silence
grew!
And the sore heart heavy with youth was a clean blade
straight in its sheath,
As we drank with a matchless dream in that chrism of
salt and dew!

*Death jams down on his spade in the bloom of our elvish
orchard,*
Even the root-curls crawl at the skeleton jokes he cracks;
*Let's make rhymes for a while, as our Youth goes out to
be tortured!*
*We shall remember a moon till they hew us under the
axe!* [5]

The war surrounded them instantaneously when they
returned to New Haven in September 1917. Student
units drilled ineptly on the campus, near Connecticut
Hall and the statue of Nathan Hale. They mounted and
remounted the preposterous wooden horses which were
the War Department's desperate substitutes for the real
thing. More imaginative than most, and knowledgeable
about the realities of war, Benét was now only mildly
amused by these new absurdities. Raised on the tales
of dead fellow-officers and the barrack-room realism of
enlisted men, he was prematurely mindful of the casualty lists. His college poetry had always been touched
by his grateful sense of the wonders of his multiple
friendships. Now he was oppressed by the imminence
of fragile mortality.

The war brought his poetry a new sobriety and di-
mension. His mood was poignantly apparent in an ac-

complished quartet of sonnets published in the *Lit*. The first three were rich with the commonplace warmth of collegiate experience, of examinations and talk and lazy mornings in the dormitory. The fourth was grim and bleak. He called it "Return—1917." His epigram was an ironic quote from the university catalogue: "The College will reopen Sept. —."

I was just aiming at the jagged hole
Torn in the yellow sandbags of their trench,
When something threw me sideways with a wrench,
And the skies seemed to shrivel like a scroll
And disappear . . . and propped against the bole
Of a big elm I lay, and watched the clouds
Float through the blue, deep sky in speckless crowds,
And I was clean again, and young, and whole.

Lord, what a dream that was! And what a doze
Waiting for Bill to come along to class!
I've cut it now—and he—Oh, hello, Fred!
Why, what's the matter?—here—don't be an ass,
Sit down and tell me!—What do you suppose?
I dreamed I . . . *am* I . . . wounded? *"You are dead."* [6]

The new burdens continued however to have a healthy effect on both his spirit and his verse. By the end of 1917 he somberly reconciled himself, for a time at least, to a noncombatant and inglorious war. He went to classes with some regularity and in the life of the community he assumed the detestable role his status as campus leader required. For the *Lit* he wrote with more realism than the genre usually received the editorials that were intended to stiffen resolve and clarify purpose. He utilized his own frustration. "It is very fortunate," he pointed out in the November issue, "that even any partial realization of the War comes to us seldom, and in snatches. For when it does come, we know the true meaning of that antique phrase, the torture of thought. There is a vicious circle around which the mind swings greyly, unlit by any flame of sacrifice or devotion, agonizing as all pains are agonizing to the very young." [7]

Even in this ponderous guise of inspirational trumpeter Benét could not disguise his bitterness and self-reproach. He demolished editorially the illusion that modern war was in any way a great adventure. "Of course," he added savagely, "there remains always the adventure of staying behind (by virtue of age or some physical defect) and having your friends killed, adventurously or otherwise." From his distress he wrung a candid rationale. "Of only one thing, out of all our muddled vision, are we truly conscious—that the War has lapped about us and is rising over us like deep water. We are all quite unprepared to make the intolerable sacrifices we must make. We shall feel pain more exquisite and rending than any we have known or shall know again. We shall fight for an end unknown to us, under a cause which we do not entirely understand. Unless we are utterly broken, there will always be the rack of thought—and we shall drive ignorantly toward a hidden and bloody consummation. Whether the thing we get will seem worth the price we pay must rest indifferent to us. For it is by such means that men buy their freedom."

Benét found more comfort in his poetry and his reading than in trying to explain the war to the Yale audience. He sold a poem to the *New Republic* and another to *Youth,* the Cambridge little magazine, and found a new market, too, in William Braithwaite's *Contemporary Verse.* A fourth poem was published in the annual anthology, *The Poets of the Future.*[8] He reread once more the exquisite verse of *Romeo and Juliet*, reviewing a new edition for the *Lit*, and found in it "not merely pleasure or awe, but a feeling of delighted and childish wonder to come suddenly again before such a work of pure and intense art as this." [9] Now, too, he had sufficient new poems of his own to submit a manuscript to the Yale University Press, whose Series of Younger Poets had already included volumes by John Farrar, Archibald MacLeish, and his own brother.

His poems were accepted in January 1918, one of the first manuscripts to be read by Carl Purington Rollins, the Press's able new typographer. When the Colonel came north on army matters he visited the Press with his son to discuss the new book. It was to be called *Young Adventure*. It would be dedicated to his brother and contain a foreword by Chauncey Tinker. Benét, weary of the recital of his gifts as a prodigy, extracted a pledge from Tinker that the foreword would be a very general statement about poetry, with no biographical material concerning its author.

But university presses move with grave dignity. The spring of 1918 came and went before the galleys arrived. Benét and Phelps Putnam took the proofs to the room of a third poet, Alfred Bellinger, and read them aloud. Bellinger's roommate, a massive football player, listened in amazement. "Wait," he said finally, "till I tell them in Nebraska I know *three* poets." [10]

Even now, however, the war continued to dominate Benét's mind. In April he learned that one of his close friends had been killed in an air engagement. "Steve Potter's death," he wrote his mother, "and the accounts of it, make me wish very deeply I could get into some active service." There were signs that the campaign to get civilian jobs with the State Department might soon materialize. Benét made one final effort to avoid the indignity of a clerkship, even in striped pants. He memorized the army's eye-chart—exactly as his contemporary, Ernest Hemingway, was doing at almost the identical moment in Kansas City—and was accepted and formally sworn into the Army of the United States. The next day, observing his newest KP at a New Jersey camp, a sergeant watched in amazement as Benét peeled potatoes. The NCO, Benét said later, decided from "the way he was carving the things he was likely to nick his nose." [11] He was summoned to another eye test—with a different chart—and promptly recommended for immediate discharge. He had served three days.

Finally there arrived the reprieve from inaction. On August 19, 1918, he went to work at the State Department. His brother was also in Washington, a ground officer in the Air Corps, and John Carter was there too for a time. The town, in fact, was full of friends, some of them career officers he had known all his life, others his contemporaries from Yale or members of the faculty. He was a clerk at State until the end of October, when he managed a transfer to the livelier job of cryptographer with Military Intelligence. Here, in an office that was virtually an extension of the Ivy League, Benét worked briefly in the mixed company of young men like himself and a group of distinguished classical scholars and philologists, under the command of the colorful Herbert A. Yardley.

There were a number of writers as well as academics in the unit, most of them older than Benét and hitherto unknown to him save by reputation; several of them would become his friends in New York after the war. Arthur Somers Roche was a captain, Tinker was there, and James Thurber. Arthur Train, who later described

73

the organization as "that dunghill of scheming and wire-pulling," was another of the officers, and Captain Franklin P. Adams was in charge of personnel. "Yet," Benét said sardonically many years later, describing the code room in 1918, "America did win the war." [12]

Even in such company Benét had a kind of compelling presence. Robert Redfield, the Chicago anthropologist, remembered being placed at a table with a number of other apprentice decoders on his first day. "Only one drew my attention," Redfield said in 1956, "because his round and spectacled face had in it qualities that made me want to know the man." [13]

Benét himself was as speedily disenchanted with Washington as Arthur Train. "At present expectations," he wrote a Yale classmate just before Christmas, "I will leave this infernal city Saturday." His eyes were not strong enough for cryptography, and he had returned to clerking in the State Department. He observed the Washington scene itself, however, with astute distaste. "The hate that goes on behind the lines is usually the worst in any war," he once said reminiscently. In 1938 he recalled with precision the Washington atmosphere of twenty years earlier, "the men in the bureaus, the propaganda men, the men with the well-shined boots and the good political connections, the wranglers and the schemers, the men who burrow and strive and breed like blow-flies in the vast intricate web of army organization behind the front." [14]

He resigned from the State Department on December 21, 1918, six weeks after the Armistice, and returned to New Haven to finish up his undergraduate work. His mood was not immediately studious. "I am rooming in Connecticut [Hall]," he wrote his friend Shreve Badger, who was waiting his discharge from the navy. "I will be damn poor—but Lord what a six months it will be!" Earlier he had assured Badger that Wolf's Head, into which the latter had just been accepted, was "one senior society which does *not* believe in prohibition!"

To his own considerable surprise, however, Benét found himself and his contemporaries approaching the academic work with unexpected zest. The war had been something of a revelation to all of them, no matter where or in what capacity or how briefly they had served. They returned to Yale with a number of questions for the faculty's consideration. "The recommencement of College," Benét wrote in his first editorial of 1919 for the *Lit*, "reveals, among its many marvels, one extraordinary —almost unique—phenomenon: the fact that the returning men, almost unanimously, wish to work as hard at and get as much out of the curriculum as possible." [15]

The College, however, was not prepared for this sobriety. The faculty was undermanned; instead of an enlarged curriculum for this new appetite, there were fewer courses available than before the war. The basic organization of undergraduate fields of study—the Major and Minor system—was, according to Benét, "an eyesore, offense and stumbling-block in the way of any consistent and reasonable plan of education." He described the enthusiasm of the veterans as "the greatest opportunity in the history of the College," fearing that it would be "lost forever" if the faculty did not provide instantaneously a new diet.

The faculty could not achieve this miracle, though it utilized the defeat in preparing for the same phenomenon in 1946. Benét and his classmates slid back to their prewar habits, Benét so successfully that as late as March 1919 there was some doubt as to whether he would be eligible for his degree in June. Many of them drifted away from New Haven that winter, or never came back at all. By February those who remained were freed of the burdens of chairmanships and offices, the campus plums now falling automatically to the juniors. They caroused their way toward June. Benét finally passed physics, sitting lordly among the freshmen while the professor made tart comments on the incompatibility of poetry and the natural sciences. He listened more attentively to Andrews' lectures on American history, and coasted through a pair of English courses. He continued to sell his new poems in New York—now to the *Dial* and *Ainslee's* [16]—and he pondered the reviews of his third volume of verse.

Young Adventure was published in October 1918. By the time Benét got back to New Haven in January 1919 the notices were beginning to appear. It was the first of his books to be widely reviewed. The critics were generous and enthusiastic, in *Poetry*, the *Bookman*, the *Dial*, the *Yale Review*, the *Nation*, and on the Boston *Transcript's* excellent book page. Louis Untermeyer found it "an astonishing performance," seeing it as evidence of Benét's "artistic maturity." Babette Deutsch spoke of its "vivid poetry . . . shocking realism [and] exquisite humor." The *Transcript* noted the extraordinary body of work which Benét had now completed at the age of twenty. "It has seemed so long since we have been reading and admiring the poems of Stephen Vincent Benét," the Boston reviewer—William Braithwaite —confessed, "that the inescapable impression of him is as of a man much older than he is." [17] Benét himself, though he never reprinted the volume's longest poem, "The Drug Shop," was justly content with this verse of his late adolescence. "I have just re-read *Young Adven-*

76

ture," he told John Farrar in 1928. "I am willing to stand by it for what it is at the time it was written."

On the surface Benét appeared to face none of the customary dilemmas of graduation. Most of his class-mates were in troubled doubt as to their careers. Benét had already launched his. He was a poet. He had pub-lished three books and sold his work in professional competition. His vocation seemed assured. Once, long before, he had told the Colonel he was going to be a poet when he grew up. His father's answer had been to escort him to the garden and invite him to name each flower. The test completed, the Colonel had agreed gravely that some day he might indeed be a poet.

Now he had survived sterner obstacles. His teachers and friends felt absolute certainty of his gifts and his destiny. "Of course it is impossible to predict how a young poet is going to turn out," Professor Charlton Lewis, himself a poet, had said officially of Benét in March, "but, judging from the poetry he has already written, and from the evident qualities of his mind, I regard him as the most promising one that I have ever known among our undergraduates." [18] Benét himself was more realistically mindful of the harsh truths of making a living as a poet. Three books and a score of sales had not brought him enough to live on for six months.

In February 1919 Benét had applied to the Graduate School for admission the following September—Profes-sor Lewis' estimate had been written as a recommenda-tion for a scholarship—but by June he knew he was weary of classes and professors. Anyway, the Colonel would retire shortly; he couldn't decently ask his father to go on supporting him indefinitely. Along with countless literary-minded young Americans in the summer of 1919, Benét therefore responded to the siren promises of America's newest industry.

The advertising agencies were insatiable for copywriters that summer. They filled the college newspapers and yearbooks with glowing want ads, rich with tributes to themselves and the young men wise enough to join their ranks. They seemed about to replace the print shops of the nineteenth century and the newspapers of the prewar period as the training schools for American literature. Sherwood Anderson, Marquand, Stallings, Barry, Scott Fitzgerald, Benét—they all wrote copy during those months after the war.

All of them save Anderson, a seasoned and resilient journeyman, were soon writing it with equivalent despair. Benét stuck it out for three months, composing soap and underwear material for Hoyt's Agency on 32d Street, in the company of several future Madison Avenue vice presidents. He was not so responsive as they to America's self-styled newest art form. He was bored by its mechanical tricks and depressed by the eight-hour day. Although he shared with the Colonel a relish for the comforts and amenities of life, like the Colonel he also lacked the acquisitive instinct which would have otherwise made advertising a more palatable career. New York itself, on the other hand, had as it always would an immense and turbulent effect on him. His imagination was both possessed and repelled by its harsh variety. Its magnitude and beauty, and its bleakness and indifference, all united with his personal situation to give his poetry its most important new stimulant since the declaration of war in April 1917.

His affair with Grace Hendrick, platonic and rather one-sided, was petering out, she seeking a larger prize than the son of an army officer, he endowing her with idealized qualities she couldn't sustain. "So there's the end of it, Nelly!" he wrote dramatically,

> Of you and your purple hat!
> And I, your impotent Shelley,
> With czars and pariahs smelly,
> Shall tapestry well [Death]'s belly,
> That gray, round Rat! [19]

In New York during the summer of 1919 his verse gathered from these various sources—from boredom, from unrequited love, from poverty, from skyscraper splendor—a new kind of robust song which brought him into closer harmony with his contemporaries and made him a spokesman for their restlessness. What he was writing were in effect modern ballads, like the one from this period which he called "Wisdom-Teeth":

> When I was a man and a very young man
> I straddled the wings of Boreas!
> For I was the high gods' drinking-can,
> My rhymes were their ale uproarious!
>
> But they poured out the posset of youth to cool
> And I shine like an empty tankard
> With a witless smile at the heavenly pool
> Where the moons of desire float anchored.
>
> The bubble of sugar I swore was love,
> The purge that I knew for knowledge,
> I'm bare of the lot, and the winds above
> Are teaching me more than college! [20]

Always, however, there was a quality which separated him from most of the young writers of his generation at this very instant when he seemed most to share their rebellion. The quality was in the title—"Wisdom-Teeth" —with its wry, self-depreciating humor. All through his mature work, which can most properly be dated from these New York poems of 1919, there ran this same thread of the nonportentous, even in the grim Nightmare series of the 1930's. As much as any single ingredient it was the one which so endeared him to so many American readers, making him the most widely read serious poet of his time. It was, similarly, the quality which separated him from his fellow poets and even more particularly from those critics who required cosmic statement and erudite disenchantment. There was in Benét an unashamed delight in the savor of poetry which would never sit well with the solemnities of the metaphysical criticism. In a sonnet called "Talk" he now, in 1919, revealed his unfashionable zest:

New words are my desire, new verbs to scan,
Chaste paradigms that never sold themselves,
And adverbs from the leaf-talk of the elves,
With dog-faced articles, unknown to man;
Low-pattered syllables that trot like sheep
Round out my mouth and mind with holy peace,
And I have found redemption and surcease
In Babylonian nouns like bulls asleep.[21]

When he collected these poems the next year in *Heavens and Earth,* he placed the New York verse in a section called "The Tall Town." Here was the record of his three months as an ad man, in lines about boarding-houses and speakeasies and prizefights and strike pickets, in the jaunty regrets for a lost love and the vivid imagery of "Lunch-Time along Broadway":

Twelve-thirty bells from a thousand clocks, the type-
    writer tacks and stops,
Gorged elevators slam and fall through the floors like
    water-drops,
From offices hung like sea-gulls' nests on a cliff the whirl-
    winds beat,
The octopus-crowd comes rolling out, his tentacles crawl
    for meat.[22]

Benét was writing the best poetry, thus far, of his career, but he was bored at Hoyt's and it was plain that
he would never become an opulent accounts executive.
A job in an office, Benét once said, "is my idea of hell
without grandeur. I would rather be kept in a cage." [23]
Henry Canby was nevertheless alarmed lest he be sucked
into the permanent bondage of a nomadic sequence of
copywriting or advertising jobs. He urged Benét to reconsider the Graduate School, arguing that he needed
an additional year to get his bearings and establish himself firmly in his writing habits. John Carter wrote about
the same time from Europe that he was coming back to
Yale for a year. He was anxious that Benét share an apartment in New Haven with him and his brother Henry.

Benét began to regret his cavalier attitude toward a
Graduate School fellowship which had been offered to
him in June. He felt no compulsion toward teaching or
scholarship, and little taste for the poverty of an instructor's salary, but by October 1919 an academic respite
seemed preferable to the flat monotony of the agency.
First from Hoyt's, and then from the Watervliet (N.Y.)
Arsenal, to which the Colonel had been assigned for his
last command before retirement, Benét began a rather

embarrassed correspondence with Dean Wilbur Cross.

"As Mr. Canby may have told you," he wrote the Dean in mid-October, "I wrote to him last week to ask if he thought it would be possible for me to recover the fellowship in the Graduate School I resigned last year— and try to make enough on the side by writing to exist. Could you tell me about it, sir—and tell me how large the fellowship is? Also, if I could get it, what courses I would have to take, when I should start, and just how much work I would have to make up?"

The Dean, who was also editor of the *Yale Review*, knew and admired Benét's poetry. Benét also had for support not only the individual testimony of Canby but also the official letter with which the English Department had sponsored Benét for a Graduate School Fellowship in March 1919. Conceding that Benét was a low-stand man in everything except English, the professors had nevertheless pressed Benet's candidacy on the grounds of his proven quality as a poet. "Benét is a genius," the committee reported in an idiom that was academically intemperate. They employed deft gamesmanship. "Yale," they pointed out slyly, "has not had the reputation of being very hospitable to genius, and you may believe that it is a wiser policy to give fellowships only to scholars of unexceptionable academic standing. I hope, however, that you will agree with us that this is an excellent opportunity to establish a better tradition." [24]

Cross therefore arranged with Dean Jones of the College that Benét should be awarded for 1919–20, despite the fact that the academic year had begun on September 25th, the Foote Fellowship of $300. Dean Jones, who recalled the physics course Benét had flunked twice, and the 55 in Spanish in 1918, and the irreverent verse in the *Record*, wrote Benét a rather pointed letter of confirmation on October 27, 1919. "I hope," said Jones, "[the Fellowship] may enable you to proceed with your work and that you may make such a record as will justify the Committee in awarding you some better Fellowship next summer."

Benét returned to New Haven immediately, taking rooms with the Carter brothers at 209 York Street. It was a bizarre shift from Hoyt's Agency. By December he had satisfied the Graduate School language requirements in Latin, French, and German and was attending classes in his four courses. He forewent the opportunity to enroll in Methods of English Study, Old French for English Students, Old and Middle English, and Advanced Old and Middle English. His schedule was obviously chosen to suit his own tastes rather than those of the Graduate School sages. He took Cook's Theories of Poetry, Pierce's Contemporary Poetry, Cross' English Prose Fiction, and Canby's Literary Composition. These were the choices of a young man indifferent to the traditional jewels of a graduate course in belles-lettres. Two of his four courses —Pierce's and Cook's—were in fact coldly labeled in the catalogue as not counting toward the Ph.D. degree. Benét's commitment to the academic world was not an impassioned or reckless one.

The poetic momentum he had achieved in New York, however, was speedily rechanneled into the productive pattern which had always characterized his Yale periods. Now there was the major difference that he was enrolled in Canby's writing course. Canby, out of sympathy with his superiors and soon to leave for New York and the literary editorship of the *Evening Post,* had none of the traditional hostility of a graduate faculty toward contemporary writers. He was, in fact, according to one of his students that year, "eternally gloomy about everything except two or three" of the young men in English 40. The latter ignited under Canby's benevolent and admiring leadership.

It was an extraordinary group—Benét, Thornton Wilder, William DeVane (later Dean of the College), Walter Millis, Phelps Putnam, Luce, and Hadden—and Canby always recalled it as the high point of a conscientious and gifted teaching career which had contained many disappointments. Canby sat casually at the end of the table, presiding in a completely pragmatic way over this mixture of highly charged undergraduates and deviant graduate students. He encouraged each student to write in the form that most attracted him, requiring only that they write constantly. "The course was wonderful," DeVane remembered many years later. "It carried itself." [25]

Luce wrote editorials and Hadden tinkered energetically with what would soon become the *Time* dialect. Benét began the novel about a California boyhood and a Yale young manhood which would be published in 1921 as *The Beginning of Wisdom*. Wilder worked on an early version of the short plays in *The Angel That Troubled the Waters*. Literary alumni of recent vintage—Canby was not a collector of celebrities—visited the class. MacLeish and Barry and John Farrar were drawn to it as much by their friends' enthusiastic reports on the lively discussions as by Canby's invitations.

Canby was primarily interested in whether or not their material would sell in a commercial market. His approach was that of an editor or literary agent rather than a professor of literature. He said very little about form or aesthetics or structural theory. He conceived his responsibility as that of providing these young writers with an opportunity to learn how to arouse and hold an audience. Stimulated by this atmosphere of professionalism, several of them had already edited a volume called *The Yale Book of Student Verse, 1910–1919*. It was published that same year by the Yale Press, with an epilogue by Bill Benét and an introduction by Charlton Lewis, the single member of the English Department whom Benét credited with having taught him much about poetic technique. In collaboration with his friend Monty Woolley, director of the student Dramatic Association, Benét also prepared for the Press an acting version of Marlowe's *Tamburlaine the Great*.

Canby's English 40 was thus in effect a vocational training in the practice of letters. "It was full of talent and ideas and ferment," said DeVane in 1954. For Benét it was a workshop which effectively consolidated the base he had been constructing through his work for the *Lit* and the *Record*. His senior and graduate years at Yale became a kind of final internship; during them he edited two books, began his first novel, published poetry in *Ainslee's*, the *Literary Digest*, Morley's "Bowling Green" column in the New York *Evening Post*, the *Yale Review*, and *Contemporary Verse*. He sold his first short stories—to *Munsey's* and *Smart Set* [26]—and participated actively in the more fully developed Yale literary renaissance, which had now matured sufficiently to launch its own little magazine.

The history of *S4N*, the little magazine which was printed in New Haven in 1919 and 1920, and then in Northampton until its demise in 1925, contained some but not all of the elements common to most of the fugitive journals of the period. It included a dedicated individual—in this case Norman Fitts, 1920—whose tenacious enthusiasm provided most of the acceleration. It provided a vehicle for a group of young men—Benét, John Carter, Ramon Guthrie, Roger Sessions, Quincy Porter, William Hanway, Fitts himself—who were personally congenial. It lacked the patron who generally figures prominently in the avant-garde world, but Fitts' drive and resourcefulness were a thoroughly adequate substitute.

S4N differed from most little magazines, on the other hand, in that its initial contributors represented several of the arts and advocated a variety of aesthetic positions. Even its title verified the lack of a doctrinaire credo. Instead of the militant banners of the species—*Blast, Broom, secession*—these young men were so unanimously uncommitted that when the first issue went to the mimeographer they had not yet agreed on a title. Fitts hastily put a parenthesis on the cover page—"(Space for Title)" —which changed by gradual stages to (Space for Name), to (S for N), and finally to the cryptic *S4N*.

In the company of the American little magazines of the period *S4N* belonged to the eclectic wing best represented by Mencken's *Smart Set* rather than to such more single-minded publications as *transition* and *Poetry*. To this degree it was particularly appropriate as the little magazine with which Benét was most closely identified. *S4N* represented the same tolerance for disagreement which was his own fundamental position both professionally and personally. There was a good deal of dispute in the pages of *S4N*, but less of the violent abuse that more often characterized the little magazines. Benét himself felt strongly about the need for professional charity.

"I don't like Joseph Lyman in the last issue at all," Benét wrote in the summer of 1921, responding to Fitts' pleas for comment on the current numbers. "There should be every room for invective and personal insult . . . —it is a neglected art and should be revived— but *only* when such insult or invective is clever, amusing, effective, or with a real point behind it. Lyman's attack on Miss Sapwood presents none of these qualities; it only suggests a little boy yelling Yah, you're another." [27]

S4N had expatriate aspects, as Benét himself was soon to have, which were neverthless subordinated to a predominantly native character. The idea had been born— on the 4th of July, in fact—in Paris, where Fitts was stimulated in the summer of 1919 by a *cercle* of poets and painters which met at the Café des Tourelles. Impressed by the "mutual inspiration" the French artists gained from weekly discussions, Fitts suggested to his Yale friends on his return to New Haven that they, too, could profit from such a device. Since they were already beginning to scatter, most of them to Europe, Fitts argued that a magazine would provide the chance "to argue, discuss, criticize, praise or condemn each others' ideas." His proposal was simple and direct. "The first of each month," he wrote in the initial issue of November 1919, "let each member write an article, short or long, in any form whatsoever, on any subject in which the writer is interested. Then I shall typewrite copies of the collected contributions and distribute them. In that way we can keep in touch with each other. Possibly once a year we can have a meeting." [28]

Benét, his name modestly established among the New York magazines, had less need for a private house organ than any of the others, but he was thoroughly in agreement with Fitts' proposition. It was exactly the kind of atmosphere he had missed at Hoyt's. He gave Fitts, during the first week he was back in New Haven, an enthusiastic endorsement, though it sounded a little like some of the papers he was already writing for his graduate classes.

"Many of the best and most original movements in art," he lectured them, "have been started by the concerted energy of a small, active group. The Preraphaelites were such a group—the Imagists also. Whatever one's personal opinions may be of either, one had, the other is having a profound influence on the most excellent creative work of its time." He quoted a stanza of Marlowe —"Join with us now in this our mean estate"—and stated that out of such enterprises as this new magazine "there may be a real American art that we have, however strugglingly, helped ourselves to make." [29]

Benét himself was for a time the major prop of *S4N*. In its first issues of 1919 and 1920 appeared the work in which he was attempting to stabilize the turbulent effects of the war and frustrated love and heady Manhattan. The Graduate School gave him precisely the respite he required and Canby had predicted. He cut classes rather freely in all but Canby's course. When he attended them it was with the detachment of a man whose mind was elsewhere. A member of Cross' seminar in fiction recalled Benét distinctly, thirty-five years later, as casual beyond the conventional intensity of graduate study. He made notes rapidly and negligently with his left hand, in French rather than English as befitted a poet who applied for a traveling fellowship for 1920–21 as early as December 1919. He clearly regarded his left hand as sufficient for scholarly chores; his right hand he reserved for poetry.

Benét was not in any way the conventionally embittered creative spirit entombed by the atmosphere of sober Germanic pedantry. He simply ignored the Graduate School, withholding himself for his poetry and his novel.

"He was drifting," John Carter speculated later, but this was far from accurate.[30] Benét was both productive and thoughtful during that year. He carefully explained what he was attempting in a note that accompanied a group of poems in the December 1919 issue of *S4N*. "The following poems or verses," he told Fitts, "are taken from a projected series to be called 'The Kingdom of the Mad.' The sonnets are a try at making something that is somewhat more dramatic and alive out of the conventional sonnet-form than fourteen perfectly smooth and faultless lines of rhymed iambic pentameter."[31]

His legend, too, was extended a little further. Now it became widely believed that when broke he instructed Carter to lock him in his room until he completed a story, which was subsequently sold for a fabulous price. In reality he was writing more carefully than ever before, profiting from the discussion in Canby's class and compelled by the authoritarian dictums of Professor Cook's lectures on the *Poetics* to frame more operative principles for himself. A contemporary could remember in 1954 the impassioned classroom declaration by Benét in 1920 that every writer possesses his own individual interpretation of the timeless situations. "The great stories must be rewritten for every generation," Benét instructed the forbidding Cook, fluently citing as evidence the variant Guineveres of Malory, Tennyson, and William Morris.[32]

Benét never had the irate mistrust of the academic world which characterized so many American writers of his generation. He had worked under several of the nation's most distinguished scholars and teachers. He was not impressed, on the other hand, by the apparatus of Teutonic methodology with which graduate students were trained. "The Ph.D., like the poor," he said once, "is almost sure to be with us, no matter what world-upheaval impends." What he valued most was character rather than learning. "That is what you have to have first," he maintained, in a tribute to Billy Phelps, "and the most scholarly thesis on the minor works of Hannah More or the rhyme-endings in Wordsworth's Ecclesiastical Sonnets won't do it for you." [33]

But the atmosphere and the ideal had made a deep impression on him. It was no coincidence that of all Willa Cather's novels *The Professor's House,* with its tale of dedicated scholarship, was his favorite. Several of his own most successful short stories—"The Blood of the Martyrs," "Schooner Fairchild's Class," "The Professor's Punch"—dealt with that same atmosphere and ideal. In "The Blood of the Martyrs," his notable antitotalitarian story, the spokesman for what Benét believed most deeply was an academic. "The truth, of course, was the truth," the tortured European intellectual reflects in his cell. "One taught it or one did not. And, if one did not teach it, it hardly mattered what one did." [34]

Benét was appalled, however, by the poverty of the academic profession. In one of his early stories, written only a year after he finished his graduate work, he spoke of "the ludicrousness of the contrast between the salaries paid American teachers and the energy, personality and wide knowledge expected of them." [35] He taught undergraduate classes several times, substituting for friends in the English Department. He enjoyed the experience, but he was not satisfied with Chauncey Tinker's celebrated epigram of the period. "The university," Tinker had said, "is the last stronghold of Bohemia." It was a Bohemia too circumscribed for Benét's taste. He was more mindful of the insecurity which accompanied the poverty, remembering that Tinker had also said that "until a man receives tenure, he should keep his bags packed at all times." Benét had seen a bully, Professor Cook, receive the homage of the profession; he had watched men as distinguished as Canby denied or passed over for promotion.

And yet in his own case the Graduate School met in full the challenge of the College faculty that it had previously been inhospitable to talent. They permitted Benét to substitute a group of poems—those published later that same year by Henry Holt as *Heavens and Earth*—for the customary academic thesis. On June 16, 1920, he received his Master of Arts degree, though "the scoundrel of a typist," he told the Dean's secretary, had caused the manuscript to be late.

From the Graduate School, too, came the much more intoxicating bounty of a Scott Hurtt Fellowship of $500 for 1920–21. Its terms stipulated that he need not be in residence at the university. In effect they were staking him to passage money to Paris and a little more to boot. From an individual member of the faculty, Edward Bliss Reed, came private confirmation of their collective interest in the young poet's career; Reed lent him an additional five hundred dollars for the trip. Benét retreated to the Watervliet Arsenal as soon as commencement was over, determined to finish *The Beginning of Wisdom* and raise a publisher's advance that would complete his European subsidy.

5. The Beginning of Wisdom

The hero . . . is sort of a human roulette-ball
& generally lands on the double zero at that.[1]

WATERVLIET ARSENAL, across the Hudson from Troy, was a fine place for Benét to work on a novel that represented an exploration of the previous twenty years. Watervliet played no part in *The Beginning of Wisdom*, which began with California, but it had the effect of turning the minds of the entire family toward the past. The Benéts had been stationed there from 1901 through 1904. To return to Watervliet now, almost two decades later, released a torrent of memories. They discussed them fully among themselves, as they did all their experiences, and Mrs. Benét reviewed them in the immense, global correspondence she maintained with other wives from the old army. The Colonel dealt crisply with them in his own more brief letters.

"When we came back to Watervliet," he told a fellow colonel who had also served there during the earlier tenure, "we found many of our old friends dead and the rest twenty years older and none the better for it."[2]

The Colonel, however, had something of the same impulse toward clarifying the past as was occupying his youngest son. He kept busy even in this year of military dismantlement. "I have named all the streets after the former commanding officers," he told his old comrade. "Farley Drive, Mordecai Drive, Shaler Court, Taylor Court, etc. The Main Avenue is Dalliba Avenue after the first C.O. Also I had a History of Watervliet Arsenal from the earlier times compiled, which is quite a monumental work."

His father's situation thus reminded Benét in a general way of the very cycles of time with which he was dealing in his novel. The vast enterprises of 1917 and 1918 were completed. The army would now be thrust backward to the oblivion of other postwar periods. The command which the Colonel had taken over at Watervliet in 1919 had already shrunk from twenty-five hundred employees to seven hundred in less than a year; it was plain that it would be cut in half again by 1921. "The lean years are here," the Colonel told his family. In the meantime the Colonel utilized his still existing opportunities. He made an extension to the shops and remodeled the pit with two electric furnaces. He added an oil furnace and a stairway and an elevator. The only person on the post who could match his energy was his youngest son.

Benét had put himself on the kind of rigid schedule that guaranteed a productive summer. He wrote all morning. In the afternoon he played three sets of tennis with his father or scrub baseball with the post kids— "who think I'm fine," he wrote a Yale classmate, "and in a class with Ty Cobb"—and in the evenings he worked some more. It rained regularly, once a day, he claimed, but the tennis court was concrete, so that even the weather had no effect on his timetable. "I have lived a quiet, working, hard-eating life," he told Phelps Putnam in August.[3]

He wrote 36,000 words during July, tore up 8,000 of

them, and by the second week in August he had finished four of the eight books into which he was dividing the novel. He was writing too fast, and despite the 8,000 words he tore up he was not cutting enough, but he was determined to have a manuscript to submit to Henry Holt before he sailed for France at the end of August. He had planned originally to leave in June; he postponed his departure in the hope of finishing the book. Now he saw that the extra two months were not going to be enough. "If I had any idea of the magnitude of the task," he wrote his sister with ironic grandiloquence, "I would have made arrangements not to sail till October, but it is too late now to change."

Benét had a number of ideas about fiction which he was anxious to test in this novel. Some of them he had evolved as he did the heavy reading assignments for Wilbur Cross in eighteenth- and nineteenth-century literature. More of them had grown out of the discussions in Canby's class. He knew in particular that he did not want to write entirely in the currently dominant realism. "It is time," he had declared in *S4N* in January 1920, when he was beginning his book, "for a considered and furious reaction against the modern realistic novel." The cult of realism, he maintained, was encouraging novels which each year grew "steadily longer" and "steadily drearier." Individuality was vanishing in a form that was becoming "as standardized and mechanical as the leading automobile manufacturers."

Benét had reached this position by a different route— antirealism—but he had arrived at a philosophy—individualism—similar to that of most of his contemporaries. "It is time for a return to color," he argued. "It is time for a return to the grand manner." A handful of the older writers, he felt, were doing good work, Conrad in par-

94

ticular, Norman Douglas, and "when not journalistically badgered," Chesterton, "most marvellously." Benét had also read Cabell with great delight. He bought *Jurgen, Beyond Life, The Certain Hour,* and *From the Hidden Way*. When the Yale Library could furnish him no more Cabell, he found other volumes at the New Haven public library. After the latter had been exhausted, he wrote Cabell's publishers for the names of three out-of-print titles. Realism, Benét conceded, had made many contributions. "It has punctured some showy bubbles and instructed us with a wholesome medicine." Nevertheless, he felt, it was not sufficient as an expression of the impulse of honor or the passion of love or the absolution of death.

"Now, God damn it," Benét cried, "we are ready for cakes and ale!" [4]

He sought therefore to make *The Beginning of Wisdom* more than just another boyhood novel, more than just another college novel, more than just another novel of personal liberation. He tried to make it all these things, and cakes and ale, and above all he tried to make it a hymn to the philosophy he and Phelps Putnam had often discussed and which Putnam had put into the verse Benét now borrowed for one of his epigrams.

> and coolly from the waste
> Now slender beauty rises strong and harsh,
> And with it comes a salt ironic taste,
> A tang of evening floating on the marsh.
>
> That beauty is not delicate nor weak,
> It can withstand all mockery and doubt,
> It is the very words the mockers speak,
> And only hardy fools can find it out.[5]

Naturally he could not do all these things. In the attempt to do them he forgot about unity, and he overwrote, and like Fitzgerald with *This Side of Paradise* he sometimes turned the novel into a scrapbook of notes and old poems and irrelevant pensées. Like most of his generation, Benét was already thoroughly aware of Fitzgerald. He was particularly conscious of *This Side of Paradise* as he worked on *The Beginning of Wisdom*. "I have had a lot of fun with the college stuff," he wrote Badger in August. "I think it is pretty accurate though somewhat local and a good deal less gaudy and Sophomore Don Juanish than F. Scott Fitz. But the three drunk scenes were a sheer pleasure to do."

It was the kind of novel which a surprisingly large number of readers of Benét's own generation felt very strongly about. They read and reread it. It was also the kind of novel, of course, which the critics instinctively treated rather harshly. Its faults were so apparent that few could resist the opportunity to deliver lectures on first novels, and poets as novelists, and undergraduate novels in general. Benét was always philosophical about the book. "The damn thing marches slowly," he told Farrar, "and in as bad order as the first parade of the Yale ROTC." A college novel, he once told another friend, is "a required project" for all young writers. Three installments from *The Beginning of Wisdom*, on the other hand, were printed in the *Bookman* the following summer and fall, so it achieved its function, belatedly, of getting him some money for his year in France. It had a respectable sale when Holt published it in 1921, and Mencken gave it a good notice. He had proved to himself that though he preferred poetry, he could also write marketable prose.

"The first novel I ever wrote," he told a young writer

in 1939, trying to persuade him to have his characters talk less and do more, "was on the struggles and soul-strivings of a very young man. And parts of it are perfectly appalling. But it was picaresque—or meant to be —and I did take him over a lot of jumps." [6]

In August 1920 Benét finished the fifth of the novel's eight books, and made a long trip to Bar Harbor to usher at a classmate's wedding. He would have preferred to spend the four days on the novel, but he characteristically put friendship first. "I wish I'd never told ——— I'd usher at his darn wedding," he wrote Laura, "but he'd have been hurt & there was no reason I could give for refusing." The classmate married, he took the train to New York and delivered the unfinished manuscript to Holt, not only anxious to get their decision about an advance but also determined to trust as little of the book as possible to the foreign mails.

He sailed for France on August 28, 1920, an early instance of his generation's restless instinct for expatriation. "Yale gave him a traveling fellowship and he is supposed to be studying at the Sorbonne," his father told a friend. "Studying what I don't know. Just studying I imagine." [7] Benét's future was staked to a novel that wasn't yet finished, and his intentions for the next year, as his father suspected, were otherwise rather vague. Just to study was as accurate a way as any to describe his plans.

Benét, whose work would always be so closely identified with America and whose major significance to the literary historians would be as one of the earliest rediscoverers of native material, in reality cared as much for Paris as for any city in which he ever lived, and rather more than for most of them. His family links with it were considerable. His paternal grandmother lived

97

her last years there. His Uncle Larry was one of the principal figures in the American colony; the Laurence Benét home at 1 Avenue Camöens was regarded by French and Americans alike as the second American Embassy. His father fled instinctively to Paris in 1923 when the prospect of William's marriage to Elinor Wylie became more than he could endure.

Benét himself was a paid-up member of the literary migration eastward, knowing France and its people better and longer and in more aspects than the majority of his more noisily expatriated contemporaries. He spent four of the 1920's ten years in France. He knew Paris as a young man on the town in the late fall of 1920. He knew it that winter as an anxious suitor, and in the spring of 1921 as a successful lover who had won his girl. He knew it as a honeymooner in 1922, and from 1926 through 1929 as a happily married father of two young children.

Benét knew Paris poor in 1920 and momentarily rich in 1929. He knew it alone and in love, gay with the white wine he relished and soberly on the wagon as he ground out short stories in 1921 for a stake on which to get married. When he read Carl Van Vechten's *Peter Whiffle* in 1922, in Scarsdale, he told his wife that it made him "violently homesick for the Rue Viscontin." He added, however, that he was happy to see he "had done practically everything on his list of what all young Americans do in France." His Paris was neither the tourist's nor the collector's of cultural experiences.

"I would rather go to Notre Dame," he told a friend who asked him in 1929 for advice on what to see in Paris, "La Sainte Chapelle, Musée Carnavalet, Musée du Luxembourg, beautiful gardens, the rose-garden at Bagatelle, on one of the bateux-mouches that run up and down the Seine, to the markets in early morning, to the

Place Victor Hugo, and wander up and down the quais (do not forget the flower and bird market, do not forget to visit the Ile St. Louis) than to the Louvre. The Louvre is a great gallery but Paris is alive." [8]

The Sorbonne, on the other hand, saw very little of him. He stuck grimly to *The Beginning of Wisdom* during the first two months. By November it was finished and mailed to Holt. Then on the 18th his *Heavens and Earth* was published in New York. His attitude toward this latest volume of poetry was a mixed one. It was the first of his four collections to be published by a thoroughly commercial house. This was made even more heartening by the fact that Holt's poetry list—Frost, Sandburg, de la Mare, Colum—was at the time a strong one. He was thoroughly aware, however, of the thinness of some of his verse, and the mere facility of much of it. *Heavens and Earth* was the collection which he pruned most harshly both for *Ballads and Poems* in 1931 and for his *Selected Works* in 1942. "It seems very motty," he told his publisher in 1928, when a new edition was being discussed. "The Helen things are all right but I'd like to cut at least ten of the other poems and repunctuate others. It needs it badly. Some of the things there make me squirm. Would revision be possible?" [9]

Yet in November 1920 it was easy for a young man of twenty-two to find in *Heavens and Earth* sufficient cause for celebration. He had finished his first novel and received author's copies of his fourth book of poems. "The early 1920's in Paris," he said many years later, "were something that will not happen again for a long time. There were fakers and nuts, tourists and people who sat at the Dôme; there were also a good many people who were doing work." For the moment Benét was among those who sat at the Dôme. "I wasted a lot of money," he confessed later, though without undue regret. When he repaid the five hundred dollars he had borrowed from Professor Reed he told his benefactor that he didn't think "anybody ever had as good a time on that amount of money!" [10] From his literary friends, however, came the sorrowful chiding always inspired in them by any momentary lapses from the impossible peaks to which they assigned him.

"Haven't heard from Steve for quite a time," John Carter wrote Norman Fitts, "but he is in Paris, drinking far too much and writing far too little." [11]

Benét, who had spent his first few weeks in Paris at his uncle's, now took an apartment near Notre Dame des Champs with Henry Carter and Stanley Hawks. Holt accepted *The Beginning of Wisdom* and sent him an advance. A festive procession of friends was constantly in or drifting through Paris that fall. The musicians—Douglas Moore, Quincy Porter, Bruce Simonds—were relatively serious-minded, but Moore in particular, whom he had known briefly in 1915 when the composer was a Yale senior, was a gay and entertaining companion. He and his bride provided a kind of merry stability for a group which included Don Campbell and William Douglas as well as Benét and Henry Carter. Campbell and Douglas were studying art and architecture in much the same way Benét was using the academic resources of the Sorbonne. "You would like this town," Benét wrote Phelps Putnam, who was restlessly employed at a foundry in Ansonia, Conn. "In fact if you ever got here it would be like rooting up the well known mandrake to get you away. It is full of liquor, amusing people & incredibly beautiful works of art."

Ramon Guthrie was in Paris that fall for a while, on his way to Italy, and Danford Barney, the wealthy professional bohemian who edited *Parabalou.* Ellen Semple was there, not yet married to Philip Barry but knowing all about Benét because Barry had talked constantly of him. Edna Millay arrived in January and she and Benét and Henry Carter did the town. Carter, as literate and witty as his brother, but less intense in his relationship with Benét, was marking time with a Paris bank job before going to the Harvard Graduate School. Through the Moores they met the convivial Richard Myers and Alice Lee, his hospitable and generous wife. Myers was a celebrated gourmet and connoisseur of all things Parisian, a talented amateur musician with a great gift for friendship and for pleasant living. Like the Moores, he and his wife kept open house for the young men, feeding them on Sundays, scolding them mildly and occasionally, seeing that they got home safely. "You have probably heard from returning Americans," Benét wrote Shreve Badger, "that I have gone to pieces in Paris and am now head of an opium-joint."

In reality, despite the merriment, he was far from in pieces. He was in fact collecting the fragments of precocity and fluency and unused talent and deep feeling about America, preparing to unite them into such bursts of finished skill as "The Ballad of William Sycamore" and "King David" in 1923, and, in 1926, into the launching of *John Brown's Body.* For the moment he exulted in the mere glory of being in Paris and having for a time sufficient money to be prodigal.

He circulated gaily on both sides of the river, linked through his uncle to fashionable and correct Paris, and through his friends and tastes to Montmartre. Sometimes the two worlds resisted each other. Having consented to attend and speak at a formal Yale-in-Paris dinner, he lingered over-long on the way with his friends at the

Ritz bar. His uncle, another speaker at the dinner, was shocked at his nephew's condition when the young alumni finally arrived. Laurence Benét carefully seated Stephen beside him. The strategy was spoiled by the presence of the celebrated and pontifical Dr. Frank Crane on the other side. Dr. Crane was appalled by his drunken tablemate. "Lead me to a Turkish Bath!" the young man cried. The evening was no smashing success from Laurence Benét's point of view, though for the young men it ended triumphantly on the left bank.

His uncle, however, was a tolerant and forgiving relative. Besides, this was his favorite nephew. Stephen dined with the Laurence Benéts grandly and in good order at Christmas, escorting a countess to dinner, he wrote his mother, and receiving from his Aunt Margaret, concerned for his dress, a splendid cane. His mother complained, nevertheless, that his letters were overly brief. " 'O,' your mother reacts," his father wrote him, " 'if he would only give me a detailed history of the day from the time he puts on his BVDs till he gets shaking between the icy sheets. What he eats, how he washes, what he studies and where, his relaxations, even his dissipations, a time schedule showing how every hour of the day is employed would not be too much.' " [12]

The Colonel himself was a trifle sardonic about their son's presumed schedule. "We are waiting anxiously," he told him, "for your Scraps from the Sorbonne and 'The Sorbonne what it is why Young Americans like it and What They Do There.' We are still unilluminated on these points." The Colonel wrote his son regularly, his letters full of shrewd judgments on what he was currently reading and news of William's successes in New York. "Be an example of righteousness," he gravely urged Stephen, "among the immoral French."

Suddenly, in fact, though it was unconnected with either his father's sly digs or his Aunt Margaret's concern for his lack of interest in correct dress, Benét did indeed become an example of righteousness. Now the Ritz bar knew him hardly at all, and in Montmartre he was only a tolerant observer of the madness of others. "Have written four short stories and 6 poems in the last month," he wrote Badger early in 1921, "and only got drunk once." He had, in fact, fallen in love. It was really for the first time, despite the frothy cynicism of his *Record* verse and the surface heartache of *Heavens and Earth*, and certainly it was for the last time.

The effect on him was remarkable, though appropriate to a temperament that was deeply romantic, monogamous, tender, and thoroughly responsible. As he informed Badger, he went back to work with zeal and persistence. He wrote short stories for money and poetry for love. The verse in particular cascaded from him, buoyant, charming songs as became a poet who had fallen in love in Paris with a girl who bore the splendid name of Rosemary. He wrote poetry to Rosemary for the rest of his life, in the *pneumatiques* with which he now employed the Paris postal system for his courting, later on scraps of paper which contained shopping lists and messages to the cleaning woman, in telegrams and anniversary cards and birthday notes, and above all in the glittering lyrics that were collected in *Tiger Joy* in 1925. Often, later, he addressed her as Jane in the love poems; Rosemary was amused by the well-intentioned acquaintances who occasionally sympathized with the dilemma of a poet's wife whose husband, they imagined, was publishing poetry inspired by his mistress.

He met Rosemary Carr at the Myers' apartment in late November 1920, courted her that winter and became engaged on St. Patrick's Day, married her in Chicago in November 1921, and thereafter never lost his sense of her beauty and goodness and his own good fortune. "Some people have names like pitchforks," he wrote her in the spring of 1921, "some people have names like cakes,"

Names full of sizzling esses like a family quarrel of snakes,
Names black as a cat, vermillion as the cockscomb-hat of a fool—
But your name is a green, small garden, a rush asleep in a pool.[13]

Rosemary Carr was indeed a creature to confirm all his poets's notions of what love should contain. She could be gay and grave, tender and remote. She was as deeply loyal as he and as responsive to writing in general and poetry in particular. She had graduated from The University of Chicago—Phi Beta Kappa, Benét wryly informed his friends, mindful of his own erratic academic record—and she was the daughter of one of the first American women M.D.'s. In 1920 and 1921 Rosemary was writing fashion notes and feature stories in Paris for the Chicago *Tribune*. Vincent Sheean, who met her in Chicago in 1920 when he was a freshman at the University, remembered years later that he had been enchanted by her beauty. "I don't mind saying," he recalled in 1957, "that she remained in my mind a long time after she had gone to Paris." [14]

Now Rosemary tried to marshall her love for Benét and her concern for his career, which was plainly in no condition as yet to sustain the rigors of marriage. Her realistic forebodings were swept aside by his ardent and resourceful courtship. "It is too incredible & wonderful," he wrote her in the first of two pneumatiques which he sent on March 18, 1921, the day following their agreement to regard themselves as engaged. "Would you prefer," he asked her, "to have been kissed in the little old back street in Paris outside of a bar, an Italian restaurant, or a printing plant?" He had returned to the approximate location of their first kiss that next morning, bent on locating the precise spot. "I stood there in the rain this morning like a fool trying to decide which it was. All might be symbolical except the Italian restaurant. I don't know what that would stand for." He had gone back to the apartment singing, to be greeted by Carter's mild curses. "Three cheers for his somnolence," he wrote Rosemary.

He settled quickly into the kind of single-minded schedule he had maintained at Watervliet the previous summer. Now he substituted lunch or tea with Rosemary for the three sets of tennis, and on the evenings when she could not see him he went to wild-west movies with French captions instead of to the Dôme. The poetry flowed singingly from him, to be published that spring and summer in the *Bookman, S4N, Parabalou,* the *Literary Digest,* and the *New Republic.*[15] "You'd make an anteater burst into madrigals," he told Rosemary in a March 21st pneumatique. The short stories were considerably more difficult. He had no illusions about being able to sell consistently such perverse fantasies as "The Funeral of John Bixby," which *Munsey's* had bought the previous year. He studied the circulation magazines, trying to master the formula.

With greater certainty he began a new novel. It would be shorter than *The Beginning of Wisdom,* he wrote his family. It dealt with a beautiful and unhappy Southern belle. "My heroine is queer," he told Rosemary. "I can't be firm with her—I know too little about her." He ground out fifteen hundred words a day and threw away most of it and began again. *Jean Huguenot* came hard, not only because it had all the attendant miseries of the second novel, but also and more particularly because he was undertaking a complex characterization that was still a little beyond him. "I should have kept it much longer," he explained to a friend several years after it was finally published in 1923—having become by then his third rather than his second novel—and he told Rosemary once that writing *Jean Huguenot* in Paris that spring was like "driving myself at a bar about 6 ft. too high." [16]

By the time he left Paris in June 1921, sailing a week before Rosemary in order to persuade her doubting family of the propriety of their relationship, Benét had nearly finished a rather unsatisfactory first draft of *Jean Huguenot*. He had a handful of short stories to try and sell in New York. He had found in Paris—quite literally—his Moores and the Myers would last richly all his life. Once heart's treasure, and the friendships established with the again he returned to the Colonel's house and the regular writing schedule it always permitted him, this time planning to write a 50,000-word novel which he hoped would finance an early wedding and a Paris honeymoon.

Benét discovered a very different kind of parental household than any he had previously known. Gone was the spaciousness of the various Commandant's quarters. The Colonel, due to retire on July 16, 1921, had begun his terminal leave in May. He was not to spend his leisure in the kind of locale he had long envisioned. "I had hoped," the Colonel wrote from Scarsdale, N.Y., to his comrade Colonel Horney, "that after my retirement we could live in the South Seas or California or some place with a decent climate and you see where I am landed. Another case of the fell clutch of circumstances."

The circumstances which thwarted the Colonel were connected primarily with his and Mrs. Benét's sense of obligation to their son William. The death of William's wife Teresa had left him with three small children to raise. The Colonel and Mrs. Benét were therefore establishing as best they could a home for Billy and the grandchildren that would allow their son to be within commuting distance of New York. It was a harsh adjustment for the elder Benéts. Gone with the spacious quarters were the strikers and the endless supply of sturdy Irish maids. In their place was a series of solitary cooks who served and vanished and were replaced with an equally impermanent facsimile.

The brunt of the housekeeping and the child-rearing fell upon Mrs. Benét and Laura. William worked a long day at the *Literary Review* and in the evenings and on week ends he was preoccupied with a novel which he wrote on the dining-room table. Living with them too, as she had for twenty years, was Mrs. Benét's redoubtable Aunt Agnes, the eighty-seven-year-old Miss Mahan. Three children and five adults in a stucco suburban house. Now they shuffled around a bit and made room for Stephen. They christened the house the Brimming Cup and settled down to make the best of it.

"I intend to write my memoirs in seventeen volumes," the Colonel told his fellow officer, "and generally do as I please if my family will allow me. And to keep on playing tennis. In this way I may reach a hale old age."

Stephen arrived in Scarsdale early in July and retreated to the garage to work, sweltering grimly on *Jean Huguenot* under a tin roof and sneezing with the smell of gasoline. Rosemary's boat was delayed by a French dock strike. Finally they had a cruelly brief reunion in New York under the watchful eye of Mrs. Carr, who had come East to supervise the meeting. Rosemary and her mother met the Benéts at the Brimming Cup and then went on to Chicago. Benét returned to the garage, encouraged by word from John Farrar that the August *Bookman* would contain the first of three excerpts from *The Beginning of Wisdom,* and wondering if *Jean Huguenot,* completed now, was going to find a home at *Harper's Bazaar.*

He had submitted it to *Harper's Bazaar* on the advice of several friends who had recently made sales there. Henry Sell, the editor, promised to read it that same week end. He told Benét he was very much in the market for a serial. "And a very nice Mammon he is," Benét wrote Rosemary, "in his shiny expensive office." But Sell turned down *Jean Huguenot,* and he gave Benét a great deal of advice about writing which Benét tried hard to understand but which didn't seem very relevant, and he began to wonder if he would ever get the money to marry Rosemary or if she would vanish forever into some midwestern void. He sent her long letters each night. "I write you so much and so wordily," he told her sadly, "because I like to pretend I'm talking to you."

Each morning he went back out to the garage. It was now so hot, he told Rosemary, that the backs of his hands perspired as he sat at the table. "Finished typing my he-and-she story," he wrote her, "and began another—Red Blood and the Woman this time but it should be interesting if I can make it plausible—it has a real plot." He played tennis with his father and they took long walks. His affection and admiration for the Colonel were as strong as ever. "Our present mode of living," he told

Rosemary, "is intimate to say the least. We are crowded into the house like sprats in a seine and have no servants. Consequently I dry dishes, split kindling etc. etc. and Father is magnificent—Belisarius in his old age running a vacuum cleaner." Benét had hay fever and now he got poison ivy, "to add," he said, "to the humor of existence." Then abruptly during the last week of July his mood became more optimistic. For the first time in his career, though he had been publishing for six years, he had a literary agent.

The agent was Carl Brandt, whose firm of Brandt and Kirkpatrick would shortly become the celebrated house of Brandt and Brandt. Benét's relationship with Brandt was the most important single professional association of his career. It overshadowed, professionally, his friendships with Farrar and MacLeish and Barry. In literary terms it even dwarfed his relationship with his brother and his father. It was appropriate that the association should have begun in the same year that he became engaged to Rosemary; the two were alike in their devotion and loyalty to Benét.

"It is true, possibly," Brandt wrote Rosemary on March 15, 1943, two days after Benét's sudden death, "that my reason for being is that I could, in small ways, be of use to him. He has given me the chance, in my time, to know the freedoms which were his absolutes. All I can hope for is to live up to his vision."

Even the initial link between Benét and Brandt in 1921 was in fact connected with Rosemary. They had first heard Brandt's name at the Myers' apartment in Paris that spring. Sidney Howard, who had dropped in unexpectedly on the Myers, for whom Benét and Rosemary were baby-sitting, and was thus regarded sourly by Benét as an unwelcome intruder on his courting of

Rosemary, had mentioned the agent when he learned that Benét was writing short stories. The young playwright urged Benét to get in touch with Brandt as soon as he returned to New York. "He's a wonderful guy," said Howard, adding that he had already sent Farrar and Barry to him. Now, back in New York, Benét diffidently spoke to Farrar about Brandt. Farrar promptly arranged for Benét to see the agent the next afternoon. In the meantime Brandt agreed to read the manuscript of *Jean Huguenot*. "Everything is easy," Benét wrote Rosemary from Scarsdale that night, "if you can get a few friends to roll a few logs for you."

Brandt, Benét told his fiancée, was "a very nice blond fat person looking somewhat like a plump blond sea lion with a soft and pleasing voice." He listened sympathetically while Benét explained that by autumn he not only had to have some money in hand but also the assurance that he could make a living for two as a writer. Otherwise, he told Brandt dramatically, he was liable to lose his girl. Brandt in turn explained that the best source of money in magazine fiction was in serials, and assured Benét that Henry Sell was not infallible as a judge of literary work. He motioned, however, toward the typescript of *Jean Huguenot*, lying on his desk.

"This," he said, "is no serial." Benét's chagrin and disappointment were transparent. "But," Brandt went on, "I'll try to sell it serially if you like." Then Brandt used *Jean Huguenot* to illustrate some of the principles of serial writing for the big magazines. The only possible market for this particular manuscript, he explained to Benét, was in such low-paying qualities as *Harper's*, *Scribner's*, and *Century*. "Because," Brandt pointed out, "the only thread that carries all the way through is the change in the girl's character. That isn't strong enough to carry the reader of popular magazines through from month to month."

Brandt paused and then went on with the instruction. "There are several serials in the book," he conceded, "and a number of short stories, but I've had books like this before and no matter how much I liked them they are the hardest to sell."

A great part of Brandt's success with young writers came from the fact that he was something of a teacher as well as a hard-boiled agent. Now, having made it clear to Benét—the author, after all, of four books of verse and a novel scheduled for publication in two months—that he still had a lot to learn, Brandt hoisted him back to his feet. He repeated that he'd liked *Jean Huguenot* very much. He compared it favorably with such current successes as, Benét wrote Rosemary, "*Moon Calf, Zell,* the last Walpole, the last McKenna, etc. etc." Brandt declared that there was no reason in the world why Benét couldn't write a serial that would sell anywhere without undue commercializing. Benét described a situation he had in mind and Brandt told him to send him a synopsis and a first installment of 10,000 words.

"I'll do everything I can," Brandt promised, "to show you how these things should be constructed so they'll sell." The agent then summed up Benét's prospects and added several more general principles. He pointed out to Benét that since his primary intention seemed to be to write poetry, which would certainly bring in no income at all to speak of, his obvious objective with the magazine fiction ought to be to get as much money for it as easily as possible. "So," Brandt reiterated, "write serials, not stories." Each single installment of a serial, the agent explained, would bring a higher price than an individual story, and would probably require less time to write once he got the hang of it. "Serials," Brandt said with finality, "are better for you than snaps and snips of short stories."

It was an entirely new concept for Benét. Brandt talked to him about the handful of basic principles of serial writing. He told him about the necessity for a sequence of rather fully developed episodes—"hangers," he called them—which would give the serial momentum and at the same time make each installment something of a unit. He emphasized that the structure should always revolve around a chase or some variation of it. That was about all there was to it, he told the young writer.

"Oh, one other thing," Brandt added, his reasoning more vocational than moral. "Whatever you do, don't get your hero and heroine into bed before the final installment, legitimately or otherwise. If you do, you'll lose a hundred per cent of your women readers and a hundred and five per cent of the men." [17]

Benét returned to Scarsdale to ponder the lessons. He knew that Brandt was already regarded as the best magazine agent in New York. This first tutorial had made excellent sense. "He knows what he is talking about," Benét wrote Rosemary that night. He had every intention of practicing the advice. It was all a trifle different, however, from the Yale literary renaissance. Brandt made even Canby seem somewhat otherworldly. The agent had told him to write something about young people, urging him to use in particular his evident sensitivity to the problems of being in love in the postwar American world. Benét went to work with a will. It was a subject on which, separated as he was from his own girl, he had a great many ideas. This became, in fact, the major flaw of *Young People's Pride* as a novel.

In a sense Benét wrote *Young People's Pride* as if it were a first novel rather than a third one. It was composed out of events which were still occurring, and from moods that were as yet turbulent and unclarified. It resembled the novels which some of his contemporaries were writing about the war, like them powerful with compelling emotion and unmistakeable authenticity but thematically and philosophically unresolved. Such of the mood as did not come from his own situation he adapted from no more than what he might have sensed the previous day in a conversation with a friend.

He observed the Long Island romances of his Yale classmates and incorporated them into *Young People's Pride*. He probed the distress of his own yearning for Rosemary and used its painful essence. The opening scene was a virtual transcript of a party Farrar had given a few weeks before. The story was rescued, however, as Thomas Beer pointed out when it was published the next year, by Benét's calm good sense and by his thesis that youth left to its own resources was quite likely to get along very well indeed.

"The young people," Beer concluded, "are moderately wild now and then. Someone takes too many cocktails. Someone starts an entanglement with his presumptive father-in-law's mistress. They dance all night. But Mr. Benét is not disturbed and he comes to no cloudy conclusions. The world, he seems to assume, will roll ahead unaltered by Oliver's awkward love affair. It is most refreshing." [18]

The influence of Cabell was noticeable in the graceful prose and urbane satire. One reviewer in 1922 would also cite it as like Cabell in its use of "the same sort of obvious tricks." Benét's friends, as always, were alarmed. "The magazines are shrewd tempters," said Thomas C. Chubb regretfully. He had admired Benét at Yale when the former was chairman of the *Lit* and he was a heeler. "Easy is the descent to pot-boiling. If Mr. Benét should go that way we have a high enough confidence in his powers to esteem it a very considerable tragedy." [19]

The primary influence on *Young People's Pride,* of course, was that of Carl Brandt. Benét kept in mind the precepts about a chase; there was sufficient excitement for the most lethargic editor. One reviewer—his future sister-in-law, in fact, the poetess Elinor Wylie—cited these deliberate fireworks as "the sleazy, meretricious fabrics of the scenario and the mystery story." [20] None of this increased Benét's regard for critics so dull as to be unaware that all this was intentional, but he was untroubled by their wrath. While he was writing it in Scarsdale in the summer of 1921 he had no illusions about its quality. "It is rather fluffy sort of stuff," he told Rosemary, to whom he was mailing the carbon of his daily output, "and I have farced it immensely."

He stayed rigidly on a schedule of about 3,000 words a day. By the first week in August he gave Brandt the synopsis and the first 10,000-word installment. "And that always makes me feel well," he told Rosemary, "to have the thing moving fairly rapidly, as most of *Jean Huguenot* did not." In the meantime there was always the manuscript of *Jean Huguenot* for display to editors. He and his brother had lunch at the Vanderbilt with Glenn Frank of the *Century,* but Frank, too, was unable to visualize it as a serial. "Anyhow," Benét said philosophically in his nightly letter, "a lunch is a lunch."

Even during those few days when he waited between installments for word from Brandt, he returned each day to the garage, to work on short stories. Like *Young People's Pride,* they too were written with the same single-minded focus upon the magazines. After one such morning's labor Benét told Rosemary that he grew occasionally weary "as to how I'm going to get my hero out of the clutches of the Band of the Purple Pants when they have tied him on the tracks of the Overland Limited." It was characteristic of Brandt, however, that he read each installment promptly and discussed it immediately with Benét. He had him change and condense the first two parts a great deal.

"Cut 50 pages out of Y.P.P. today," Benét wrote his girl. "Petty infanticide. The dear child is so changed from the first draft that it's like going to bed with your sweet little baby a Caucasian and waking up and finding him a nigger. But this ought to be the last operation—pretty near."

As Benét grew more certain of the method, the changes required by Brandt became increasingly minor. "I am willing," Benét told Rosemary, "to turn Y.P.P. and its author inside-out upside-down or any way at all & throw my immortal soul into the bargain for a sufficient amount of cash." The agent told Benét the final three sections were fine. Brandt encouraged the young writer as much as he could during this difficult period of work and separation and no tangible success in sight. The agent was also unfailingly realistic and candid. He told Benét he was certain to make money sooner or later. He cautioned him, on the other hand, that despite its improved structure *Young People's Pride* was going to be restricted in its sale because of the presence of what Benét described to Rosemary as "the immoral lady."

Benét had not been able to sterilize his novel sufficiently. The immoral lady—Rose Severance, mistress of one of the young people's parents—was a mature and well-drawn characterization. She was sufficiently well-drawn, Brandt grumbled, to make the serial unaccept-able to the *Saturday Evening Post*. She would not, how-ever, prevent the editors of *Pictorial Review* or the Hearst publications from giving it a serious reading. Brandt, characteristically, did not press Benét to alter the portrait of Rose. Benét felt that the six exhausting weeks had been well-spent.

"I've learned something about that sort of construction, writing it," he told Rosemary. "The next serial I do I'm going to do with my own idea and write it as I like but with Y.P.P. construction." He was hopeful that he could master the formula and nonetheless write meaningful fiction. "I've got the idea and it ought to be real if I can handle it. Trouble with Y.P.P. is, some of it's real but much of it's rubber stamp."

Benét was particularly heartened by Brandt's confi-dence in him. "He seems to believe in my stuff, which is really encouraging." Now that the serial was finished and making the rounds of the editorial offices, Brandt advised him to catch his breath with some more short stories. He had talked him up to George Lorimer at the *Post* and was anxious to get Benét on a solid footing with some one magazine. Suddenly things began to break for Benét in a breath-taking sequence of good fortune. "The combination," he had written Rosemary in early August, when their situation seemed most bleak, "has been too elaborate so far—it must be just a couple more numbers till the lock clicks open."

Now Henry Sell, at *Harper's Bazaar*, conceded that having held *The Beginning of Wisdom* so long before re-jecting it, he ought to pay some kind of option. They set-tled on $250 with the understanding that Sell would get first look at the new serial. The Poetry Society announced that its $500 prize for the year's best volume of poetry was to be split between his own *Heavens and Earth* and Sandburg's *Smoke and Steel*. Holt told him that it looked like *The Beginning of Wisdom,* which had finally been published in late September after several last-minute delays, would probably sell 10,000 copies. October was turning into a kind of bottomless cornucopia of good news.

Sell telephoned that he would use *Young People's Pride* as a five-part serial in *Harper's Bazaar*. Brandt phoned him in Scarsdale that he had sold a story called "Goobers—à la Française" to *Delineator* for $200. "Another editor fooled," Benét told Rosemary. A day or two later the agent called to say he had sold a second Paris story, "Mad Americans," to *Metropolitan* for the same price.[21] Henry Carter even chose this moment to pay back a loan he received from Benét in Paris.

"Money collected today," Benét wired Rosemary on October 19. "Make plans accordingly. I love you darling."

There was now so much interest in Benét's work, in fact, that Brandt cautioned him to abandon his plans for staying abroad indefinitely after the marriage. "You can make at least twice as much money," Brandt told him, "by being here right now. In a year or two you can go and live anywhere you please—you'll be absolutely fixed, but we've got to nurse this thing along personally for at least a year more." He advised Benét to get married immediately, take three months off for a honeymoon, and get back to New York by March 1922. It was welcome advice.

Benét hurriedly wrote Rosemary to get her passport and they fixed the marriage for November 26. He rounded up his ushers, wrote a final short story whose idea had appealed to Ray Long of *Cosmopolitan* when Benét outlined it at lunch, and rushed to Chicago. He arrived several days before he was supposed to, bringing with him Brandt's check for $1794.10. "That is the final, net, five star sum we have," Benét told Rosemary jubilantly. It was blood money, earned by sweat and heartache in a garage with a tin roof in the heat of a Westchester summer. Those who later reproached Benét for the romantic climaxes of some of his short stories forgot what he had endured and triumphed over between July and November of 1921.

He and Rosemary were married at a thoroughly conventional Ivy League kind of wedding, and they came East that night in a drawing-room on the Twentieth Century, but to all intents and purposes he had rescued his princess from a tower. It was no wonder that ever after he believed firmly in happy endings.

6. Ballads in Grub Street

There was a lot more hackwork you could live on then than there is now.[1]

BENÉT'S willingness to accept Brandt's judgment that he should live in New York rather than Europe had important implications for the nature of his career. His susceptibility to expatriation in 1921 was considerable. It was both mixed with and reinforced by his painful separation from Rosemary and by the mutual joys they had shared in Paris. "But we're going back," he wrote her from Scarsdale in July 1921, "sink or swim, live or die, survive or perish!"

Nor was Benét enamored of the United States. His letters were full of distaste for a general atmosphere in which prohibition was the symptomatic quality. "It is different, expensive, unamusing, sweaty and efficient here," he told Rosemary. He felt the same ambivalence toward New York that he had experienced in 1919 as an ad man. Now his uneasiness was increased as he became more familiar with Manhattan literary life. He had given poetry readings, participated in the Wanamaker Book Fair, and gone to Farrar's *Bookman* luncheons. He had joined and attended, largely at the urging of Laura and William, the Poetry Society. None of it had overwhelmed him.

"I hate New York literary people," he exploded to Rosemary, "except for a handful. I hate all the literary backbiting and posing and general nervous hurried air of going somewhere faster than anybody else. . . . They remind me of fleas in their attitude toward life and art. Jumping educated fleas. What do they know about Art? They only know the particular prejudices of their clique. . . . fraternity politics all over again."

He discussed the respective merits of Europe and America with his friends. During the summers of 1921 and 1922 he saw a good deal of a group which included such rising and amusing young writers as John Weaver, Donald Ogden Stewart, Thomas Beer, John Peale Bishop, and Robert Nathan. Their affection for most of the national institutions was no warmer than his. They were content to live with them, however, arguing that one could get abroad for a part of each year or for six months every two years. Farrar, on the other hand, was the principal spokesman for a more militant wing which insisted on New York rather than Paris as the capital of the forthcoming renaissance. Benét incorporated the general dispute into one of the early episodes of *Young People's Pride*. The direction in which his own instincts led was plainly evident.

"Bunny Andrews sailed for Paris Thursday," says Ted Billett longingly. "Two years at the Beaux Arts," and for an instant the splintering of lances stops, like the hush in a tournament when the marshall throws down the warder, at the shine of that single word.

"All the same, New York is the best place to be right now if you're going to do anything big," says Johnny uncomfortably, too much as if he felt he just had to believe in it, but the rest are silent, seeing the

Seine wind under its bridges, cool as satin, grey-blue with evening . . .

"New York *is* twice as romantic, really," says Johnny firmly.

"If you can't get out of it," adds Oliver with a twisted grin.

Ted Billett turns to Ricky as if each had no other friend in the world.

"You were over, weren't you?" he says, a little diffidently, but his voice is that of Rachel weeping for her children.

"Well, there was a little café on the Rue Bonaparte —I suppose you wouldn't know—."

Brandt's however, was the most persuasive voice. He had already displayed his magic. "That man," Benét told Rosemary, "can chirr-up checks out of thin air." The rest were arguing from emotion and instinct and ego, like himself; only Brandt was talking demonstrable practicalities. Benét and Rosemary therefore honeymooned deliciously from Paris south to Marseilles and down to the Italian Riviera. "This incredible town," he wrote his brother from Le Puy in March 1922, "is full of black basalt and running water. The white wine is superb." From his father came entertaining letters about the various domestic crises at the Brimming Cup and reminiscences of his own European travels. The Colonel inserted an ironic aside or two regarding Stephen's literary fame.

"Your Mother," he told his son, "wrote the Newark women that you had wedded a wife and were in Europe but that you had always been a clean good son, and the cutest baby she ever saw and when you returned to this country it would be your dearest wish to read for the

Newark women. Rosemary will know full soon the disabilities which are entailed by being the wife of a Public Character."

They lingered rather longer than they had intended, or than Brandt had recommended, but they were back in the United States by late spring. Rosemary went out to Chicago to see her parents; her father was ailing. Benét returned to the Brimming Cup, using it as a base from which he searched the area for a home for himself and his bride. He put an advertisement in the *Literary Review;* then he ranged northward as far as Carmel, east to Long Island, across the river to Staten Island, up the Hudson to Tarrytown. "From now on," he wrote Rosemary, "strange way-stations shall know me, and dubious news-agents be terrified by the number of cakes of milk-chocolate I buy to stay my journeys, my feet shall be set in the lovely sands of Quogue, I shall laugh, crying 'ha-ha, $100 or bust!' in the high places of Amagansett."

He read all the new fiction, enjoying Huxley's *Crome Yellow* in particular, and he gingerly renewed his membership in Manhattan literary life. "Let it not Blind you, my de-ar Wife," he told Rosemary, "to my Truly Serious Purpose, My Strenuous Vivid Seeking for a Real Nest For Just Us Two." As it had been for the past two years, his principal concern was with the rigors of magazine fiction. Brandt was making good his pledge that editors would soon begin to buy regularly. During the second half of 1922 the stories Benét had written the previous summer continued to be sold and published. In addition to *Delineator* and *Metropolitan,* they appeared now in *Cosmopolitan* and *Redbook.*[2] The first installment of *Young People's Pride* came out in the June *Harper's Bazaar.* He was something of a celebrity, interviewed by lady reporters who asked him questions cosmic and inane.

Brandt assured him that he would earn between five thousand and seventy-five hundred dollars during the coming year. All he had to do was keep on writing the short stories. It sounded easy but Benét already knew different. "The short story," he confessed to Rosemary, "was never exactly my forte." He was an instinctive poet, knowing and possessing the form since childhood, relishing its richness of scope, fascinated always by its technical abundance and problems. He had to discipline himself to the short story.

"Finished another short story today," he told Rosemary in September 1921, "a very short one, thank God, only 4000 words. I tried to copy Millay-Boyd in it and rather produced the effect of an elephant trying to walk the tightrope—I am not at my best in the flippant sentimental." Even now, in mid-1922, his work sought after by editors, he made discouraging false starts in some instances and in other cases he laboriously finished stories that proved thoroughly unsalable.

"I am writing a silly story for the Cosmo," he told Rosemary in June 1922, "about a doctor who created a lady out of dirt. I do not think much of it, but it may bring us GOLD." He sketched a heaping mound of money-bags on the margin of the letter, but the story brought not gold but rejection. Brandt phoned the next day, Benét told his wife, "& said he didn't like my 'Dr. Faustus' at *all*." But it took as long to write a silly story as a good one. Even the good ones were by no means automatic sales. His Cabell-like parable, "The Barefoot Saint," had traveled from desk to desk. "Carl has for the nineteenth time nearly sold it," Benét wrote his wife, "this time to Frank of the *Century*, but don't breathe or it will probably pop open again. That tale has won more editorial praise and less cash than anything I ever did." [3]

Benét's problem, as with most magazine writers, was always plot. He had an inventive and ingenious mind, but the demands he was making on it were large. More and more, as he had done unsuccessfully with the Faust legend, he began to improvise the central situation from his vast reading. He blended the Restoration period and classical mythology into a tale called "The Golden Bessie," about the seventeenth-century daughter of a miser, who was dipped—nearly—in gold paint, and he returned to his favorite Spanish Main for a first-class story, "Snake and Hawk," which N. C. Wyeth illustrated for the *Ladies' Home Journal.* In another story he freshened a conventional love story by reviving the legend that lovers once prayed before the Venus de Medici.[4] In some cases Brandt relayed to him the specific needs of a certain editor.

"C. wants a love-story—modern," he told Rosemary in July. "Says Ray Long is howling for them." Again Benét renovated a timeless legend, this one the tale of the maiden who bade her three suitors compete for her hand by act of prowess. The trivial plot was redeemed by freshness of style, some effective comment on the American rich, and intriguing incidents. The story did not appeal to Long after all, however; it finally went to *Redbook* instead of *Cosmopolitan.* The blurb made recognition of Benét's growing status, describing him as "an author whom people are talking a lot about these days."[5]

Cosmopolitan did, however, buy several of his stories during this period.[6] Ray Long was at the height of his success, commanding with enormous prices the most proficient magazine writers of England and America. He featured Benét's ingenious and melodramatic "Elementals" in the April 1922 issue; Benét received a number of letters from rather simple-minded readers who wanted to put themselves to the same elaborate test he had devised for his fictional lovers. Long was generally indifferent, however, to the kind of fresh, occasionally satiric characterizations which continually and exasperatingly thrust their way into Benét's short stories.

"She considered him," Benét wrote that summer of one of his heroines. "He Faced Facts so firmly. An enemy might have said that those facts lay always somehow on the fringes of sex and that he had not only Faced them continually but even dragged them out when nobody else would have found them there to Face—a slick, blond collie never weary of exhuming the same disreputable bone." It had a prose vitality which compensated for the winded plot, but it had to be sold to the poorer-paying *Harper's Bazaar*.[7] Benét did his best to harness these troublesome instincts.

"This damn man in my story is strapped on an operating table," he wrote Rosemary. "I must leap and either save or kill him. I'd much prefer the latter, but I'm afraid he's worth more money living than dead." Brandt had become thoroughly aware of his client's wayward humors. He reversed the earlier prescription, now advising Benét to postpone any new serial for the time being and stick to short stories; their comparative brevity would allow him less room for license. Benét stubbornly put together a backlog of half a dozen marketable stories. Then he celebrated Rosemary's return from Chicago and their assumption of housekeeping—first in a Scarsdale cottage for the remainder of the summer, and then in a 57th Street apartment—with a burst of notable poetry.

He had written only two poems since their return to America, one a piece of light verse which, astonishingly, was bought by the *Ladies' Home Journal* for almost as much money as his various books of poetry had previ-

125

ously earned, the other a brief lyric, "Oh, Tricksy April," which he never republished.[8] Now he abruptly and joyfully dipped into his Southern memories for a pair of ballads which reassured his startled friends, who had imagined him the permanent captive of the circulation magazines.

The American past had never been displaced in Benét's consciousness, neither by his distaste for contemporary aspects of that past, nor by expatriation, nor by the Graduate School indoctrination in English belles-lettres. Each one of these seemingly incongruous agents had in fact supplied its own particular stimulant. In Paris he became the friend of Douglas Moore, who was already determined to compose American opera. In the Graduate School he worked with Henry Canby, who was more interested in American than English literature.

The effect of Benét's dissatisfaction with the current national scene was to drive him back to its more appealing heritage. Magazine editors, on the other hand, were insisting that he write contemporary material. Now his instinctive reaction was to alternate the burden of commercial fiction with the sweet release of an earlier America. He had sentenced himself to magazine fiction, after all, in order to support the periodic indulgence of poetry. It was thus wholly natural that the first work he did during the late summer and early fall of 1922, "The Ballad of William Sycamore," should bear the subtitle "1790–1871."

The poem was published in the *New Republic* in November.[9] It was an initial step in the formation of the most durable aspect of Benét's achievement and reputation. Hitherto his work had been known and valued in the two dissimilar literary worlds of moderately avant-garde poetry on the one hand and slick fiction on the other. Each was an area of literary extremism; each was an area in which achievement and reputation are lightly bestowed and abruptly withdrawn.

"The Ballad of William Sycamore" erected a bridge between these extremes. It appealed to sections of those two earlier audiences and simultaneously attracted an audience that was both nonliterary, in contrast to the avant-garde world, and intellectually literate, in contrast to the world of *Redbook* and *Metropolitan* and *Every-body's*. It was the audience which had previously valued and enshrined the work of Irving and Longfellow and Lowell and Mark Twain. It was the audience which would, by its persistent pressure and in opposition to formal literary criticism, thrust *John Brown's Body* and "The Devil and Daniel Webster" and *A Child Is Born* into the national literature. Benét made his first substantial contact with that audience through "The Ballad of William Sycamore," which became a standard entry in anthologies and texts.

"I knew this writer and he was my friend," said the Kentucky poet Jesse Stuart in 1957, recalling the excitement with which he had first read the William Sycamore ballad as an undergraduate in the late 1920's, "before I ever met him." [10]

It was a poem which tempted its readers to sing it or chant it or at the least to read it aloud. It was the kind of poem which one reader wanted to share with another. There was the foot-tapping beat and compulsive chant of the authentic ballad, united with Benét's buoyant sense of a robust, brawling, fertile America. It joined Benét to the innumerable Americans who shared his uneasiness about the contemporary scene but who nonetheless felt a profound kinship with the national origins and refused to concede that its values had dissolved.

This was an unashamedly sentimental ballad, and its images and episodes were familar ones. If it was the beginning of Benét's role as a national poet and storyteller, it was also an inaugural step toward the mistrust of his work by those professional critics who would label him a cinema poet. But the more temperate and judicious would concede his achievement. In 1948 the *Literary History of the United States*, no friend to the popular and well-rewarded writer, confirmed "The Ballad of William Sycamore" as "the incarnation of the pioneer spirit set to perfect American transposition of the old ballad music." F. O. Matthiessen, the most sensitive and creative literary critic of Benét's generation, and a man who was often equally displeased by Benét's political moderation and popular fiction, regarded it as notable work. In a year of national disenchantment, of debunked heroes and shabby leadership—"the Harding administration," Benét said once, "would have sickened a buzzard"—Benét was mindful of more luminous national objects.

> The hunters's whistle hummed in my ear
> As the city-men tried to move me,
> And I died in my boots like a pioneer
> With the whole wide sky above me.
>
> Now I lie in the heart of the fat, black soil,
> Like the seed of a prairie-thistle;
> It has washed my bones with honey and oil
> And picked them clean as a whistle.

And my youth returns, like the rains of Spring,
And my sons, like the wild-geese flying;
And I lie and hear the meadow-lark sing
And have much content in my dying.

Go play with the towns you have built of blocks,
The towns where you would have bound me!
I sleep in my earth like a tired fox,
And my buffalo have found me.

As the climax of the ballad made clear, and the final
stanza in particular, Benét had by no means declared a
truce with contemporary America. To the extent that
modern America was in opposition to earlier America,
the seat of current values was in the cities whose urban
culture was so at variance with the frontier past.

In "King David" he joined his contempt for persisting
American fundamentalism with his own singing and blas-
phemous impudence. He was melding into a personal
style the disparate influences of Lindsay and Browning
and Kipling and Morris. If "The Ballad of William Sycamore" was a preliminary tuning, "King David" was a
major enterprise. Even more than "William Sycamore,"
it extended his position as a writer who could appeal to
professional and lay tastes alike. The award to it of the
Nation's poetry prize for 1922 involved recognition of a
significant kind. This was one of the major laurels of the
period, competed for each year by several thousand poets
who included not only the inevitable amateurs but also
such accomplished writers as William Ellery Leonard,
Babette Deutsch, Clement Wood, Allen Tate, Max
Bodenheim, Leonora Speyer, Genevieve Taggard, and
John Gould Fletcher. Even the one hundred dollars

which constituted the cash award was itself an indication of the status of the *Nation* prize; in the prevailing condition of American poetry a hundred dollars had virtually Nobel dimensions.

The response to "King David" by Benét's peers, when it was published in the *Nation's* issue of February 14, 1923, was immediate. From England, John Drinkwater wrote instantly to congratulate Benét personally. From Chicago, Edgar Lee Masters wrote the editors that "King David" was "a miracle" for which he honored them and its author. "He does not need to go further," Masters declared. "He is there now." Witter Bynner, who had himself competed for the prize, called it "an extraordinarily fine poem, the best I have seen from him." [11]

The editors also received what they called a "mass of correspondence" from readers. It "poured into the *Nation* office." They printed several pages of it in subsequent issues: the wrath of a Catholic educator who canceled his school's subscription, the sorrow of a pious citizen who grieved that Benét had written his poem "so well that the *Nation* was in honor bound to award it the prize and publish it," and the standard query as to what effect "this collection of obscenity, irreverence, and utterly bad poetic metre would have upon some sweet young girl or upon the cultured ladies of my household?" [12]

A poem that could so arouse the poetically apathetic American middle class, and so delight his colleagues, was solid achievement, and comfort for the fictional abuses he had committed during the previous eighteen months. Benét, rarely content with his seriously written work, was well pleased with both "William Sycamore" and "King David." When Burton Stevenson asked permission in 1924 to include some of his verse in a new anthology of modern poetry, Benét wrote him that he thought these two were "the best things I have done for some time." What he achieved in "King David" was a blend of several characteristics that had previously been separately displayed in individual work. There were the charming high spirits as well as what Matthiesson later termed the anti-Victorianism of such superior light verse as "For All Blasphemers."

> Adam was my grandfather,
> A tall, spoiled child,
> A red, clay tower
> In Eden, green and mild.
> He ripped the Sinful Pippin
> From its sanctimonious limb.
> Adam was my grandfather—
> And I take after him.[13]

There was also the shrewd characterization that had been a liability to his magazine fiction, the portraits of Uriah and Nathan as much as of David. To the lyricism which his poetry had always contained, and the technical virtuosity in which he had been so precocious, was added the shrill jazz of the decade's music. "King David" possessed them all, a kind of perfect miniature of his talent, a prophecy of *John Brown's Body,* a promise of the prose beat of "The Devil and Daniel Webster." It marked the end of literary adventuring and the beginning of major achievement.

> "Why should I grieve for what was pain?
> A cherished grief is an iron chain."
>
> He took up his harp, the sage old chief.
> His heart felt clean as a new green leaf.

His soul smelt pleasant as rain-wet clover.
"I have sinned and repented and that's all over.

"In his dealing with heathen, the Lord is hard.
But the humble soul is his spikenard."

His wise thoughts fluttered like doves in the air.
"I wonder is Bathsheba still so fair?

"Does she weep for the child that our sin made perish?
I must comfort my ewe-lamb, comfort and cherish.

"The justice of God is honey and balm.
I will soothe her heart with a little psalm." [14]

"William Sycamore" and "King David" gave Benét a poetic acceleration which he had difficulty in restraining. Weeks after he had reluctantly put poetry aside, bending himself again to another period of bread-and-butter writing, new poems continued to intrude. None of them had the scope of the two ballads, for he was pressed for time, but neither were they fragments of light verse or stanzas of epigram. It was plain that his imagination had now matured to a point where it could encompass his talent. His work was moving beyond the merely poetic. He was beginning to envelop his technical mastery with larger and more durable conceits. Satiric analysis and philosophical poise gave new substance to such poems of 1924 and 1925 as "Snowfall" and "Carol: New Style." His sonnets had a compact unity, as in the one called "X-Ray" which the *New Republic* published in May 1924.[15]

Smile if you will or frown, wear silk or serge,
Play age or youth, it will not help, my dear.

This is a place where truth is made too clear
For idle minds to watch that Truth emerge.
The penetration of this light is just,
Inhuman, and most mercilessly pure.
From its assault upon your house of dust
Only the naked scaffold will endure.
Beneath the perfect candor of this ray
All mortal comeliness lies overthrown,
And even human blood is merely grey,
And ribs and joints are beautiful alone
As the weak flesh contests but cannot stay
The passionless search for the eternal bone.

But the major part of his energy was diverted to making a living. His weariness with magazine fiction was as evident as his new poetic vigor. Most of the short stories he wrote in 1923 and 1924 were mechanical and superficial; the freshness that had disguised "The Golden Bessie" and "Snake and Hawk" was lost to the trivialities of the synthetically sophisticated. *Redbook* became the principal market for the least commonplace of his stories. The rest trickled down to such less demanding magazines as *Metropolitan* and *Liberty*.[16]

As his work became increasingly stereotyped, his editorial value rose, from $200 a story to $250, to $400, now to $500. Only once during those eighteen months was he able to cheat a meaningful story from the formula. "Uriah's Son," published in the May 1924 issue of *Redbook,* was an effective piece of work. It was an indulgence, however, and Benét even doubted that it would sell. "I've just finished a story that you won't care to publish," he told the *Redbook* editor, "for it's not my usual sort."[17]

To his surprise they bought it immediately. It was a

reminder that it was not the taste of magazine editors but the natural inability of writers to constantly freshen the formula which accounted for the drabness of the popular magazines. "Uriah's Son" was included in the O. Henry Memorial Award volume that year, the first of a number of such awards to his magazine fiction. He was gradually taking his place with such craftsmen of the genre as Wilbur Daniel Steele, Booth Tarkington, and Richard Connell.

A short story of from five to ten thousand words, however, no matter how trivial, sometimes took him a month or more to write. Each new story was pure speculation. Even if Brandt succeeded in finding a buyer, which he couldn't always do, it might be weeks before the sale was made. With his first child expected in the spring of 1924, Benét therefore looked around for some kind of strike that would make hack work more profitable. The classmates whom he met in the Yale Club were thriving in the stock market. He knew writers who were already enjoying from personal experience what Scott Fitzgerald would soon discuss in his celebrated *Saturday Evening Post* article, "How To Live on $36,000 a Year." [18] Benét's share of the literary boom was thus far less prodigal. "It seems silly to pay in driblets," he wrote Edward Bliss Reed, sending him fifty dollars toward what remained of the five hundred he had borrowed in 1920, "but what income I have is so fluctuating that I'm forced to."

For a time in 1923 he wrote brief columns on books and the literary scene for *Time*.[19] In those days, he said later, to be a *Time*man was no automatic entree. Often when he asked for *Time's* free tickets at the box office he was told stiffly that "the New York *Times* man is already in the theater." Publishers, similarly skeptical about the magazine's status with consumers, required him to return all review copies. He got the job through Briton Hadden, whom he liked and admired, but the pay was low and the hours restricting, and he had absolutely no interest in that kind of career.

John Farrar, however, was also writing occasionally for *Time* during this period, and since he too was sometimes covering the Broadway openings, it was natural that they began to consider theatrical entries of their own. Farrar, prodigiously energetic, and restless even in his triple role as *Bookman* editor, assistant to the publisher George Doran, and *Time* columnist, had already written a one-act play about the war called *Nerves* which Monty Woolley directed for the Yale Dramat in 1919. It was published by Samuel French in 1922 and successfully produced by a New York amateur group. A number of people urged Farrar to lengthen it for a possible professional production. Farrar and Benét talked it over; what could they lose? They worked on it evenings during the summer of 1923, Farrar doing the major revisions and Benét concentrating on the dialogue and the outlines of the individual scenes. By early September they had added two more acts and a number of new parts. Farrar began to show it around. Benét and Rosemary spent a couple of weeks at the shore, their hopes rising and falling in response to the tone of the messages from Farrar. Most of the notes and telegrams had the large cloudiness of preliminary skirmishing. By the end of September Benét was in a state of wry frustration.

"It may be going to be put on in the Hippodrome with a chorus of diving elephants," he wrote Ethel Andrews, "or it may be in Lee Shubert's wastebasket—I can't find out."

Then, as if in reproduction of those splendid weeks in 1921 when all news was good news, their enterprise began to catch fire. Winifred Lenihan was looking for a vehicle. They hastily enlarged one of the female parts for her. A pair of young producers, William Brady, Jr., and Dwight Wiman—the latter a Yale contemporary—put up some money. Kenneth MacKenna, who would play the male lead, pledged some more; Farrar and Benét each put in a little. Brady and Wiman began to cast and Benét, always excited by the theater since his work at Yale with Monty Woolley and the famous theatricals which John Berdan had directed at Alpha Delta Phi, began work on a second play. Again Farrar joined him, but neither here nor with Nerves was it a genuine collaboration. In the latter Farrar was the principal author; now Benét did most of the writing.

They interrupted work when Alice Brady hired them to doctor yet another play, this one a vehicle for Grace George and C. Aubrey Smith. Benét and Farrar accompanied the show on its out-of-town run, but there wasn't much to vet; it closed before reaching New York. The experience itself was instructive, however, and Grace George told Benét she was looking for a play for the fall season. Benét went back to work. This would be an historical drama, another offshoot of his interest in the American past. It was based in part on a 1903 novel by Alfred Henry Lewis called *Peggy O'Neal*. Benét retitled it *That Awful Mrs. Eaton*. The central part—written with Grace George in mind—would be that of Peggy O'Neale Eaton, second wife of Andrew Jackson's Secretary of War and the provocative object of the President's chivalry and the capital's social outrage. The title invited jest, and Benét himself later described it to his brother as "that awful awful *The Awful Mrs. Eaton*," but when he finished it in the early winter of 1924 he was overcome despite himself by the optimism which always surrounds Broadway.

"All theatrical business is chancy & dilatory," he wrote his mother-in-law in January 1924, as much for his own restraint as for her information, but he added that there were many indications that 1924 would be "a first-class year." This was more than a graceful reference to his mother-in-law's prospective grandchild. William Brady, Sr., had read *That Awful Mrs. Eaton* and liked it. He would produce it with Grace George as Peggy Eaton, a part she claimed long to have relished. From the authors' points of view this was a giddy prospect.

Brady was the most open-handed theatrical magnate of the period, his productions a legend of opulence. Few leading ladies could match Miss George as a box-office draw. There was, however, many a hitch. Miss George, with a fine disregard for chronology, decided that the part was too old for her. Brady, whose periodic gaiety was as monumental as his productions, vanished on a prolonged tour of the most expensive speakeasies. The spring and summer of 1924 dissolved in his capers. In the midst of these hectic ventures, on April 6, the Benét's first child was born. She was christened Stephanie Jane, the Stephanie, Rosemary explained later, for Stephen, the Jane because Benét insisted that some part of his daughter's public title must include the private name by which he celebrated his love for his wife.

In the meantime *Nerves* lurched through difficulties which were more commonplace than those which attended the senior Brady's production. The principal problem with the war play was a theater; most of the good ones were controlled by the Shuberts. Then in early August, just as Benét was planning a New

Hampshire vacation at the Moores with Rosemary and Stephanie Jane, both *Nerves* and *That Awful Mrs. Eaton* began to take shape simultaneously. Young Brady announced that he would start rehearsing the former on August 18 and would open on September 1. His father, "who is now entirely sober," Benét wrote Rosemary, "and wealthier than I have ever seen him," declared that the Jackson play would begin rehearsals on August 25 and open September 15.

"So," Benét concluded on August 14, "as far as I can see both plays will have to be rewritten before next Monday."

In the middle of these twin revisions Brandt phoned him that *Cosmopolitan* wanted a Christmas story from him right away for the December issue. "Naturally," Benét wrote at his wife, "I snapped at the chance—but Judas!" He had also agreed earlier to write a monthly drama column for the *Bookman*, commencing with the October issue; now other people's shows began to open with him in attendance as critic. "When you see me again," he told Rosemary, "I will be wearing straw in my hair."

The senior Brady, not to be outdone by his son, decided to start the *Mrs. Eaton* rehearsals, with Katherine Alexander replacing Miss George, on August 18 instead of the 25. Opening night would be pushed forward a week, to September 8. Benét rewrote the entire second act of *Nerves* the next evening, working on into the early morning in the kitchen so that the upstairs tenants would not bang their displeasure on the ceiling, as they had done before when he typed late. He and Farrar then rewrote the third act that week end. The word was now definite that *Nerves* would open at the Comedy Theatre on September 2. The Comedy was the right size, Benét wrote his wife, and the rent was low. Vocational optimism was overtaking his normally realistic nature. "We can make money there on low receipts," he explained, "and if it's a big hit we can move."

Now the senior Brady suddenly announced that *Mrs. Eaton* would have a one-night trial performance in Stamford, Conn., on September 4th—"Lord knows why!" said Benét—and return to New York for additional rehearsals before opening on the 8th. They finished the new third act of *Nerves* late Sunday afternoon and began rehearsals that night. Casting for *Mrs. Eaton* was completed and then a new postponement occurred when Brady senior lost his option on the National Theatre to a higher bidder. "Some Yiddish bootlegger," said Brady, now loftily on the wagon.

"So," Benét told Rosemary on August 21, "we now open on the 15th or 22nd—or indeed almost any time."

The leading man confided rather bitterly to Benét, whose immunity to tantrums made him a confessor to all parties in both shows, that he anticipated a phone call late some night informing him that the play would open without rehearsal the following day with Jefferson instead of Jackson as the hero. In the meantime the war play was in process. Benét went from *Eaton* castings to *Nerves* rehearsals and back to his typewriter for more rewriting. In the intervals he attended as *Bookman* critic the openings of two musicals and a drama called *The Werewolf*.

"*Nerves*," he wrote to Rosemary, "is getting along finely. During the last 2 days, [Winifred] Lenihan has threatened to quit, Bill has threatened to quit and Johnny has left the theater in a rage declaring he would never come back. After which, all settled down and was calm. I think we're on the right track and if there aren't too many temperamental explosions, the show ought to look pretty good the first night." Now the senior Brady solved his theater problem by holding dress rehearsals for *Mrs. Eaton* at Fort Lee, New Jersey, in the Paragon Studios whose glass skylights had been the first ever built for the indoor production of motion pictures. Having dealt ingeniously with the one dilemma, Brady created a new one by falling magnificently off the wagon.

Somehow Benét found the time to meet Rosemary and Stephanie Jane in Worcester and bring them back to New York. His father sent him his best wishes for the various openings. "Your mother," said the Colonel, "hopes you have got some new clothes and when she comes to New York she wants you to display them. I tell her the law of our family has always been 'Women and children first.' But in this case, there should be enough for all."

The Colonel's choice of a clothes image with which to express his optimism about the theatrical ventures was an unfortunate one. Everybody involved very nearly lost their shirts. *Nerves* opened three nights before *What Price Glory*. Its rather collegiate, sentimental version of life on an American squadron was no competition for Sergeant Quirt and Captain Flagg. It closed after three performances.

The failure of *That Awful Mrs. Eaton* was less easy to explain. Benét himself shrugged it off as poor theater, blaming himself for having put in too much local color and having confused the audience with historical intricacies. In mid-July, however, a stock company had produced it with enormous success in Detroit. Benét himself had been there to see the enthusiastic reception and to receive in person the congratulations of Senator Couzens. In New York there was public apathy and sour notices. Benét gave his own unreserved endorsement to

What Price Glory, describing it in his *Bookman* column as "the most exciting theatrical experience in New York." He included in his review a brief paragraph on *Nerves*, whose run he described as "sudden."

"In any case," he told his readers, "it seems to us that few authors could have been more fortunate in the acting and directing of their first play than the authors of *Nerves*, and our gratitude to a splendid and long suffering cast and management is very sincere. With which few words we declare the polls officially closed." [20]

Benét covered the entire season for the *Bookman* that year, in essays that were lively and generous.[21] He had profited professionally from the experience as a playwright; in later years he and Farrar enjoyed recalling that the sets for both plays had been Jo Mielziner's first New York ones, and that *Nerves* had given Humphrey Bogart his first New York notices. Benét's love of the theater was genuine and permanent. Eventually it materialized most fully in his work for radio fifteen years later. Farrar always credited much of his friend's great success with serious network drama to those months of exacting theatrical experience in 1924.

But now, in the autumn of that year, George Doran told Farrar that he'd fire him on the spot if he wrote any more plays. Benét for his part recognized that since he himself had no employer he would have to provide his own discipline. He concluded that he had better get on with more certain ventures, though his mind was always attracted to the stage. "Think of play [I] would like to write in afternoon," he once noted in his diary, "instead of working on short story."

Thus, in the fall of 1924, Benét was more broke than at any time since 1921, though he was a thoroughly established writer to whose work a number of editors were responsive. His name was worth featuring on the covers of the circulation magazines. He had published, if one included such limited editions as *The Ballad of William Sycamore* and *King David,* six volumes of poetry and three novels. He had collaborated on two Broadway plays and published his poetry in virtually every American magazine that printed verse, and yet at one point during the winter of 1924 his bank account was down to $35. Being broke was no novelty. In the past it had never bothered him particularly. But it was newly unpleasant to know that his being broke meant that his wife and daughter were also broke. He endorsed in full the Colonel's domestic doctrine of women and children first.

Nineteen hundred and twenty-four had been an entertaining year—lugubriously so at times, but entertaining nonetheless. It had been enriched by domestic happiness and the new pleasures of parenthood. Otherwise it had fallen distinctly short of the high hopes he had expressed for it in January to his mother-in-law. Brandt welcomed him back to magazine fiction, though he reminded Benét that his absence from the field would probably mean a cut in story price for a time. Benét began to plan a novel that had been at the back of his head for a long while and on which he had already done a little work. He had always wanted to write about the eighteenth-century Florida of his Minorcan ancestors. He had a fine title. He would call it *Spanish Bayonet.* Perhaps Carl could sell it as a serial.

7. The Literary Life

*Steve never hated anyone so far as I
knew, but he hated cruelty and ignorance.*[1]

In 1925, when he was twenty-six, Benét, like so many
of his generation, was often more concerned with appearing older than his years rather than with worrying
about the passage of youth. He grew a mustache, trying
to get rid of what he called his beardless-wonder look.
This was a decade, after all, when youth seemed limitless; all other generations, they knew, had grown old
quickly, but it seemed as if for them youth was going
to last forever.

This was a generation which inherited its earth early.
Achievements and experiences which had previously
been reserved for one's thirties had been theirs since
adolescence. War, travel, marriage, parenthood, the big
money and the smash hit—if one hadn't quite encompassed them all, there was certainly the illusion that one
was just about to. It was a time when things which had
been traditionally elusive came easily instead.

Although Benét shared most of the characteristics of
his generation, and all of its major experiences, he differed from many of his contemporaries in this one respect. Literary success, it was true, had come readily

and, a casual observer might have concluded, without too much effort. The things he honored, however, had been increasingly hard won. He competed bitterly for his bride and there had been the possibility that he would not win her. He wrote his poetry, the only part of his work which he valued, at the cost of long hours of hack work. The hours and the imminence of defeat left inevitable scars. When his generation's youth did indeed vanish, to be replaced by layers of distress in the 1930's, he was rather better prepared than most of his contemporaries.

Even now, in 1925—with or without the mustache— he seemed to have a premature serenity on which his friends and family drew limitlessly and often without being fully aware of their dependence. The friendships were multiplying, but always at the center were the ones he had made at Yale and in Paris, with Douglas Moore and his wife Emily, with Dick Myers and Alice Lee, with Farrar and MacLeish and Sidney Howard, Evarts, Don Campbell, Phil Barry and Ellen, Shreve Badger and John Andrews and the latter's sister Ethel. It was revealing, too, that there were so many others, whom he thought of as no more than acquaintances, who regarded themselves as his friends. From him they received a sense of friendship deeper than relationships which should have been more intimate.

Later when they tried to assess his quality, whether they were friends or acquaintances they all cited the same characteristics—warmth, wit, generosity, loyalty, wisdom—but at the same time, like his family, they rather took him for granted. There really appeared to be, except to the unusually perceptive, so little that was truly remarkable about him. His own description of himself was one they would have endorsed with affectionate amusement, though on reflection they would have footnoted it sharply.

"I will wear glasses and probably a brown suit," Benét told a college dean who was to meet him at the railroad station and escort him to his lecture. She had never seen him before, and had inquired nervously how she was to recognize him. "I am not quite sure what I look like," Benét told her, "but I have several times been taken for an insurance salesman." [2]

The nondescript appearance—slightly seedy, Benét would have called it—vanished as soon as he began to talk. "He is one of the most sparkling conversationalists I have met anywhere," said Billy Phelps in 1930, and despite Phelps' notorious exaggeration and his partiality to celebrities, this particular enthusiasm was verifiable. It was the characteristic at which they all marveled. A reporter who interviewed Benét that same year was impressed by the ease with which he and the poet conversed. "He talks quickly," the newspaperman noted, "one line following so closely upon another that the effect is of many nearly finished sentences." [3]

Indeed he loved to talk, the playwright Norman Rosten remembered, and there was nothing he didn't enjoy talking about. Edward Weismiller, another of the young writers who became so indebted to him, retained the same image, recalling Benét's "habit of sitting stretched out in an easy chair, a cigarette in the exact center of his mouth, the ash cascading down the front of his blue serge suit as he talked animatedly without removing the cigarette." [4]

Inevitably they measured him against his professional colleagues, trying to define the qualities which somehow made him as memorable as other writers who by their more apparent charm or good looks or greater fame

145

should have overshadowed him. "Steve was as articulate as MacLeish," decided Christopher LaFarge, comparing these two poets who had so influenced his own work, "but he could never be didactic." Philip Barry's wife Ellen, who knew him well for almost twenty-five years, remembered best his wit and his sense of fun, and the excitement he could inject into every situation, whether it was a trip to Florida or no more than a movie at the neighborhood Trans-Lux. In this he reminded her of Scott Fitzgerald, but with Fitzgerald she always felt the darkness and threat of excess. In Benét there was delight in life without the destructive abandon. "This was his wisdom," she reflected once, "and probably also a result of his wisdom." [5]

He had no illusions about the uncertainties of life, however, and—rather more than all but his most intimate friends suspected—he had a fondness for the gamble and the long shot. Gradually he restrained this speculative impulse as his domestic responsibilities grew heavier, but he never entirely surrendered it. Always in his philosophy there was something of the crap game's quick roll. "Life's too brief and insecure," he told Rosemary in 1921, "not to play everything you have on the appearance of Little Joe, even when you have no logical reason to suppose he will emerge."

He was a brave man, as he would show increasingly during the travail of his maturity, and like any man of courage who is also intelligent there were many things he feared, but he feared most the torpor of security and passivity. "It does really seem to me," he told Rosemary just before their marriage, at a time when tactically he ought perhaps to have been stressing his reliability, "that you get more out of things by alternating feasts and semistarvation than a continual safe existence in Childs restaurants."

The remark was a reminder that he was a man who valued all his senses. When he and Robert Nathan later referred to his public role as that of "the good gray poet," they did so with conscious mockery, aware always of the sensuality that lay beneath the laborious surface of conforming respectability. Despite the efforts of others of his friends to elevate him to bloodless sainthood, he was deeply responsive, as both his work and his life showed, to sex, good liquor, rich food, the violent beauty of nature, strong colors, jazz.

In 1925 it was to be expected that such a temperament would be weary of budgets and overdrawn bank accounts, of circumscribed living and the amiable, ceaseless deadlines of magazine fiction. "We are going to make a little money this year," he told Rosemary, who had taken Stephanie Jane to Chicago for a brief visit with the Carrs, "if I have to bust myself. Then—think of it, Jane—if we do, we might play for six months or so, in Paris or somewhere, anywhere for me, so you were there." His life was a rich one, however, even in the small apartments of these years—now they were living further downtown, on 15th Street—for the life contained his wife and his work and his daughter and his friends.

He had made his peace with New York, taking long walks now each morning along 2nd and 3rd Avenues, through the Park, sometimes as far as 125th Street to have a late breakfast and ale with Hervey Allen. His friends' wives would see him as they did their marketing, his long legs and slightly stooped shoulders identifying him from several blocks away, his pockets stuffed with newspapers and small packages, gifts for Rosemary and Stephanie, his sharp eyes digesting the city deceptively from behind the thick, sleepy glasses. More often than not his mind was also in combat with a spavined plot or an awkward characterization, but as always he twisted away from the magazine fiction at intervals, escaping into the poetry that grew steadily more assured.

For a month, when Brandt had sold two stories simultaneously, he labored pleasurably on two very different pieces of work. The first, "The Mountain Whippoorwill," was a part of the same lode which had mined "William Sycamore" and "King David." It was printed in the *Century* in March 1925, one of the last major publications of a great magazine which was now dying. From England the novelist and poet L. A. G. Strong wrote him almost instantly, asking permission to include it in his annual anthology of distinguished magazine verse. "It was a pure delight to read," Strong told him, "the most exciting long poem of the year." [6]

Like the two earlier ballads, "The Mountain Whippoorwill" was instantly cherished, to be reprinted and memorized and recited. It was identified with Benét until it became, like *John Brown's Body* and the classic short stories of his maturity, a kind of entree by which strangers—like the southern girl who to his intense embarrassment once greeted him at a cocktail party as Mr. Whippoorwill—imagined themselves his friends because they had loved his writing. He subtitled it "A Georgia Romance," but it was equally an echo of the boyhood summers in North Carolina in 1913 and 1914.

"I was trying to adapt the strict ballad form to a contemporary American subject," Benét explained later, "vary it as I chose, and use colloquial speech—get the note of the boxwood fiddle into it, if it could be done. I had heard the mountain fiddlers in the North Carolinas, and their tunes stuck in my head." Benét, who was writing in answer to some questions from an anthologist, was as always impatient with both critical theory and self-diagnosis of the creative process. "Of course I didn't draw up these rules on paper before I wrote the poem, any more than you say to yourself, 'I will now have a blue-eyed child with a Roman nose and a hare-lip.' But I was trying to think back to the fiddle music and the speech." [7] The unabashed zest and simplicity of "The Mountain Whippoorwill" appealed to the tastes of a decade which was attracted to primitivism; its raucous music and triumphant climax endeared it to those other readers who normally mistrusted poetry:

> Oh, Georgia booze is might fine booze,
> The best yuh ever poured yuh,
> But it eats the soles right offen yore shoes,
> For Hell's broke loose in Georgia.
>
> My mother was a whippoorwill pert,
> My father, he was lazy,
> But I'm hell broke loose in a new store shirt
> To fiddle all Georgia crazy. [8]

The second sustained poem of this period was altogether different, a sonnet sequence which he called "The Golden Corpse" and dedicated to Don Campbell. Here he recorded the portents of dissolving youth, and honored its memories before they should be forgotten or distorted. Both the technique and the content were part of the new maturity which was gradually crystallizing in his verse, the lines now wrung of the loose wordiness, the stanzas more firmly declarative.

The lively new *Saturday Review of Literature*, which his brother and Henry Canby were erecting to replace the *Literary Review*, featured the sonnets handsomely in the issue of May 2, 1925. Often the lines were as sharply etched as those verses of Frost which Benét was now

touting to such skeptical friends as MacLeish, who recalled many years later that Benét had been the first
among them to value the New England poet:

> Therefore, in neither anguish nor relief,
> I offer to the shadow in the air
> No image of a monumental grief
> To mock its transience from a stony chair,
>
> Nor any tablets edged in rusty black.
> Only a branch of maple, gathered high
> When the crisp air first tastes of applejack,
> And the blue smokes of Autumn stain the sky.[9]

But that was about all the poetry he could afford for
now—"The Mountain Whippoorwill" and "The Golden
Corpse"—if he was to pay the rent and the grocer and
the premiums on the insurance policies he so scrupulously increased annually, and if he was indeed to make
enough money this year so that he and Rosemary could
play for six months. Now, when his publisher urged him
to get together for the fall list a new collection of his
verse, he was painfully reminded of the corrosive effect
of magazine fiction upon his productivity. To give the
collection more substance, in fact, in the section he
wanted to call "Fiddlers and Pirates," he had to reach
back to 1916 for "The Hemp," which would not disgrace
"William Sycamore" and "King David" and the "Whippoorwill." Even with a padding of blank pages, and
others with no more than four lines of verse, the volume
would come to no more than a hundred and twenty
pages.

"Seen in cold type," he wrote his wife sadly in June,
when he read the galleys, "it looks like a pretty small
book for five years' work."

The quality of the poems, however, as even Benét admitted, was high, though he himself would concede no more than "pretty even." He had signed a new contract since the publication of *Jean Huguenot* by Henry Holt in 1923. Now he was with the prosperous and growing house of George H. Doran Company. Farrar, along with Stanley Rinehart one of Doran's principal editors, worked on the new collection. He arranged for a special limited edition as well as the regular one, the former "quite doggy," Benét told Rosemary, "with vellum covers." There were innumerable sessions in which the editors, not content with the modest *Poems and Legends* which was Benét's original intention, considered various alternative titles.

"I am tired fussing about it," Benét wrote his wife, "and said either *The Singing Sword* or *A Sword Upstairs, The Dark Side of the Moon,* or *3 Bags Full* were O.K. with me." Then, impatient with the editorial brooding, Benét decided that he'd reserve *The Singing Sword* for a novel. He told them to use *Tiger Joy.* He took it from Shelley's "Prometheus Unbound."

> Oh, gentle Moon, thy crystal accents pierce
> The caverns of my pride's deep universe
> Charming the tiger, joy . . .

Tiger Joy was published in September 1925. Despite its slimness it received the best critical reception of any of his collections to date. In one important respect the invading burden of magazine fiction had clearly worked to the great advantage of his poetry. No longer was he able to write it constantly, with that fluency which in the past had produced so much that was merely publishable rather than transparently permanent. Now, since *Heavens and Earth,* he had been compelled to husband his poetic gifts, reserving his energy for genuine effort and frugal completion. Coupled with the new lyric resources of his courtship and marriage, this accounted in large part for the finished authority of *Tiger Joy*. It was, as his brother told him, by far his best book of short poems as yet. The volume was dedicated to Rosemary, with the stanzas which had been printed in the *New Republic* in May under the title "Riddle."

If you were gone afar,
And lost the pattern
Of all your delightful ways,
And the web undone,
How would one make you anew,
From what dew and flowers,
What burning and mingled atoms,
Under the sun?

Not from too-satin roses,
Or those rare blossoms,
Orchids, scentless and precious
As precious stone.
But out of lemon-verbena,
Rose-geranium,
These alone.

Not with running horses,
Or Spanish cannon,
Organs, voiced like a lion,
Clamor and speed.
But perhaps with old music-boxes.
Young, tawny kittens,
Wild-strawberry-seed.

He liked the title. *Tiger Joy,* he told Rosemary, expressed "the quality I should like to get in my poetry. I am hoping this is a year I can do some real work in and if so I intend to ride it." He thought himself that "The Golden Corpse" was the best individual verse in *Tiger Joy.* A number of the reviewers agreed, but all of them found a great deal to praise. Mark Van Doren, who felt the four ballads had, "in an exciting degree, the merits of their type at its best," speculated hopefully that Benét might soon write a backwoods epic. This was characteristic of the new note of large expectation which *Tiger Joy* extracted from its readers.

Now they likened him no longer to Browning and Morris but to the sturdier—and more currently fashionable—Thomas Hardy. Gone in large part was the tone of reproach which even the most friendly critics had previously used. "For," said one of them, "he now has . . . something to say. We respond. We care not at all for a few lines that are weak or a few phrases that seem too raw. Better unchastened virility than affectation." Even *Poetry,* partisan spokesman for a wing to which he had never really belonged and from which his magazine fiction had certainly separated him completely, found qualities to admire. Their reviewer cited "a sparkling yeasty humor" and a "fine narrative sense." [10]

Tiger Joy was the first of his poetry collections to be discussed without reference to his role as a prodigy. It received a sobriety of assessment which indicated that he had survived precocity; he was receiving new status as a seriously regarded young American writer. The conservatives of literary criticism did him the compliment of identifying him with the disturbing group which included Fitzgerald, Floyd Dell, and Ben Hecht. Vernon

153

Parrington made disapproving notes on the work of all of them as he prepared the third volume of *Main Current in American Thought*.

Benét, however, was already at work on a novel that would in part remove him from the group Parrington stigmatized as Youth in Revolt. "I am at present sweating over a costume-book to be called *Spanish Bayonet*," he wrote his friend Bob McClure in April 1925, "and trying to crib all I can from *Henry Esmond* without being detected." It was characteristic of Benét that in a long letter he spoke only once of his own work and then with depreciation. The qualities he might have borrowed from Thackeray he had in reality possessed for some time, a regard for accuracy and the conviction that an historical novel must depend on its fictional characters rather than on what Benét once called "the stuffed personages of history." Doran gave him a small advance. While his wife and daughter were with the Carrs he put himself on the harsh schedule of 10,000 words a week.

"Don't know if I can," he told Rosemary, "as I have to think till all the wheels go around before I can visualize people in wigs and purple panties."

Benét's determination to write an historical novel that would be not only accurate but plausible was an additional stage in the slow process by which he was adjusting the necessities of the commercial market to the central but still dormant strengths of his basic gifts and his sense of America. Acute readers detected the process when *Spanish Bayonet* was published in February 1926.

"*Spanish Bayonet*," said Thomas Beer, "represents an episode of conditioned importance. The novel of the American past begins, here, to escape from the ordinary settings as, with Mr. Hergesheimer, it escaped from the ordinary inflections of the elder historical novel. How far can the thing go on? Are we to have nonpatriotic and unflattering tales of early Alabama, early Missouri, and perhaps, at last, of Puritan New England? Mr. Benét's resolute and impenitent appearance in this field arouses a hope that he may look for more material and so do as well again." [11]

Even Beer, a sensitive writer who was as familiar as Benét with magazine restrictions, could only guess at the history of *Spanish Bayonet's* composition. Benét, riding the lessons of four years of formula construction and the new stimulant of material that absorbed him, felt from the beginning that the book was going well. "Yesterday," he wrote Rosemary in early May, "I finished the first 10,000 words of *Spanish Bayonet* and will start typing tomorrow. The last part seemed fair enough while I was writing it and I hope," he added cautiously, "it won't slow up too badly in typescript." He was working with far greater care and much higher hopes than normally accompanied his magazine fiction.

"The first 12,000 words are nearly all typed," he told Rosemary three days later, "& I am finishing up today and starting on the second section. I really am inclined to think that some of it isn't so bad . . . —I think it moves—and the writing certainly seems better on the whole than any prose of mine since the B of W."

It was revealing that in the final clause Benét first wrote "is better" and then crossed out the "is," replacing it with "certainly seems." This was more than his characteristic diffidence about his work. It was also an indication of the hopes he had for the book, a kind of superstitious talisman by which he might ward off disappointment or failure. He finished the second section but he felt it wasn't up to the earlier part. "[It] will need a good deal of revision," he told Rosemary.

While he was revising the second weeks' work, he got a phone call from Brandt. *Pictorial Review* was suddenly anxious to get hold of an American costume serial at once. They had heard he was working on one. "I haven't the slightest hope that S.B. will be what they want," Benét wrote his wife, "but it won't hurt to show it to them." The familiar, disruptive factor of editorial whim had been added to the other problems of composition. The situation resembled the one which existed in the summer of 1921, when he was submitting the separate installments of *Young People's Pride* to Brandt's suggestions. The agent's knowledge now of exactly what *Pictorial Review* was looking for—Vance, the editor, had explained his requirements explicitly—meant that Benét was no longer alone with the manuscript. Then he abruptly indicated that the likeness to 1921 was to be no more than superficial.

"Carl said he thought the book got off to a grand start," Benét wrote his wife on June 2, "but of course wants a happy ending, which I am not going to give him."

Benét was feeling a kind of commitment to *Spanish Bayonet* which was a new note in his attitude toward his prose. He had always regarded fiction as an expediency. Now he experienced some of the same sense of proprietorship which attended his poetry. "I am praying it will be good," he told Rosemary frankly, abandoning superstition and diffidence. "It gets sort of confused in the middle but the death of the monkey strikes me as being well told."

What was happening was part of a process that had begun with "Sycamore" and "King David" and "The

Mountain Whippoorwill." This was the perilous and by no means automatic transition from natural aptitude to acquired craft. He had begun with talent and motivation, but many have that. Now these were being united with something that was professional pride but more too. It was the quality which the critics had detected in *Tiger Joy*. He had something to say and the will to say it properly.

Spanish Bayonet, as Benét now recognized, had too melodramatic a base to be wholly the book he realized too late it might have been. He was nevertheless determined to protect what was sound in it. "I knew the last part of S.B. would annoy them," he told Rosemary, when Brandt relayed the displeasure of *Pictorial Review* with the death of the heroine, "but Caterina is going to stay dead."

Now, while he waited the results of Brandt's further negotiations with the editor, he turned dutifully to short stories. He wrote three of them in two weeks, "which isn't so bad for me," he told his wife, but they were sorry things and he told his father that one of them, "this stupid diamond-robbery story," was the worst work he had ever done. He had postponed beginning the stories as long as he was working on *Spanish Bayonet*, he explained to Rosemary, "as I was trying to keep in the mood of the book." He could no longer switch from work he valued to what he once savagely called "the work that crawls in the hand." [12]

With *Spanish Bayonet* completed, for the moment, his mind worked restlessly over the theme of a more ambitious novel. It would be called *Hotspur*, he wrote his wife, a modern novel about a young Fortunatus. "It has possessed me all day & I can't get rid of it—it would not be a pretty book but I wish, in many ways, I had thought of it before I started S.B. However, that way folly lies, and if I really want to do it as much as I seem to now, I can after S.B. is out of the way. I wish you were here so I could talk to you about it."

He could not keep to his resolve. "I've been taking notes on *Hotspur*," he admitted a few days later, on May 20, "whenever I thought of anything. His full name is Thomas Clovelly Hotspur. The story is written in the first person by his friend Snipe Wiggan. It won't be a pretty story, but I think it has points." In this frame of mind it was natural that he should soon be thinking of poetry. Suddenly, with a brief sentence of aside in a letter devoted otherwise to news of friends and his own expectant delight at the return of Rosemary and Stephanie, Benét disclosed the full extent of his ambitious ferment.

"I have a swell idea for a long poem. The only trouble is, it would take about 7 years to write & I'd have to read an entire library first."

The long poem which would become *John Brown's Body*, conceived in June 1925 out of the excitement and frustration of an eighteenth-century historical novel, could for the moment have no more substance than the fragmentary notes for *Hotspur*. Until he finished the current short stories his larder at Brandt's was ominously bare. "Maybe Carl will sell 'Handmaid' yet," Benét told his wife, "but that and the awful 'Fire and Snow' are the only two left." On June 5, encouraged by Rosemary, who thought he would have better working conditions there, Benét accepted the MacDowell Colony's offer of a studio for three weeks and took the train to Peterborough, New Hampshire. "I went to bed at nine-thirty," he wrote her the next day, "and rose at seven-thirty. Am I not a good boy?"

He was amused to find that the atmosphere of scrupulous quiet and enforced creativity did not agree with him. "I am still very sleepy," he told Rosemary, "and haven't started to work yet. The quiet, of course, appalls me and the birds in the morning sound like airplane engines. I am a city child. I saw a squirrel today and Mr. Novik saw a partridge. Either he has better eyes or a weaker sense of veracity. Darling, I miss you like hell."

Soon he was thrust back on schedule despite the birds and the quiet. Brandt wrote him that *Pictorial Review* insisted that the ending of *Spanish Bayonet* must be more romantic. The agent did his best to anticipate and divert Benét's wrath. "I think what they will want you to do," he comforted his client, "would mean a minor compromise and, of course, would only have to hold for the serial. The whole situation looks good to me." Benét disagreed. He was maddened by the editorial pressure; his anger was complicated by the clear knowledge of what a sale to *Pictorial Review* would mean during the next year in the lives of his wife and daughter and himself.

"This morning," he wrote Rosemary from Peterborough, "[I] sent Carl 3 alternative plans for ending the serial & otherwise keeping Caterina alive. One I wouldn't mind doing so much but as it is the gloomiest I imagine *Pictorial* will choose one of the others. I am still biting my nails with fury at the whole tribe of magazine editors —but if we can get 10,000 it seems silly not to grab it if I can change it back in the book. Carl will let me know as soon as possible what price they will give & if they will be satisfied with anything less than wedding bells."

Brandt kept him cheerfully abreast of developments in New York. "Thank you for your letter," he wrote Benét on June 23, "which, with certain slight editing, I have used to put before the *Pictorial Review* as your thoughts on the last installment." Brandt postponed his own verdict on the trio of alternative endings until he heard from Vance. "I do think," he told Benét, "that Andrew must go north and that the best way is that Caterina should be left in the south somewhat with the idea that Andrew, if he comes through the war alive, will come back."

Benét, licked by the reality of the ten thousand dollars he might receive, started to revise the final section. "I have been trying to get the 2 girls together," he told Rosemary bleakly, "and made a draft but tore it up as unsatisfactory & will try again." He kept at it through the end of June, spurred on by Brandt's encouragement and *Pictorial's* obvious interest. He made a hasty overnight trip to New York to discuss the changes in person and went back to Peterborough the same day. His situation was both bizarre and depressing. In the woodland studio of a utopian colony presided over by the austere Edwin Arlington Robinson, and peopled in part by literary innocents at work on five-act verse tragedies, he compelled himself for a bait of $10,000 to water down a good novel into a palatable mediocrity. His principal allies, as always, were his wry humor and the Benét sense of the ridiculous.

"A strange woman in a white dress," he wrote his wife, interrupting the sequence of the letter, "has suddenly stationed herself with an enormous black camera out in the road and is taking a picture of this studio and, as far as I can see, of my neck. I wonder who *she* is? It is an AliceinWonderland incident—perhaps she will turn into a sheep or a chessman—I would not be surprised."

His fellows at the Colony—colonists, Mrs. MacDowell called them—never sensed his desperation. Years later they recalled instead his friendly, easy manner, "so open to everyone," one of them remembered, "that he made the place very agreeable." In an atmosphere that encouraged temperament—sometimes with great success—Benét was distinguished by his calm good nature. The rather harassed young secretary of the Colony, herself an aspiring writer, remembered with eloquent emphasis thirty years later that Benét "did *not* complain of shortage of hot water or lateness of delivery of luncheon." Though he quite clearly preferred the periphery of any group, one of them noted, "his warmth, his sensitivity, and his generosity" usually made him the center. "I used to wish he would return and everything he wrote had afterwards for me an added warmth." [13]

Benét was interested in the other colonists as he was always interested in people. He listened as effectively as he talked; his letters to Rosemary were full of shrewd portraits of the composers and novelists and poets. He was wary at first of Mrs. MacDowell's principal lion. "I am still very scairt of EAR," he wrote his wife, "but it may wear off." Soon, in fact, he and Robinson began to talk easily, the latter's formidable reserve broken by Benét's simplicity and charm and by the older man's affection for his brother Bill and his friend Douglas Moore.

Robinson told Benét a number of his celebrated stories, and confided that he couldn't understand how some of their colleagues were able to write when drunk. "I've never been able to," he said reflectively. There was a certain consolation for the grim cannibalism Benét was performing on *Spanish Bayonet* as he listened to Robinson. Riding back to the Colony one night from a movie in town Robinson eyed the heavens.

"There is something about those stars," he told the

younger writer, "that mystifies and humiliates me more and more as I grow older. They keep making me suspect that it doesn't make a damn bit of difference whether I finish the poem I am writing or not." [14]

The entire atmosphere of the Colony, Benét decided, was rather like being on a ship; the chief interests were food and walking. He never attained, however, the serene state of suspension from worldly interference for which the Colony was celebrated. This was, after all, the second time in the past four months that he had been separated from his wife. He told her he felt as if he hadn't seen her for ten years. His loneliness was aggravated by the presence of a newly married writer and his bride whose company Benét enjoyed but who held hands and called each other Honey. "Huuh, said he from his artistic sty," Benét wrote Rosemary, "where is my honey?" Each mail brought new reminders of *Pictorial Review*'s insistence that there be a happy, romantic, and thoroughly unreal ending for *Spanish Bayonet*.

Benét sketched out in detail the synopses of the three alternative endings and mailed them to New York. None of them was sufficiently a surrender. They would be content, as he had originally suspected, with nothing less than wedding bells. Benét tried once more and then some time toward the very end of his three weeks at the Colony he could make no more concessions. He packed and went home to New York. "I would rather be with you on the hottest of 57th Streets," he wrote Rosemary, "than working here with God and Mrs. Mac-Dowell in the middle of the surf-pounding pines."

The colonist assigned to Benét's studio arrived the next day, before the staff had done the customary tidying that followed a departure. Benét's successor therefore found the Wood Studio exactly as Benét had left it.

The table and chair were set diagonally across the middle of the room, facing a wall. Benét had moved them from their place by the window in order to wrestle undistracted with a happy ending. In the end he had not been able to stomach the happy ending. He had gone as far as he could with the dismantlement of a good book. The relics of his combat were observed by the new colonist.

"As he had created unfinished pages that did not suit him," the new colonist recalled, "he had crumbled them and fired them into the corner beyond the sofa. There were enough of them to fill a bushel basket." [15] Among the relics—though the new colonist, an essayist for the *Atlantic Monthly,* had no way of knowing this—were ten thousand dollars which now he would not receive from *Pictorial Review.*

8. Goodly Fellowship

*And God knows we were all going crazy in
New York and about one jump ahead of the sheriff.*[1]

BENÉT's unwillingness to alter *Spanish Bayonet* to the
requirements of *Pictorial Review* meant major economic
distress for himself and his family. The concentrated period he had spent on the novel, as well as the weeks of
fruitless revision, had cost him the chance of building a
backlog of short stories at Brandt's. For the moment their
only income was the small one which came from Rosemary's new job at *Vogue;* a good share of that went to
the girl who came in to look after Stephanie.

Since committing himself to writing, five years before,
Benét had published two collections of verse and three
novels. He had written thirty-four short stories—about
two hundred and fifty thousand words—and sold all but
two of them, for a price that averaged slightly below five
hundred dollars per story. Both his verse and his prose
had won national prizes. Several of his ballads were already semiclassics in the national literature. He had been
industrious and productive, and his professional growth
had been consistent, and yet during the last half of 1925
and the first months of 1926 his situation was fundamen-
tally as insecure and discouraging as that of an unknown

and unpublished writer arriving in New York at the age of twenty.

When Benét put Rosemary and Stephanie on the train for Chicago in 1926, for their annual visit to the Carrs, he had five dollars left—in the world—after buying the tickets. He lived on the five dollars until a small check arrived from his mother; he immediately mailed fifteen dollars of it to Rosemary. His predicament was not unique; it was not even unusual. It was a commonplace in the practice of American letters, as it had been for five generations. His state of mind was made no easier by an encounter about this time with Louis Untermeyer's young son Richard. The boy had just been admitted to Yale as a member of the Class of 1929.

" 'Ten years after your class, isn't it?' he remarked pleasantly," Benét told his wife, "& I felt senile." The boy regarded his father and Benét not only as contemporaries of one another now, but as equally interesting relics. "Of course," he told them, in 1925, "you people made a lot of *experiments* in poetry—but you really didn't have much to say." [2]

So in the summer of 1925, back in the heat of Manhattan, Benét turned to precisely the kind of wearying hack work about which Henry Canby had warned him as long ago as 1919, the jobs so meager in their reward and so expensive in the time they dissipated. For the *Bookman* he wrote several pieces of literary journalism. One was an imaginative account of the manuscripts in the Morgan Library. There was a poignant vividness in his response to the various items. He envied his old favorite William Morris, whose handwriting in the first few pages of "House of the Wolfings" was "like his Golden Type, at once beautiful and clear; later on it grows more hurried as the fever of the tale takes hold of him." Then he speculated as to which of the holdings one would choose above all the others.

"I should turn first," Benét wrote, "to two pages of manuscript more than four hundred years old, the manuscript of a poem, 'London, thou art the flower of cities all,' written by W. Dunbar, poet and 'skotte' . . . on the second page, before the poet sat down to write upon it, some idle fellow outlined the watermark on the paper —the ramping figure of an absurdly fiery horse—so that when Dunbar came to use it, he had to write his lines around the horse and did so, carefully. . . . I can see W. Dunbar, 1501 . . . lacking the money to buy another sheet, going ahead on his poem. The manuscript may be far less important, in a literary sense, than many another here, but it is the first I should choose for our Christmas tree." [3]

He reworked for the *Bookman* that staple of the literary essayist, "My Favorite Fiction Character"—his was Doctor Watson—and he did a pair of articles on detective stories and authors' wives. All of the pieces were competent; none of them had the slightest connection with his basic gifts or professional direction. As exercises they were a vocational regression. He wrote several reviews for the *Saturday Review of Literature*. His comments on MacLeish's *Nobodaddy* and *The Pot of Earth* were interesting, and showed his own considerable familiarity with T. S. Eliot's work and with *The Waste Land* in particular, but as criticism the writing shared the *Saturday Review*'s general tendency to indiscriminate enthusiasm. [4]

None of these chores could match the professional degradation of an assignment he received, gratefully but without vast pride, through his friendship with Stanley Rinehart. He rewrote as a novel for George H. Doran Company the melodramatic Broadway thriller *The Bat,* on which Rinehart's mother, Mary Roberts Rinehart, had been a collaborator. The fact that the novel was published anonymously was an indication of Benét's distaste for the extremes to which literary recession had pushed him.

He ground out several more short stories, but he was weary of the pretense of light-hearted modern romance. His mind was still on the themes he had tapped lightly in "William Sycamore," and the long poem which he had gloomily told Rosemary it would take him seven years to write. Benét looked around for help. He had already received an advance on *Spanish Bayonet.* His brother was as broke as he; it never occurred to him to borrow from his friends. Without much real hope he went down to Pershing Square for a talk with Henry Allen Moe, secretary of the John Simon Guggenheim Memorial Foundation. Moe—"a grey-haired Buddha," Benét said afterward—encouraged him to put in an application for one of their fellowships. If his project was accepted, he would receive a grant of $2500.

Benét was purposefully vague in the outline of his project. "What I said in my 'plan,'" he explained later, "boiled down to this—that I was sick of writing short-stories and wanted to do a long poem on some American subject. I told them I had several ideas—including the Civil War one—but couldn't say which one I'd take." [5] Benét wrote Wilbur Cross at Yale in September 1925, asking him to write a letter of recommendation.

"It would mean a year in which I could write what I want," Benét explained to the Dean, "preferably verse,

167

which has no market value, instead of writing what the magazines want, which, unfortunately, boils the pot, so I should, naturally, like to have a stab at it."

The Dean was pleased to write for him, and so were Edna Millay and John Masefield, and Benét put it out of his mind as much as he could and went back to the he-she stories. Soon, he knew, he would have more than a wife and a three-year-old daughter to care for; now a second child was due in the fall. Women and children first, as the Colonel said. But Brandt told him frankly that his lack of interest in the magazine fiction was pretty apparent; each new one was increasingly difficult to sell.

He and Brandt talked his situation over. Benét told the agent that he wanted to write some stories he could be interested in. "I've got to have some fun doing these things," he told Brandt. If he were going to do modern stories, they had to have something more than just sentiment. He didn't propose to violate the various taboos, but what he wanted to work with, Benét said, was material that would be outside the conventional situations. He didn't know exactly what they'd be; he knew what they wouldn't be.

"Why not," said Brandt, who by now had considerable confidence in Benét's capacity and persistence. "The love stories aren't selling, and you're sick of writing them anyway. Why not. Let's try it." [6]

Benét put aside the contrived romances of office girls and Long Island heiresses, and the mannered toughness of Manhattan sophistication. He wrote during the late winter of 1925 and the first four months of 1926 a group of short stories in a new mood and idiom. He abandoned the flippancy on which he had made most of his magazine reputation. He turned back, in much of the work he did during these months, to the American past, to the towns he had known as the nomadic child of an army family, and to those earlier periods he had possessed through his reading and his imagination. He began to give to his stories, freed from the jargon of the falsely contemporary, some of the poetic prose which fifteen years later became his singular voice in magazine fiction.

"He was the only one of us," John Marquand said many years later, "who could write a story for the *Saturday Evening Post* and make it read like literature." [7]

Benét's objective with these 1925 and 1926 stories, though he did not thoroughly clarify his intentions, even privately, for several years, was no less a mission than to break to his individual talent the mold of American mass audience fiction. "We have our own folk-gods and giants and figures of earth in this country," Benét said once. "I wanted to write something about them."

Two ingredients were essential if Benét was to reproduce in marketable prose the success he'd already had with some of his verse. He must work with the American past, which would permit him nostalgic evocation as well as the display of his moving convictions about the national character. He must also—even more difficult— somehow inject into commercial fiction the fantasy so important to what was best in his poetic imagination.

It was not an easy assignment. The renaissance in American letters which was then occurring—primarily in Europe, but with important native and New York aspects—had no connections with the large circulation magazines. The bulk of the thoroughly mechanical material which was later siphoned off into radio soap opera, or its successor the TV situation comedy, was in 1925 and 1926 the fixed diet of the big slicks and their lesser competitors. There is an air of outrage and disbelief in those introductions which Edward O'Brien wrote during the 1920's for his annual collections of the best American short stories. O'Brien's target was always the popular journals. What O'Brien had been unable to effect through persistent attempts to establish higher standards, Benét was undertaking as a single, vulnerable, commercial writer.

The first indication of his restless experiment emerged in a *Collier's* story, in late January 1926. The story was called "The Odor of Sanctity." [8] As was natural at the beginning of a complex revision, the story was little more than a sketch, a kind of uneasy scenario of what was to follow. Only two thousand words long—a structure thoroughly uncharacteristic of his work either then or later—it was closer to fable or essay than genuine narrative. It ended with a clumsy final paragraph in which Benét sought the fantasy he was anxious to introduce into his fiction. The sketch as a whole was damaged by conflicting strains of satire and bathos. The protagonist was a caricature; he couldn't possibly serve as the folk hero whom Benét had to create if the elements of reality and fantasy were to be effectively joined.

He had, nevertheless, attempted the fantasy. He had taken a tentative step into the post-Civil War America of small towns and national serenity. Gradually he began to get his footing. The May 1926 issues of two very different magazines carried stories in Benét's new, still partially blurred voice.[9] Brandt, whose efforts for Benét consistently went beyond his 10 per cent reward, had with prophetic insight placed one of the stories with *Country Gentleman*. Benét's first sale to what was in effect the rural edition of the *Saturday Evening Post,* with a circulation of one and a half million, was an important step.

The association did more than raise Benét's story price and bring him into the outer orbit of the *Post*. It gave him an audience and editorial staff which were more friendly to his new treatments than the subscribers and editors of, say, *Cosmopolitan* and *Redbook*. Two of the magazine's young associate editors in particular were immediately responsive to Benét's work. Ben Hibbs and Robert Reed later became senior editors in the Curtis hierarchy, Hibbs as editor of the *Post*, Reed of *Country Gentleman*. Hibbs, according to Brandt, was in 1926 "like Benét in having an eagle on his shoulder." [10]

Brandt's labors were even more vividly dramatized by the nature of the second magazine in which he placed Benét's other May story. Unable to dispose of "The Shadowy Crown" to any of his regular buyers, but mindful that Benét ought to be encouraged at this point, Brandt refused to give up on the story. He sold it—in certain respects at a distinct loss to himself—to the *Elks' Magazine*. Here again, though in this case the magazine was of little consequence, and its national circulation small, the audience would be a sympathetic one. If worse came to worst, the *Elks' Magazine* could also be counted on for further sales during this difficult transition period.

"The Shadowy Crown," like "The Odor of Sanctity," was another piece of retrospection. Benét, discarding the awkward, omniscient point of view, used the town doctor as narrator. This gave him an opportunity for literate comment on the characters and situation, and for intimate knowledge of the town's habits and values. That the form was resolving itself was shown by Benét's introduction of a specific name for the town, a name he retained in subsequent stories. He called the town Freestone. The name was symptomatic of what he was seeking. It included in its source-words both liberty and permanence. It also permitted his ironic examination of the reverse of these qualities as exhibited in the semi-rural America of a generation earlier.

The story itself, with its theme of the exceptional individual in an unexceptional environment, was a fresh one. Benét, on the other hand, had not yet mastered the problem of a situation for his material. "The Shadowy Crown" had a bookish quality, an inevitable excess of the literary as he ducked away from the stereotypes of magazine plots. Some of the dialogue was overquaint—what Benét later condemned in another of his stories as "too damn itsy-bitsy"—and he had to resort to desperate breaks in the time sequence to squeeze out the necessary wordage.

Country Gentleman, on the other hand, very definitely had the best of the May bargain. "The Sobbin' Women" was the first of these new stories in which Benét demonstrated consistent grace and confidence. The story represented the completion of tentative experiment. Benét would write better stories than "The Sobbin' Women"—and many, from necessity or weariness or haste, that were inferior to it—but this one would never shame its superiors. Years later both Hibbs and Reed remembered the story distinctly, even recalling it as the first they bought from Benét. "I wish," said Reed in 1954, "we could have paid him what it was worth." [11] "The Sobbin' Women," above all, inaugurated a satisfactory solution to the troublesome problem of a narrator. Benét created what he called a "frame"—the story was told by a village sage whom the author termed the Oldest Inhabitant—and he preserved this frame for some time in his later stories of nineteenth-century America.

There was a clarity of story line and a localized stability that had been missing in "The Shadowy Crown." The bookish quality remained—the legend of the Sabine women, after all, was a Roman one—but the nature of the heroine and the circumstances of local terrain made this credible. The types whom Benét would use with vigorous national pride emerged for the first time. Here were the bound girl, the hedge parson, the fabulous pioneer. The folk-hero quality was developing, blurred because it was shared by seven brothers, but nevertheless taking shape.

Benét was sufficiently at ease now—and sufficiently liberated from the vulgarity of magazine wit—so that his own sly, tart humor began to flow into the material. It was as if "The Sobbin' Women" had fully released the flow of fresh prose that had been inhibited by an act of will since 1921. His plots were still the ones that would meet the rigorous requirements of editorial buyers. Boy still met girl, and eventually boy would get girl, but in the five to ten thousand words that lay between these two unalterable events Benét continued to unbend his style and strengthen his narrator.

"They say growing up in a small place makes for a limited view of things in general," said the Oldest Inhabitant in "The Lucky Fist," published in *Collier's* in late June 1926. "Maybe so, but it seems to me that where you haven't so many things to look at you're apt to get more juice out of what you do see." [12] As the title indicated, Benét was exploring in this story what would become one of his favorite themes. He wrote of Luck and its nature with vivid force.

Ham's fist was something to look at. It was big and blunt and strong, but there was more to it than that— a sort of driving force like the force you imagine in the head of a hammer combined with a curious quality that was almost grace. The little red-blond hairs on the back of it shone in the light as he flexed the fingers slowly and shut them up again in a hard stone clump . . . For an instant, in the shimmer of the lamp as I watched it, it seemed to change to something incredible and a little dreadful, a lump, a hard, shining ball of solid, actual gold.

As had happened in all the earlier stories, here too, in "The Lucky Fist," Benét showed that he was still marked by the five years of servitude to standard plot and one-dimensional character. The symbol of the lucky fist was almost submerged in the maneuvers of boy separated from girl. The necessities of fast-moving narrative corrupted similarly his second *Country Gentleman* story, "Miss Willie Lou and the Swan," but there were glimpses of his informed sense of the period.

[They] came from England . . . and settled in Virginia a while. But then they got the itch to be movin' west—and when families moved then they moved like the children of Israel. The Faithfuls took cuttin's from their garden and wines from their cellar and barrels of leather-bound books. They brought their slaves and huntin' dogs and their blood horses . . . to that wild, raw border country, and they settled down to make a place that'd be the spittin' image of the place they'd left in Virginia . . .[13]

This had been Benét's most productive period since the first weeks he spent on *Spanish Bayonet* in the spring of 1925. He had written almost a dozen short stories; one, "The Sobbin' Women," was the best work he had yet done in the medium.[14] Four of the stories were cited in both the O'Brien and O. Henry annual rolls of honor. In this mood of speculation—his hopes riding, after all, on a small foundation grant intended to underwrite a project as unlikely of success as an epic poem—Benét attempted a story that was recklessly counter to a basic prohibition of the editorial mystique. He used a biblical situation in which one of the disciples was the hero and Christ a subsidiary character.

"Eleven leaderless men," he began the story "True Thomas" in the April *Good Housekeeping*, "without wealth or rank or power, who had followed a carpenter and now found themselves, since his death, suddenly set at war with the greatest and most able civilization in the world." [15]

Benét was beginning to give his talent for fiction its first real airing. He had the storyteller's traditional power, in the overworked but meaningful phrase, of bringing the past to life, of vivifying a commonly held legend. "So Judas was dead already. And He was dead. Utter good and utter evil had finished together and left only human flesh to take up the burden that had broken a god." The ultimate theme of the story was characteristic of Benét's profound confidence in mankind.

> "He is God—He is very God!" cried James in an ecstasy.
>
> "He is man," said Thomas to himself. "Thank God, He could be man as well."
>
> But, loving the others suddenly, he did not say it so they could hear.

It was an extraordinary performance for a writer who six months earlier had seemed creatively spent and perhaps fit for no more than a long period of literary journalism. The O. Henry judges placed "True Thomas" among those American stories of 1926 "ranking highest." O'Brien gave it his three asterisks of distinction. It was unlikely that the Guggenheim judges were reading *Good House-keeping* and *Country Gentleman* and the *Elks' Magazine*, but these stories were more eloquent than the letters from Millay and Masefield and Cross. In April the list of grants was released. Benét was on it. He was jubilant.

"It is a good graft," he told Phelps Putnam, urging him to apply for one. "They are very decent. They give you $2,500 in four yearly installments and tell you to run off and roll your hoop. Then they don't bother you any more." Once again he had recovered from seeming disaster. "Don't worry!" he wrote Rosemary in Chicago. "I enclose herewith 2 checks for $50 apiece and will send them to-night by airplane mail. I phoned Stan [Rinehart] & he very kindly gave me $750 advance on the new *Spanish Bayonet* royalties, so you see everything is all right. S.B. by the way has sold over 7,000 net (excluding the 800 or so review or free copies) so besides *this* check we will get at least $900 more from it during the year, so that's nice, isn't it? The gross sales are over 8,000."

The success of such stories as "The Sobbin' Women" and "True Thomas," not only in terms of his own satisfaction with them but also as promises of further editorial acceptance, did not reconcile Benét to magazine fiction. Throughout his career he objected to the extremes of editorial perversity which during his lifetime controlled the American short story. "I think [Edward O'Brien] is just as prejudiced in favor of the formula formless story," Benét said later, "as the big-magazine-editor of 1925 was prejudiced against it." [16] Brandt, he knew, found it much harder to sell these less conventional situations. He himself chafed that they took so much longer to write than the more trivial ones. Mindful of Brandt's problems, and doubtful too that he and Rosemary could live for a year on $2500, even in France, Benét manufactured several very commonplace stories before they sailed.

"I wrote another story yesterday," he told Rosemary, "and am typing it today. It is . . . a dear little candy-laxative of a tale about a sweet little girl named Sally and I do not see how it can fail to sell—it is so cheap." [17]

Benét's bitterness about the rigidity of editorial taste was softened but not erased as his liberation came closer. "I shall try to console myself as best I can," he assured his wife, on the day following her departure for Chicago, "by trying to start one of my celebrated, bright, gay stories of gay, bright, dumb young people." It was another of those periods, however, when everything was falling smoothly into place. "Erd [Brandt], thank God," Benét told Rosemary, "has sold that terrible Belinda story to *Liberty* for $600. The ravens are often dilatory but they do seem to come along sooner or later."

As always when his spirits were high and there was money in the bank, he indulged himself with verse. The last writing he did before they boarded the *Caronia* was a pair of poems. Neither "Archimedes' Last Foray," published in the *Saturday Review of Literature* in mid-June, nor the *New Yorker's* "After Attending a Seance" was first-class work.[18] Benét never reprinted them. "After Attending a Séance," however, did mark an abortive beginning of the important association he would have as a poet with the *New Yorker* in the 1930's. It was also a reminder that Benét was not only aware of but also technically interested in those forms and themes of contemporary verse which his own verse seldom reflected. More than anything else it was a hearty cock of his thumb at the U.S.A.

There are cigars beyond the grave, it
  seems,
Cigars and anecdotes and dogs and
  gin
(Or something very like it). There
  are dreams
And all the latest Gershwin and Berlin.
There is no sin, of course—no genuine sin
(But something very like it), but
  there's work!
And Rotary-clubs for every cherubin . . .

He and Rosemary stayed up till 2 A.M. the first night at
sea. "It seemed so delightful," Benét wrote his parents,
"to be anywhere that was relatively cool." The foghorn
troubled Stephanie for a time; she was reassured when
they explained that it was merely the boat talking. Alice
Lee Myers met them at Le Havre and drove them to
Paris. The Myers had found them a fine apartment on
the rue Jadin. It belonged to Mrs. Jean Lamont, an
American friend of both the Myers and of Bill Benét.
Both its comfort and the fashionable address, Benét
wrote a friend, were beyond their station. Mrs. Lamont
was renting it to them until her own return to Paris in
May. "It has a bath and no concierge," Benét told
Shreve Badger, "thus reversing the usual procedure."
Mrs. Lamont had hospitably left champagne and wines
for Benét and Rosemary, and books and toys for their
daughter.

They were suddenly weary, conscious at last of the
insecurity of the past five years. "When we got to this
marvelous place," Benét wrote his brother, "we simply

sank into it, as into a goosefeather bed and relaxed."
They investigated the new American Hospital, where
Rosemary would be delivered some time toward the
end of September, and Benét went out there again to
see Carl Brandt, who'd had two serious operations for
appendicitis while on a business trip to England and
the Continent. The good news, this time of a particularly ironic kind, continued to come in. Brandt had
sold the English serial rights of *Spanish Bayonet* for one
hundred and fifty pounds. For British readers Caterina
would die as planned. Benét began to think about the
long poem. "I have a nice little room on the 6th floor,"
he told his brother, "all swept & garnished."

9. John Brown's Body: One

Money buys the time to do your work well.[1]

THEIR son was born at the American Hospital in Paris on September 28, 1926. He had threatened an earlier arrival, and for a time, Benét wrote his friends, it had seemed he might be named either Caronia or Chemin de Fer. He was christened Thomas Carr, however, an amiable and healthy baby whose arrival signaled a kind of recommencement and renewal of all their lives. "I am doing some work," Benét wrote Shreve Badger, "and expect to do more when Jane gets back from the hospital."

They settled comfortably into the new atmosphere. Stephanie played each day in the nearby sandpiles of the Parc Monceau. "She alternates French and English with great unselfconsciousness," Benét told Robert Nathan. The three-year-old became a particular favorite of Mrs. Lamont's cook, who had been left behind for them along with the champagne and the wines. The Benét domesticity was confusing to the woman's Parisian conception of Americans. "Jeanne," Benét wrote his parents, "is very entertaining on the subject of American marriages —never having worked for undivorced Americans before." He settled pleasureably in the sixth-floor room. From the window he could see his family when they walked in the small park. He resumed the research and planning he had tentatively begun in New York in late June and July.

His sense of the project, like the plan he had submitted for the Guggenheim fellowship, was a broad one. This was characteristic of all his work; even editors had become adjusted to his unwillingness to tie himself down. The quality he most valued in writing was movement; he had learned that for him an outline tended to freeze movement. The general shape of the poem was nevertheless already clear to him. In the fall of 1926 he visualized twelve parts; in its final form, thirteen months later, it in fact contained ten units, the eight books preceded by the invocation and the slaver prelude.

His conception of the organization was in part a reflection of the long talks he'd had with the composer Douglas Moore about the use of American material. He deliberately maintained a loose form, he said later, seeking the structural fluidity of a musical composition. For the moment his working title was *Horses of Anger*. His mood was one of careful and luxurious exploration. For the first time in six years he was free of deadlines; the Guggenheim check would arrive each quarter. "I don't know how or when it will ever get finished," he said in November 1926. "However, I am glad to have the chance to experiment with certain things I have always wanted to try." [2]

He read steadily, with the extraordinary speed and retention which had confounded his contemporaries at Yale. Several of them were in Paris during the next year—Chubb, MacLeish, Donald Ogden Stewart, Douglas Moore—and watching him go through the resources of the American Library reminded them of the wagers they had won by betting classmates that he could read an entire book on the train ride from New Haven to New York. Now, instead of James Branch Cabell and Chesterton, he read the regimental histories he had brought from New York, and he reread for the first time since boyhood the *Battles and Leaders of the Civil War.* He read diaries and memoirs and autobiographies, and all the collections of correspondence.

For the portrait of John Brown he relied particularly on Villard's biography; for the political and social history of the period he studied Channing and McMaster. He read all the various lives of Lincoln, especially Sandburg and Hay and Lord Charnwood. He shaped several of his battlefield episodes from *Four Brothers in Blue,* the participant account of life in the Army of the Potomac. Wherever possible he went back to original sources; all during the rest of his life editors asked him to review new Civil War material, knowing that he had acquired the background of a professional specialist. The historian Samuel Eliot Morison, writing in 1930 to ask permission to quote from *John Brown's Body* in his own *The Growth of the American Republic,* told him that the poem's historical narrative was accurate in every detail. Douglas Southall Freeman, reading the poem while he researched the same period for his *R. E. Lee,* was full of admiration. "He could have fortified even his casual adverbs with footnotes," said Freeman.

Benét found the research a vast pleasure. "Good source books," he said once, "make the most fascinating sort of reading." [3] He was working, however, almost ten years in advance of American scholarship. A decade later both the New York publishers and the university presses would be printing immense quantities of Americana of every description. Eventually there would be a Civil War Book Club, and a History Book Club, and magazines devoted exclusively to the national past. In 1926 a student of that past had to track down a large part of the material on his own.

"Why doesn't somebody write a good life of Lee," Benét suggested to Farrar in 1927, midway through his own project. "There ought to be a really first-class life of him, neither the biographical-novel nor the old kind —and there isn't. And now is the time when somebody could do it with a little perspective. The writers are being well taken care of but the Civil War people aren't and a lot of them were damn interesting. You could write a superb novel around Forrest—there are the Grant memoirs but there is no great life of Grant—etc. etc. But Lee is a crying need. And it would take brains, for he's something of an ungettable man. For that matter, Davis would be quite a stunt to exhume from the legend." [4]

Benét took notes on the reminiscences of Mrs. Roger A. Pryor, and *The Diary of a Southern Girl*. He used John Beauchamp Jones' *A Rebel War Clerk's Diary*, again almost ten years before it was republished in a general edition, and the memoirs of Letitia Macdonald. All his rigorous sense of the importance of accuracy responded to the duties of sound research. "Well, for the record—" he always prefaced the debate of conversation. Here, too, he was trying to establish the record of conflicting testimony. "It is worthy," he said once, "to assemble facts, to put truth in the face of legend, to investigate impartially, to throw new light on an old problem." [5]

He became one of the regulars at the American Library, housed ornately on the rue de l'Elysée in a former palace of the Papal Nuncio. "He read everything we had on Lincoln," one of the librarians remembered years later. They recalled him arriving once a week with an armful of books and leaving an hour or two later with an equal load.[6] From the New York publishing houses the Library received exhibition copies of most of the new books, and these were available for circulation for six weeks before being returned to America. Here Benét read *Elmer Gantry* and *The Sun Also Rises,* both of which he admired, and *Show Boat,* and, in French, the novels of Proust, "who is almost ideal for me," he wrote John Carter, "as he is as long as Trollope and a lot better." These were evening diversions, however, like the French detective stories and the old Edgar Wallace novels which he trailed through the second-hand bookstalls. His working day was built around the Civil War and its people.

"I wish I had about a million books on the Civil War that aren't in the American Library," he wrote his brother, "but then I am having trouble enough with the ones I can use—people lie so, especially when they are writing their reminiscences."

He envied the writers who worked the same field in later years. "We are getting better and better sourcebooks on American history all the time," he said in 1939, "and we are lucky to have them." [7] For the moment he did his best to check himself constantly. "I want to be as accurate as possible wherever I can," he told John Farrar, warning his editor that if the poem were ever finished he would probably be making corrections right up to publication time. He had read all the current historical studies which took their lead from Strachey and Gamaliel Bradford. He respected the research of these two, and of such disciples as Philip Guedalla, but he had little use for the bulk of this new school of history.

"A good many of our recent biographies or semi-biographies—or biografictions—whatever you choose to call them," he said in 1932, "have [been] rather like Mark Twain's reconstruction of the dinosaur, 'three bones and a dozen barrels of plaster.' The author might not always take the trouble to find out just what his subject did and when he did it—for that often requires a tiresome amount of research. But, as regards what the subject thought and felt, there the author was not merely all-wise but all-seeing. . . . A few footnotes, a dash of Freud, thick paper, a dashing jacket—and *Passion on the Wind, or the Life of Chester A. Arthur* was ready for the trade." [8]

Benét was anxious to avoid any such improvisation in his own portraits. "These little things are hell to check on," he told Farrar, explaining why this was going to be so long a project, "and I have had a lot of grief trying to do so." He worked every day, surmounting for the first time his hostility to early rising. When a friend remarked that he kept hours as regular as an office worker, he replied—it was one of the few times he spoke of his writing habits—that a long poem was a 9 A.M. to 5 P.M. proposition. He likened the problems to the composition of a novel.

"When you set out on a long poem," he said, "it's not possible to write only when you are feeling fine. You have to write so much every day or you'd never get the thing done. Short poems are a different matter." [9]

By Christmas he had finished what he still regarded as the first of twelve sections. He rarely mentioned what he was working on during this period unless his friends questioned him persistently. Few of them were particularly enthusiastic about his project. It was not a year in which many of his generation were exploring the American past or approving its present. Most of them sympathized with the waves of anti-Americanism which the French were exhibiting. MacLeish was preoccupied with French poetry. Tom Chubb talked to Benét about the poem in 1927, and later admitted that he tried to dissuade his friend from a Civil War theme; Chubb argued that it was thoroughly unpromising both as to subject and success. The only person besides Rosemary to whom Benét showed the approximately one thousand lines of the first section was Ramon Guthrie. "He seemed to think there might be something in it," Benét wrote his brother in January 1927, characteristically reserved about his own work.

The days slid by, sponged up by work and reading and the placid delights of a happy marriage and fulfilled parenthood. There were people and scenes to remind them pleasantly of the gaieties of their courtship and honeymoon in 1921 and 1922, yet the pattern of their lives now was very different from the conventional image of Americans abroad. Alice Lee Myers came in sometimes to sit with the children so they could go out for an evening; all their pleasures were similarly domestic. Their friends were mostly other married couples with young children—the McClures, Charles Child the artist and his wife, Dick and Alice Lee Myers, and the Moores—and McClure later remembered with nostalgia "the quiet evenings together *en famille*."

Child once described their circle as composed of the handful of Americans in Paris who were not having marital difficulties. Moore read aloud the comic opera he was writing about contemporary America, with its refrain, "America *shall* be saved!" They played involved word games and admired one another's children, and Benét began to put on weight alarmingly as a result of Jeanne's cooking. "What a contrast," McClure recalled, "between

Steve's Paris years and those of some other young American writers we knew at that time, notably Fitzgerald and Hemingway." [10]

Benét was as immune to the anti-Americanism of some of the literary expatriates as he was to that chauvinism of the industrialists whom he and Rosemary met at Uncle Larry's. He refused to be disturbed by the hostility of the French, who were alternately excited by the closing chapters of the Sacco-Vanzetti case and the recall of the war loans. When interviewers asked him later why he had gone to France to write an epic poem about the Civil War, Benét invariably replied, quite truthfully, that it was because living was cheaper there than at home.

Through Brandt they were invited to various literary cocktail parties, but Benét had seen his fill in New York. He endured a single of Louis Bromfield's celebrated luncheons and returned gladly to the rue Jadin. The stable nature of his and Rosemary's lives during this period, and the lives of most of their friends in Paris, was a confirmation of his beliefs about the permanence of American values. He had done Montmartre in the fall of 1920, and with immense enjoyment; now he enjoyed other pleasures, all of them of an essentially simple and familiar kind. "It takes more than traveling," he explained later, "to make a man an expatriate." [11]

Benét differed at this time from those millions of Americans who never fled America during the 1920's only in his regard for ideas and the arts. He read all the expatriate magazines of the period, and he puzzled his way conscientiously through Gertrude Stein. He was linked to the avant-garde currents through his friendships with MacLeish and John Peale Bishop, both of whom he saw regularly. He valued and honored the work that the serious-minded members of that group were doing, and unlike some of them was never willing to repudiate it later. So far as his nonliterary creed was concerned, however, his values and aspirations were more homely and in certain respects more durable. It was to this, as much as to the more dramatic differences, that McClure referred when he contrasted Benét's Paris period with Fitzgerald's and Hemingway's. His mood was eloquently apparent in the moving stanzas called "Hands" with which he briefly interrupted work on the long poem that winter.

> My wife's hands are long and thin
> Fit to catch a spirit in,
> Fit to set a silver snare
> For something lighter than the air.
>
> My brother's hands are long and fine,
> Good at verse and pouring wine,
> Good to spend and bad to hoard
> And good to hold a singing sword.
>
> My own hands are short and blunt,
> Being children of affront,
> Base mechanics, at the most,
> That have sometimes touched a ghost.
>
> I ask, between the running sands,
> A blessing upon four hands,
> And, for mine, an iron stake
> They can do their best to break.
>
> Now God the Son and God the Sire
> And God the triple-handed fire,

Make these blessings come to be
Out of your civility
For four hands of courtesy.
AMEN.[12]

It was an ideal state of mind in which to write a long poem celebrating the solidarity and permanence of the Union. "I hope it has in it," Benét wrote Farrar in 1927, "some of the landscapes, sights, the sounds of the people which are American. I am tired, not of criticism of America, for no country can be healthy without self-criticism, but of the small railers, conventional rebels. We also have a heritage—and not all of it wooden money."

Benét's passionate feelings about America had been partially concealed from him in New York. They had emerged during occasional periods of well-being, taking the form of the Sycamore and Whippoorwill ballads; then they were cloaked again for long periods by the pressures of Manhattan poverty and the offense of his fiction. In Paris the various stresses were removed. Both his emotional and his intellectual attachments to America were cultivated simultaneously, the one by the separation from his native country and by the version of America which he and his friends were living in Paris, the other by his reading in the national past. "Living abroad," he said in 1928, "has intensified my Americanism." [13]

When Ethel Andrews visited them in Paris in the late winter of 1926 she heard Benét speak of these things. "I never realized how strongly I felt about the United States," he told her, "until now, living so long away from it." She might have forgotten the entire conversation, she said many years afterward, except that it was only a few months later, in October 1927, that she read his "American Names" in the *Yale Review*. She realized then, reading the poem in New York, that he must have been writing it during that very period when she talked to him in Paris. Like the ballads and the short stories, "American Names" became another of those revered national statements which would be his public identification.

> I have fallen in love with American names,
> The sharp names that never get fat,
> The snake-skin titles of mining-claims,
> The plumed war-bonnets of Medicine Hat,
> Tucson and Deadwood and Lost Mule Flat. . . .
>
> I shall not rest quiet in Montparnasse.
> I shall not lie easy at Winchelsea.
> You may bury my body in Sussex grass,
> You may bury my tongue at Champmédy.
> I shall not be there. I shall rise and pass.
> Bury my heart at Wounded Knee.[14]

"American Names" was an outcropping of the long poem, a symptom of the energy and involvement with which he was now working. He was interrupted briefly by word from Mrs. Lamont that her plans had changed; she would need the rue Jadin apartment in January rather than May. They moved during the Christmas holiday to suburban Neuilly. "This apartment is comfortable," Benét wrote his brother, "large and quiet and we have taken down the hand-painted oil picture of the assassination of St. Whoozis, and the alabaster bust of an unknown French lady of the presidency of Sadi-Carnot, and the two black memorial urns that erstwhile made the salon so tastefully French."

There was a Bois for the children and the neighborhood was less bustling than the rue Jadin. Benét had to walk ten blocks a day for the cigarettes he chain-smoked while he worked; he was profiting, he told his brother, from the enforced exercise. "My damn poem is getting ahead," he added briefly, "though every time I sit down to it I wonder if anyone else will ever be able to read it without falling asleep." Now he worked in a small room with two porthole-like windows through which, he said, most of the heat from the stove nevertheless escaped. By early March he was typing the third section. "Sometimes I think it is good," he wrote home, "& sometimes I wonder who will read it but the typesetter—but I shall finish it or explode in loud fragments of *Battles & Leaders of the Civil War*."

Now their lives were even more remote from the American Paris. Neuilly was at the end of the bus line, inconvenient to get to and almost unnecessary to leave. Rosemary ventured into town more often than he, in search of copy for the monthly Letter from Paris which she was contributing to *Town and Country*. The only real breaks in their suburban routine, however, were when Henry Canby stopped briefly on his way home from a P.E.N. meeting in London, and an evening with Carl Brandt, back for his annual European trip. Once they went out to dinner with the Guthries and the Sinclair Lewises, but they were content with unfashionable Neuilly. "They can put up seven more modern-art cafés on the Left Bank," Benét wrote Don Campbell, "all full of red marble and pitchbin, and I won't care." Even the general atmosphere was more stable.

"France is just as good as it ever was," he told Campbell. "We have passed through two peaks and two depressions of pro-American and anti-American feeling and are now back on the good old comfortable basis that all Americans are crazy but worth being polite to nevertheless. Which is really much more liveable than being looked at as if you were the Massachusetts executioner or kissed by mistake for the Spirit of St. Louis."

By mid-April, still visualizing twelve units, he had finished the fourth section. As he retyped it he began to see the final structure more clearly. He moved the invocation from its original setting in the third section and revised it as a separate unit. He retitled the poem *John Brown's Body* and now he decided on eight books rather than the dozen sections. He blended the finished groups so that by the late spring of 1927 three of the books were completed. Both his brother and Henry Canby wrote several times that they were anxious to publish any available fragments as soon as possible in the *Saturday Review of Literature*. Benét was hesitant.

"Some of it could be printed separately, I think," he wrote Bill at the end of April, "though I don't know how much—maybe the invocation or some of the John Brown part in particular. But I'm afraid the effect of the thing, if any, is a mass effect."

In early May he paused again to retype what he had done to date—one hundred and thirty-five pages—and to catch his breath. "It's a queer start," he wrote his brother, "& sometimes I think it will be the most colossal flop since Barlow's *Columbiad*." He mailed them the "Invocation," however. They used it immediately in a June 1927 issue, the first public indication of what he had been working on for twelve months.[15]

By then the Benéts had moved to the country for the summer. They rented a house near the Myers' at Bizy, fifty miles from Paris in southern Normandy. It was designed for two families; Mrs. Lamont and her two young children rented the other half. The house had four bedrooms and no bath; Benét said he would rather be cool than cleanly. There was a tennis court up the hill which he was invited to use, but instead he stayed on his nine to five schedule. Mrs. Lamont remembered that the only time they saw him was in the evening. "I am at present extinguished," he wrote Robert Nathan, "under the tall foolscap of this long poem." By the first of July he had finished the sixth book. He told Farrar that it would be completed by August, but cautioned him not to expect the manuscript until fall. "I'll have a lot of going over it to do," Benét explained.

Now the mail brought word of the excited reaction to the "Invocation." There were approving letters from readers and congratulations from friends and colleagues. A lady who was a friend of John Brown's grand-niece wrote to say how much she was looking forward to the complete poem. "I'm afraid she will not greatly care for what I say about the old man," Benét told his brother. "He had his points but he was a queer proposition."

He finished the final book in mid-August and took a week off to visit his brother and Elinor Wylie in England. He returned to Bizy to begin the revisions and continued work on them after they moved back to Neuilly. They rented for the winter a small, three-story house—two and a half stories, really, Benét wrote his family—with its own garden. They were only three blocks from the Bois and two from the river. For the next two months Benét worked over the manuscript without interruption. At the end of that time he told his brother it was finished and apologized for not writing since August. "I was sweating at John Brown's damn body whenever I had a minute, trying to get it off." He sent one copy to New York, for Brandt and Farrar, and the carbon to his parents. He asked his brother if he'd read it in manuscript rather than wait for proofs.

"I am very anxious to see what you think of the whole bloody thing," he told Bill. "I am still too close to the damn thing to see the wood, if any, for the interminable array of trees. The bulk of it looks fairly impressive, just as bulk, but I don't know how it will strike as an evening's reading. I'm telling the family to send the carbon on to you, if you want it. It will look cleaner in the proof but then—well, you can see that I am suffering from the usual pains of the afterbirth."

While he waited anxiously for the reaction to the manuscript—"biting my nails," he told Bill—Benét began to work on some short stories. His fellowship had been renewed in June for six months, to permit him to finish the poem, but the extension was almost up. "Mr. Guggenheim goes out of my life on January first," he wrote his brother, "and will be mourned with appropriate ceremonies."

His sense of obligation to the Foundation was immense. He always emphasized that without its help he could never have written the poem. For the rest of his life he uncomplainingly read the numerous applications from other poets which Moe submitted to his judgment. "The Guggenheim Fellowship," Benét told an interviewer in 1930, "provided me with leisure to write the sort of thing I felt was worth while, and I did so, not thinking of results." He was even more emphatic in private. "It damn near saved my life," he told Phelps Putnam.[16]

Canby asked him to review jointly two new volumes of verse, one by Phelps Putnam and the other by Donald

Davidson. Benét wrote a thoughtful estimate of both books, his assessment of Davidson's *The Tall Men* a restatement of a part of his own intention in *John Brown's Body*. "Mr. Davidson," said Benét approvingly, "sets himself beside the Masters of *Spoon River* and the Neihardt of *The Song of the Indian Wars* and the other explorers and colonizers of certain parts of American ground, who are now reclaiming that ground from the artificial throstles and hawthorn of those who could not see the sky as it was for all the English poetry that had been written about it." [17] He read Robinson's new long poem, *Tristram*, and wrote Bill that it was "a fine thing, full of beauty and force and a curious fretting intensity. I'm glad it's had the success."

He spent most of the late fall of 1927, however, on several new short stories, "for a little of that cash," he told his brother, "that we all of us need." In his present mood it was impossible to resume the modern love stories. Benét picked up as if without interruption the narrative frame of the Oldest Inhabitant, which he had last used eighteen months before, and the material of American history. Brandt sold the first new story to *Country Gentleman* almost as soon as it reached New York. Hibbs and Reed were delighted to get "The Fool-Killer," postponing a scheduled story to make room for it in the November issue. The story contained more stretches of effective prose than even "The Sobbin' Women" or "True Thomas." It was crammed—over-crammed, in fact—with passages that confirmed Benét's absorption in native American types. Still writing in the loose, full style of *John Brown's Body*, he virtually over-powered the story with the abundance of his exposition and reflection. But there were neat lines of satire, and a realistic evocation of the period. "It was a bad time for fools and wildcats, and a good time for huskin' bees and pride in the land you'd cleared. And the men and women, for the most part, was hearty and strong and fool-despisin', like the time."

Lem Burdick, the fool-killer, was a part of Benét's creative extension of American folklore, a variation of Bunyan and Fink and Davy Crockett. Peter Vane, the story's hero-inventor, was similarly related to the Lincolnesque legend. Benét was again freshening the standard components of historical fiction. "He'd had two wives in his time," says the Oldest Inhabitant of the fool-killer, "but wives didn't last long with him, though he took good care of his stock."

Benét wrote two more stories while he waited to hear about the poem. Brandt handled them exactly as he had a similar pair in 1926. One of them, "The Lucksmith," he sold to *Country Gentleman;* the other, "The Giant's House," he placed as before with the *Elks' Magazine.*[18] *Country Gentleman* hired as illustrator for "The Lucksmith" the same artist who had done the drawings for "The Fool-Killer." The editorial care strengthened the continuity and series-effect which Benét himself had inserted not only through the consistent use of the Oldest Inhabitant as narrator but also of the same foil—"the young man in white flannels"—in both stories. Once again, in "The Lucksmith," Benét explored the intangibility which was permitting him a degree of fantasy in his magazine fiction.

"Luck's like gold," said the Oldest Inhabitant dreamily. "It's where you find it. And it's like gold another way too. One man'll walk over a piece of lucky ground and never so much as pick up an old safety-razor blade. And another'll go to sleep there, some dark night, and when he wakes up in the mornin' he's turned into John D. Rockefeller. Yes, luck's a curious thing."

In "The Giant's House," on the other hand, his memories of Army garrisons still stirred by the work on the long poem, Benét created his situation from the traditions of Ordnance and gun-making. He gave the narrative additional strength by his imaginative use of a young boy's memories. "The world grows smaller as you grow up in the world. Mind and all that—but the mere matter of height has something to do with it. That's one reason children are apt to be fond of small people—and why stories like 'Jack the Giant Killer' have lasted so. Because children actually do live in a giant's house—a house not built for them. And the giants may be friendly or unfriendly—but a certain gulf remains."

All three were good stories, their quality again verified by the various asterisks and citations of the O'Brien and O. Henry rolls of honor. They would provide a few months' income to replace the Guggenheim quarterly check. Brandt also wrote him that "Bon Voyage," one of the worst of the stories he had done in the spring of 1925, had finally been sold to *College Humor*. Benét himself was still not fully comfortable with the form, preferring, so long as he had to write prose, the more fluid structure of the novel, and hopeful always of the secondary profits of serialization. He began considering a new piece of historical research, this time into a period that lay between the pre-Revolution months of *Spanish Bayonet* and the Civil War of *John Brown's Body*. His conception of the new novel, in fact, was as a successor to *Spanish Bayonet*. By the first weeks in 1928 he had a very general outline in mind.

"It would deal with the nephew of SB's hero," he wrote Brandt, "and would take place principally in the time of the Tripoli pirates. The scene would be America, the Barbary States and possibly France. Jefferson would appear in it and possibly a glimpse of Napoleon. Dr. Gentian [the villain of *Spanish Bayonet*] would reappear for a scene or two. This hero is a stronger character than his uncle and more of a maker of events. There should be something of the development of a great New York trading house and something of young America feeling its oats and finding herself on the sea. But it isn't a sea story . . . It should run to about 100,000 words. My working title is *The Silver Dollar*—an actual silver dollar plays something of a part—but I am not very satisfied with it. I have not the plot very clearly yet but see several scenes, including the first scene and the last. That is generally the way I do."

Before it had really begun, however, his working schedule for *The Silver Dollar* was interrupted—pleasantly—by letters from New York about the manuscript of *John Brown's Body*. Brandt, in fact, who read it over a week end, sent Benét an enthusiastic cable on Monday morning. Bill Benét and Farrar were equally excited. Benét was pleased and relieved by their warmth, though wary of its extravagance. "Thanks inordinately for your letter," he wrote Bill. "Only I wish the book were that good." He was particularly encouraged by Farrar's judgment that the poem had unity.

"You lose the feel of the whole," Benét wrote back, "working on a thing of that size for so long, and can see nothing but the parts." He had scrupulously avoided discussing the poem as long as he was working on it. Now for an instant he was uncharacteristically communicative about his work.

"I tried to put America in it," he told Farrar, "at least some of the America I knew. If I did so, some of it should stand till a better man comes along. I feel rather curiously about it myself. I think my best work so far, perhaps, is in it and yet it is more detached from me than anything I have ever done. It seemed to me a thing of that sort should be tried. A poet of greater faculties would have avoided my failures in it and my superficialities—and there are many of both—but what I have done, I have done to the extent of such capacities as I have."

Benét was skeptical of some of Farrar's praise. "As for genius," he said, "I don't know—but it did take persistence. Incidentally, if any criticisms, either of details or the whole, do come to you, please tell me them. When that thing was finished, I felt as if I had given birth to a grand piano." He urged Farrar, with several plausible arguments, to consider an immediate spring publication for the poem, though as usual he was willing to defer realistically to professional judgment. "If, after this, however, it still seems to you and Carl that a Fall date is preferable to a late Spring or early summer one, go ahead on that basis. You know the state of your lists and the various publishing conditions better than I do."

Farrar was anxious to set type immediately from the manuscript. Benét, conscious of the mechanical difficulties of printing a long poem, reluctantly cabled permission. He insisted, however, that he had to be given an opportunity to read the galley proofs in detail. "There are a number of checks on actual facts and some revisions," he explained, "that nobody else could do for me. If I tried to do them now on the one old working copy I have—in which some of the corrections on yours are missing—it would take quite as long as sending galleys over and back and probably get into an awful tangle as regards page references etc as well. Also it will be the greatest help in the world to me to see that thing actually in type—it changes the whole appearance of the poem and makes errors stick out like sore thumbs. So, if you will, send me the galleys when you have them, and I will get them back just as soon as I possibly can."

The immediate effect of this correspondence with Farrar was to send Benét back to short stories. The fact that *John Brown's Body* was not to be published until the fall of 1928 meant in turn that the unwritten *The Silver Dollar,* which he had visualized for October 1928 publication, would have to be pushed forward to the spring of 1929. He must depend again on short stories for most of his 1928 income. "I certainly cannot count on the poem," he told Farrar, "large Siamese child though it is."

As his tone indicated, Benét had no real qualms about the next few months. Those last three stories were the kind he at least got some pleasure out of writing, and all of them had sold readily. He prepared for a couple of months of hard work, not by any means intoxicated with the prospect of no relief from magazine fiction, but aroused as always by the problems to be solved. "I certainly felt when I had finished the poem," he told his parents, "that I never wanted to write another line as long as I lived—and yet I won't be sad to start. Writing is a funny thing, when you've got the habit of it."

And then suddenly there was an end to the bonanza of good fortune which had begun with the original *Country Gentleman* sale in early 1926 and continued on through the Guggenheim award and the productive months of *John Brown's Body*. He was more exhausted than he realized by the long struggle of concentration.

He was ill all through the winter of 1928, a sequence of grippe and trench mouth and frightful colds which laid him up completely. "I was sicker than I thought," he admitted to Farrar. Just as he was back on his feet in early April there was tardily delivered to him in Neuilly a telegram from Westtown, Pennsylvania, which was several days old and whose statement was so gross that for an instant it was incomprehensible. The Colonel was dead.

He had died very suddenly on March 30. There had been no warning and no real illness. He was seventy-one years old and apparently in excellent health and then he had a heart attack. Benét wrote a hasty note to John Farrar by the next boat. He asked Farrar to turn over to his brother immediately the $500 due as an advance on *The Silver Dollar*.

"Will you arrange with Bill and Carl," Benét asked Farrar, "so that if there is any necessity for it Bill can take this check and use it as he sees fit. I don't imagine that such an emergency will arise, but as you know, sometimes when people die suddenly, the estate is tied up until the will is proved, and there may be no ready money available." It was a gesture of composed logic under stress which the Colonel would have valued. There was no point in his returning to America for the funeral. He was broke; to borrow the money from Doran or Brandt would simply be to deprive his family of future earnings in order to indulge his own grief. "The contract is very generous," he ended the hasty letter to Farrar. "Thank you again, John. I will write at more length, later. I cannot, now."

The Colonel's death was a staggering blow. Benét answered the letters of condolence with polite composure. Only to a few close friends did he speak with any candor of his grief, and then briefly. "Nothing in life," he wrote Farrar in early May, "can ever make up for that particular relationship, or fill that place. He understood me completely. And he was the best man I ever knew or am likely to know. I am glad it was sudden—for him. He would have hated the slow thing. For me—well, there is no use talking of that." It was the longest comment he ever made to anyone but Rosemary. Thereafter, however, he was noticeably affected by the deaths of his friends' parents. He always wrote them immediately and in what were for him exceptionally personal terms.

"I remember my father saying to me," he told Bob McClure in 1936, "'We always think of our parents as immortal,' and thinking of it again when I got the news of his death. And yet that is the way we are bound to think of them—especially if we love them. There is no philosophy to soften the shock. He died within twenty-four hours and I have always been very glad of that—it was eight years ago but it does not seem so long."

For once the short stories were a blessing. He recovered himself throughout the late spring and early summer of 1928 with an intensity of work that produced seven stories that were all immediately marketable. One of them—"The Story about the Anteater"—was a moving account of a happy marriage which represented not only therapy but testimonial.[19] "But work does help, I know," he wrote his brother. "It is the one thing." Years later, when the *Reader's Digest* asked him to do an article in a series of theirs called The Most Unforgettable Character I've Known, Benét could not oblige, he told Brandt, with any remarkable Indian guides or wise old priests. "I'm afraid the person who influenced me most," he said to Brandt, "is still my father." [20]

He had been particularly conscious of the Colonel as he worked on *John Brown's Body*, remembering not only his creed of duty to the Union, but also the descriptions he had given of the occasions when his own father had introduced him as a boy to Grant and Sherman and so many of the Union generals in Washington. Benét was comforted that at least the Colonel had read the poem in manuscript, and approved it. From unused fragments of his *John Brown's Body* research he now composed two short stories with the Reconstruction as their setting. "Let me recall as I can," the narrator of "Candleshine" begins, "that old, drowned South of my youth, where I was born and ran wild as a rabbit in a lost brier-patch. It was a strange place and strange time, that South of the first decades after the Civil War. A time of bitter memories . . ." [21]

He even managed from this same block of material the vexing editorial delight of a seasonal story. "Green Christmas" had as its theme, in the holiday season of 1877, Benét's profound convictions about the Union. "Yes, we followed the state," says a former Confederate major who had served with Wade Hampton. "But we must all live under one roof now—the best man we ever had said so." [22] Benét was particularly pleased by the sale of "Green Christmas" to the *Ladies' Home Journal*, for it raised his story price to a new high of $700. Brandt sold the *Journal* two other stories, both contemporary trivialities which Benét provided as ballast for the historical material. [23]

The last story he did in mid-1928 was a compromise between these two areas of his magazine fiction. "Two White Beans," in part as a consequence of the attempted compromise, was poorly constructed, its narrative awkwardly broken between an effective account of Caribbean filibustering and the small town to which one of the survivors escaped. The reader was jerked from one character to another—each of them well drawn—so that his interest was scattered without control. The vivid portraiture and the topical quality—this was a decade, after all, which seemed always to have Marines in Nicaragua —made it nevertheless acceptable to *Country Gentleman*, partial as they were to the freshness and vigor of Benét's work.[24]

The bungled structure of "Two White Beans" was symptomatic of Benét's impatience to get back to the manuscript of *John Brown's Body*. The galleys arrived in May and he worked on them without interruption, knowing the urgency with which they were needed in New York. He persuaded Farrar to allow him a final check on the page proofs just before publication. "I have altered quite a number of lines," he wrote the editor, "and made some cuts and additions and tried to catch all the errors. Probably some have escaped me but I have tried to work so no important corrections will be necessary in the page-proof."

He was very gloomy after he mailed the galleys. He had put in two years of the hardest kind of work and now that it was done he felt a deadening sense of anticlimax. The last six months had been painful and exhausting, made difficult by his own illness and wretched by the death of his father. "We are all well here as far as the health of it goes," he told Farrar. "For the rest of it I cannot speak—the loss is still too near." He was convinced now that the poem was a failure. "It's a damn shame to have wasted the Guggenheim money that way," he told a friend who visited them in Neuilly. "No one will read it." [25]

10. John Brown's Body: Two

*Never did I think I would return to New
York with any money left after tipping the
Library-steward. But it will be a very pleasant
—and novel—sensation.*[1]

In New York the group of men who now assumed
custody of *John Brown's Body* were anything but gloomy.
Dan Longwell, promotion manager for the newly merged
house of Doubleday, Doran, took the manuscript to
Fisher's Island, in Long Island Sound, to read on a week's
vacation. Longwell, an astute and sensitive judge of mass
taste, who in the 1930's launched the new *Life* for
Henry Luce with such success, was deeply affected by
the poem. He had been partial to Benét's work ever since
he tried in 1921, as a young bookstore manager, to persuade readers to buy *The Beginning of Wisdom* instead
of *This Side of Paradise.* He was particularly affected by
John Brown's Body, however, for it confirmed and extended all his own militant convictions about America
and his special interest in the Civil War. He read it aloud
in the lovely setting of the west side of the Island; he
went back to New York convinced that thousands of
Americans would feel as he did about it.

It was a confusing scene to which Longwell returned
at Doubleday, Doran. The merger was so recent that

most of the executives were still preoccupied with its details and their own futures. Longwell took advantage of the situation, he recalled later, to set up "in the most high-handed way" a sales campaign of real proportions. He handled the whole thing personally; he gave to it the same kind of treatment by which he had promoted so successfully in 1925 such a seemingly special book as Margaret Kennedy's *The Constant Nymph*. "Unlike most publishers," according to Edna Ferber, several of whose own books profited from Longwell's handling of them, "Dan Longwell knew books not only as merchandise but as a form of creative art. He was sympathetic, intuitive, and shrewd—a rare combination." [2]

Longwell talked *John Brown's Body* constantly during the spring and early summer of 1928, anxious to lubricate the kind of word-of-mouth excitement that so often precedes a best-seller. He got blurbs from Lawrence Stallings and Morley and James Boyd. He labored over the jacket; as illustrator he hired Frank Leslie Sandford, who had recently done a fine cover for him for a book called *American Bandwagon*. Longwell furnished Sandford with a detailed prose description by Christopher Morley of the Virginia hills, urging him to translate Morley's rich prose into his own work. He told the artist to use throughout a blend of gray and blue for his basic colors. Longwell wrote all the advertisements himself; he placed them carefully and prodigally. "I spent a lot of Doubleday's money," Longwell said with satisfaction many years later.[3]

Farrar, assured now of Longwell's devotion to *John Brown's Body*, and knowing that Longwell had no equal in book promotion, went to work on the newly organized Book-of-the-Month Club. Every New York editor was mindful that the startling success of Robinson's *Tristram* the previous year had been directly linked to its distribution by the Literary Guild. Farrar persuaded his friend Dorothy Canfield Fisher, one of the Club's judges, to read the poem in proof. He sent Benét a copy of Mrs. Fisher's enthusiastic letter. Benét, still gloomy, was cautious.

"I am glad, of course," he wrote Farrar, after thanking him gratefully for the labor he was so clearly putting on the book, "that she seems to like J.B., but of course shan't count on anything from either of the book-clubs until I read the advertisement in the papers, if then. The ways of all committees have always been a profound mystery to me and I have seen too many things of that sort fail to click at the last moment. And if I had all the money I might have made on flukes I'd have broiled Rolls-Royces for breakfast. There is nothing like thirteen years of the so-called literary life for exploding Alnaschar's castles."

Benét was still oppressed by a sense of failure with the poem, and anxious to rid himself of it by getting on with *The Silver Dollar*. "J.B. will go or it won't go," he told Farrar bleakly, "and by the time it comes out, I hope I'll be too busy writing something else to worry much about it. In ten years more I ought to be able to do something if I have the brains. How long it takes to learn even the A of composition let alone the B's and C's."

On June 14, however, Farrar's optimism was vindicated. "John Brown Book of Month for August," the cable to Neuilly read. "By next mail send us list critics friends associates who might be interested deluxe edition. Farrar." Benét was properly stunned. He frugally cabled a two-word acknowledgement—"Swell. Benét"—and then wrote Farrar a long letter. "Your cable arrived early in the morning," he told Farrar, "and I propped one eye open to read it. It left us quite breathless. I really did not expect such a thing, in my usual sour way, and was most pleasantly taken aback. That is swell. I know you must all have worked for it hard—you in particular—and my gratitude to you all is very genuine. I had of course envisaged the possibilities as I do of everything from sudden death to being adopted by a Rockefeller but was no less astonished for all that." Benét then momentarily recovered his instinctive and acquired caution. "Now," he added, "it remains to be seen how many of these B of the Mo subscribers, with their exchange and substitution privileges, will take advantage of the glorious privilege offered them. And you can trust me not to bank on any extraordinary figures. Now couldn't you get a law passed by Congress, making the compulsory reading of JB a prerequisite to American citizenship? I wouldn't put it past you, after this. I babble."

Benét had trouble putting together an impressive list of prospective purchasers of a deluxe edition. "All the people I know," he explained to Farrar, "are either in the game themselves and get their books free or else are too poor to buy them." He was much more concerned about the poem itself. "What actual publication-date will there be now—August first? and if so, and you should be unable to send me page-proof in time, will you see to it that somebody of intelligence checks it over? The corrections I made in galleys do seem important to me and I am nervous as a witch about them—especially the Whitman, the Dedication and prefatory note and "Bury me where the *fences* hold the land" in John Vilas's last speech. Will you let me know about this as soon as you can?"

Farrar had not stopped with Dorothy Canfield Fisher.

He sent proofs of the poem to a number of other prominent literary people, including E. A. Robinson. Robinson's letter about *John Brown's Body*, a copy of which the editor sent to Benét, was, as the latter commented, "very Robinsonian." The older poet, severe and judicious as always, told Farrar that "parts of it are very fine and parts of it are as bad as possible." Robinson reconsidered the second adjective. "Bad isn't exactly the word, for Benét knows what he is doing. Mistaken might be a better word." He regretted that a poet of Benét's gifts had not taken more time. Benét was both philosophical and acute in his response to the praise and the criticism.

"Of course I agree with the dictum," Benét told Farrar. "Poetry should be written in bronze. And I could have taken a couple more years to JB with advantage. But not, I think, with enormous advantage. I am not built that way. As it was I did my damndest to smooth out the roughest of the verse. But ten years work could not have made some of the prosier passages much less prosy. The fault there is not only in me but in the nature of both subject and medium. As it is, I am content that he thinks some of it good. That is much from him. If the poem is to stand eventually, in any sort of way, it will do so because of a few passages in each Book and the mass-effect of the whole. The faults are many and glaring. But I could do no better, given such brains as I had. Now it is out of me and I am anxious to do something different and more disciplined."

Farrar, alert to the possible effect of a *John Brown's Body* success upon the sales of Benét's earlier verse, arranged for Doubleday, Doran to take over the earlier volumes—*Young Adventure* and *Heavens and Earth*—from the Yale University Press and Henry Holt. Benét, his mood still one of self-criticism, told Farrar he certainly wanted to do a lot of cutting and emending if there were to be any new editions of the 1918–20 poetry. He couldn't conceal, however, his excitement about the prospects for *John Brown's Body*.

"There are ten thousand questions I should like to ask you but I know our letters will cross so I won't. However tell me a lot—for like Pepys I am with child to hear of this strange thing. Now I shall get this off on the first boat. Meanwhile much gratitude and many many thanks to you and to all."

In New York Dan Longwell adjusted his campaign to the new development. Earlier in the spring he had sent a copy of the poem to Stanley Morison, the celebrated English typographer who redesigned the London *Times* in 1932. Morison designed for *John Brown's Body* a stately volume, tall and narrow. When the Book-of-the-Month Club designation was made, Longwell reasoned that he was now dealing with a different audience; subscribers might be wary of so ornate and unfamiliar a design. He had the book squeezed down to novel size; it could also be sold for novel price.

During the next two weeks the feeling grew more and more strong among the editorial staff that with a little luck and some good reviews they might be about to effect a tour de force of publishing. The success of *Tristram* in 1927 had proved that on rare occasions a long poem could be sold in large numbers. Robinson, on the other hand, had the advantages of great critical prestige and a quarter of a century of publication. They speculated that the presence of Benét might give added impetus to the promotion campaign. Farrar urged him to come home, and to arrive in New York on publication day.

Benét was reluctantly willing. He disliked leaving Rosemary and the children, but the trip would give him a chance to see his mother and Laura and visit Rosemary's parents in Chicago. He could also look around for a home for his own family; what with Stephanie almost ready for school, and no boys Tommy's age near them in Neuilly, it was time they thought about moving back. He agreed to deliver some lectures Farrar had arranged, and to go with him up to the Breadloaf Writers' Conference in Vermont. He was leery, however, of their major publicity dream. "I'd rather not arrive," he told Farrar, "on exactly the day the book comes out. It seems too pat." Benét was thoroughly skeptical of any magic that might accompany his presence.

"There are some people," he argued, "whose personalities can arouse interest in their work. I am not one of them. My work is the best of me, and I would rather lie behind it, as perdu as possible. And experience has taught me that this is the best course I can follow. Writing should speak for itself—if it cannot, it is lost. And as for me—I am not even a foreign author. I do not speak Czechoslovakian, I never was bitten by a lion or caught a strange species of tortoise while flying over the North Pole. And I've lived in New York long enough for most of the professional literary gang to know who I am without wanting to know any more. You can lionize Trader Horn and introduce Leon Feuchtwanger. But you can't do much to me except raise the remark, 'I didn't know he'd been away.'"

He booked a second-class passage on the *Ile de France*, sailing from Cherbourg on August 8. He was newly startled by Farrar's latest statistics on the effects of the Book-of-the-Month Club designation on the size of the first edition. "65,000!" he marvelled. "My God!" It was supremely ironic that his first popular success, after seven years of deliberately writing for the market, was evidently going to be the work he had thought least likely of success. "I am all for larger and larger editions," he wrote Farrar just before he sailed. "I have had so many of the first & only kind."

Even before the *Ile de France* docked in New York the warm hand of Doubleday publicity reached out to embrace Benét. One of the firm's young gentlemen rode out on the cutter with a reporter in tow. "He gave me cigarettes," Benét wrote his wife, "the reporter interviewed me, then they took me up to the sundeck of the first class where I was photographed in every possible expression of stupidity by slightly unwilling photographers who shot first and inquired what it was all about afterwards."

Farrar met him on the dock with more reporters. His mother and sister arrived. He had lunch with them and then was escorted to Alan Rinehart's apartment, where he was interviewed by additional reporters. "I was tired enough by then," Benét told Rosemary, "to say anything." Not until the next day did he really have a chance to absorb the sensation of being back in New York. A newspaperman asked him, inevitably, what impressed him most about America after being away for two years. Benét said the new buildings had changed some blocks beyond recognition. Familiar districts were now entirely strange. Early that second morning the same young gentleman from Doubleday conducted him on a tour of the firm's celebrated Garden City plant.

"I saw John [Farrar]," Benét told his wife, "the special edition, the bindery, numerous directors & everything but the Rajah's Ruby." His author's copies of *John*

Brown's Body had already been mailed to Neuilly, but he inscribed a copy at Garden City and had it sent to Rosemary in case the others were delayed. The actual sales since publication on August 8, eight days before, were 52,000 copies including the Book-of-the-Month Club. Five hundred copies, he was told, had already been bought that very day.

"The press has really been remarkable," Benét told his wife, "space everywhere & some of the praise so overdone it makes me feel ashamed."

Benét mentioned casually as they were leaving Garden City that he wished he had a detective story to read in bed that night. George Doran himself promptly fetched him a parcel of a dozen new ones. "If you want a white elephant," the publisher told him jovially, "we'll get it for you." Benét was delighted by the success and its holiday atmosphere, but, as he had told Farrar earlier, thirteen years of the literary life had given him a realistic balance. He had no illusions that the poem was the artistic perfection which so many of its reviewers had maintained. "A long poem without a flaw," he said later, "has never been written." [4]

He did what he could to discourage its presentation as an epic. From the beginning he himself had used instead the word cyclorama. With time his own judgments on the poem became the most responsible ones. It survived, as he had predicted it would, on the basis of notable individual passages in each book and the cumulative effect of the whole. Later commentators found intricacies of imagery and theme which had escaped the hasty reviewers; they found a grandeur of scope and a unity of narrative which its early detractors had denied. [5] It was having in the late summer of 1928, however, an extraordinary reception.

"The *Transcript* passed on it," Benét wrote Rosemary, "the *Times* & *Tribune* were yes&no, the *Literary Review* of the *Post* more unfavorable than favorable. But practically everything else was favorable—& the *Tribune* gave it the whole front page of *Books*." Even when the first excitement had settled there were remarkably few second thoughts or hindsight reservations. "There should be dancing in the streets," said Leon Whipple in the November *Survey*, "that we have found and fostered a poet of such courage and invented a way of broadcasting a hundred thousand copies of his poem." [6]

Herschel Brickell declared in the *North American Review* in October that "whatever its minor faults, it is in the large a distinctly fine achievement, and its popular success a literary event of no small importance." Benét's achievement was honored by judicious peers as well as excitable reviewers. "Mr. Benét's poem," Robert Morss Lovett wrote in the *New Republic*, "is an epic in intention, in scope, in sense of racial consciousness. It may not win the medal of the American Academy, but it will be crowned by the Grand Army and the Confederate Veterans, and by those who feel the spell of the past of which they remain the survivors." [7]

Allen Tate, his approval restrained by the offense to his regionalism of the sympathetic portrait of Lincoln, conceded nevertheless that *John Brown's Body* was "the most ambitious poem ever undertaken by an American on an American theme." Despite the Lincoln he was impressed by the portraits as a whole. "If professional historians," said Tate, "particularly those of the Northern tradition, will follow Mr. Benét's Davis, a distorted perspective in American history will soon be straightened out. Nowhere else has Lee been so ably presented . . ."

This kind of assessment, as judicious as his own when he completed the manuscript, was more meaningful to Benét than the extravagance of friends or the near hysteria of some of the reviewers. "He is what a poet for this work must be," said the *Outlook's* James Boyd, who had himself done distinguished fiction in the same area, "a man of good heart and courage, sardonic and tender, sensitive and rugged, a man of salty gusto and high desire." [8]

The book was having a range and warmth of response which had not occurred in American poetry for three generations. The poet to whom he was most frequently compared was Whitman. As the London *Times* pointed out, however, with a clearer perspective than could exist in America, its reception was actually more reminiscent of Longfellow's. Readers of *John Brown's Body* reacted as American readers had not reacted since the publication of "Hiawatha" and "Evangeline" in the 1840's and 1850's. For the rest of his life they wrote him letters about the book, from every part of the country—and when he died, and afterward, they wrote his widow as if in mourning for a dear friend. In 1928 and 1929 there were scores of requests to autograph the owners' copies. Benét answered each one in longhand.

"Thank you for your letter," he wrote from Neuilly in January 1929, in a reply that was characteristic of all of them. "I should be very willing to autograph your copy of *John Brown's Body* if you are willing to take a chance on sending it over here. The French mails are sometimes a trifle uncertain—especially with packages. Or, if you prefer it, I could write a slip to put in the box." [9] There were other letters which were longer and more personal. They wrote to thank him for an experience they had never before received from a book, and for the justice of his intepretation, and for articulating their own emotions about America.

He got letters from relatives of some of the historical figures he had used. A son of the man who supplied John Brown with rifles wrote to verify Benét's details. The daughter of General G. K. Warren of the Army of the Potomac told him how much she valued the description of her father. His phrase "Greek-mouthed" was more apt, she said, than any she had ever heard. "It was a pleasure to hear from you," Benét wrote Miss Warren. "As regards the adjective, I suppose it was the two things together. I thought General Warren a fine-looking man and the particular incident struck me as being comparable to something from the *Iliad*—that is, one individual chief like Achilles or Hector changing the scales in a battle, by personal valor or sagacity. I should like to have drawn fuller sketches of so many of the leaders, North and South. But space did not permit." [10]

From the South in particular came a stream of mail, almost all of it an expression of gratitude for the fairness of his portraits and his informed presentation of Southern values. A Texan wrote to say the poem had been approved by every veteran to whom he showed it. There were many letters from amateur students of the Civil War, all of them marveling at his accuracy and research. Sectional cranks wrote to quarrel with his picture of the Confederate prison at Andersonville. He answered them patiently. He had based his description on the official report by a Confederate medical officer, but he read the partisan literature which the Old South now mailed him in defense of the prison's notorious Commandant.

"Thank you for sending me the pamphlet concerning Major Wirz," Benét wrote a Southern lady, "which I have read with great interest. I have received several letters concerning my characterization of him in the poem and intend to go over the evidence in the case. Naturally, I do not wish to say that he was guilty if he was not. On the other hand, Andersonville was a pretty bad business, even with every extenuating circumstance taken into account. As you will probably have noticed, I chose an example from each side, to show what life in a military prison is generally bound to be. At the best, it is bad." [11]

There were letters of congratulation from his professors at Yale, from Phelps and from Edward Bliss Reed, and Tinker called the Invocation "the finest lyric verse of our time." There was a letter from Monty Woolley, and notes from colleagues and fellow poets. "It made me so proud of you," Edna Millay wrote him. Harriet Monroe wrote from *Poetry;* the poem, she said, "quite bowled me over." Stark Young was impressed by technical qualities and cadences that reminded him of Yeats. Once a friend of T. E. Lawrence told Benét the latter had admired the poem; another time, to his profound astonishment, Noel Coward told him how much he had enjoyed it.

Dudley Fitts wrote in the avant-garde *Hound & Horn* that the descriptions of Bull Run and Gettysburg were comparable to parts of the *Aeneid.* "A fine achievement," Fitts concluded, "worthy of honest praise and a long popularity." [12] From the Boston novelist Robert Grant, dignitary of the American Academy of Arts and Letters, came an invitation to deliver the Phi Beta Kappa Poem at Harvard the next spring. Sinclair Lewis cited it in his Nobel Prize speech in 1930 as evidence of the American literary renaissance. "The first book that I read by the bearer of this name," said Justice Holmes, referring to one of General Benét's publications, "was a treatise upon Military Law; the next, with many years between, was an epic poem!"

In Atlanta a young newspaperman named Ralph McGill, later to become editor of the *Constitution*, bought dozens of copies for his friends. "I still don't know anyone who has caught the essence of the Civil War as well as he," McGill said years later. "Frequently here at the office one or two of us will relax around coffee by reading some portions of it out loud. Sometimes when we are visiting, one with the other, we will pick up that book and read from it for hours after dinner when we are sitting around discussing books or poetry." [13]

The historian Douglas Southall Freeman, mailing Benét complimentary copies of the first two volumes of his *R. E. Lee,* told Benét in 1934 that he hoped they would be accepted "in partial payment of the debt I owe you for *John Brown's Body.*" Samuel Eliot Morison described it as "that great book." In Rhode Island a woman once asked him to autograph a copy that was warped from constant reading. Some one else sent him a copy for signature in which every single line was marked and emphasized by the owner's comments. Another wrote him that the book "has become like an old friend to be seen and appreciated at intervals." Robert Nathan, after a visit to Phillips Exeter Academy, told Benét that the poem was required reading in the senior class. "How does it feel to be a classic?" Nathan inquired.[14]

Years later, when he was weary of requests to recite it from the lecture platform, Benét was heartened when a young Iowa graduate student told him that a girl in Michigan had once read aloud to him the lines from Melora's song. During World War II he got letters from servicemen who had read the poem overseas; now he was articulating another generation's Americanism. When Vincent Sheean came back to New York in 1942 after the Tunisian campaign, he told Benét about a regular army major who had a copy of *John Brown's Body* with him during the entire trip across the Atlantic. On the troopship the major quoted passages by heart to Sheean, and illustrated their conversation, "à propos of almost any subject that came up," said Sheean later, by reference to the poem. Days afterward, after the landing, Sheean met the major's outfit when it completed an engagement with the French. The major still had the copy of *John Brown's Body*. "It was at least as important to him as his .45," Sheean told Benét, "and maybe more." [15]

John Brown's Body was the biggest moneymaker that Doubleday had during all the prosperous ten years from 1924 through 1934 when Dan Longwell was their promotion manager. In 1928 and 1929 alone it sold 130,000 copies. Even more impressive was its sales durability. Longwell successfully defeated a proposal that it be issued in Doubleday's dollar edition, and the results supported his thesis that it would continue to be bought at its original price; between 1930 and 1933 Americans bought an average of 6,000 copies a year.

In addition to the regular trade edition there were a high school edition and a college edition, each at the same $2.50 price. The former was initiated in 1941, and by 1957 there had been eighteen separate printings for a total of 91,000 copies in this one edition alone. The college edition was first issued in 1929, with an introduction by Henry Canby. During the next twenty-five years there were forty-four printings. Between 1941 and 1957 the college edition sold 87,000 copies.[16]

The poem was read and discussed and analyzed in classrooms in every state in the Union; it was required reading at the University of Alberta in Canada. Four hundred and eighty-seven institutions—high schools, colleges, universities, country day schools, teachers' colleges, prep schools—used one or both of these special editions. Undergraduates wrote Benét every year for help with the term papers they were preparing on "*John Brown's Body* as a National Epic."

One had to go back to the schoolroom poets of the nineteenth century, to Bryant and Whittier and Longfellow, to Lowell and Holmes, to find an American poem which had been read in such numbers and with such absorption by so many Americans. Its impact was multiplied and extended through its use in other mediums. Parts of it were recited innumerable times on the radio, in all kinds of versions that ranged from brief readings to hour-long adaptations. Passages were once used to celebrate Lincoln's Birthday on the Rudy Vallee Hour, when the latter was America's favorite radio program.

Raymond Massey read it over a national network as World War II approached, and in England the BBC produced it. When General Wavell addressed the Academy of American Poets on their fiftieth anniversary, he quoted from *John Brown's Body*. There were Ph.D. dissertations written about it, and solemn theses in fulfillment of the requirements for the degree of Master of Arts. In the 1950's it was taken three times across the continent by Charles Laughton and Paul Osborn, in a version that played to capacity crowds in every kind of theater and auditorium and ancient opera house.

It brought Benét a great deal of money in 1928 and 1929—about $25,000—and there rarely was a year thereafter when it didn't earn him from five hundred to a thousand dollars in book royalties alone. It made him a national figure at the age of thirty, known to thousands of Americans who knew the name of no other living American poet. He was alternately touched and exasperated by its enshrinement as an American classic. "And there it is and could be worse," he wrote in 1941, when his publishers issued an annotated edition with footnotes and scholarly apparatus and an editor's essay on the causes of the Civil War:

> With notes and preface and the rest
> And every kind of teacher's aid
> To harry schoolboys into learning
> The unpremeditated verse,
> Written because the heart was hot
> With quite a different kind of burning.
> And that is the revenge of time,
> And that, they say, the workman's pay.
>
> It may be so, I wouldn't know.
> I wrote it poor, in love, and young,
> In indigestion and despair
> And exaltation of the mind,
> Not for the blind to lead the blind;
> I have no quarrel with the wise,
> No quarrel with the pedagogue,
> And yet I wrote for none of these.
>
> And yet there are the words, in print,
> And should an obdurate old man
> Remember half a dozen lines
> Stuck in his mind like thistle-seed,
> Or if, perhaps, some idle boy
> Should sometimes read a page or so
> In the deep summer, to his girl,
> And drop the book half-finished there,

Since kissing was a better joy,
Why, I shall have been paid enough.
I'll have been paid enough indeed.[17]

The immediate beneficiaries of the success of *John Brown's Body* were those whom Benét, with a sense of duty which was both inherited and instinctive, regarded in various ways as his dependents. He was more shrewd and realistic about money than his older brother, but he was no less generous or extravagant than Bill. He established his mother and Laura at the Hotel Judson for the fall and winter. He got presents for Rosemary and the children. "Do you need any money?" he wrote his wife. "If you do, let me know and I can cable it any time."

He bought some bonds for Rosemary and put them in her safe deposit box at the Guaranty Trust. He told her to send her mother a check for a thousand dollars. "Say it's from you or from both of us as you think tactful," he wrote Rosemary. "What's the use of all this cash if I can't do what I want with it?" He applied for more life insurance and in the intervals between all this he was entertained at Doran's penthouse and looked up Douglas Moore and John Carter and all the other old friends who were in New York. He talked to people about possible houses in New Canaan and Philadelphia and on Long Island, and he gave a reading at the Barbizon and spent a couple of days at the Breadloaf Writers' Conference in Vermont.

Breadloaf, one of the early instances of an enterprise that soon became an American institution, was largely the creation of Farrar. "I gave a few conferences (God save the mark!)," Benét told Rosemary, "read, [and] talked foolishly before classes." His youth, which took most of the Conference members by surprise, as well as the aura of his extraordinary success and his modest willingness to help in whatever way he could, combined to make him as warmly regarded here as he had been at MacDowell. The Director, Professor R. M. Gay, was planning a sabbatical year in France. Benét answered his questions and made suggestions about where to live. He and Gay took a long walk along the lovely country road and discussed poetry. "I remember him as definitely boyish, slight, fragile, and shy in manner," said Gay, who never met him again. "I have perhaps never known a man for so brief a time whom I liked so much." [18]

Benét went back to New York, to further publicity maneuvers, and additional luncheons, and dinners with his mother and Laura. He was anxious to get back to Neuilly. Tommy had been sick, Rosemary told him, and though she wrote in a day or two that the little boy was fine again, Benét resented each new day in New York. He was delayed by the long Labor Day week end. The Doubleday staff urged that he stay a while longer to make up for the missed opportunities of the holiday. He went out to Chicago to see Rosemary's parents, and was escorted through the Chicago bookstores by yet another young gentleman from Doubleday. Finally, on September 6, he at last saw his way clear to book passage, having fulfilled every conceivable responsibility to his mother and Laura and Rosemary's family and Farrar and the house of Doubleday, Doran and his public.

"All well Chicago," he cabled to Neuilly. "Sailing *Berengeria* nineteenth. Whoopee. Love. Steve."

In six weeks he had been transformed from one of a large group of promising young American writers into the major popular poet in the United States. He had been feted and lionized till he was heartily sick of handshakes and adoration. He had made a lot of money and would obviously make more in the next few months. He had also spent more money—by far the greater part of it on other people—than he and his family had lived on in France for two years. He had signed books and read aloud and delivered lectures.

The entire nature of his life had been changed and the future pattern of his career established. He would never again be able to travel second-class, though he would often wish it and sometimes his finances would require it. Instead of being a young writer whose work was ahead of him he was a literary figure to whom writers very little younger than himself would now turn for aid and comfort and advice. He could no longer be identified simply as Bill Benét's brother, or young Benét, or Steve Benét. He had become Stephen Vincent Benét. It was a transformation which had occurred, quite literally, almost overnight. It was small wonder that he was only superficially aware of the alteration as he boarded the *Berengeria*. Besides, he was too glad to be going back to his family in Neuilly to worry about it.

The household at Neuilly and the nature of the family's final ten months in France were also dramatically changed by the success of *John Brown's Body*. They had two servants now, and all the harassments of an over-extended budget were wonderously removed. They were able at last to do a little of the traveling they had not been able to afford since their honeymoon six years before.

They accepted Philip and Ellen Barry's invitation to visit them at Cannes, having refused twice in 1927 because they had lacked the money to get there from Paris. For a week Benét and his wife were a festive part of the circle which Fitzgerald was preparing to describe in *Tender Is the Night*. "Their villa," Benét wrote his brother, "is a demi-Paradise. We led a gay life, swimming, talking, going around in large cars and drinking at appropriate intervals. You would like those people and I hope to see a lot of them when they get back to America."

Back in Neuilly they had many callers themselves. "We have been beset by visitors," he told Bill, "& are expecting a lot more." The feeling that he should be left alone while he did his work was gone; the friends trooped through on their ways to Rome or London or Berlin, or back to America. "Jean [Lamont] is still here for a little while," Benét wrote his brother, "though expecting to go to Switzerland next week or so. Or maybe it's Italy. I can no longer keep up with where people are going." Leonard Bacon was in Paris briefly, he too on his way somewhere else. They had dinner at the Crillon and a cousin of Bacon's appeared, Waugh-like, with a tame bear. "It caused an incredible sensation," Benét explained, "especially when it went up in one of the elevators, and the Crillon will never be the same again."

If his resumption of work was thwarted by gaieties in France, it was equally interrupted by tragedy at home. Elinor Wylie died suddenly on December 12, 1928; Bill Benét, not yet forty-five, was a widower for the second time. Stephen, who had great regard for his sister-in-law's poetry, and a kind of chivalrous disregard for the gossip about her private life, was grief-stricken for his brother. "There isn't a minute when we aren't thinking of you," he told Bill. "You have done so much for me, ever since I could remember at all."

He made a special trip by plane to England to gather

up the belongings Elinor had left there, having intended to collect them herself that spring. He wrote his brother long, thoughtful letters, full of comfort and gossip from Neuilly and Paris, knowing that the affection and the trivialities were the best solace he could offer. He looked up all his half-forgotten literary alliances on the Left Bank when Bill, now an editor of Payson & Clarke, asked him to keep an eye out for promising young writers. He endured another luncheon with the ubiquitous Louis Bromfield, who tried his patience, in the hope of adding to Bill's list, and he read all the new French novels and poetry for possible translations.

He wrote similar letters of comfort to his mother, trying to console her for the decision to at last place the ninety-two year old Aunt Agnes in a sanitarium. He spent a great deal of time with his children, making up for the weeks he had been in America and those long months of the nine to five schedule. He was delighted by both of them; he was much the same kind of wise and indulgent father that the Colonel had been. Stephanie, he told his brother with delight, had the two qualities he claimed to be most lacking in himself—industry and a liking for society—and he listened gravely to the long stories she told him in French.

She instructed him on the Vice of Gluttony and questioned him about the holy references her teacher made so constantly in school. Stephanie explained to him, he wrote Bill, that "the Holy Ghost is one of God's other names just as I am Monsieur Benét as well as Poppa. At least I think that's what she thinks but who can tell? I always used to think of him as something like the gas, which God turned on when he needed it, as well as I can remember. I find religious instruction for the Young rather hard." Tommy, at two and a half, was more in-

226

terested in machines and gas pumps. Benét resigned himself to long sessions with the *Book of Knowledge* in search of answers to his questions. The little boy grinned constantly, Benét said, and thus acquired whatever he sought. He had Rosemary's Irish look, Benét told Bill, and spoke nothing but French. When he was put to bed, Benét wrote home, he said cheerily, "A demain!"

There was little time for work amid so many pleasant distractions. Benét was mindful of his sloth; like most writers he was also restless without a project in hand. "After all," he wrote his old teacher, Edward Bliss Reed, "*John Brown* was finished a year ago, except for certain revisions, and it is time I got back to work." He was still spent, however, from the long haul of the poem; without the customary financial pressure it was doubly hard to take hold of anything. "I'm hoping to do some more verse," he told Reed, "but not another 367-page one very soon. Next time I'll be more laconic if I can."

John Brown's Body continued to sell amazingly, leading the best-seller list month after month, and he bought stocks and bonds and sometimes in the evenings he wrote a little poetry. "I have been trying to write a sort of ode," he told Farrar, "at least it acts like an ode." He could not recover the driving concentration of 1926 and 1927. During that period, when a friend asked him what he did if he couldn't keep the poem going, he said he just stared at the wall until something happened. Now, he wrote his brother, he worked on "some jingles" after dinner and read the detective stories which Doran continued to send him.

He was also conscious that the reception of *John Brown's Body* had placed new responsibilities on the use of his talent. Even the single short story he wrote during the first six months of 1929 was an indication of his consciousness of his new role. "The King of the Cats" was a richly imaginative exercise, full of sharp satire and affronts to the formulas of magazine fiction; Brandt was fortunate to sell it even in the modest market of *Harper's Bazaar*.[19]

Occasionally Benét did some casual research for *The Silver Dollar*, but again he missed the pressure of necessity and the creative excitement of a project that possessed him. Farrar, anxious to capitalize on *John Brown's Body* with a new book for 1929, prodded him gently by mail. Benét conceded his sloth and sought to remedy it. Then, sensing that a novel was unlikely this year, Farrar suggested that Doubleday publish "The Barefoot Saint" in a limited edition.

Benét tried to discourage the idea. He cabled that the story didn't seem worth book publication. Having read and reread the manuscript three times, he wrote Farrar a long letter. "It is a nice little story for the time when I wrote it," he told the editor, "but it is prettyfied and it is too much like Cabell. I'd really rather you didn't do it. It seems to me too slight to deserve a deluxe treatment. You need for that a story you can read in an hour but which you keep remembering for a long time. And 'The Barefoot Saint' isn't that. It is just a pleasant imitative piece of colorwork."

Benét was troubled by his own stubbornness, knowing his debt to Farrar and his obligation to the firm itself; he was also, as always, reluctant to be difficult. "Please don't think I am just being perverse about this. I was exceedingly fond of the story when I wrote it and mad to have it published. But I have some perspective now, and it really isn't worth it. I know you would do everything for it in the way of format—but if the stuff isn't there, the stuff isn't there. And it does seem important to me to have something for the deluxe people to work on that won't look too much like a Cinderella in its fine clothes."

Farrar assured him that the book would be a very modest enterprise; it wouldn't be promoted lavishly or falsely. "Okay under those conditions," Benét finally cabled at the end of March, after many letters, "though would prefer I wrote something better." The story, which had wandered from editor to editor for seven years, was now bought promptly by the *Saturday Review of Literature*. They printed it in the issue of April 20, 1929, and Doubleday brought it out that summer.

The manner of its publication—the magazine featured it impressively, and the book was a handsome one—was a measure of Benét's new status, but, as he himself had said so emphatically, the story was not a first-class one. Its effect was to make him even more conscious of his obligations. He began work on a new short story that would perhaps redeem it. He did not finish "The Treasure of Vasco Gomez," however, until late that summer; in July they sailed back to America, having at last obtained the necessary papers to take one of the French servants with them.

"We are starting to wander around express companies and such," he wrote Bill, "trying to figure out whether to pack Corantine [the maid] in a wooden crate and ship her by the little swiftness or to get visas for all the four bookcases stating that they are free of tuberculosis and unlikely to become a public charge once they get to America."

Even as they prepared to leave France, *John Brown's Body* continued to spill new bounty. News of the award to him of the Pulitzer Prize for poetry arrived one Saturday night in a cable from Bill. The telegram was

229

delivered in the middle of dinner; since their guests were both on a diet he and Rosemary postponed their toasts. "However," Benét wrote his brother, "we have since drunk to you, ourselves, and the maker of Mr. Pulitzer." They sailed on the *Ile de France,* this time first-class and accompanied by a servant. "It is really fantastic," Benét told his brother, "to have so much happen about one book and makes me feel like a Ralph Henry Barbour boy."

1a. Brigadier General Stephen Vincent Benét (1827–1895). The poet's grandfather, later Chief of Ordnance, United States Army, as a young lieutenant shortly after graduation from West Point.

b. Colonel James Walker Benét (1857–1928). The poet's father, a career officer in the United States Army from his graduation from West Point in 1880 until his retirement in 1921.

c. Colonel Benét's "Only" Children. Laura, Stephen Vincent, and William Rose, in 1900.

d. Mrs. James Walker Benét (d. 1940). The poet's mother, photographed in 1915 when the Benéts were stationed at Augusta.

2. Colonel James W. Benét, U.S.A. (Ret.). In 1927, the year before his death

3*a*. Stephen Vincent Benét at the age of four, sitting in the breech of a 16-inch gun at the Watervliet (N.Y.) Arsenal, where his father was stationed from 1899 to 1904.

b. Two years later, on the lawn in front of Officers Row at the Watervliet Arsenal.

c. In 1907, aged nine.

4*a*. Stephen Vincent Benét and his brother, William Rose Benét, stand together on the Yale campus in the fall of 1915, the younger Benét a freshman, his older brother, a member of the Class of 1907, already a well-known poet and an assistant editor of *Century Magazine*.

b. Yale Literary Magazine Board, 1919.

Robert M. Coates, managing editor; J. J. Schieffelin, memorabilia; Thornton Wilder, book reviews;

Donald M. Campbell, editor's table; Stephen Vincent Benét, chairman; Frank P. Heffelfinger, business manager.

. Benét in 1921, just before his marriage to Rosemary Carr.

6*a*. Benét's uncle, Laurence V. Benét, managing director of Hotchkiss et Cie.

b. Carl Brandt, Benét's literary agent and close friend from 1922 until the poet's death in 1943.

c. Benét and his wife Rosemary, in Paris in 1928, just after *John Brown's Body* had been finished.

7a. The stone studio on Henry Canby's country property in Killingworth, Conn., where Benét wrote most of *Western Star*.

b. Benét reads to his two oldest children, Tommy and Stephanie Jane.

8a. Rosemary and Stephen Benét in 1934, a few months after their collaboration on *A Book of Americans*.

b. Benét and his publishers, John Farrar and Stanley Rinehart, posed for a publicity photograph, rejoicing over the great success of "The Devil and Daniel Webster."

9. The Benét family at their summer home in Stonington, Conn., during the summers of 1941 and 1942.

10. Benét and Raymond Massey, who acted in and read several of the poet's wartime radio scripts, stand obediently for an NBC photographer in June 194[...]

1. *Life's* photograph of Benét, taken in 1942 in connection with the magazine's publication of his Fourth of July radio script, *Listen to the People*.

12*a*. Benét's son at the exhibition of his father's books and manuscripts in the Yale Library in 1944. (Photo by Elliott Kone.)

b. The Liberty ship *Stephen Vincent Benét* after its launching in San Francisco in 1944.

11. The Wages of Cinema

*This place is the new Klondike for all
literary and aesthetic gents—they all go
around sniffing, but pocketing checks.*[1]

WITH the earnings from *John Brown's Body*, Benét once
told an interviewer, he confidently expected in 1929 to
subsidize a couple of years of writing additional poetry.
However, he continued wryly, "I invested in good, sound,
New Era stocks." [2] They returned to the United States,
in fact, just in time to observe at first hand the collapse
of the stock market and the departure of prosperity.
By the end of 1929 his financial position was not very
different from what it had been in 1926, save that he
now owned a great many bonds of doubtful value. So
far as his immediate hopes for financial security were
concerned, *John Brown's Body* might just as well have
received the public apathy of most poetry.

They lived very comfortably for a month or two, when
they first got back to America, in Leonard Bacon's enormous house at Peace Dale, Rhode Island. "We are
grander than we have ever been," Rosemary wrote Ethel
Andrews. "Steve is trying to be worthy of being lord of the
manor. Do come and see us here—we'll probably be in
a garret in New York next fall." Now, in the late summer
of 1929, with a seemingly assured income ahead and his

creative lethargy behind, Benét reproduced briefly the same early stages of productivity which had preceded the composition of *John Brown's Body*. He did two thoughtful reviews for the *Saturday Review of Literature,* and he kept the pot boiling at Brandt's with a light and frivolous tale for the *Ladies' Home Journal* called "The Prodigal Guest." He finished the first-class story he had begun in France, "The Treasure of Vasco Gomez," with its vivid portrait of the psychology of possession, and he wrote for the *New Republic* a pair of excellent short poems.[3]

In each of the new poems, the first he had published since *John Brown's Body,* Benét attempted with considerable success to extend the range of his lyricism. Both of them, "Bad Dream" in particular but "Song" as well, had a weight of melancholy that was new to his verse; 1928 had been a year of death and pain as well as royalties and honors. In "Song" he played subtle variations on what might have begun as a piece of light verse for a child's bedtime. In "Bad Dream," however, his mood was more bitter.

> Out of the stroke, the change,
> The body locked in its death
> Like a stream locked in the ice,
> The whiteness under the cheek,
> The lips forever set
> In the look that is always strange
> Because we remember yet
> How they spoke, how the mere breath
> Was enough to make them speak.

With the approach of school in September they moved to New York, to an apartment on 93rd Street. To the minor disruptions of the shift and the homesick sulking of the maid Corantine, no longer the jewel she had been in Neuilly, was now added the major catastrophe of the stock market crash. Their rootless migrations from apartments to rented houses and back to more apartments, plus the requirements of two active children, had made both Benét and his wife anxious to own a home of their own. Benét was thus doubly responsive to a Hollywood offer of a twelve-week contract at a thousand dollars a week. The United Artists assignment was a promising one, a movie about Lincoln with Walter Huston in the lead and the celebrated D. W. Griffith, of *Birth of a Nation* fame, as director.

They decided that the children had been through enough dislocation during the past three years. Benét, though he did not relish the separation, would go out alone for the three months. "Well," he told his brother, who was just back from a speaking tour, "some lecture & some write for the movies and I say it's spinach anyhow, no matter how it's boiled." He and Griffith left for the coast together on December 2, in the splendor of drawing-rooms on the Wolverine. They worked all through the journey, cutting about one-third of the original script.

Benét was pleased to find Griffith easy to get along with and easy to work with. To his relief it was even possible to kid him a little; he was neither a prima donna nor a stuffed shirt. He consoled himself with the thought that after all he had worked in advertising, and written a play for William Brady, Sr. Not much could happen to him in Hollywood that hadn't already happened in New York.

Benét arrived in Hollywood at the climax of the industry's most irresponsible and unstable era. The conversion to sound had brought staggering profits and the destructive knowledge that the most trivial material would be richly rewarded at the box office. New executive and financing alignments were forming and dissolving almost simultaneously. "It was," Benét told his friend Christopher LaFarge, "the zaniest of its various periods." [4]

Benét was fortunate to be working for Griffith, one of the great directors and a man of professional and personal integrity. Griffith, himself possessed of abundant charm, was much taken by Benét. He went to considerable pains to make the young poet comfortable. He entertained him week ends, and together they visited the incredible homes of the director's millionaire friends. He took him out on the town, accompanied by the two young ladies whose twin presence was always required by Griffith's exhaustless appetite for dancing. He explained the workings of Hollywood and brought Benét to the various preliminary conferences. "I am giving my celebrated imitation of a piece of furniture," Benét wrote his wife. "I don't know why anything happens and don't try to find out."

Actually he learned very quickly, as was demonstrated both by his effective script—Griffith wanted him to stay on for another picture—and by his subsequent comments on movie-making in general. He watched with dismay, however, the intrigue that was gathering around Griffith. He identified the principal conspirator rather readily— "a Yale man [and] a son of a bitch," he told Rosemary— and he speedily declared himself on Griffith's side. "I continue to like him," he wrote his wife, "and really to think a lot of him, in many ways. He's all right. And he can produce loyalty."

Benét attended a mammoth celebration at the Hotel Roosevelt in honor of Griffith—a sure indication that there

234

was backstage dirty work going on—and to his own and Griffith's astonishment was introduced by the master of ceremonies, along with Eric von Stroheim, Colleen Moore, and Donald Crisp, as another of D. W. Griffith's personal discoveries. "The place was packed," he wrote Rosemary, "& everybody talked about when they wanted to fire Mary Pickford from Biograph because she wasn't pretty enough & when Chaplin got $5 a week, until I felt I had been there too."

This was the palatable side of Hollywood, clearly phony but pleasantly extravagant and briefly entertaining. The work was something else. Benét, determined as always to give good value for money received, labored hard on the script. Then began the conferences and revisions and interferences. Griffith he didn't mind; it was the others who enraged him. "I think we're about through," he told Rosemary, "& then Mr. Griffith has a new idea. The trouble is—he's generally perfectly right." The various executives, however, were not only persistently wrong but sometimes malicious. "There is a tragedy going on here—D.W.G.'s. And there is comedy. Lord, what comedy! If it didn't make you so mad."

Then they were delayed, when Griffith became ill during January. Benét continued to work on what was now the fifth version he had participated in. Griffith's foes—"the money men," Benét told his wife—took advantage of the director's absence to hamstring the production as much as possible. "I've got a respectable thing," Benét told his wife in mid-January, "and I think a good story. I'm damn sure they won't use it but will try to cheese it up with love interests and negro comedy characters—but when I've presented it to them, my literary conscience will be clear. If I were working with Griffith alone, I think I could get him to do what I want

—but the endless ramifications of this business will probably succeed in producing a half-baked opus, neither one thing nor the other—and then they'll wonder why it failed."

Benét spared his wife the worst of his wrath, though at the end of January he wrote a blistering letter to Carl Brandt. "The next time you sign me up on a 12 week contract to come out here for any amount of money, there is going to be a good deal of blood flowing around the Brandt office. Of all the Christbitten places and business[es] on the two hemispheres this is the last curly kink on the pig's tail." He told Brandt that the executives who talked about Screen Art were as bad as the shanty Irish and the fugitives from the cloak and suit trade.

Benét sent along the 10 per cent he owed Brandt for the previous four weeks' salary. "I enclose a check, due you, for 400 more drops of Uncle Tom's blood. Don't waste it on riotous living. I worked for it." He passed on to Brandt some news of other friends inside. Sidney Howard—"lucky Sidney," said Benét—had finished his contract and was departing immediately. Arthur Hammerstein, asked by Griffith how he was getting along, had replied, "Just ready to jump in the river." Benét's anger was directed at the misuse of time and talent.

"Nowhere," he told Brandt, "have I seen such shining waste, stupidity and conceit as in the business and managing end of this industry. Since arriving, I have written four versions of *Abraham Lincoln,* including a good one, playable in their required time. That, of course, is out. Seven people, including myself, are now working in conferences on the 5th one, which promises hopefully to be the worst yet. If I don't get out of here soon I'm going crazy. Perhaps I am crazy now. I wouldn't be surprised."

The deranged quality of the period was heightened when somebody forged his name in New York to a $600 check, and was then made ugly by a story in *Variety* that Considine, the producer, had ordered changes in Benét's script for the good of the producton. Benét was merely amused by the embarrassment of the Guaranty Trust, which had to restore the financial loss, but the second episode touched off an uncharacteristic harshness. He felt that Considine, deeply involved in the current maneuvers at Universal, had taken a pot shot at him in lieu of a direct attack on Griffith.

Benét, normally easy-going and tolerant, and impervious to personal attack, was thoroughly aroused. His professional reputation was something else again. "This story must be retracted at once," he wired Brandt, "or I will sue. Please get busy on this immediately. Get in touch with Authors' League." Considine backed down, telegraphing his denial to *Variety* the next day. "All serene," Benét told Brandt. "Drop matter."

The brief skirmish was symptomatic of what Benét objected to in Hollywood. He knew that there were in Hollywood inumerable men of talent and honesty, for he had worked with some and met others, but it was plain that as a rule they were almost invariably victimized by interference and officious supervision. Once, after a particularly destructive story conference on *Abraham Lincoln,* he phoned a friend who had been in Hollywood for some time: "Aren't there any men of principle in this goddamn town?" "No," said the friend, and hung up. Benét's feeling as a craftsman was the one he described later, discussing a colleague's account of script-writing, as "the puzzled wrath and impotence of the writer who wants to do work, after all, no matter how much he is paid, and can't find out how it is to be done. For he has come to a land where a story isn't a story but a conference." [5]

He was interested in the technical problems and he had no patience, then or later, with the thesis that Hollywood and adult movies were somehow absolutely incompatible. "What [Max] Miller has left out of his book," he said in 1936, commenting on Miller's embittered account of life in the studios, "is the fact that good pictures are made, from Mickey Mouse to *The Informer*." He was impressed by the scripts which men like Oliver Garrett and Dudley Nichols were filming, and he cited the two former newspapermen in 1930 as "doing original work for the screen which hasn't been thought of in some other form—novel or stage play—first." [6]

He attempted that same kind of freshness in his own script for *Abraham Lincoln*. Despite the concessions and the intrigue he was able to give some distinction to the film. There was nothing he could do, however, about the executive insistence that the cast be inflated with superfluous bit parts. One version from which he managed to cut sixty pages, he told his wife, had "every historical character & incident in it except Millard Fillmore repairing the White House plumbing." Nor was there anything he could do about the beautiful young mulatto who was suddenly written into the slave ship scene at a conference —"scantily clad," the script read, "showing her slim, sensuous figure." Nor could he prevent the vulgarity that required Mary Todd to appear in a ballroom gown "cut very low for the time."

But he protected some of the sense of Lincoln as a folk-hero, and he captured the mysticism of the Lincoln temperament. He managed a sardonic portrait of Mary Todd to accompany her breasts. "You and Mr. Lincoln,"

238

said a friend of the lady, "will make a great man." He had assessed the Hollywood instinct for the colossal; he sought to control it in his scene directions. "Open out on a ballroom," he wrote. "Ballroom should not be too de luxe and there is a good deal of pioneer atmosphere." He made longhand changes in the final script right up to rehearsal time, all of them intended to make the dialogue less literary and declamatory.

"Well," said the midwife who delivers Lincoln, "he'll know who his paw is, anyhow, and that's more'n his ma knows about her paw."

There were brutal, realistic touches, as in the bucket brigade disposing of negro corpses on the slaver, and the captain's harsh line, "We won't make much money this trip." Many of his best touches were in the staging. "They are the religious, kindly sort," he wrote of the women who attended the passing of Ann Rutledge, "who love death-beds." It was characteristic of Benét that, having just lost a lot of money himself, he should then devise a scene in which Lincoln's horse was repossessed by the sheriff.

"On the whole," Benét told his wife after the script was finally okayed, "I don't think it will be such a bad show when Griffith gets through with it. Not as bad as we thought for a while." Considine now told him it was the greatest script he'd ever read. "No thanks to him," said Benét sourly. They urged him to stay on through rehearsals, on an extended contract. "I won't," Benét told Rosemary, "& I know damn well they can't make me. I'd do it if you were out here, but not as it is." Griffith wanted him to start work on another story, this one about the Alamo; the director promised him not only a higher salary but also a percentage of the profits.

Benét, however, wired his wife that he would be leaving at the end of the week. "Will not stay here for another picture so don't believe papers." He delayed his departure several days when Griffith asked him to stay over for one final conference, "with the great god Schenck himself," but on February 8 he was finally released. He drew his final thousand dollars. "Meet me Chicago next Friday," he wired Rosemary, "and how glad I will be. Love and rejoicings. Steve."

The rejoicing was short-lived. Benét was severely ill throughout the spring and summer of 1930 and again during the first half of 1931. California's damp climate, coupled with the susceptibilities which remained from childhood scarlet fever, brought on the arthritis which would cripple him so sorely for the rest of his life. He was using a cane when he got back to New York in mid-February. He passed the next six months of 1930 and the winter and spring of 1931 being treated by various doctors; they speculated with various diagnoses and various remedies.

The only satisfactory relief came from sun and rest. They spent both summers in Rhode Island, this time renting a house in Peace Dale from their friend Pierre Hazard. In 1930 they stayed on in Rhode Island until November before going back to the city, hoping that the sea air and quiet life would provide a cure. Benét, as always, was reticent about his personal affairs. He rarely mentioned his situation; only his extreme stoop and obvious stiffness betrayed his pain. "The wages of sin-ema," he remarked wryly to Alfred Bellinger when the latter asked about his health.

The effect on his work, however, was clear evidence of his distress. Two reviews, a pair of short stories, some light verse in the *Delineator*, the Phi Beta Kappa poem called "The Island and the Fire," and the brief "Hymn of a Reveler" were the extent of his published work in 1930 and 1931.[7] It was his most unproductive period since leaving Augusta at the age of seventeen; it was, in fact, the only prolonged stretch of nonpublication he had experienced since 1915. It occurred at the very time when his new reputation had made possible new opportunities. A more devastating piece of professional bad luck would have been hard to devise. His weariness was evident in an uncharacteristic refusal to oblige his publisher's request that he read at the Barbizon.

"I'm afraid I'm not yet up to facing an audience," he told a Doubleday official in September 1930. "I'm a lot better but still seem to get unduly tired for the silliest reasons."

His ill health was made the more poignant by the creative vitality and purposefulness he had shown in Hollywood, and by the effectiveness of one of the two 1930 stories he did manage to finish. Again Brandt used the *Elks' Magazine*, this time for a forceful treatment of the nineteenth-century folk-heroes of the American rivers. Benét called it "Little Golightly," another of his imaginative projections of the national relationship between the forces of turbulent American nature—the forests, the prairies, in this case the rivers—and the American character.[8]

It was an agonizing eighteen months in every sense, for his mind was as robust as his body was frail, tumbling with the image of a new long poem about the settlement of the West. Even the atmosphere of Rhode Island was a constant stimulant. "Some of the life," he told Bob Mc-Clure, "is nearer the best of early America than anywhere else I happen to know. It may not seem so to the natives but it certainly does to the visitor." He went up to New York from Peace Dale for several days in the late summer of 1930, to see a doctor and attend a showing of *Abraham Lincoln*. Both experiences were frustrating; the doctor was bland as ever, and several damaging changes had been made in the script after the final version was approved. He had a long talk with Dan Longwell, however, who was as always responsive to Benét's ideas about America.

Longwell suggested that the problems of research and narrative might be clarified if Benét had a fairly large and detailed map to work from. Longwell, whose acquaintanceship among students of Americana was extensive, told him about an excellent cartographer at one of the western universities. Benét thought the suggestion over and wrote Longwell about it in the fall. The scope of his conception and the excitement of the project were clearly evident.

"It would really be an enormous help to me," he told Longwell, "if such a thing could be made. What I want particularly is the main routes Westward, the Nollichucky Trace, Delaware Water Gap, the Natchez Trace, the route or main route North through the Five Nations and Sir William Johnson's country, then the Oregon Trail, the Sante Fe Trail, the line of the Southern Pacific and Union Pacific, the Chisholm, and finally the Lincoln Highway indicated."

In "The Island and the Fire," the poem which he read at Harvard in June 1930, and which the *Saturday Review of Literature* published in October, Benét made a tentative step into this material which would finally emerge as the posthumous *Western Star*. "The Island and the Fire," in fact, had a little of the same relationship to *Western Star* as the "Invocation" had to *John Brown's Body*, though its roughness of verse and cloudiness of

statement were reflections of the discomforts and post-
ponements within which it was written.

O spirit, weary with the love of earth,
Broken beneath her riches,
Your wounds are bound at last, your wounds are healed
By fire and salt, by darkness and the tide . . .

Benét never incorporated "The Island and the Fire"
into *Western Star,* however, and he insisted on a number
of changes before he permitted it to be published. He
made additional minor revisions for its publication in
his *Ballads and Poems* in 1931. This volume of selections
from all his previous volumes of verse occupied most of
what little strength he had during the fall and winter
of 1930. He weighed and rejected the earlier poetry with
the self-criticism which had developed in him since the
success of *John Brown's Body.* One of the reviewers
complained that he had "left out much that might safely
have been included." The critic conceded, however, that
"in pruning it down to the lowest levels he has made a
notable book." [9]

It was characteristic of Benét that he did not attempt
major alterations of any of the poems, even though some
of them had been written as long ago as adolescence.
He either omitted poems altogether or included them in
essentially their original form. "One cannot rewrite, after
fifteen years," he said in a brief Note, "without changing
the work completely." This was more than a reflection of
his newly critical attitude toward his work; it was part
of his basic honesty. He would stand on the record.

Ballads and Poems, published in February 1931, in a
regular trade edition as well as a limited printing of two
hundred and one copies, was thus a representative selection of all the verse he had written, save for *John Brown's*

Body, during the period from 1915 through 1930. It was well reviewed—"one of the finest books to appear in years," said *The Outlook*—and in a depression year its sale was a respectable one for a volume of short poems. Benét was scrupulous in his insistence that it not be an exploitation of the success of *John Brown's Body.* He refused to write an introduction for the volume, and he balked at Doubleday's effort to disguise the book as something it wasn't.

"I've been thinking over your suggestion of either *American Ballads and Poems* or *American Names* ever since I got your letter," he wrote Harry Maule, who was the book's editor, "and hope you won't think me pig-headed for not wanting to use the word American with this particular book. It's rather hard to explain, but, in the last analysis, this book *is* a compilation, a great number of the poems in it are not American in subject, and I simply don't feel, after a good deal of considera-tion, that that particular adjective belongs on the title-page. I know *Ballads and Poems* has no particular kick in it . . . But I don't think American belongs on it—too many Greek girls and knights. Sorry."

Gradually Benét began to recover his health. He could work for longer stretches now and by the spring of 1931 he was more free of pain than at any time since the beginning of 1930. In April he finished the first short story he had written in more than a year. "American Honeymoon" was a crisp, satiric portrait of contemporary manners; Benét was not surprised when it was rejected by the circulation magazines. He was pleased to have it bought in July by *Harper's Bazaar.*[10] "That's very nice of Charlie Towne," Benét told Brandt, "and I'm delighted." It was a reminder, however, that magazine restrictions had not changed during his absence. He was almost broke now, the Hollywood money dissolved by months of inactivity and heavy medical bills. He set to work on material and situations which he hoped he could keep within the taboos.

"Here's some light summer reading for the chewing-gum trade," he told Brandt in June 1931, enclosing a new story. "Try and get it swallowed by some large editor."

It was a bitter period, as his tone indicated, for it meant a return to the fictional trivialities he had fled five years before. Such stories were now all the more distasteful to manufacture because in the interval he had enjoyed the eighteen-month security of the Guggenheim Fellowship, the creative satisfaction of *John Brown's Body,* and the brief financial prosperity of 1929 and 1930. "I have cut about 800 words of this story," he wrote Brandt in December 1931 about a story which had been questioned by an editor, "and that is all I can or will do. If Hartman isn't satisfied with that, tell him to send it back. There has to be a certain development and progression in fiction whether editors like it or not. The last story they almost took, they thought was too short. In fact, they're all crazy."

His bitterness was apparent even in the most stereotyped of his fiction itself. "Nobody ever looked unhappy in snapshots," reflected the central figure of his "Days of Sunshine," which Maclean's published in January 1932, "nobody ever looked regretful. The people were always about to do something interesting." [11] One of the stories he wrote during the summer of 1931, "The Crime of Professor Sandwich," Brandt was unable to sell anywhere; another, "A Death in the Country," made all the familiar editorial stops before finally being sold to *Harper's.*[12] It was one of the best stories he had yet written, a moving and adult account of growth through pain, and

Harper's paid it the editorial compliment of printing it immediately, ahead of material that had been bought earlier, but it became a symbol to Brandt and Benét of the hazards of writing fiction that was too good for the market.

"I am busy," he kidded Brandt, at a time when the agent was urging him to come up with something salable, "on my plans for turning 'A Death in the Country' into a five-act drama in blank verse to be produced by the Associated Morticians of America."

Benét was nevertheless a thoroughly professional writer. He did not often produce work that was unmarketable or limited to the quality magazines. The rest of the stories which he wrote during this initial period of new health in 1931 and 1932 were harshly tailored for the trade; they were sold readily to *Pictorial Review,* the *American Magazine,* the *Saturday Evening Post*—his first sale there—and *Delineator.*[13] "Here is a story," he wrote Brandt, enclosing a new one, "with, at least, a worthy moral." He felt well enough now to accept a lecture assignment at Wellesley, and in 1932 he undertook some reviewing again for the *Herald Tribune* and the *Saturday Review of Literature.*[14]

Despite the short story sales, however, he could do no more than hold his own financially. Editors did not pay until stories were published; most of them now had heavy backlogs of material, bought for friendship's sake in many cases to encourage writers through these depression months. Often it was six or seven months between the time of a sale by Brandt and publication of the story. Benét was still being treated expensively by doctors, and now too, in the fall of 1931, they had to find a larger home; Rachel, their second daughter and third child, was born on October 22. "Weight 9 pounds 10 ounces," Benét wrote his friends, "and quite enter-prising."

They moved from the 95th Street apartment, renting a house on 69th between 2nd and 3rd Avenues. It was more comfortable and nearer the center of things. "We like the house," Benét wrote Bob McClure, "and it has a backyard where I am going to plant grass-seed and tulips." It was owned by the Rockefellers, Benét ex-plained, "but hardly one of their choicer properties. It looks like something you build out of those pink stone building blocks when you are a child and has more waste hall-space than the Grand Canyon." It was, how-ever, he added, "abnormally quiet," and his arthritis seemed to benefit from the antique register-heat.

As his domestic responsibilities increased, on the other hand, his expenses naturally went up. Stephanie and Tommy were both in private school, the doctors' bills continued, and though Brandt managed to ward off any cuts in his story price, neither was it likely that prices would go up. His long walks each day showed him a New York that was in trouble. Shutters were up on the stores all along Madison Avenue. He was sick-ened, he wrote Bob McClure, by the 1932 conventions of both political parties—"the nadir of the United States of America," he said—and he himself was going to vote for Norman Thomas.

By October 1932 he felt that a whole period of his own and the national life was dead and finished. "I think fifteen years are over," he concluded. "I didn't think they were till this Fall." He was working hard, and he felt well again, but both the times and his luck were bad. He spent the late spring and all of the summer of 1932 on a short story which turned into a novelette. As always his problem was the disorder which invariably

247

developed whenever his imagination was aroused by a situation originally designed to be formula fiction.

"This is merely to let you know that I am not dead," he wrote Brandt in a brief note in July, "and have been working on the long story. It's taken more time than I expected for I rewrote the second section completely and, I think, improved it a good deal. I think I have something, if I can get it the way I want, and do it right. At least I feel I want to more or less shoot the moon with it, and that takes time. I'm in the third section now. It will certainly run 30,000 words, maybe 40,000. If I could, I'd get it about the size of Willa Cather's *The Professor's House*. But I don't know whether that will be feasible."

The note betrayed the pressures under which he worked. There could never be any true structural or thematic compatibility between a conception that was part magazine serial and part something as sensitive as *The Professor's House*. "It was a pleasant and healthy summer," he told Bob McClure in October, "though I have had more trouble with this stinking novelette than I've ever had in my life. I now think I've done it from the wrong point of view and ought to do it over again from another, which is always a help when you've written The End and sighed. The trouble with it is that one character in it is too good to throw away, and so are some of the scenes, but the whole thing isn't baked right. Writing is sometimes as enjoyable as prickly heat."

He had to break his concentration repeatedly in order to write something immediately salable. "Here's a vapid little short short story you might be able to work off," he told Brandt. "I have been trying to work [the] long one but it hasn't quite jelled." It never did jell; four months of hard work was gone, with very little money earned during that period and none to come in later as its fruit. When his brother asked him for a loan in the early fall of 1932, Benét was unable to help him.

"I wish to God I could!" he wrote Bill. "Maybe some money will turn up in the next week or so and if it does, I'll ship some along. But just at the moment I'm stony, with a $260 insurance premium to pay and the children's school bill ahead, if we send them back, not to speak of the rent and the coal."

His difficulties were made worse by the closing of the Chicago bank where Rosemary's mother had her account. It looked as if Rosemary would have to rescue Mrs. Carr with the little which remained of the money she had inherited after her father's death the previous year. "I'm sunk not to be immediately helpful," he told Bill, "and God knows I wish I could be. But I just haven't got it—and if I don't get some soon myself, we'll probably be out in the Park."

He was further discouraged by executive changes at *Country Gentleman* which brought in editors less sympathetic than Hibbs and Reed to his Oldest Inhabitant stories. He was no more able now than in 1925 and 1926 to improvise one synthetic story after another. "We continue to exist," he wrote Dick Myers in Paris, "one jump ahead of the sheriff, me writing short stories to run between the fashion-drawings and the article on how to cook bullock's-heart for a formal Valentine dinner, in the better women's magazines." He went back to the American material, and he was particularly pleased with "The Yankee Fox," which he finished in December 1931. It was turned down not only by *Country Gentleman* but also by the regular buyers of his contemporary stories. Again he talked his situation over with Carl Brandt.

"I should like you to think over the possibility of getting a new market for this variety of story," he wrote the agent. "It is much more my kind of story than a story like 'Serenade,' and, if it were possible to make some sort of profitable connection, I could do a series on the line of an American *Puck of Pook's Hill*—though hardly, as you will agree, with the same ability. Nevertheless, it seems to me that a series of rather simple, romantic stories, American in background, with a certain fairytale quality might have a chance of appealing to the larger market in this particular time, when nobody very much wants to read about the depression any more. Would the *Post*, with its new color-work, be interested in such a series?"

Brandt, as always, was tireless in his efforts, but 1932 came and went without any editorial response to the idea. "I've only sold one story in the last four months," Benét told his brother. He was desperate enough now to tell Brandt to negotiate with Hollywood when the latter talked to the agent about Benét's doing another picture. Nothing came of it; it was just Hollywood talk. "There is nothing like the movies," Benét wrote Dick Myers, "except soap culture and zymotic diseases."

The short stories that he valued continued to receive awards and honors in the annual O. Henry and O'Brien selections, but, as he told Brandt, "I usually have to pay the rent about the time somebody gives me a medal or a testimonial." He began to shop around for the hack work which he had not done since 1925. In this one respect his situation was more advantageous than in 1925. The success of *John Brown's Body* had created for him a new professional resource: lecturing.

He disliked being away from his family, and he detested the general atmosphere of the lecture hall, but he did a conscientious and workmanlike job; he was always asked to come back again the next year. It was relatively lucrative—in 1931 he was asking, and sometimes getting, $350 a lecture—but it always left him weary and often ill. He kept his humor and his perspective despite the easy adulation. "As for the fee," he wrote the dean at Wellesley, when she confessed that their budget was overtaxed, "I will come for $150— modestly between Mr. Frost and Mr. Eliot, if that will be of any assistance."

Norman Foerster invited him to spend ten days at the University of Iowa in the spring of 1932. He gave several lectures and held conferences with the young men and women from the Writers' Workshop. He was a great success, and almost twenty-five years later Wallace Stegner could still remember his impact. "His lecture," said Stegner in 1955, "was probably the first I had ever heard that bent poetry to the uses of exposition, and at twenty-one or twenty-two I was so excited by it that I went pouring up afterward in a most uncharacteristic state of euphoria to tell him with fervor that I wished I had written that." [15]

At Iowa Benét met Paul Engle, whose work would be so affected by his own, and he formed other friendships with the young poets and novelists. He liked the atmosphere at Iowa, with its intelligent and balanced program in the creative arts; though he had little sympathy with the critical position of most literary humanists, he acquired considerable respect for Norman Foerster, director of the School of Letters. He drank prohibition liquor with the graduate students, and read to them from the galleys of MacLeish's new *Conquistador*, and talked about poetic technique. He resented the time it took from his writing, however, and though he was fairly well paid—$500 for the ten days—a large part of the money was spent on traveling. "God did not make me to be an influence," he told Rosemary. "He meant me to sit on my rear and write."

There were only just so many lecture engagements available each year, however, and there was only one University of Iowa. He wrote several more Oldest Inhabitant stories and the reaction was the same; nobody wanted them. "The winter has had its usual animations," he wrote Bob McClure, "recently grippe, an unusual number of babies among our friends and acquaintances, and the almost constant breath of the sheriff on the neck." He talked with MacLeish, now the editor of *Fortune*, about doing an article for them on children's books. Dan Longwell collected some statistics and background material for him about the juvenile field. "Well," Benét told his brother toward the end of 1932, "this is all perfectly mad and I have faith in the United States and art, but if present conditions keep on, I'm afraid I'm going to be in a hole. I should say a rather long one, too."

12. Younger Poets
and Other Americans

*. . . at least there is somebody in the White
House who isn't afraid of his shadow.*[1]

GRADUALLY things began to get better. Just as 1932
had seemed to close out one period for himself and the
nation, so 1933 was slowly launching a new one. "I can't
say it's been a bad winter," Benét wrote Bob McClure
in March, "for we've all been well so far and the children
have gone ahead at school." He was still scrambling
financially from one month to the next, he told McClure,
and 1932 had certainly been an ill-chosen year in which
to increase his life insurance premiums, but the sense of
disaster was lifting. "That incredibly lengthy corner
seems to have been turned," he said.

The change was signaled in a small way by the sale of
an Oldest Inhabitant story to *Pictorial Review*.[2] "Young
Lochinvar" was not one of the best of his American tales,
but it was a gay and lively sketch of the meeting between the Oldest Inhabitant and aviation. He was even
more encouraged when "The Yankee Fox," the excellent story he had written in December 1931, was finally
bought by *Woman's Home Companion* and published in
June.[3] The *Saturday Evening Post* had brooded long

over "The Yankee Fox," and Benét amiably made several changes for them before legitimately snarling a bit when they finally turned it down.

"The other comment," he wrote Brandt when the latter passed the *Post*'s note on to him, "seems to me a little foolish. I have already specifically stated that it was the sort of country where people went out with their hounds whatever errand they happened to be doing. Naturally they'd take the hounds with them, when they went on a lynching-party. And, in this case, they'd certainly take them not because they didn't know where the hero was—but specifically to humiliate him by chasing him out of his house with the descendants of the hounds his grandfather had brought from England. Hasn't anybody on the *Post* ever seen a Southern possum hunt or a Southern mob? What a lot they've missed."

It was heartening to have the story sold, however, and in the summer of 1933 the *Post* did buy his new "The Bagpipes of Spring." [4] This was a contemporary story of Park Avenue, better than the worst of his magazine fiction but not comparable to the American material. Even here the *Post* was skittish. Brandt urged Benét to keep his temper with them; it would be worth it, the agent reminded him, to get established there. "Thanks for your nice letter," Benét wrote back from Peace Dale, "and also for the good news about 'The Bagpipes of Spring.' Why does the *Post* always fuss about prices so—however, you're perfectly right and I'll be glad to have the money. Can you get it for me as soon as possible as I have to pay the rent."

He finished an article for *Fortune* on the United Press, though now he had to row with Ralph Ingersoll, the managing editor, when the latter seemed to be fiddling a research assistant out of his pay. Two other new stories were sold to the *Delineator*. "I know one thing," Benét wrote Paul Engle, who was at Oxford now as a Rhodes Scholar, "the dead weight, the black chill of last winter, that lay on the spirit like frozen blood, is gone." [5] He was heartened by the President's inaugural address, his earlier mistrust of Roosevelt lessened now like that of most American liberals.

He still met shocking poverty and distress as he walked the New York streets each morning before settling down to work, and one day he saw a very respectable-looking old man take off his shirt and carefully wash it in a stream in Central Park, but it was encouraging to have national decisions as positive as the March closing of the banks. Benét watched a handsomely dressed citizen who left the Guaranty Trust that morning with tears running down his face; Rosemary told him about a woman who brought $6500 in gold to the bank when it reopened. Yet the slow, sluggish restoration of national confidence was unmistakeable. "Things are popping and boiling," he wrote Engle, "things are happening, there's a different smell in the weather. How much of it is Mr. Franklin Delano Roosevelt, I don't know—I think a good deal. I'm for him, for one."

Benét's sense of relief, as always, was accompanied by new verse. He was still hard-pressed financially, however, and the poetry he wrote in 1933, save for an ode to his grandfather which he did at the request of the University of Georgia, was uncharacteristically connected with the perennial burden of his debts and bills. It was equally connected with his private life, for now he was reading aloud in the evenings to his children, and it was also linked in part to the abortive research he had done in 1932 for a *Fortune* article on juvenile litera-

255

ture. All these factors solidified in May 1933 when he attended an exhibition of children's books at the New York Public Library. "Superb," he noted in the diary he had just begun to keep, and the stimulant of the exhibit stayed in his mind over night. "Think of doing book like English *Kings and Queens*," he noted the following day.[6]

He phoned John Farrar, who along with the Rinehart brothers had left Doubleday, Doran to form the new firm of Farrar and Rinehart, Inc. He and Farrar had lunch two days after the Library exhibition, and discussed the idea. Benét now thought of calling the book *Presidents and People*. Farrar encouraged him to go ahead with it. Benét talked it over with Rosemary; they decided to do it together. Benét had begun work on a novel that winter—he had owed Doubleday one since 1928, when he accepted an advance on *The Silver Dollar* —and now he scrupulously wrote Dan Longwell of his plans. He was badly stuck anyway on the novel, he told Longwell, which he was thinking of calling *James Shore's Daughter*, and he hoped that a spell of light verse would give him some perspective. "I don't think it will take time away from the novel," he told Longwell. "The two things are so different."

Benét's conception of the book included good illustrations as an absolute necessity. He talked it over with Charles Child, who had returned from Paris and settled in Bucks County. Child did some sketches and they all had lunch together—Farrar, Child, Benét, and Rosemary—at the Benéts. They decided to go ahead with it. "Thought of children's book," Benét wrote in his diary two days later. "Ought to be very amusing if we do it right."

He and Rosemary agreed to divide the men and women, he to do the former, she the latter. Benét wrote his first one on June 5, "a jingle," he noted in his diary, "about Peregrine White & Virginia Dare," and every day thereafter for the next two weeks he wrote at least one and sometimes two. He spent a couple of days with Child in Pennsylvania, and they talked some more about the project. "He was a wonderful collaborator," Child said later. "Wonderfully flexible, and no excessive pride or ego or vanity." Child had the normal mistrust of writers held by most artists; though he had known Benét since the days in Paris, he was startled by his fairness. "Steve never made any special demands or insistence on priorities."

Child in turn drove up from Pennsylvania to Rhode Island in July, after the Benéts had again rented Tom Hazard's house, and they worked out some more of the sketches. Sometimes Child would make the drawing before Benét wrote the text, on a suggestion from the poet. "How about an Indian," Benét might say. "He's standing to one side, looking toward the reader." Benét and Child agreed that what they wanted was enough bite in both the text and drawings so that there could also be the adult appeal which all good juvenile material possesses; they rejected an earlier image of the book as a primer. He and Child enjoyed the collaboration; the verse and the illustrations reflected their merriment. "This sanctimonious old sneak," Benét wrote of Daniel Drew,

> Pretended to be poor and meek,
> But all he cared for, first and last,
> Was making money just as fast
> As he could get it in his claws,
> In spite of justice, right or laws.
> He toiled not, neither did he spin,

257

But how he raked the dollars in!
(The process suffers various changes
But still occurs, on Stock Exchanges,
Where there are things called bulls and bears.
And people sell what isn't theirs
To buy Amalgamated Pup
Because they think it's going up,
And then, with quite a sickly frown,
Find out it's really going down.
They didn't know, but someone knew
And someone got the money, too,
Someone, in fact, like Daniel Drew) . . .

He worked hard on some of the verse; the ones on Lincoln and Lee he wrote and rewrote. Others came easily, done in a single sitting with no more than a change or two the following day. He wrote the ballad of the clipper ships and the one he called "Western Wagons" with gusto and roll. He gave to the individual portraits the kind of shrewd, relevant moral which a child would understand and its parent savor, and some, like the one on Jefferson and the final stanza on Lincoln and the interpretation of Grover Cleveland, were fresh and acute as characterizations. "They call you rascal?" says Jefferson to the reader.

They called me worse.
You'd do grand things, sir,
But lack the purse?

"I got no riches.
I died a debtor.
I died free-hearted
And that was better.

"For life was freakish
But life was fervent.
And I was always
Life's willing servant.

"Life, life's too weighty?
Too long a haul, sir?
I lived past eighty.
I liked it all, sir."

They worked all through July and August, trying to
get the volume, which they'd decided to call *A Book of
Americans,* ready for fall publication. "This kid's book
has taken a lot of time," he wrote Brandt in early September, "but I'm feeling fine and like work." The verse
and the pictures were finished by the middle of September. Benét spent a day at Farrar's office looking
them over. "Most pictures superb," he wrote in his diary
that night. "Hope they don't overenthuse the book." The
limited edition was ready for signing at the end of
October. "Really looks very well," he concluded, "and
like an entertaining book."

The trade edition was published on Armistice Day.
It got good reviews—"moving, lasting poetry," said
Lewis Gannett in the *Herald Tribune*—and it sold surprisingly well. "It tided us over a poorish financial
period," Benét wrote Paul Engle. Passages from it were
anthologized regularly, and printed and reprinted in
such columns as F.P.A.'s "The Conning Tower." It was
done in braille, and several of the stanzas were set to
music; it was still in print twenty years later. Like many
readers, Benét himself was always partial to Rosemary's
lines about Nancy Hanks.

"You wouldn't know
About my son?
Did he grow tall?
Did he have fun?
Did he learn to read?
Did he get to town?
Do you know his name?
Did he get on?'"

Benét always stressed to interviewers that his wife was the author of those stanzas, and of "Jesse James" as well as all the women in the volume. He emphasized, however, that it was he who wrote the dedication. "To Stephanie, Thomas, and Rachel," it read, "our other works in collaboration."

Benét was occupied that summer with other people's verse as well as his own. In June he was asked by George Parmly Day, head of the Yale University Press, if he would accept the editorship of the annual competition called the Yale Series of Younger Poets. Benét told Day he'd be delighted. He still owed the Press a great debt, he said, for *Young Adventure*. "The Series has always been an interesting one," Benét added, "and most certainly deserves carrying on, especially in these times, when it's harder than ever for younger writers to get their work in print."

Benét had become increasingly conscious, ever since his trip to Iowa, of these professional dilemmas of young American poets in a depression period. His friendship with Paul Engle—whose first volume, *Worn Earth,* had just been published in the Series—had made him even more aware of literary obstacles which were more severe than he and his contemporaries had encountered in the early 1920's. In Rhode Island he had met the young Providence poets who were publishing their work in *Smoke*. His old teachers at New Haven were constantly sending talented undergraduates down to New York to see him. "I think the public, or rather the very small poetry-reading public," Benét told George Day, "is or can be interested in young unknown writers." He brought the point of view of a writer to his new editorial chair. "But," he cautioned Day, "it takes a little advertising."

The Series was a well-established but rather local one. During its initial period, from 1919 through 1924, there were two volumes published each year on the basis of semiannual contests. In 1924 Edward Bliss Reed, Benét's former instructor, became editor. Reed initiated the policy of having a single winner, though he continued to hold two contests each year. Now it was decided to have a single competition, with manuscripts due in the spring, and the winning entry published in the fall. Benét received the thick parcel of poems in late June.

"I have prayerfully read the fifteen mss.," he wrote the Press on July 4, "and have finally decided on *Girl in the Mirror* by Shirley Barker as the best candidate. It's the most ambitious book of the lot and the best unified—and she has narrative ability and a very good feel for New England. Also, as she seems to be a junior at New Hampshire, considering what her age must be the book really shows promise, though, like all beginning writers, she is influenced." [7]

It was the inauguration of an enterprise which Benét continued for the rest of his life. During his editorship the Series achieved and maintained national status for the first time; the Press, revealingly, felt it necessary to appoint poets as prominent as MacLeish and Auden as his successors. The quality of the winning verse was considerably improved during Benét's tenure; this in turn encouraged a better grade of submissions. Benét wrote a brief foreword for each volume; this, too, increased the prestige of the Series and the circulation of its books. He worked hard over the manuscripts each year, reading all of them rather than permitting the Press to make a preliminary selection. He made constant suggestions about the format and promotion of the Series, and he sent copies to friends like MacLeish and Phelps and Hervey Allen in order to stimulate interest.

Each year he wrote many of the unsuccessful contestants personally; each year he spent a great deal of time finding commercial publishers not only for previous winners but also, often, for the rejected authors. "Nobody before or since," said a member of the Press in 1955, "has done anywhere near the amount of work as Editor that Steve did." [8]

For many of the contestants Benét was their first and often their most durable connection with the professional literary world. They relied on him for every conceivable kind of counsel; some attached themselves permanently to him. They sent him subsequent work for criticism, sought his advice on publishers and agents, and came to see him when they visited New York. They brought their girls and fiancées around to meet him, and he wrote letters in support of their applications for fellowships and for jobs. Edward Weismiller, to whose *The Deer Come Down* Benét awarded the prize in 1936, had a relationship with him which was typical of those that developed from the Series.

"It seemed to me that I owed the real beginning of my 'career' to him, as indeed I did," said Weismiller in

1956, "and then I would not have put the word in quotation marks. He was a very wise person, utterly kind; only seeing him and having him glad to see me, willing to talk to me, meant a great deal to me. A great man, talking to me as though we were both quite ordinary people! Obviously it was possible to be a poet and a human being too; I had hoped it was, but how, at that age, is one to know?" [9]

All of them, even those whose manuscripts he rejected, were impressed by his breadth of taste. In an artistic area of intemperate partisanship he was as responsive to the new metaphysical poets as to the more traditional lyricists and narrative writers who were closer to his own work. He had little patience on the whole with proletarian verse, finding it imitative and poorly disciplined, but he patiently read the denunciations and the philippics. During his editorship Benét gave the first recognition and publication to poets as diverse as Norman Rosten, Muriel Rukeyser, James Agee, Margaret Walker, and Joy Davidman. His decisions and manner, the poet Frank Merchant remembered, were "remarkable for being free of any literary factionalism." [10]

His basic editorial principal was that the Series should not only reward present achievement but also try to encourage poets who seemed to have promise of further achievement. His judgment was astonishing in retrospect; each of his choices continued to be a productive writer. "What I keep looking for," he told one of the young poets, "is the live nerve, the live person speaking." [11] In 1934 the Press suggested that they ought to screen the manuscripts first, since there were now more entries than ever before. "Don't worry about overworking me," Benét wrote back. "I'd be glad to read 50 manuscripts in the hope of getting a good one." He dealt, patiently but without false encouragement, with the grievances and ill temper of disappointed contestants.

"I realize the difficulties you speak of that poets have these days in getting their work published," he told one of them in 1933, "and I am sorry to add to them. However, the Yale Press has room for only one book a year in its Younger Series, and I have to pick the one that seems to be that best. Yours didn't seem to me to be that best and that is all I can say. Except this—I could wish that instead of using the Hamlet frame, you had invented a frame of your own. Of course, it is up to every man to do his work as he sees fit. But if you could create a symbol of your own for the thing you want to say—well, that would be doing something." [12]

Muriel Rukeyser remembered his extraordinary kindness when the Press was publishing her *Theory of Flight* in 1935. Her manuscript was a difficult one typographically. "He saw the book through every detail," she remembered later, and she recalled with equal gratitude his flashes of insight when she came to his home to discuss her work with him. "Your interest," Margaret Walker wrote him in 1941, after a long correspondence which followed the rejection of her manuscript, "has encouraged and reassured me in an unmeasurable way." [13]

In 1934, when he was reading the second year's poems, Benét insisted on a redivision of the financial arrangements. "I have been thinking about the Yale Series," he wrote Eugene Davidson at the Press, "to this effect. It seems rather disproportionate to pay me $250 for reading the mss. when the lucky boy or girl who wins the competition can only make, at the most, $100 if he completely sells out the 500 copies of his book. I therefore suggest that you pay me $150 and pay the winner of the competition the other $100 as an outright prize, exclusive of any royalties his book may earn in addition. After all, I'm old and tough."

Davidson agreed, but the next year urged Benét to reconsider and take back the extra hundred dollars. "No," Benét replied, "I very decidedly want the $100 to continue going to the poet." In 1934, when he awarded the prize to James Agee, he argued successfully that both the Series and Agee's book would benefit if Mac-Leish wrote the foreword. "I'll pay him for it," Benét explained to Davidson, "and it seems to me it would be pleasant to get a little variety in the prefaces, now and then. In this case, particularly—as MacLeish knows Agee while I've just met him." MacLeish agreed, and Benét sent him a check for seventy-five dollars; this left him an equal sum as payment for having read forty-two book-length manuscripts.

Benét was particularly mindful of the urgency of financial reward, for his own work continued to receive august honors that had no immediately negotiable value in a depression year. His short stories were winning citations. He received an honorary degree from Dickinson College, and the annual Roosevelt Medal for distinguished poetry. "I don't know quite what you do with a medal," he wrote Basil Davenport, when the latter congratulated him on the award, "except carry it around in your upper breast-pocket and hire somebody to shoot you in it, so you can say afterwards that it saved your life—but it is very nice of them and I am pleased to get it."

Now, with the Yale Series behind him until the next year, and *A Book of Americans* completed and published, he went back to work in the fall of 1933 on *James*

Shore's Daughter. He had begun the research months before. The entries in his diary were brief and repetitive. "In public library most of day, reading Gustavus Myers' *Great American Fortunes* and books on the 1900s." He was hoping to make this novel not only a statement about a specific period in American history but also a comment on the nature of the American rich. He had seen rather more of them than most middle-class American writers.

A few of them were his friends; many of them were his acquaintances. He had attended a university which belonged to them and been a member of their societies and their fraternities. He had rented their apartments and houses and now, in New York, his children had their offspring as classmates. He had read with interest Bob McClure's unpublished fiction about the California variety; he and McClure analyzed them in their letters. "Whenever anything touches the rich," he wrote McClure, "they immediately retire behind their secretaries into their money like a hermit crab retreating into its borrowed shell."

He began writing at the end of January. From the beginning *James Shore's Daughter* was a painful and wearing task. He was anxious to write a novel that would not shame *John Brown's Body;* this could not be another *Young People's Pride.* And yet, so far as his fiction was concerned, he had done little but write and rewrite *Young People's Pride* during the past ten years. He had evaded, through the American material, some of the restrictions of formula fiction; he had written passages of imaginative exposition and fragments of genuine characterization. Always, however, his principal objective had been to sell in the popular market. He had learned a great deal about construction, but some of it was related to the plausibilities of jerry-building. Now he was attempting a major fictional truth after a decade of minor compromises.

He was thirty-five now, with a wife and three children to provide for. He had permitted himself to become committed to a style of living and a burden of responsibilities that were closer to those of his Yale classmates than to the characteristic writer or intellectual. There were private schools, and a maid, and a good New York address; there were Rhode Island summers and Brooks Brothers clothes, and one had to return the dinners and entertainment received from friends who lived on their unearned incomes or were as prosperous as the Barrys. He was thirty-five, and it was a hard time of life and a difficult year in which to write a novel that would have artistic strength and a meaningful statement.

Benét knew now a desperation that had never previously attended his working hours. He labored morning and afternoon on the novel, day after day. He shortened his walks and he worked in the evening, and even the arrival of good weather did not lessen his resolve. "A lovely goddess day," he noted in his diary, "spent chiefly indoors by me, still working on the infernal J.S.D. But there is a kind of work that makes more work."

There were days when he wrote no more than three hundred words, though he had often written a ten-thousand word short story in three sittings; there were days when he spent seven hours at his desk and wrote almost nothing at all. "Worked morning afternoon and evening, getting satisfaction out of writing but very little ahead on the book." There were other days when he did no more than try to clarify the theme and structure. "Spent 6 hours hard thought on book," he wrote in

267

his diary in May, "but go nowhere. Nothing really accomplished."

He was reaching for a wisdom and artistic purity which, save for *John Brown's Body,* he had not cultivated in a persistent way for ten years. It was not easy, at thirty-five. He almost gave it up. "Thought of junking novel completely but kept on finally." In May, as he had told Longwell, he became so bogged down, still on the first section after three months, that he withdrew to *A Book of Americans.* In September, back in New York after the Peace Dale summer, he returned to *James Shore's Daughter.* "Reread mss. of novel, seeing what it should be but not how to make it so."

He was tired and discouraged. He had worked all summer on the children's book; he had enjoyed the work, and he was satisfied with the book, but there should be some respite. There was none. There was instead the awkward, slippery manuscript of *James Shore's Daughter.* "For some reason," he noted in September, "very fogged all day—probably letdown after book finishing. But must get back to work at once for finances never worse & plans all uncertain." He resumed the dogged labor. By October he had revised and finished the first two parts of the novel. Now there were days when he was so tired that he fell asleep at his desk. It took him a week to get the third part started. "Worked hard, morning & afternoon, getting nothing done—to my desperation."

Finally he saw the proper form for the third section. At the end of the month, at half past one in the morning, he finished that section. He began the fourth and final unit the next morning. He was feeling now, with unfamiliar weight, the strain of those multiple tasks by which he earned a living as a professional writer: the interruptions to do a review, or give a reading, or hastily revise an old short story in the hope that Brandt could sell it on the strength of the Roosevelt Medal publicity; the delays and humiliation when he went downtown to borrow some money from Carl, the letters to answer, the young writers' manuscripts with the notes asking him if he'd mind reading them. "I would give a lot," he wrote in his diary now, "to get any kind of real peace & stability to do my own work."

He finished the fourth part and again he uncharacteristically went over the manuscript for painstaking revisions. "Know I can finish it in a few days, if I ever get a few days." He completed the revision at the end of November, "at 11:40 AM," he noted. He had put himself through a punishment that all but a handful of fellow writers would have regarded as cruel and unnatural; a few of his contemporaries, had they chosen, could have reminded him, sanctimoniously but with truth, that the cruelty of his labor had been magnified for him precisely because for ten years he had let it become so unnatural. Even so he wasn't content. "Not what I want," he concluded after one final reading of the manuscript, "but the best I can do. It should be a masterpiece in a small way—and it is not." He took it down to Brandt's office and that night, he said, he sat coma-like in the living-room after dinner, and at 10:30 went to bed.

His travail with *James Shore's Daughter* was not over. Brandt telephoned in a day or two; he doubted very much that the novel could be sold serially. Again there was the same new note of weariness in Benét's diary, altogether alien in him and carrying with it a forbidding sense of uneasiness. "This whole time," he wrote, "is a silly period during which people give me gold medals but I have no money to live on and no time or place to do my work—and little likelihood of getting either."

A few days later he got Brandt's check for $225, representing Doubleday's advance less the agent's 10 per cent, "which goes immediately," Benét noted, "on rent etc." He was cheered the next week when Dan Longwell told him how much he admired the book. He continued to take a special care with the manuscript. He gave a set of galleys to his Uncle Larry, and another to his cousin Andrew Jones, both of whom had lived abroad a great deal; Uncle Larry had known the various European capitals during the period of which his nephew was writing. He told Stephen that the story was an interesting one and that all the historical details over which Benét had sweated were correct save one: James Shore could not have had a private telegraph line in Paris at that time. He also remarked dryly that although Stephen included a great many French phrases when his characters were in Paris, he employed no German or Italian ones despite several scenes in Rome and Switzerland. Benét took the hint; in the galleys he cut a great deal of the French out of the dialogue and exposition.

He was still depressed when he finished checking the galleys in February, though he made a number of changes and then checked the page proofs as well. "It's too well written & not well enough constructed. However the critics thought [Sinclair Lewis's] *Work of Art* a good book & they may think so of this." His gloom deepened when Longwell told him at the end of March that publication had been postponed for three weeks. Benét had hoped to know by the first of May whether or not the book was going to make any money. "I have seldom felt more depressed or at my wit's end than I do now." His author's copies arrived in the middle of April. "I think it looks swell," he wrote Longwell, "and am very pleased with the way you've done it. I couldn't ask for a better presentation. I don't know what the great American public will think of it, as a story, but anyhow, you've done your job. Thanks."

There was a well-organized parade of publicity. He was interviewed and did a broadcast and signed the limited edition; there were lunches at the Algonquin. None of this was a help in getting on with new projects, but he was in no condition to work. He was staking more on this book than on anything he had ever written. He hoped that it would reprieve him financially; he longed for an interval of peace from debts and bills. If he could also get a little ahead on money, he could spend the summer on the long poem about the settlement of the West. It was six years since he made his first notes on it, and he was no further along on it now than he had been then.

As much as anything, however, he was looking to *James Shore's Daughter* to restore his professional self-respect and assurance. For the moment he lost the poise of a writer who had published earlier and more consistently and in greater quantity than any of his contemporary peers. "Sleep badly," he noted on April 23, two days before publication, "wake early. Have sort of buck-fever about book, wondering about its reception."

There was a cruel indecisiveness to the reception. *James Shore's Daughter* did not meet the partisan vindictiveness that withered Fitzgerald's *Tender Is the Night,* published that same year under somewhat the same personal circumstances for Fitzgerald as *James Shore's Daughter* represented for Benét. There were good reviews in the Sunday *Times* and *Tribune,* a bad one in the *Sun,* and a hedge by John Chamberlain in the influential daily *Times.* "Will bring in no cash customers," Benét noted glumly after reading Chamberlain. The book sold slowly for the first few weeks. Benét could justify only the mildest extravagances. He bought his wife a chiffon nightgown, and he got a bookcase for the house; he bought a dozen plants at Macy's for his garden, and a fielder's glove for Tommy.

In mid-May, however, Longwell telephoned to say the book was going better. By the first week in June sales had passed ten thousand copies. "Not bad," Benét wrote in his diary, "but a bad year nevertheless." After all, the five hundred dollars he'd gotten for *The Silver Dollar* in 1928 would come out of these current royalties; he'd had another $250 in late 1933, and a second $250 in February. The bills could be paid, but there would be no summer of poetry. The book had been a major effort. It was his best novel, the finest piece of long prose he had written, though subsequent lovers of his work rarely rediscovered it. The writing, as even he himself conceded, was tight and finished, the structure, though the past tense made the narrative occasionally sluggish, was better than he had thought it. It was a mature and thoughtful book, and as near a full use of his prose talent as he had yet achieved. "The style," said Herschel Brickell in the *North American Review,* "is admirable; he writes with poetical economy and insight." [14]

A number of the reviewers, to Benét's relief, stressed that the novel was "worthy of the poet of *John Brown's Body.*" His sexual realism, essential to the milieu he was describing, was offensive to the *Catholic World,* though their reviewer found it otherwise "a solid piece of fiction." The English reviewers were warmly enthusiastic, and only here and there, from the New York *Post* and the *New Republic* in particular, were there the sour, party-line charges that a novel about the past was necessarily and automatically an escapist retreat from the present.[15]

It was satisfying to have completed a book that had given him so much trouble. In May and June of 1934, with the bills paid, he was able to work with more peace of mind. The challenge of *James Shore's Daughter,* and the way in which he had met it, did not, however, encourage him to undertake now a similarly ambitious project. Instead he withdrew to short stories. His spirit had been shaken by the demands he had put upon himself.

"I've been over [the manuscript]," he had told Dan Longwell in February, "as I'll never go over anything again."

He was almost cheerful as he returned to hack work. He sent Brandt four new stories during the next ten weeks. "God be with you," he told Brandt of one of them, "if you try to read it!" The bills were paid, but new ones were coming in. There was a flurry of Hollywood negotiation in July. Brandt sounded him out. "I'd be glad to adopt *Dotty Dimple* or the works of the Marquis de Sade," the author of *John Brown's Body* and *James Shore's Daughter* wrote back, "for $1250 a week. So don't hesitate."

13. Angry Poet

Taxi strike going on but don't see any of it in this neighborhood. . . .

THE middle years of the 1930's, and of his own thirties, thus became for Benét a period of personal and professional crisis. The artistic duress of writing *James Shore's Daughter,* and the plain reality that he simply could not afford that kind of labor financially, nor perhaps temperamentally, invited him to slip permanently into the role of proficient hack. It was a tempting fate.

The luster of *John Brown's Body* would always give him a vocational edge over his competitors. It would be easy to rationalize his compromise from year to year, on the basis of domestic responsibility and momentary expediency. There would be the fragmentary notes for the long poem on the settlement of the West as occasional consolation; he could tinker with the poem for a few weeks every year or so. There could be Hollywood sorties in the winter and a writers' conference or two in the summer as a purge. That kind of an American literary career was being practiced by many of his contemporaries; from Washington Irving to Ben Hecht there was ample precedent for the self-limitation of one's talent.

Benét walked the very center of this particular professional road from time to time, and he was never completely removed from its environs, but from 1935 until his death he also traveled another route. He came to this alternative path as a result of various conditions. The insistence of his creative instincts was an important factor. So was his boredom with formula fiction, and his deep feeling about America; so, too, were such elements as his friendship with Archibald MacLeish, his profound admiration for Franklin Roosevelt, his appalled horror at totalitarianism, and his devotion to the concept of freedom. It was not an easy road, and none of these factors could ever have been much more than temporary irritants without his own determination to chart such a route.

"It is one of the hardest things in the world," he said later, "for the popular writer who has made a success at one sort of thing to branch out into another field. The bread-and-butter pressure is all the other way. 'Give us some more of your delightful stories about Southern mountaineers—or New York policemen—or Andaman islanders.'" [1]

Benét had learned this truth each working day from 1925 until this present moment. His stories about the American past had been resisted by every editor save those at *Country Gentleman* and the *Elks' Magazine*. He was encouraged and rewarded to remain faithful to the light contemporary material of his initial magazine successes. As a poet he was identified with the loose, folk verse of *John Brown's Body* or the rollicking wit of "King David." Editors urged him to maintain the familiar forms and tone; even the circulation magazines solicited verse from him for national holidays and tributes to Washington and Lincoln and, once, to Colonel Lindbergh. "Sorry," he wrote Brandt in 1931, when *Country Gentleman* had offered him a large price for such a poem. "I have tried to make Mr. Washington come down off his monument but with no success."

Benét was an acute and pitiless analyst of his own situation; he had begun to keep a diary for that very reason, as its candor and self-examination showed. "There comes a time in the life of every writer," he said once, "when he has said the first things he had to say and cannot say them over again in just the same way—and yet he must go on writing." [2] For him that time came in the mid 1930's.

Ever since 1915 his primary preoccupations had been the twin and frequently conflicting ones of a poetry that was largely subjective and the private relationships of his family and friends. His concern with politics had reached its peak during adolescence, when he created a temporary socialism from which to challenge the Colonel's benign conservatism. Like most of his generation he then became indifferent to politics as an undergraduate and later as a young man. He was thoroughly uninterested in the presidential campaign of 1920, Tom Chubb remembered, and such occasional political rallying-points of the 1920's as the Sacco-Vanzetti case got only the mildest response from him.

As late as 1932 he washed his hands of both major political parties and made the negative gesture of voting for Norman Thomas. Chubb felt that it was the rise of Hitler which aroused Benét to a public literary role. In reality, however, he could not insulate himself in 1933 and 1934 against the grim depression winters in New York. Long before he was fully aroused by totalitarian savagery he was stricken by the sight of white-collar workers

276

wielding relief shovels in their shabby overcoats. "They were not used to digging," Benét wrote McClure. "You could tell by their shoulders."

MacLeish, far better informed about the national scene than most American writers of the period, was living in New York now. The two couples were congenial and saw a good deal of each other socially. MacLeish's own poetry was shifting from the personal concerns of his early verse; now he was formulating his concept of public speech as the role of the poet in time of national emergency. In the fall of 1933 Benét spent a long dinner and evening with MacLeish, Farrar, and Hervey Allen. "Talk about really doing something about what we believe in," Benét noted in his diary, "both as regards literature and democracy."

At the same time his friendships with young writers were acquainting him with a literary generation which was obsessed with politics as his own at that age had been engrossed by aesthetics and individual self-fulfillment. They brought for his inspection and verdict not only their manuscripts but also their plans for new magazines and their manifestoes of protest. Benét was impressed by their conviction and touched by their confidence in him, which he characteristically regarded as misplaced. He was also skeptical of their optimism.

"Have lunch with ——— and his earnest wife at Automat," he wrote in his diary in 1934. "They are eager idealists &, like most e.i.'s, somewhat disingenuous as to the means they take to bring about the Kingdom of God."

He knew more about American history than any other major contemporary novelist or poet save Dos Passos. His creed as a liberal was grounded in his confidence in the American heritage and the good sense of the American

277

people. "No," he told Paul Engle, when the latter inquired about his politics, "I am not a revolutionary." From the beginning he was thoroughly hostile not only to fascism but also to Marxism. His convictions about liberal American government were as strengthened by the hostility of native communists to F.D.R. as by the similar hatred of the President by the American rich. "At the moment," he said with satisfaction in 1936, "every element I dislike most in the country is allied against Roosevelt." Much of his political thinking began in this pragmatic, intuitive way.

"Govt. starts selling gold abroad," he wrote in his diary in 1933. "All stuffed shirt Wall St. people against it—so feel rather for it, while knowing nothing."

He was diffident about his own ignorance of geopolitics, which was by no means as complete as he imagined or pretended it to be. He regretted, however, the grim self-assurance and monomania of the new literary generation. "The life of a young radical," he noted in 1935, speaking of a young poet, "strikes me as dreary, or rather ———'s life does. He is too busy thinking about economics to laugh." Benét was doubtful of all panaceas and wary of doctrinal infallibility.

The 1930's were a time of pundits and wise men. Benét instead thought of himself as a rather confused liberal. He suspected that most Americans, when their self-interest was not too much involved, were very much like himself in their confused liberalism. He shared with his friend Robert Nathan a kind of urbane good-will, though soon his own liberalism became increasingly militant. In a letter to Nathan, congratulating him on the canine hero of his current fantasy, Benét summed up in an epitaph of light verse his doubts concerning the various loud certainties of the period.

He was no Lippmann, I can see,
Nor Heywood Broun, nor Dotty T.
But he seems rather more like me.

For he was liberally inclined
But lacked their comprehensive mind.
They know who's who. They know what's what.
But he and I, I fear, do not,
Who sniff the legs of grief and mirth
And run bewildered on the earth.

For he was liberally inclined
But lacked the trained-dogmatic mind.
And yet liked living, wet or dry.
And so do I, and so do I.

As his political and social involvement became more and more broad Benét came to regard liberalism as a specific and definable creed, difficult to practice but essential to American principles. "If you're a liberal," he told a friend who was regretting its necessary ambiguities, "that means you're always out on a limb. It isn't very comfortable, on the limb, but then God never intended liberals to be comfortable. If he had, he'd have made them conservatives. Or radicals." Out of an historical perspective more extensive than the typical liberal's he found strength and verification. When Philip Barry despaired of America because of the vituperation of Roosevelt, Benét reassured him with tales of the invective which continually surrounded Lincoln. "His wide reading," said Barry's widow many years later, "made him much more knowledgeable about politics than Phil or the rest of our friends." [3]

Benét seemed to his friend Christopher LaFarge, the

poet and short story writer, to be almost the ideal representative of a demanding political position. "He had a truly liberal mind," said LaFarge in 1954, "which liked to entertain and examine other people's ideas." LaFarge remembered that Benét would not argue; he would only discuss. There was nevertheless a realistic quality in his thinking which made his liberalism a permanent creed. "Roosevelt has made his purpose plain," Benét rejoiced in his diary in 1934, "and united all the pigs and Bourbons against him, which is fine." It was this same realism as much as his knowledge of history which made him so mistrustful of the native communists.

"I'm not very sold on Marxism as a doctrine," he wrote Paul Engle in 1935. "They have built it into too cast-iron a theory, and life seems to take pleasure in fooling cast-iron theories. Also, the leading professors over here are a little too witch-burning to suit me."

He was invited out to the University of Iowa again, in the spring of 1935. The long train ride across half the continent was a tonic and confirmation. "As always, traveling these miles," he told Engle, "I was impressed once more. My God, the cows, the chickens, the fruit-trees, the ploughlands, the abundance, depression or no depression! It is just so completely different from any European scene—the enormous backlog of energy possibility, in spite of any number of mistakes and lots of crooks."

In the meantime, however, he saw in New York and at Peace Dale the less attractive side of the American scene. He met people, he said, who regarded even Paul McNutt as a red; he was equally angered by the distorted coverage of the Washington news by the New York press. His and Rosemary's active social life took them into homes where the most obscene innuendoes about Roo-

sevelt were regarded as documented fact. His sense of
what was valuable in America was deeply offended.
"It is curious," he noted in his diary after a summer in
Rhode Island, "how many Eastern people really behave,
once they've had money for 2 generations, with a sort
of would-be Divine Right." There was a violence now
in his reactions which replaced the earlier placidity.

"At Westbury," he wrote in his diary in 1933. "Go to
overstuffed, stupid ———'s for lunch. Where are you
going for the summer? Oh, what a party we had. We
missed you at Palm Beach, etc. Enormous estate. [They]
have made the supreme sacrifice by opening the golf
course for charity. Goyas, etc.—but God, what human
beings."

His sense of justice caused him to make a kind of foot-
note to this outburst. "Much better rich than ———,"
he noted a few days later of another host, but even here
his acceptance was qualified. "If one has to have [the]
rich, which may not be necessary." All but a handful of
his friends were rabidly hostile to the New Deal. Only
at the Century Club, and not always there, was he likely
to find himself belonging to the majority. His objection
to the anti-Roosevelt group was, as LaFarge pointed out,
that they would not discuss; they would only argue.
Benét joyously won their money when they challenged
him to bet against Landon in 1936, but often there were
bitter quarrels. "The election is in full swing here," he
wrote McClure in 1936, "but New York, thank goodness,
is a fairly impersonal place and I don't get into as many
fights as I would have in Rhode Island."

Ethel Andrews—married now to John Harlan, cor-
poration lawyer and future Supreme Court justice—was
startled to see a Benét who was aroused in an entirely
new way. When she was the hostess she tried to keep the

conversation off politics. Benét's identification of the opposition was harsh and bitter. "It is horrible," he wrote Paul Engle, who was still in England, "to see the nervous violence of the comfortable ones once they get the idea that one cent of their precious money is being touched. It makes you feel degraded. The patriots and lovers of America who put their money in Newfoundland holding companies—the descendents of signers who talk about people on relief as if they were an inferior breed of dog. What a sorry class of rich we have here—their only redeeming feature is their stupidity."

The state of the nation became more and more his primary concern. "Try to write after dinner," he noted in his diary, "but waste time in idle thought about political situation instead." What he hoped for, and this was the appeal for him of the New Deal, was simply an America of more genuine opportunity. "If we could have fifteen years of decent government, Federal aid and Robert Moses," he told Engle, "this would be a good city to live in. They might even build new schools."

The letters he wrote to Engle were an important release for him. He took special pains with them, filling two and three single-spaced pages with detailed descriptions of national events and acute characterizations of contemporary motives. Always he ducked the mantle of sage and pundit. "All this is subject to change without notice," he told the young poet after making some tentative predictions, "and I never pretended to be a prophet anyway." Now, too, his short stories had additional comment on the current political and social scene. For the first time he began to give to his stories of the American past a sustained contemporary relevance.

He wrote, in "A Man from Fort Necessity," a good story about the young Washington. It was published in

282

the *Saturday Evening Post*.⁴ The parallel between the hatred of Roosevelt and Washington was apparent. "You can say that he wants to make himself a king or a dictator, if you like," says the innkeeper who had served with Washington in the French and Indian Wars. "Every man to his own brand of politics. But you'll have to say it outside; not in my house. He's a man that likes his way; yes, I'll grant you that. I don't give a shinplaster for a man that don't, myself; other people may be otherwise minded. But as for that New York newsletter and what it says about him, you can put that right back in your pocket while you're drinking my liquor."

In the spring of 1935, his mind preoccupied with the native fascism of Huey Long, Benét wrote an even more detailed parable for the times. In "Silver Jemmy" he drew the parallel between Jefferson and Aaron Burr on the one hand and Roosevelt and Long on the other. The contemporary implications were harsh and telling. "He talked to me for some time," says the New Orleans aristocrat after an audience with Jefferson, "of his belief in 'the common man' and 'democracy'—beliefs which we know to be both subversive and impossible of realization . . . his influence is rapidly waning and his doctrine of 'the common man' has roused much resentment among the better educated. It seems likely that he will be the last President of this present confederation—and that the nation will then either fall apart of its own weight or give rise to some dictator." ⁵

These were the months, after all, in which the Liberty League was born; these were months in which some of the hostility toward Roosevelt, and particularly among the class of whom Benét saw so much socially, became pathological. Many Americans in 1935 were questioning the utility of a democracy, weighing various alternatives.

One of his friends announced emphatically that she would move to England—she didn't—if Roosevelt won in 1936. Benét listened to the tirades at Manhattan dinners and on Rhode Island beaches. Now, in "Silver Jemmy," he translated them into an historical perspective.

"It is the first time *you* have known them," the old creole tells his son, "the cries and the wild voices, the prophets of calamity. And yet they come not once in the life of a nation but many times. Your sons in their turn will know them, and their sons also."

Cosmopolitan, which eventually bought the story and finally published it in May 1936, was fearful of its theme and tone. They argued first that it needed more romance and a lighter touch. Benét made cheerful concessions to their anxiety about the love interest, but he refused to tamper with its basic statement. When a *Cosmopolitan* editor protested to Brandt that the story was too intellectual, Benét became thoroughly exasperated.

"If patriotism is intellectual," Benét wrote his agent, "so is the banking system—and Father Coughlin can fill Madison Square Garden by talking about the banking system, not about cuties. In other words, this happens to be a time when people are interested in things which might have been considered intellectual in '28. And any editor with brains can tie this story into the present with a ten word blurb. Doesn't the Cosmo think that a few men might like to read the magazine once in a while? This is a man's story, as I see it—but I'm damned if I think that's a defect, in principle."

The editorial timidity was chronic; it was not confined to *Cosmopolitan*. The *Saturday Evening Post* bought his notable antitotalitarian story, "The Blood of the Martyrs," but Benét was irritated by their attempts to soften its indictment. "Illustrator has done his best," he noted, "to portray all possible European types & thus avoid damages." Wesley Stout, successor to George Lorimer as editor of the *Post*, aroused Benét in memorable fashion when he objected to the opening paragraphs of "Schooner Fairchild's Class." [6] Stout's prose, as he denounced Benét's characterization of the story's central character in a letter to Brandt, was more oratorical than editorial.

Benét, Stout told Brandt, had created in Lane Parrington "not an individual but a stuffed shirt, an effigy of the conservative cause. It is a tract worthy of the immaculately conceived Harry Hopkins. I care not how ridiculous he may make his Parrington, as long as he does not offer him as a symbol of the blasphemy of opposing those selfless, consecrated knights of the Holy Grail." Stout thereupon suggested that the *Post*, which was then paying Benét $1250 a story, would nevertheless buy "Schooner Fairchild's Class" if the characterization of Lane Parrington was altered. Benét would have no part of it.

"I can't make any revisions," he wrote Brandt. "I wouldn't know where to begin if I wanted to. . . . The whole thing is pretty surprising to me—and pretty disappointing. Because if the *Post* is going to want the opinions of its editorial page stuck willy-nilly into its fiction—if you have to class-angle a story for the *Post* as you'd have to for the *New Masses*, only in reverse—there's no point in my trying to write for them. I can't work that way. Any magazine can make its own rules—but that seems to me a stupid policy for a general magazine. Where does Stout think he gets his three million circulation? From the Union League Club?"

Some of this kind of editorial pressure was removed when Ben Hibbs became fiction editor of *Country Gentle-*

man in 1934. Now Benét's Oldest Inhabitant stories were again welcomed there; his price rose gradually during the rest of the decade to $1500, and in 1934 and 1935 *Country Gentleman* bought and published four of his American tales.[7] The most interesting characteristic of these new stories was the confirmation they gave that Benét could not be labeled a merely regional or period writer. Beyond their common quality of a recurrent narrator they resembled each other only in their imaginative evocation of the American past. They might deal with the antebellum South or post-Appomattox bitterness, with the flatboat legends of the Mississippi or the covered-wagon caravans pressing across the mountains. He would write a clipper-ship story and a hunting story, a trotting story, a steamboat story, and a story about Yankee peddlers. Benét was roaming unrestricted through a hundred years of American history, the first genuinely national American story-teller since Washington Irving, more richly talented than the latter and thoroughly free of Irving's uneasy sense of American inadequacies.

Benét varied the historical fiction, as always, with a coating of trivialities, most of them published in *Redbook* and the *Delineator*.[8] "This is the Xmas story to Mr. Vetluguin's specifications for *Redbook*," he wrote Brandt in August 1935. "If he likes it, stick him for it." Here too, however, as with the more substantial material of the American past, there was editorial perversity. *Redbook* also craved revisions and simplification.

"I think that is a little whimsical on Mr. Balmer's part," Benét told Brandt, when the agent sent him the *Redbook* suggestions, "[but] Vetluguin is a good egg, I'd like to please him, and if you consider it absolutely necessary, I'll make the revision. But I would like to point out to him or to Mr. Balmer that I have to have a little fun writing a story of this sort or it isn't going to be any good. I'm perfectly willing to work to any sort of specifications, but I think I ought to be allowed to put in my own doors and windows. If you revise and revise, and put in this and take out that, it gets to be like the movies and the thing goes dead and flat."

Neither in the historical material nor in the contemporary situations could he be entirely free of the taboos and restrictions. This long period of concentration on short stories, extending almost without interruption from April 1934, when *James Shore's Daughter* was published, until the late spring of 1935, had given him a legitimate sense of financial security. "I've made some money," he wrote his brother, "paid up the back bills and hope to be a little flusher this winter than I was last." His ideas about contemporary issues frustrated and truncated by the circulation magazines, but enjoying a reprieve from old debts, he began his most productive season of continuous poetry since *John Brown's Body* eight years before.

The poems Benét wrote in 1935 and 1936, of which the most permanently distinguished was "Litany for Dictatorships" and the most immediately famous the Nightmare series in the *New Yorker*, had their origins in Benét's various anxieties. His major anxiety was the perilous condition of human liberty in the twentieth century. He examined a number of different kinds of beleaguered freedom: political freedom in the "Litany"; artistic freedom in the stanzas to Vachel Lindsay called "Do You Remember, Springfield?": technological freedom in the "New York" poems, and personal freedom in all of them.

The result was a group of poems, most of them written

between the spring of 1935 and the late winter of 1936, which he could collect with satisfaction in *Burning City* in June 1936. They gave new status to his role as a national writer. In 1948 F. O. Matthiessen would cite "Ode to Walt Whitman" as evidence of Benét's grasp of the American heritage; in the "Litany," Matthiessen felt, Benét recorded the issues "more affectingly" than any of his contemporaries. The *Nation* reported, quite rightly, that although the book lacked the high peaks of *John Brown's Body*, his growth was impressive. He was, said his fellow poet Donald Culross Peattie, "as nearly the national poet as any one has been since Whitman." [9]

Broad as his topics were, their original source was always the deeply subjective one which had been Benét's chief poetic strength since 1915. It was the quality which separated both him and these poems from the characteristic literature of protest of the 1930's. "She does not make the mistake of many young revolutionary poets," Benét had said approvingly of Muriel Rukeyser, "in thinking that a political statement is a poem because it is a political statement." [10] Nor did he himself make that error; he could not, since the poetic tradition in which he wrote was a personal one. Always, despite the grandeur of his subjects—Walt Whitman, the decay of a civilization, the preservation of democratic values—always these poems were superior to the conventional verse of a dialectic because of the intimate, nonportentous, unoratorical quality. Always there was the same relief from rhetoric which he gave to so brief a poem as "Sparrow."

> Lord, in your mercy let me be a sparrow!
> His rapid heart's so hot.
> And some can sing—song-sparrows, so they say—
> And, one thing, Lord—the times are iron, now.
> Perhaps you have forgot.

They shoot the wise and brave on every bough.
But sparrows are the last things that get shot.

Thus the poems of 1935 and 1936 were not only statements on the great questions but also intimate lyrics which examined his own situation as his thirties came to an end. Each group contained fragments of the other; this too gave the best of them a permanence that was rare in the social art of the 1930's. A basic theme, rising above the social declarations, was the recurrent celebration of the practice of poetry. He presented this statement in the large outlines of Whitman and Lindsay, and in the slighter verse of "Thanks" and "Reply," where the celebration was private and immediate, and deeply moving in its candor.

> It is a long time, long.
> And so much wasted, yes.
> And other men, oh, yes,
> All the clever, better-placed men.
> And so much bad work for bread,
> The work that crawls in the hand
> And that I would do again.
>
> A long time, very long, yes.
> And the lateness beginning, yes.
> And everything that you say
> And the door shut with a weight.
> O lightning, o forked bough,
> Raining from the great sky,
> The fire burns in the hand
> Even this late.

This, too, was part of the origins of *Burning City*. Benét was feeling in his late thirties, under the stress both of conditions peculiar to his own situation and of others common to all men in this decade of tension, a compulsion to restate the moments of his life. He looked back to one war in "Short Ode," ahead to another in "1936." There was a poem to his daughter and there were lyrics in which the presence of his love for his wife was dominant and tender. He celebrated the retention of his poetic gift—"The fire burns in the hand / Even this late" —as if in gratitude that it should still exist despite the uses to which he had sometimes put it. When an interviewer asked him why he had written "Litany for Dictatorships," Benét replied that he wrote it because he had to. The beginnings of the New York series, as he noted in his diary, had been the repeated nightmares of his own sleep. He described the poems as angry poems.

"Feel much like writing these days," he noted in August 1935. He wrote steadily all that summer and fall, the "Litany" in mid-July, "Girl Child" and "For Those Who Are as Right as Any" at the end of the month, "Sparrow" and "Old Man Hoppergrass" in August, and "Do You Remember, Springfield?" and "Memory" in October. All through the last weeks of November and before and after the Christmas holidays he worked on "Notes to Be Left in a Cornerstone." He finished it toward the end of January. The *New Yorker* bought it immediately, enclosing their check for four hundred and eighteen dollars. "Highest price ever got for a poem," Benét wrote in his diary. "Quite stunned."

The *New Yorker's* response was characteristic of the impact which these poems were having and continued to have. He mailed "Litany for Dictatorships" to the *Atlantic Monthly* in mid-July; two days later Edward Weeks telephoned to say that he would pay a hundred and fifty dollars for it and planned to break open the September issue to make room for it. Benét began to think in terms of a collection of the poems. Farrar and Rinehart, to whom he had shifted completely when Dan Longwell moved from Doubleday to the Luce organization, were immediately anxious to get the book on their spring list. By the middle of December 1935 the jacket had been designed by Charlie Child.

Now, with the book a visualized reality in both his own and his publishers' minds, Benét was pressed again; his bank account grew thinner and he wrote once more for a deadline. The *New Yorker* check for "Notes to Be Left in a Cornerstone" went immediately on the back rent, fuel, and phone bills. The winter brought ominous warnings about his health. "Try to work afternoon & evening but with no success. The cold seems to freeze up the vital juices. Also have a continual pain in the back." By February the easy, buoyant mood and circumstances of 1935 had vanished. "I must finish this infernal book—get so I dream about it—but I will not do it sloppily."

He completed "Ode to the Austrian Socialists" at the end of February, however, and in March "Short Ode" and "Complaint of Body, the Ass, against His Rider, the Soul." By the end of March the grotesque race between time and money reached a climax. "Must finish book— must also make some money." On April 11, the day he finished typing the manuscript and making final revisions, his bank balance was down to two dollars.

"Hand to mouth for last 3½ years," he wrote in his diary, "& still going on. Should be used to it but am not— takes my courage now. You lose, in time, the first flair, when it is exciting to be broke, work days at a stretch, and redeem finances by some coup."

In April he got a check from Doubleday for four hundred and fifty dollars of current royalties on *John Brown's*

Body. It was not even a respite; he paid the New York State income tax with it the same day. In early May, when he was proofreading the galleys of *Burning City*, his resources had again almost vanished; this time his account had shrunk to three dollars. The children's tuition had to be paid by June. He was encouraged by the publication of the book—"seems solid," he conceded—and by the high praise of most of the reviewers. What should have been a triumphant professional moment, however, was made wretched by poverty and self-reproach. "This degrading, humiliating and constant need of money is something that stupefies the mind and saps the vitality. Will I ever get free of it & be able to do my work in peace?"

Burning City sold well, yet he was still so broke in July that they had to remain in New York; the children spent a couple of weeks with Rosemary's relatives in Richmond. He borrowed two hundred and fifty dollars from Brandt. "Try to work on story in evening but no go. Owe lots of money. Am so tired of things being like that." He finished the new story on July 9 and sent it downtown to Brandt. "Will you give me a buzz on this?" he asked the agent. "I'm afraid it's a little long but I tried to get a lot of things in." Brandt read the manuscript and telephoned Benét immediately. "It's a honey," Brandt told him. He would send it to the *Post* right away.[11]

Benét had gone back in this story to the American nineteenth century, his imagination aroused by passages in Van Wyck Brooks' *The Flowering of New England*. As he did so often, he also found a portion of his situation in a timeless legend that was as much universal as American. The particular legend he chose was a poignant clue to his frame of mind in June and July of 1936. During those weeks he, too, would have entertained a proposition from Satan. The hero of "The Devil and Daniel Webster" was the New England statesman, but the author's kinship was with Jabez Stone, the bedeviled farmer who worked a rocky strip of New Hampshire land.

"The Devil and Daniel Webster" consolidated the national role which had been slowly materializing for Benét ever since the publication of the ballads of 1922 and 1923. Though he wrote the story in ten days, it was in a very real sense the product of ten years of labor. Its realistic fantasy and extraordinary plausibility came from a decade's drafts and revisions of those fifteen Oldest Inhabitant stories which preceded it. In Daniel Webster he had found an ideal folk-hero. Webster was ambiguous enough for productive characterization, less remotely sacred and frozen than Lincoln, majestic in his strengths and weaknesses, national in his values. Just as Longfellow rehabilitated Paul Revere, so too had Benét revitalized another tarnished hero.

Americans responded to the story in a way that astonished the *Post,* who published it in the issue of October 24. Soon the magazine wooed Benét and Brandt with an attractive contract that pledged four stories a year for $1750 for each story. When Benét stopped off at Brandt's office he found himself, he said, "quite the white-headed boy. *Post* depending on me, etc." His publishers brought out the story in hard covers; it went through eleven editions during the next twenty years and was still in print in 1957. There were deluxe editions from fancy presses, with elaborate illustrations. It was precisely the kind of permanent classic which Benét had once denied "The Barefoot Saint" to be, "a story you can read in an hour but which you keep remembering for a long time."

When it was given the O. Henry Memorial Award as the best American short story of the year, Harry Hansen, the editor of the series, reported that it was one of the rare occasions when all the judges were unanimously of the same opinion. "Second and third readings," said one of them, "convince me of its fine chance for as near an approach to immortality as a short story can attain." [12] It was as widely anthologized as any single American tale by an American writer. It reached continuous and additional audiences as operetta, one-act play, and full-length movie.

Benét had begun with no more than a title, taken from the work sheet on which he listed phrases that seemed to have the promise of a good story in them. Not until several months later did he read Irving's "The Devil and Tom Walker," which was often supposed to have been his inspiration. All he had was a title, "The Devil in New England." His initial conception, harassed by bills as he was, after the publication of *Burning City*, and anxious for a quick sale, was to have the Devil come to a modern small town. "Then I tried shifting it back into the past," Benét explained later. "It seemed a good idea but I didn't know what I'd have him do when he got there." [13] It was at this point that he first visualized Webster as the Devil's antagonist.

"I had always thought of him," Benét said in 1941, "as an orator with one hand stuck in the bosom of his frock coat, till I read of him in Van Wyck Brooks' *The Flowering of New England*. Then he began to come alive and I read more about him." [14]

He did a good deal of research on Webster in late June of 1936, as was indicated not only by this story but also by its successors in the *Post*, "Daniel Webster and the Sea Serpent" and "Daniel Webster and the Ides of

March." [15] Once he had fixed on Webster, the rest, he said, was easy. "Webster's strong point was oratory," he explained, "so naturally he'd have to meet the Devil in an oratorical contest and win." [16] The enormous success of the story required Benét to discuss it publicly in a way that he rarely did with his work.

"It's always seemed to me," he said later, "that legends and yarns and folk-tales are as much a part of the real history of a country as proclamations and provisos and constitutional amendments. . . . 'The Devil and Daniel Webster' is an attempt at telling such a legend . . . I couldn't help trying to show him in terms of American legend; I couldn't help wondering what would happen if a man like that ever came to grips with the Devil— and not an imported Devil, either, but a genuine, home-grown product, Mr. Scratch." [17]

After the publication of "The Devil and Daniel Webster" Benét became a story-teller to the nation. He could now write for the largest magazine in the United States stories about leprechauns and sea serpents, and about Nazi tyranny and American responsibilities. He wrote for the biggest audience that any American writer of his stature had ever possessed. For many of his readers his political and moral values were their only encounter with this particular set of national convictions.

His personal as well as his professional status was consolidated by "The Devil and Daniel Webster." The early summer of 1936 was the last period of truly desperate financial pressure which he had to endure. It ended dramatically in August, when, Jabez Stone-like, he found temporary prosperity: two more stories were sold to the *Post;* one of the studios unexpectedly bought the movie rights to a story called "Everybody Was Very Nice" for twenty-five hundred dollars; and Rosemary inherited a thousand dollars from an aunt whom she scarcely knew. "Thus ends," Benét wrote in his diary, "one of the strangest weeks in our lives." Thereafter his income rose rapidly on the strength of the Daniel Webster success; it leveled off at between twelve and fifteen thousand dollars a year for the rest of his life.

There were still the nightmarish intervals when insurance and rent and tuition came suddenly due at a time when he was caught between stories. And, as his income grew, he assumed new responsibilities. Now he gave his mother additional funds; when he was flush he sent her checks for two or three thousand dollars. He increased his contributions to charity; he gave generously to most of the antifascist organizations. He never knew complete freedom from financial tension, but "The Devil and Daniel Webster" gave him an earning power which now at least was more realistically in balance with his responsibilities.

He had discovered and disciplined his fiction talent in the big slicks, though he'd had to escape the prison first. "[Writing]," Benét told the short story writer Pauli Murray in 1939, "is a job to be done, like any job—it's a profession to be learned, like any profession. It isn't learned in a month or a year—it takes time. But it can be learned." For evidence—though he was without that kind of vanity—Benét could have referred Miss Murray to back issues of *Country Gentleman* and the *Elks' Magazine* and *Cosmopolitan*. More particularly, however, the story was public verification that now he was what could not have been anticipated on the basis of his earlier work for *Metropolitan* and *Redbook* and *Liberty*. He had become an important and revered American man of letters.

14. Man of Letters

*Finish the damn review and
send it off by boy.*

NONE of the multiple aspects of Benét's role as an American man of letters was unique to him. Each was duplicated separately by other writers of his generation. There were few of his contemporaries, however, and no one of his public and professional status, who undertook as many facets of the role. Those who lectured rarely edited; Benét did both. Those who served as counsel to younger poets and novelists did little reviewing; Benét did both. Those who were active in the affairs of such guild organizations as the National Institute of Arts and Letters were apt to be indifferent to political groups; Benét was prominent in both spheres.

Thus, one year, Benét noted that although it was only July he had already been asked to write a poem about the Great War, another about San Juan Hill, and a preface for a volume of Napoleon's correspondence, not to speak of requests to address the National Convention of Women's Clubs, adapt *The Man without a Country* as an opera libretto, and serve on the Pulitzer Prize Drama Committee. He declined the Pulitzer assignment on principle, disapproving of past coercion of their judges, and he was able to avoid the other invitations as well, yet in any given year from the middle of the 1930's until his death he was involved with half a dozen undertakings which related to his professional life but were not connected directly with his own writing.

Most of these activities—editing, lecturing, reviewing —brought in a minor but important share of his income. Each of them extended the range of his influence in the trade itself and within the society as a whole. The novels on which he reported favorably to Farrar and Rinehart, Inc., as their principal reader, were apt to be the novels which were then published by that increasingly important firm; the poets whom he selected for the Yale Series were the ones whose work thereupon received critical attention. The volumes which he co-edited with Carl Carmer for Farrar and Rinehart's Rivers of America series were widely bought; his voice was even more distinctly heard in his lectures and reviews.

He was fulfilling a role which only William Dean Howells had performed with equal scope in the twentieth century. Like Howells the fact that he lived in New York meant that he was at the very center of the life of his profession. It meant, too, that he was thoroughly available to colleagues and to aspirants. "In the last week or so," he wrote his mother in 1940, "I have advised a gent to get married and a gent to change his publisher and a gent to rewrite the Lincoln portion of his book."

Though he was primarily identified with the world of commercial publishing, Benét exercised an influence on avant-garde writing through his editorships and his friendships. When Valentine Gammell, patroness of *Smoke*, was planning to withdraw her subsidy from the poetry journal it was Benét who persuaded her to continue it. "Little magazines," he told Mrs. Gammell, "are the way to keep poetry going." He discouraged her plans to devote an entire issue to his own work; the function of the magazine, he said, was to publish new verse. It was also Benét who convinced Mrs. Gammell that *Smoke* should be open to poets of every kind, and particularly to what its sponsor unforgivingly termed the School of Unintelligibility. "They ought to be given a chance to prove they're good," he told her after reading some new verse which she had planned to reject. "This is a good poem." [1]

A large part of this side of Benét's professional life was practiced in private, through his correspondence and through what he wrote in his reader reports and said in his reviews. A portion of it necessarily had to be performed in person. His fondness for public literary life had never been great; as he became increasingly a celebrity he disliked it even more. "Too many people, too much talk," he noted in his diary after one such affair. "Oh God, these interesting people, these open mouths." He had a similar distaste for the rituals of literary publicity. "Go down & have informal pictures taken by Pinchot," he wrote, "i.e., lean over bookcase that isn't mine to read book I wouldn't be caught dead with."

His patience with ladies who kept salons and those who inhabited them was scanty. He was repelled by the bad manners, superficial taste, and bogus values of artistic enthusiasts. He had never quite recovered, he told Rosemary, from the woman who once introduced herself to him at such a gathering. "O, Mr. Benét," she had said, "you really must be some young God from Olympus come back to earth again!" What he enjoyed most were the small parties which he and Rosemary exchanged with the LaFarges, and the Moores, the Barrys, the Farrars, the MacLeishes, Dick and Alice Lee Myers. He endured the banquets and publishers' teas through his instinctive willingness to oblige his friends and a reliance on an extra drink or two. "I must say," he wrote his brother once, "that cocktails improve the intelligentsia."

He was invariably hospitable, on the other hand, to the young writers who virtually queued up to his door. "I would doubt very much," said the publisher William Sloane, who as a Farrar and Rinehart editor worked closely with Benét, "whether any young writer or editor ever went to Steve without being warmly received and helped to the utmost of his ability." [2] His own work might have profited had he lived somewhere less accessible than the East Sixties; his considerable services to American letters would have been sharply reduced.

From the moment Farrar and Rinehart began business in 1934 Benét was their most valued reader. "John Farrar consulted him almost instinctively," said Sloane, "particularly on fiction manuscripts." Benét's relationship to the firm was basically that of the literary adviser in an English publishing house; his authority was far greater than that of the typical reader in an American firm. He read anywhere from ten to twenty manuscripts a year for Farrar. The reports were never perfunctory; in a page or two of single-spaced typescript Benét presented an orderly sequence of analysis, appraisal, and suggestion. "These reports were masterpieces of their kind," said Sloane, "and almost always when Steve's verdict was favorable and we undertook the book, what he said about it provided our publishing approach and even often the actual words used in the catalog or the flap of the jacket."

Frequently Benét talked personally to the authors,

making suggestions and encouraging them to go ahead with revisions. Whenever Farrar himself or one of the editors felt they had made a literary discovery, they asked Benét to check their judgment. Other publishing houses frequently asked his opinion on manuscripts: Bobbs-Merrill, his classmate Tim Coward at Coward-McCann, Henry Holt when Sloane became trade manager there. He maintained a friendly relationship with Doubleday even after transferring to Farrar and Rinehart. He did an occasional report for his friend Basil Davenport at the Book-of-the-Month Club; had he lived, he would have become one of its five judges. Macmillan once sent him a long religious poem about the Virgin Mary; they were doubtful of its appeal as a trade book. Benét told them it was good work with an excellent chance of a substantial sale. Macmillan accepted his recommendation; during the next fifteen years they made twelve printings and sold thirty-eight thousand copies of Father John Lynch's *A Woman Wrapped in Silence*.

To this kind of work Benét brought an unusual combination of professional skills and experience. He was a shrewd judge of popular taste; he knew a great deal about narrative technique. His own achievement as poet and short story writer gave his opinions and reports a weight which few editors could match. His conception of the editorial function was both flexible and clear. "True criticism," he said once, "creative criticism, is one of the most difficult of all the arts. It must instruct without patronizing, judge without prejudice, know the best of the past and yet know what the new is about."

Benét's patience with a worth-while manuscript was limitless; his expectations were realistic. The writers and editors whom he helped were permanently grateful. "I owe a good deal to Mr. Benét," said the author of one of the volumes in the Rivers series. "His help made a good book out of a mediocre manuscript." They found him reasonable and consistent, and full of shrewd insights. "Just treat it as what it is, the spine of New England," he told a writer who was having trouble with his Connecticut River assignment. He was firm with the tendency of local pride to make the volumes a history of an entire region. "Write it your own way," he told another of the Rivers authors, "but keep in sight of the water." [3] Farrar and Rinehart got good value for the $750 they paid Benét annually as co-editor of the series.

"I suppose the only way to describe Steve," said William Sloane in 1957, thinking back to his editorial association with Benét, "would be to say that if I had a chance to be some other person whom I had known in my lifetime, I would prefer to have been Stephen Benét, not anyone else." Like most of the others who worked with him, Sloane's relationship with Benét was almost entirely a business one. It was an extraordinary response to a man who himself regarded his efforts as merely part of his job.

Even the audiences to whom he lectured felt some of that same kinship. Most of them were startled by the warmth they experienced, for he seemed at first an unimpressive figure without promise of excitement. They were dismayed by his diffident manner as he waited to be introduced by the evening's chairman, the latter inevitably more assured than Benét, his suit better fitting, his shoulders more square. Benét's air of fatigue and nervousness seemed to forecast a dry and spiritless evening.

"Then he spoke," a man who heard him lecture in 1937

at Iowa State College recalled, "and it all changed in that instant, & I realized that here was a man of deep sincerity, intellect &—I believe—a voice with great power. It was a memorable evening." [4]

Each listener concluded that Benét's effectiveness was limited to his or her sensibility alone; their response identified his lectures as personal and untheatrical, delivered by a craftsman discussing his trade. He talked to audiences as far apart as the model young gentlemen of West Point and the chattering ladies of the women's clubs. He spoke to earnest graduate students and blasé undergraduates, to innumerable book-fair visitors, to thoughtful meetings of Phi Beta Kappa and festive gatherings of Alpha Delta Phi. Even at a Kiwanis lunch in Iowa City to which Frank Luther Mott took him he was asked, to his dismay, to give an impromptu talk.

He lectured at many of the colleges and universities in the East—Middlebury, Wilson, Bryn Mawr, Wellesley, Williams, Amherst, Yale, Gettysburg, Harvard, Russell Sage, Brown, New York University, Columbia—and he made three separate trips to Iowa, twice to the University and once to the State College. He talked at the University of Chicago. He lectured as far west as Minneapolis and as far south as St. Augustine. He talked to high school students in and around New York and to the lads at Phillips Exeter Academy; he answered patiently the latter group's fearful questions about the Marxist tendencies of American writers. At Yale they were impressed by his urbane wit, which they approvingly likened to the *New Yorker;* in Iowa they responded to his simplicity and lack of affectation.

"What I remember," said one of his listeners twenty years later, "was the confident radiance of his person and the feeling he communicated of something I do not know how to describe, and for lack of a better phrase must call spiritual energy." [5]

Those whose judgment was more professional, and who could compare him to the great stars of the lecture circuit, had much the same reaction. "Of those who visited Iowa during my chairmanship," said Professor J. Raymond Derby, whose tenure at Iowa extended from 1930 through 1939, "Mr. Benét was emphatically the most effective. I have never seen [his techniques] equalled by an author-lecturer." [6]

Benét's success as a lecturer was not an automatic or easy one. Both his reserve and his instinct for privacy were offended by the entire process; he also had to work hard on the lectures themselves. He spent three or four days preparing a new one, and he was always doubtful of his success. "Lecturing, on the whole," he wrote his daughter in 1942, after a trip to Minnesota, "is not my favorite dish." His daily schedule in New York was normally so crowded that inevitably he wrote the lectures under pressure. "When I do make a speech," he warned a sponsor who wanted a copy beforehand, "I have to prepare it very carefully—and want to. I'd rather be over-thorough about it than otherwise." [7]

Normally he read poetry as part of the lecture, either his own or his contemporaries'; he tried always to make it a meaningful experience. He believed that poetry should be sung or chanted; many of his listeners were reminded of Vachel Lindsay. "Poetry," he told the monologuist Florence Locke, who had asked permission to give readings from *John Brown's Body*, "is not something to be read with the eye alone, it is something to be heard with the ear as well. When you read words on a page—unless you can hear them sing in your mind as well—you have only grasped half the intent of poetry. It has always been my belief that we needed great speakers and sayers of verse, exactly as we need great interpretative musicians—to give us not only the words but the music behind the words." [8]

Benét's own adaptation of this conception was personal and vigorous. "He tipped his head back and chanted," remembered one of the staff at Breadloaf, where Benét lectured in 1935 as well as 1928, "his voice having a volume surprising in so meager a man and a quality that sounded like a butcher sawing a bone. But it was oddly effective, probably because of his air of complete sincerity, and, after the attitudinizing and affectations of some poets we had heard, was very refreshing." [9]

His lectures and readings—"call it a lecture-reading," he once told a prospective sponsor, "like the *Herald-Tribune*"—brought him anywhere from forty to three hundred and fifty dollars. Normally he earned between a thousand and fifteen hundred dollars a year from them. Carl Carmer recalled that he and Benét, though they were co-editors of the Rivers of America series, met most frequently on trains that were carrying them to or returning them from the lecture circuit; Carmer likened this phase of the contemporary writer's situation to the wanderings of gypsies. It increased Benét's perspective on America; it preserved him from the provincialism of New York literary life. The cost to him physically, however, was considerable. Each year he returned home more weary; each year he set out with less gusto.

"Do I have to do any speaking?" he asked when notified in 1937 that Yale wished to award him an honorary degree in June. He compared the process to those other burdens which he regarded as necessary evils. "If I haven't been having grippe," he wrote his cousin Andrew

Jones, "I have been speaking, which is worse." What he preferred, if he had a choice, was the kind of seminar discussion which took place at the University of Iowa. It was the only aspect of his role as a public figure in which he felt real confidence. "Round table at 11 A.M.," he noted in his diary. "Liked talking there & did well."

His relationship with the young writers whom he met in that atmosphere, or to whom he talked individually after reading their manuscripts, was a more intensified version of his effect upon an audience. He himself, mistrusting the dilettante and the casual amateur, was thoroughly comfortable with their youthful intensity. His limitless appetite for reading meant that he was apt to be better informed about current writers than their instructors; his receptive breadth of taste meant that he was sympathetic to the new and strange. At a time when the professors of literature were still indifferent to Faulkner it was reassuring for graduate students to hear Benét confirm their liking for the southern fiction. One of them recalled being so excited by his interview with Benét that he ran most of the way back to his dormitory. Years later, no matter how different their own work was from Benét's, they remembered as mature professionals the help he had given them as unknown young men.

"His visit [to Iowa]," said R. V. Cassill in 1957, "marked a crucial turning point in my life. It was not merely that I gave up writing poetry soon thereafter and turned more resolutely to fiction, and it was not enough to say that he encouraged me, was kind, was instrumental in bringing me into working contact with Wilbur Schramm, Paul Engle, and others who were of great help to me for the rest of my college days. By some democratic magic he granted me the right—waiving all questions of merit or postponing them to later judgment—to think of myself as an artist. I have always felt the debt very deeply."[10]

The circle of Benét's literary retainers multiplied each year by a kind of fixed law of dependency. They came into his orbit through the lectures and seminars, through the Yale Series, through his relationship with Farrar and Rinehart. One poet would send another to him; they dispatched their roommates and their friends. His name was valued at Fisk and Howard and Atlanta, wherever talented young Negroes were in need of professional help. He served as a judge for the annual Hopwood Awards at the University of Michigan, and for the Shelley Award; for several years he read batches of poems for each issue of *College Verse* and chose the winning entries.

Always he sought the good work and the promising work rather than the merely acceptable. He protested the judicial apparatus of numerical averaging by which the Hopwood Awards were made. "That particular system," he wrote the University of Michigan officials, "seems to me to make for mediocrity. I'd rather have anybody's first choice than two or three people's second choice."

It was this kind of candor and realism which made him so successful with young writers. He stressed the technical aspects of writing; he urged them to think in terms of structure. He told the young novelists that writing fiction was like building a house; it was a question of getting everything into its place. "I can teach anybody with a moderate literary bent how to write a sonnet that scans," he said once, "or a short story that might sell."[11]

At the same time, however, Benét emphasized that the final ingredient was the intangible one of talent. He never pretended there was any substitute. "Nobody," he maintained, "can teach an original creator of the first or second rank, though he might help him to avoid certain mistakes." His prescription was always the same. "It is writing that teaches a man how to write." He suggested concrete exercises and he stressed again and again the need for clarity. "Don't use four adjectives when one will do," he told George Abbe after reading some of his fiction. "Don't use five long words to say, 'We were happy.' 'It rained.' 'It was dark.' Write of the simple things simply." [12]

He read the manuscripts carefully. When he discussed them or wrote letters about them it was always by specific reference to particular passages; he did not issue large aesthetic commandments. " 'Artistically' means nothing," he told a young novelist, "and is another two-dollar word in the wrong place. If you want to describe her hair, describe it. But don't tell me it was done artistically. It doesn't *mean* anything." He quoted from the manuscript to illustrate his point. "Words. And big words. Overdressed words. And yet vague, unprecise, giving no picture. Simpify, simplify. And don't use the thunders of the Last Judgment to drive a nail." [13]

He spoke those painful truths which are kinder than the bogus praise but more difficult to say. "He may have an unusual and interesting personality," he told a mother who had sent him her son's poetry, "but, so far, that personality has not got into his verse." He invariably apologized for his candor, but the principle seemed to him an inviolable one. "I'm sorry if this seems harsh criticism," he said once, "but if criticism is to have any value, it must be honest." Always he reminded them of fundamentals. "Fashions change in the novel as in other forms of art," he pointed out, "but there is still no substitute for actual story-telling." [14]

Benét sought nonetheless for something to praise, knowing it was fruitless to destroy a young writer's confidence. "A little success is good for all of us." Even here he tempered the applause. "Nor am I telling you," he cautioned Pauli Murray after congratulating her on an improved technique, "that these two sketches are works of genius, nor that you will get them accepted right away, or even that writing will be easy for you from now on. It won't and you will probably make several bushels of mistakes."

The young men and women were conscious of the nature of his method. "Since you scowl without malice," Norman Rosten wrote him in 1942, sending a group of new poems, "I shall be delighted to get your reaction." What Benét gave so generously was a blend of friendship and instruction. "You know how good it was for me when I was living in New York," Paul Engle wrote him from Iowa in 1941, "to come to your house and see the children. You were the only person I knew when I came to N.Y. Right now I wish I could talk over my next book with you."

Benét was impatient with laziness or evasion. "You've got to get to work," he told a young poet who had been idle and discouraged, feeling herself out of step with current poetic values. "You must read more of the modern poets, to learn what your own technique should be." He never concealed from them the role which luck would play in their futures, and the accidents of timing and coincidence. He talked to them realistically about the problems of the literary market. "After all," he said, "writing is a business." He presented them with the frustrating paradoxes of composition. "Labor over a style," he pointed out once, "and you spoil it; yet without work, you never acquire one." [15]

His generosity to young writers, and the effective way in which he implemented it, originated in forces more complex than instinctive kindness. It was surely a partial compensation for the mechanical quality of so much of the magazine fiction he had written in the past, and which even now was frequently required of him. Perhaps, too, it was an aspect of what a cynical friend once described as his lame duck compulsion; a few of the young men and women he labored with were not so much writers as vocational waifs. More particularly, however, it was a tangible acknowledgment of the help he had himself received in the past, from his family, from Henry Canby and others on the Yale faculty, from Brandt and Farrar and Dan Longwell. He taught through example and conference and lecture; he taught by correspondence and he taught, too, in the pages of the *Saturday Review of Literature* and the *Herald Tribune*, where hardly a month passed in which he did not publish two or three reviews.

He adjusted himself realistically to the modest critical standards of those publications; his reviews were discriminating, but as a rule they lacked the bite and force of either his lectures or his comments on individual manuscripts. He accepted the journalistic doctrine that book reviewing should be approached as an area of news coverage. He described the book and he sought to arouse the reader's interest. His evaluations were generous and his depreciation mild. Only occasionally did he deliver in his reviews the kind of frank judgments which made him so effective with young writers. "Most of the authors in this book," he once wrote impatiently in the *Saturday Review of Literature*, "write the short story as if they were writing with mittens on." [16]

Normally, however, he was asked to review the major

volumes of any particular publishing season, and often he chose the books himself; he wrote the notices for Sandburg and MacLeish and Freeman. His endorsement of such colleagues as Faulkner and Wolfe and Farrell, still treated a little gingerly by these middlebrow journals during the 1930's, was acute and emphatic. He wrote one of the first testimonials to Fitzgerald's achievement, several years before the Fitzgerald revival, and his comments on volumes that dealt with writing itself were always lively and shrewd.

"In the end," he said in the *Saturday Review of Literature*, discussing books and courses on how to learn to write, "it is your own laborious practice, your own deep-seated desire, and your own material, when you find it, that will make you a writer, not any book, any course, or any single criticism. I am sorry to be dogmatic but that is the McCoy. The class is dismissed for the day." [17]

He wrote twenty or more reviews each year during the late 1930's and early 1940's. In time he shifted increasingly from the *Saturday Review of Literature* to the New York *Herald Tribune;* the pay was better, and he was apt to get more space. He averaged about five hundred dollars a year from the work. He was one of Lewis Gannett's Monday guest reviewers in the daily *Herald Tribune,* in addition to his Sunday reviews. In 1940 and 1941 he and Rosemary did a series of literary profiles for Irita Van Doren's Sunday section.

As a reviewer Benét was an editorial comfort, according to Mrs. Van Doren; he was quick and reliable, and his copy came in on time. He wrote his reviews without malice and he did not use them as outlets for spleen or vanity. Several times he refused to comment on books he had already read and disliked a great deal. He was wary of inflexible critical principles, as he was wary of all dogma, and his effort was always to assess a book in terms of its author's intentions.

It was characteristic of his approach to reviewing that he did not find such a novel as *Gone with the Wind* a bad book, as did the ill-tempered and unrealistic, nor a timeless classic, as did the majority of the reviewers. "It is a good novel rather than a great one," he maintained, "by the impalpables that divide good work from great." He tried to be both workmanlike and generous. He did not regard his judgments as imperishable. "I had a tough time doing it," he once wrote Henry Canby, enclosing his notice of Elmer Davis' *Giant Killer*, "thinking so much of the book really good and yet so much of it mistakenly planned. Incidentally, if you think another reviewer would find things in it I haven't found, don't hesitate to call on one." His harshest verdicts were for material that was unprofessional. "The book would have been improved by cutting," he declared of a history of the Lee family, "and the writing is sometimes—well, sloppy." [18]

Reviewing, like all these compartments of his role as a man of letters, was nevertheless an additional invasion of his working schedule. He permitted it because of a mixture of those same motives which allowed him to be overgenerous with the time he surrendered to young writers. A review was also, on the other hand, a tangible assignment which one could solve by labor and competence. It could be launched and completed in a single day. It was not slippery and wearing, like a short story; one need not stare desperately at the wall in search of a situation or chainsmoke through two and three false starts. It was a kind of vocational narcotic which he resisted but which had at the same time a portion of the therapeutic compensation that accompanied the relationships with young poets and novelists. "——— comes in to have his story looked at," he noted in his diary. "Must get to my own work."

He owned a sense of duty which required and was satisfied both by the private aid he gave to unpublished manuscripts and the public judgments he exercised upon the published ones; good work should be endorsed, bad work should be denied. All of these motives, as well as the gregarious fraternalism that was basic to his temperament, found a major outlet in his membership in the National Institute of Arts and Letters and, later, its inner unit, the American Academy of Arts and Letters.

15. Academician

Get wire I have been elected to American Academy. This insures wreath for my grave but little else.

BENÉT was elected to the National Institute of Arts and Letters in 1929, at the age of thirty-one. The election brought him at an early age, professionally, into the single American organization which was entrusted by federal charter with the responsibility of maintaining and extending the arts on a national scale. He entered the Institute at a crucial period in its thirty-year history. His election was part of a grudging concession by such senior men of letters as Hamlin Garland and Robert Underwood Johnson that the new literary generation was a reality which required recognition.

It was not an easy surrender for a generation of writers who were not only professionally conservative but also deeply offended by the literary values of the current American renaissance. The group which was now in its thirties—Benét's generation—had in various proportions given its allegiance to such repugnant spokesmen as Lewis and Dreiser and Pound. The senior men in the Institute and in the American Academy of Arts and Letters, a kind of upper chamber which drew its fifty members from the Institute's two hundred and fifty, had no intention of seeming to endorse such freaks. And yet short of a calculated policy of deliberately allowing the Institute to perish, they had to make the best of a distasteful situation. By 1930 a significant cluster of new elections had been made. From their unappetizing successors the older generation chose six men and one woman. Their hopeful reliance on such ingredients as Eastern birth, Ivy League education, and Anglo-Saxon parentage was painfully transparent.

The new members, in the order of their acceptance, were Sidney Howard, Edna St. Vincent Millay, Benét, Philip Barry, and Lewis Mumford. Despite the presence of Frost and Masters, there was no authentic representative of the new poetry—Eliot, say, or Cummings, or Hart Crane—though Benét was sufficiently tainted so that one member declared he would not vote for him under any circumstances. Each of the seven had certain negatively redeeming qualities in addition to the strengths of pedigree and alma mater.

As a group, though they had all lived and worked abroad, they were not strongly identified, at least professionally, with the expatriate Americans. Rather they represented what might be called the New York wing of the literary renaissance of the 1920's. They were linked with such successors to the *Century* as the *Bookman* and the *Saturday Review of Literature* rather than such expatriate heresies as *Broom* and *transition* and *secession*. Each of the seven was in his various way a gentleman or a lady by the professional and personal standards of the Institute and the Academy. Each had received sufficient but not unseemly popular success.

It was an irony which would shortly be observed in wounded disbelief that among the seven—and he a graduate of Yale, a student of their own Wilbur Cross and their own Billy Phelps, a brother indeed of one of Johnson's own assistants on the old *Century*—was the individual who would become a major conspirator in the reformation of the Academy in the late 1930's. By excluding Fitzgerald and Sherwood Anderson and Ring Lardner, they had planned their self-protection and decent perpetuation. In point of fact they had encouraged their own conquest by the election of Benét.

From 1929 until 1931, however, Benét was successively preoccupied with the Hollywood assignment and the months of poor health. He appeared in every way an unlikely revolutionary. As the decade ended the official agency of American letters seemed destined to retain into the 1930's the deification of the past and the hostility to the present which had generally been its characteristic since its establishment in 1898. The only persistent ridicule of its status and dignity came from the increasingly disreputable Mencken.

The Academy, whose funds supported the Institute, had as its principal financial support Mr. Archer M. Huntington, the artistically minded son and heir of Collis P. Huntington. Archer Huntington, who had earlier made gifts and endowments in the neighborhood of a million dollars, gave an additional $100,000 in 1927. In 1929 he was newly generous. A gift of $700,000 would now erect a two-story exhibition hall to the rear of the spacious quarters on 156th Street. So solvent was Huntington that his bequest was made good despite the darkness of October 1929. The new building was opened in November 1930. The Academy now possessed, and shared with the Institute, an auditorium seating seven hundred and fifty in addition to the original building and the new gallery.

There was every likelihood, as the 1930's began, that Huntington's tangible warmth would continue. His second wife, the sculptress Anna Hyatt, was elected to the Institute in 1927 and would pass to the Academy in 1932. In 1930 the Academy made the passage easier by awarding Mrs. Huntington the Gold Medal, in recognition of "special distinction" in her field. The Academy's principal full-time administrator, Mrs. William Vanamee—as well as the librarian, Colonel Frank Castro, Jr.—were both in effect employees of Huntington. Huntington himself, not unnaturally, was on excellent terms with his fellow men of letters.

He encouraged them to use his box at the Metropolitan. He entertained them and their wives, "a most delightful host," said Hamlin Garland, now the dean of American letters, "gay, witty, and sympathetic." In the councils of the Academy his influence was a sober and conservative one. He warned his colleagues to be wary of assuming any national function other than that of establishing and maintaining a roll of honor. The older members were readily persuaded. "I felt the force of his words," confessed Garland, who had at first thought Huntington's program too negative. "After all, it does not matter how the current comment runs. America needs an organization which is not striving for the immediate." [1]

The damage, however, had been done. Throughout the early 1930's the new members persistently urged the nominations of their contemporaries; one or two of them had to be accepted each year. Many of the new members lived in or near New York; they went uptown regularly to the meetings, often on the special bus which picked them up at the Century Club. Gradually during the 1930's the elections began to reflect the persistence of themselves and such older allies as Van Wyck Brooks. Henry Canby,

317

elected in 1931, joined Brooks as their principal authenticator, the two older men constituting a kind of middle generation whose personal and professional sympathies were with the younger men but whose slight seniority made the new points of view less unpalatable to the oligarchy.

It was a trying period, nevertheless, and a very special temperament was required to withstand the sheer weight and oppressive sluggishness of the majority and of the atmosphere. A young man like Benét, decent, gregarious, well bred, conventionally anxious to please his elders, might have been expected to slide gradually into a dulled acceptance of the prevailing Institute mores, stupified by their plausible and pleasant amenities. This had been the conventional manner of absorption, the younger rebels transformed into company men without ever being aware of the transformation. From Benét's point of view, however, no matter how presposterous its behavior the National Institute of Arts and Letters was the major existing agency of guild obligation. At times his tolerance very nearly deserted him.

"Arrive hour late at Institute," he wrote in his diary in November 1933, "where stuffed imbecile R. U. Johnson & other incompetent old men try as usual to elect mediocrities and suppress ability."

The perpetual wrangling, however, began to produce a new kind of nominee. They traded and bartered till two o'clock in the morning; they shifted the elections from literary drabs and Nicholas Murray Butler's college president friends to men and women like MacLeish and Carl Sandburg and Charles Andrews, Ellen Glasgow, Walter Lippmann. A kind of rebel party, uncoalesced as yet, was forming. This weight of junior influence was one the Institute had never previously granted to any of its junior generations. In this case it was conceded rather than bestowed. These younger men, after all, possessed a fresh version of the traditional evangelicisms of American letters. Most of them were in the process of newly discovering or meeting for the first time such phenomena as America itself, democracy, the common man, the literary heritage of Melville and Mark Twain and Whitman, socialism, political activism. Through the Institute they were able to make a kind of single warhead of these various drives.

Benét continued to accept each laborious assignment which was thrust upon him. Throughout 1933 and 1934 he served on a committee chaired by the theatrical producer, Winthrop Ames, and charged with making recommendations to the governing Council. The group met frequently, usually at Ames' Beekman Place home, and dealt pleasantly with their business after luncheon or dinner. "Got slightly boiled," Benét noted regretfully in his diary after one such gathering in January 1934.

Once he had demonstrated his willingness to live with committee life, Benét was rarely left idle by the Institute leadership. In February 1934 he was asked by Augustus Thomas to serve on the nominating committee for the Department of Literature. In January of the following year he was working, this time with Clayton Hamilton as well as Thomas, on a special Fact-Finding Committee. Their objective was to locate some method of elevating or counteracting the generally commonplace awards which were being made by the Pulitzer Committees. Benét, as a consequence of his work on that particular committee, was in turn appointed chairman in May 1935 of the committee on awards for the Institute's own prizes. He stubbornly fought for the award of the Gold Medal to Charles Andrews. "Curious politics of committees," he noted in his diary.

Gradually the younger men moved from the mechanical assignments of the lesser committees into those areas that established the tone and direction of the Institute. In May 1935 Benét was appointed vice-chairman of the nominating committee in the Department of Literature. This group, so obviously central to the nature of the Institute, was chaired by Canby. The shift in control was moving rather more rapidly.

Benét was now elected in January 1936 to a vice-presidency of the Institute, along with Herbert Adams, Winthrop Ames, Jonas Lie, Albert Spalding, and Deems Taylor. Canby was named secretary, and Arthur Train treasurer. Wilbur Cross was succeeded as president by Walter Damrosch. In 1937 Benét became not only chairman of the nominating committee for Literature, succeeding Canby, but also chairman of the even more important equivalent committee for the Institute as a whole. The kind of submissive awe which the ruling management of American letters had received for so long from Hamlin Garland and the majority of his literary generation was completely foreign to most of the new members of the Council.

This loose union of men of different ages and varied artistic background—Damrosch, Canby, Brooks, Benét, MacLeish, Train—had in common a kind of attractive worldliness, a fondness for the upper-class amenities of metropolitan living, individual histories of conscientious professional labor and achievement, and an instinctive affinity in politics for Roosevelt and the New Deal. They also possessed a temperate individualism that immunized them on the one hand from current literary radicalism but made them nonetheless sensitive to any domination by such essentially nonprofessional men of letters as Butler or Huntington, or such obedient creatures as Johnson and Garland.

They began to meet socially, usually at Damrosch's rather luxurious home in the East Eighties, often at Arthur Train's, sometimes at the Century Club. Benét's vice-presidency, renewed annually during the 1930's, made him a permanent part of the Council. He was also a perennial member of the important Committee on Progress. In 1937 he was one of the chief architects of a plan to launch two fellowships of $2500 each. The proposal was approved in outline by the Council, but there was a division of opinion as to whether or not members of the Institute should be eligible. The idea was therefore killed in committee.

This, however, was the kind of undertaking which Benét and the others were continually pressing. Benét's broad acquaintanceship with young writers, many of them belonging to entirely different schools from his own, made him more aware than most of his colleagues of the current difficulties which handicapped the young men and women. He himself had been rescued professionally by the Guggenheim Fellowship. He was genuinely offended that the Academy's income should be used primarily for maintaining the buildings and for exhibitions of the work of dead members and lavish dinners for the living. Such projects as the celebration of Virgil's two thousandth anniversary, which the Academy undertook in 1931, did not move him greatly.

This mood, which was shared by a growing minority that included most of the younger men who were at all active in the Institute's affairs, was richly dramatized by Huntington's most current generosity. In 1935 Huntington surpassed himself. He made the Academy a fresh gift of $500,000 for its endowment. Benét, committed to the concept that the Institute and the Academy should use their considerable income for the professional welfare of American letters in general, was now made the more restless. In 1937 two MacDowell Fellowships originated in the Council and were accepted, each carrying a grant of five hundred dollars. The evolution, however, was slow and sometimes seemed imperceptible even to men as realistic as Benét. His sense of their obligation was specific and certain.

"If an Institute like ours is to mean anything," he told an associate, "it cannot be just a pleasant club or a source of self-gratification to its members. It must help the body of art. It must keep the new work coming along and recognize the good work already done, not always widely popular with the public, but done by the enduring people." [2]

Such a conception was difficult enough to state in the prevailing climate of the Academy. It was even less easy to maintain. "Sorry," Benét wrote once when asked to second the nomination of a moderately well-known writer of the period, "but I do not feel able to second Mr. ———. The woods are full of him." The younger generation was grimly mindful of what Benét called in 1939 this "much-vexed question of Elections to the Institute." As chairman of the nominating committee in the Department of Literature Benét tried, as the decade ended, to estimate the success of their efforts.

In a report to the executive body of the Institute, Benét reminded them that the Constitution restricted election to those "qualified by notable achievements in Art, Music, or Literature." As evidence of their efforts to meet this standard he analyzed the period from 1933 through 1938 in the field of letters. He pointed out that thirty-seven new members were elected during those five years. He used several gauges, including the incidence of prizes and awards, to measure the reality of achievement among the thirty-seven.

He explained that of the members elected to the Institute prior to 1933, and still living in that year, fifteen were included in at least one of four widely used anthologies. Of the members of the Institute elected in the brief period between 1933 and 1938, on the other hand, fourteen were represented. Here was a significant correlation. Benét emphasized the significance with as much tact as he could command. "In other words," he told his colleagues, "since and including 1933, we have elected almost as many members whose work rates inclusion in these highly-selective anthologies as belonged actively to the Institute before."

The point could hardly have been missed by the various generations of the Institute. Benét summed it up. "It would certainly seem to indicate that the elections of the Institute during the last seven years have been on the right basis, that the men elected to the Institute have been men of distinction, and that the Institute has been choosing its members in strict accordance to its constitution."

Benét, as always, was shrewdly realistic. "That we have made omissions is also undoubtedly true. A Melville or a Molière will, now and then, not be elected to an institution such as ours. Human judgment is fallible." The new guard of American letters could nonetheless indulge itself in some legitimate self-satisfaction. Between 1937 and 1939 they had elected, among others, Thomas Wolfe, John Dos Passos, Stuart Chase, Ezra Pound, Joseph Wood Krutch, Charles Beard, William Faulkner, and John Steinbeck. Their judgment and recognition were not only professionally valid but also in several cases considerably in advance of the academic and popular verdicts which subsequently confirmed them. The three contemporary writers who were most conspicuously absent—Dreiser, Mencken, and Hemingway—had all been offered election and refused. Even Benét, not given to hasty or excessive exultation, was well pleased with his research and its reception.

"Attend meeting of Institute Council," he wrote in his diary the next day, "and astonish the boys by giving some statistics on Institute elections. Meeting satisfactory."

It was the last satisfactory meeting within either the Institute or the Academy for some time. The startled elders absorbed the implications of the new trend in elections. They belatedly realized that their choices for the Academy were after all restricted, by the constitutional amendments of 1904, to members of the Institute. Previously this had presented no problem; the Institute had been in every sense an incubator for the Academy. Now this range of selection was being rapidly limited to the men sponsored by Canby and Brooks and Benét and their allies.

From the point of view of the senior Academicians it was a thoroughly unsatisfactory situation. Archer Huntington, with the warm approval of Butler, made his move. They would amend the amendments. From now on it would no longer be necessary to limit themselves to the pool of Institute membership. They would establish for themselves the legal right to elect anyone to the Academy. In this way the members of the Institute would have neither vote nor voice in the choice of Academicians. They almost got away with it.

On October 26, 1939, notice of the proposed amendment was sent to all the Academicians. "Academy trying to put things over," Benét wrote in his diary. "All due to personal pique of Nicholas Murray Butler. Disgraceful exhibition of old-man pettiness." Damrosch and Benét, both of them members of the Board of Directors of the Academy, discussed the situation privately and planned their strategy as best they could in view of their scattered strength in a Board that was composed largely of Butler's people.

At a meeting of the Directors on November 28 Damrosch presented a resolution which denounced the Huntington proposal. Phelps made a conciliatory speech. The display of resistance, however, provoked Huntington and his followers into near hysteria. Huntington resigned on the spot, "in," according to Benét, "a pet." He furthermore announced that he would never enter the Academy doors again. Butler, for once a rather anticlimactic actor in an executive drama, followed the benefactor from the room. Mrs. Vanamee, weeping, submitted her verbal resignation and withdrew in the wake of the other two. Benét was now doubly disgusted. "All a lot of nonsense, as nothing will be done till January."

At a conference in early December the anti-Butler faction decided, despite Benét's protests, to stall for time; they would assess Butler's next move and attempt to gather votes. Gradually their resistance stiffened. They prepared a slate of officers with which to oppose the Butler candidates, who would otherwise be automatically re-elected in January. Damrosch was the presidential choice of both Brooks and Benét. In early January they persuaded the conductor to accept the assignment. "I think we are lucky to have such a candidate," Brooks wrote Benét.

The Council of the Institute met for dinner at the Century Club on January 9, 1940. After a long discussion they finally decided to turn down the Academy's demands. "Got mad & made a speech," Benét noted. "Damrosch excellent." Now there were additional meetings. Benét joined Canby, Train, and James Truslow Adams at Damrosch's house to discuss the impasse. A week later, in early February, they met again, this time with a number of other Academicians.

"Cowardice and pussyfooting of old, successful men," Benét noted. "Still want handout & would rather do anything than fight." The three major exceptions, he felt, were Damrosch, "who has guts and will fight for a principle," Charles Warren, the constitutional lawyer and historian of the Supreme Court, and of course Van Wyck Brooks. The timidity of the majority of the Academicians was assessed by Butler, who had been re-elected with his officers and Board. On April 12, 1940, Butler made a gesture of supreme contempt for his opposition.

Under Butler's leadership the Directors of the Academy passed the new amendment. Three of the anti-Butler faction were absent from the meeting. In the minutes Mrs. Vanamee asserted that "there had been no criticism or protests received from any of the members of the Academy" after the announcement of the proposed amendment. This was so emphatically false that Benét wrote a crisp and detailed letter to the Board.

Benét pointed out that it was, "or should be," well known to the Board that in point of fact a large number of Academicians had protested the passage of such an amendment. He charged the Board with having failed to call a general meeting of the members to discuss the amendment. The Board's behavior, said Benét, was "an arbitrary and undemocratic action, contrary to the principles on which the Academy was founded and contrary to the best interests of the Academy as a whole."

Damrosch promptly had copies of the Benét letter sent to all Academicians. "This amendment is an illegal one," Damrosch assured his colleagues, "and can be so proven in court." He urged the Academicians to sign the Benét letter as indication of their approval of its position. "It is naturally of great importance," Damrosch pointed out, "that we demonstrate to the present Board of Directors that we are not in sympathy with their action."

At the next election, consequently, the Damrosch slate of the officers was voted in, Phelps withdrawing his compromise candidates as soon as he saw that the Damrosch group was firm. Butler resigned as president. Mrs. Vanamee and Colonel Castro departed to enjoy their pensions in Florida. Huntington made good his melodramatic pledge. He never again entered the Academy he had built for the arts and letters in America.

Now the plans and ideals which had been so long delayed and buried, in committee and Council and Board, began to jell. A period of extraordinary activity was starting. The men of letters began to implement the principle which had been enunciated, and continued to be enunciated, by such members as Benét. "All of us know," Benét told his colleagues, "what money and recognition mean to the serious artist. Money buys the time to do your work well. Recognition by people who know what work is gives you confidence to go ahead."

The major instrument of the Institute's new role was its program of grants to workers in the various arts. Eighteen thousand dollars was appropriated by the Institute, "to help young writers, musicians, and artists." Benét insisted that this initial program should be neither

327

charity nor usury; he resisted successfully the proposition that the money be restricted to loans for the needy. His conception of their responsibility was a multiple one. The Institute, he argued, had a definite obligation in the area which in England was traditionally covered by the Civil List pensions for indigent artists. It also had a similar obligation to provide a treasury of outright grants and small loans to cases of immediate distress.

The Institute had as well, Benét maintained, the responsibility of recognizing the younger artists and rewarding the mature. This was the region which Benét saw as their primary goal. His philosophy was quite evidently a stubborn resolve not to accept half a loaf. "Go to Academy meeting at Damrosch's," he wrote in his diary for January 5, 1942. "Get $5000 for grants, making $10,000 in grants for this year. That makes up for a lot of dull meetings I've sat through." Benét was anxious that wherever possible they should avoid mere duplication of existing agencies of literary subsidy and reward.

"A grant," he reminded his colleagues, "is not given on the basis of specific work, like a Guggenheim Fellowship, for which a particular work is to be done, and it is not given like the Pulitzer Prize for a specific work which already has been done—but for the whole work of the recipient." The philosophy of the Institute and of the Academy, Benét hoped, would be in all ways more speculative and more imaginative than the principles of existing prizes and fellowships. In this way they could compensate for the relatively limited funds with which they were working.

"I have no doubt," Benét told the Institute, "that we shall make mistakes in some of these grants. Anybody is bound to do so. But, in all modesty, it does seem to me that we are better qualified to give such grants than almost any other institution. For our judgment is judgment by men who work themselves, who know what work is."

Thus they undertook without compensation save guild pride an assignment which would inevitably expose them to considerable labor, sure abuse, and probable error. They abandoned the security of rewarding only the safe and the aged. They attempted to underwrite with their cash and their professional status not only fresh ability but also the difficult and elusive gifts of the avant-garde. "He is a talented young man whose work is not commercial," Benét said in May 1941 of a poet who had applied to the Institute for a loan. "It is extremely advanced and experimental and I doubt if he ever makes any money. Nor does it strike me that he is a budding Joyce. Incidentally, his [poetry] would give some of our more elderly members the screaming meemies. However, I consider it part of our duty to assist the young and experimental."

The loan was made—one of several from the Institute by which this particular poet was enabled, quite literally, to survive—and, as Benét pointed out to the members in connection with yet another similar case, "we have helped a good man to get on with his work." The committee on grants, supported by an increasing majority of the membership, achieved during the 1940's an impressive degree of professional objectivity in their awards. It became impossible to isolate a specific school or coterie of fiction or poetry and argue plausibly that no other schools were being supported by the Institute. They established a standard of judicious detachment in the first awards of January 1941 and maintained it scrupulously. Damrosch made an excellent speech, Robert Moses gave the guest address, and Benét presented the awards.

The size of the grants was increased in 1942. One thousand dollars apiece was awarded, without strings, to Norman Corwin, Muriel Rukeyser, Hermann Broch, and Edgar Lee Masters. "The purpose is two-fold," Benét explained in announcing the grants, "to encourage younger artists who have shown real ability, and to give practical recognition to more established artists who are doing distinguished work for which the monetary reward is small."

Throughout the decade the grants continued to reflect Benét's image of them as recognition both for new talent and for a mature body of achievement. Between 1943 and 1946 they went to writers as diverse as Carson McCullers, Karl Shapiro, Eudora Welty, Tennessee Williams, Norman Rosten, Jean Stafford, Gwendolyn Brooks, Kenneth Burke, Malcolm Cowley, Arthur Laurents, Marianne Moore, Arthur Schlesinger, Jr., and Irwin Shaw; between 1947 and 1949 to Nelson Algren, Eleanor Clark, Robert Lowell, Bertolt Brecht, Dudley Fitts, Harry Levin, Genevieve Taggard, Allen Tate, Léonie Adams, James Agee, Alfred Kazin, and Vincent McHugh.

The recipients were a cross-section of professional endeavor in fiction, criticism, scholarship, and poetry. There were critics new and old, difficult poets and poets of the conventional lyric, naturalists and symbolists and traditional story-tellers. There were almost as many women as men. There were a number of southerners, as was appropriate to a period of creative abundance in that region, but there were also writers from every other area of the country. The ambitious titles of both the Academy and the Institute had been made considerably

330

more meaningful than ever before; their intentions and realizations had become truly American and National.

The ten years of vigorous reformation were both a symbol and a vehicle for Benét's principles. All of the energy and resolve which were fragmented into his other separate roles as man of letters were united in his leadership of the Institute and the Academy. He enjoyed and profited from the friendships with such men as Brooks and Damrosch and Train; his warm instinct for club life was in this club strengthened by the professional framework.

The elevation of the two organizations was a miniature of the national restoration during those same years; the management of letters had been recaptured in much the same way that the federal government had been restored to the citizenry. For Benét it had been an arena for political as well as literary action; they had commandeered the Huntington money for guild improvement as the President had confiscated private wealth for public betterment.

Had he lived longer, Benét would have become president of the organization, but through the program of grants in particular he was permanently enshrined. It was an association in which he took great pride; it was an association which supplied him with the kind of outlet that paralleled the political memberships more characteristic of his generation in the 1930's. Its aims were more realizable, however, than the aims of the political fronts. Benét's Americanism was nowhere more evident than in his sponsorship of a democratization of the Institute and the Academy.

He made incongruous alliance with James T. Farrell; the rather fastidious son of Yale and the Regular Army was united with the belligerent Chicago naturalist on the basis of their common concern for the free exchange of ideas and the necessities of the arts in a democracy. Farrell, suspicious of everything that Benét represented socially and professionally, was more startled than Benét by their relationship.

"He was quite a serious man," Farrell recalled many years later, still astonished to find sobriety in a literary wing he had long despised, "and interested in the economic problems of writers. I talked with him about this at [the Institute]."

As an American man of letters Benét's influence thus extended from the far right to the far left. Like, again, William Dean Howells, he was himself a trifle left of center. It was an appropriate position for a writer whose values were those of the majority of his countrymen.

16. Western Star

*Birthday—39. Must have ½ Western Star
completed by 40.*

THE rewards of being a man of letters were largely in
the form of influence and prestige, neither of which
Benét valued particularly. His joint earnings from lecturing and editing and reviewing barely paid the New
York and Rhode Island rents. "Academy of Poets started.
Wish they'd give *me* $5,000," he noted in his diary
after reading of the newly established grant. He still
continued to depend on short stories for the major part
of his income. During the second half of the 1930's, however, there was a profound alteration in his relationship
with the circulation magazines.

Not once during the last three years of the decade did
Brandt have to rely on the second-line magazines for
sales. Benét's work no longer appeared in *Liberty* or
Redbook or *Woman's Home Companion.* Eighteen of
his new stories were published during 1937, 1938, and
1939.[1] Thirteen appeared in the *Saturday Evening Post,*
two in *Country Gentleman,* one in *Collier's,* one in the
Ladies' Home Journal, and one in the *Atlantic Monthly.*
The purchase of "A Tooth for Paul Revere" by the *Atlantic* was the single forced sale at a loss; all his regular
buyers turned it down as too much of a fantasy. Each

333

of the other seventeen stories, with the exception of "Schooner's Class" and "Into Egypt," was bought by the magazine of Brandt's choice, for prices—including the two that were rejected by the *Post*—which ranged from $1250 to $1750.

It was even more significant that only one of the eighteen stories was in the stereotyped formula Benét had formerly employed in at least two-thirds of his magazine fiction. "A Cat Named Dempsey," which the *Post* bought without hesitation, was a facsimile of the trivialities he had once written so regularly for *Metropolitan* and *Everybody's*. The other seventeen were divided among four significant categories; each was a notable example of magazine fiction at its most expert and adult.

The majority—"A Tooth for Paul Revere," "O'Halloran's Luck," "Oh, My Name Is William Kidd," the two new Webster stories, "Johnny Pye and the Fool-Killer," "Jacob and the Indians," "The Die-Hard," and "A Man from Fort Necessity"—were folk-tales of the American past. Two of the stories—"Doc Mellhorn and the Pearly Gates" and "Henry and the Golden Mine"—were modern fantasies. "Among Those Present" was contemporary satire, a vivid characterization done in the first person and reminiscent of Dorothy Parker and Ring Lardner; it was an excellent statement of Benét's complex feeling about New York and its effect upon the young men and women whose talent drew them to it. The remaining four stories were in certain respects the most important, overshadowing the charm of the American material, the richness of the fantasies, the bite of contemporary satire.

In this final group he extended the contemporary comment he had initiated in 1936 with "The Blood of the Martyrs." Two—"Greatness" and "The Last of the Legions"—were parables of the times in which he used episodes from the European past to illuminate the European present. "I thought of my man at the villa," reflects the Roman centurion as he and the legion prepare to leave Britain, "and how he might die in peace, even as Agathocles had said. But all the time, the moss would be creeping on the stone and the rain beating at the door. Till, finally, the naked people gathered there, without knowledge—they would have forgotten the use of the furnace that kept the house warm in winter and the baths that made men clean."

"Into Egypt," on the other hand, was a direct and moving indictment of totalitarian persecution, made plausible by the realistic portrait of a young fascist officer. The fourth story was a triumphant blend of all of them, in which he projected successfully the tempting, difficult fantasy of a future civilization. "The Place of the Gods" rose above the level of tour de force where most such stories remain; the new, postwar wilderness of America had its origins, as it were, in Benét's imaginative sense of the precolonist America of the sixteenth century.

Even Benét granted these stories some merit. For the first time he consented to the publication of a handful of them in book form. *Thirteen O'Clock* was published in 1937, *Tales before Midnight* in 1939. Of the twenty-five stories in the two collections, fourteen had originally been published in 1936 or later; several of the earlier ones had first appeared in such quality magazines as *Harper's* and the *Century*. "I have been trying to write the kind of short stories I like to write," he told an interviewer in 1939. It was characteristic of him that when he talked about his magazine fiction he said nothing of the editorial resistance which had been the prelude to this new level of achievement. "Fortunately," he said

335

instead, "magazine editors are giving me considerable liberty." [2]

The publication of *Thirteen O'Clock* and *Tales Before Midnight* was the first formal literary presentation of Benét in the storyteller role by which he had made his living since 1922 and with which most of his working time had been occupied. The reviews were both respectable and respectful; there were a number of warm acknowledgments of his achievement and some critical surprise at the high level of his performance. Everybody, however—the reviewers, Farrar who encouraged him to allow the collections, Rosemary who read the galleys and congratulated him, the public who bought more copies than was customary with short story volumes—everybody was more pleased than Benét.

He eliminated stories ruthlessly when he made the selections for *Thirteen O'Clock,* leaving out a number from *Country Gentleman* that might have been included and several from *Harper's Bazaar* and the *Elks' Magazine.* He spent several weeks revising the token selection which he did tolerate; he made additional changes in the proofs. He altered the title of "The Place of the Gods" to "By the Waters of Babylon." The only three he really approved of in *Thirteen O'Clock,* he said, were "The Devil and Daniel Webster," "Glamour," and "The Curfew Tolls."

He was more pleased with *Tales before Midnight,* all but two of whose stories had been published in 1937 or later. Even here he was diffident and scrupulous. "Look over old stories & discover I wrote a good many bad ones." It was his eighteenth book, however, and something of a milestone; the hard core of political creed and contemporary indignation gave the group an impressive unity. "I think they made a handsome book of it," he wrote his mother, "and I am glad to have the collection together."

Even the inevitable reviews by fastidious critics who deplored his tendency to write for money did not discourage him. When Robert Nathan told him how much he admired the stories, Benét answered with a cheerful reference to a bad notice he'd received. "I had just read a review of myself by an able young man," he told Nathan, "and was wondering whether I couldn't write because of (a) native incapacity or (b) because the machine was running down."

In point of fact his fertility and competence had been joined for the most propitious use of the medium of his career. His sensitivity to the past was now put to the even richer purpose of clarifying the present. He wrote these tales of totalitarian denunciation rapidly, once he conceived the situation, but always there was a period of blocked ferment which might last anywhere from ten days to a month. All kinds of factors and individuals contributed to his creative process during those preludes.

In the middle of November 1939, "money getting low," he struggled typically for a new story. "Try to think of story," he noted on November 15. "Try to work on story," two days later, "don't get anywhere." And on November 18, the same four or five hours of wrestling at his notes. "Try to work—no ideas." The exhausting germination continued on into the last days of the month, a kind of dry heaves of composition. "Try to work—get nowhere. Money running very low. . . . Try very hard to think of story, but don't. Money extremely low. . . . Cold. Don't get anywhere."

Then, abruptly and with splendid relief, the whole painful ordeal ended. A kind of sweet fruitfulness began. "Start idea for story 'Into Egypt,'" he noted on December 1. He finished the initial draft—10,000 words—the next day, and on the third day he typed it. Rosemary read it with pleasure and approval, though Benét simply noted that "she seems to think O.K."

The exhausting labor had been attended, however, by other elements than the need for money and his own resolve to sweat dryly until an idea came. On November 14, one day before he began work, he had read in the *Times* the appalling dispatches from Berlin. "Killing Jews in Germany," he wrote in his diary. On November 18, during the fourth day of his search for an idea, his mother telephoned him from Pennsylvania. She, too, was thoroughly upset by the Nazi genocide and anxious to discuss it in detail with her son. On November 25, the ninth day of his sterile gestation, he walked downtown and back. On the way he stopped at Louis Cohn's House of Books, to see if the dealer had any new Americana for him. Cohn, worldly and cosmopolitan, as familiar with Paris and Berlin as with New York, was in a terrible state. He and Benét discussed the new Nazi horrors. For ten more days these three encounters sat in his subconscious, along the still unlubricated tract of his indignation. Then on December 1 the various forces were freed. "Start idea for story, 'Into Egypt.'"

On December 5 Brandt telephoned him. He liked the story very much. Five days later, on a Friday afternoon, the agent's secretary called. Would he please come to the office some time on Monday, at his convenience, and talk to Mr. Brandt. Benét gloomily read the signs. "Damnfool *Post* probably doesn't like story." He stewed through the week end. On Monday his suspicions were confirmed. The *Post* had rejected "Into Egypt" because, they explained to Brandt, they had been getting so much material on Jews. "This is pretty silly," Benét concluded in his diary, knowing perfectly well that the magazine's fundamental objection had been to the story's unequivocal and controversial position and theme.

The painful travail of November was now prolonged in different form. Ten more days went by, the bills continued to come in; at last Brandt telephoned once more. He had sold the story to the *Ladies' Home Journal* for $1500. "Get check," Benét noted on December 29, "and pay school-bills." A process which began on November 14, when he read the morning *Times,* ended almost seven weeks later when he spent the payment. The sequence of frustration, labor, and fulfillment was reproduced each time Benét began and completed a major short story from 1937 through 1942; he wrote at least half a dozen each year and sometimes eight or nine.

The process was a punishing one. The physical and mental strain was immense. It contributed to a nervous breakdown in 1939; he spent several weeks in the hospital. It contributed also to his general disrepair. His arthritis returned; the cycle of doctors and dentists resumed. "Feel perfectly terrible," he wrote in his diary in June 1937. He tried body exercises and massages and new vaccines. He slept on a board and he tried wearing a corset; his back became more stooped and the periods of pain longer. "Arthritis is a funny disease," he said ruefully. "There is everything from chaulmoogra oil to radiotherapy. I have tried most of them, but am always willing to try something else." [3]

He had arthritis of the spine, his doctor explained later. He couldn't even move his neck freely. "He suffered a great deal," said the doctor. "His endurance and patience were extraordinary and exceptional." [4] Margaret Farrar, whose friendship with him and Rosemary was now very nearly as close as her husband's, remembered that as his arthritis became worse he seemed to develop a deep, warm chuckle which replaced his former rich, high-pitched laughter. The deterioration of his body, and the new grief when his mother died in 1940, were similarly accompanied by a creative energy more prolonged and productive and at a higher level of accomplishment than any since—and including—*John Brown's Body.*

His "Nightmare at Noon," published in the New York *Times* in June 1940, was a genuine literary event. It excited the reading audience as had none of the verse prophecies and warnings of such contemporaries as MacLeish and Millay. The Lunts, knowing that Philip Barry was a friend of his, asked the playwright to talk to Benét about letting them do a dramatization of it. It was produced on radio, a high point in the brief poetic renaissance the networks were then enjoying. That same year he shocked the lovers of his lyric poetry with the brutal "Minor Litany" in the *New Yorker.* Bernice Baumgarten, Brandt's principal assistant, told him that everybody she met was talking about it; his wife told him she hated it.

> This being a time confused and with few clear stars,
> Either private ones or public,
> Out of its darkness I make a litany
> For the lost, the half-lost, for the desperate,
> For all those who suffer, not in the flesh. . . .
> This occurs more or less than it did in the past times.
> There are statistics. There are no real statistics.
> There is also no heroism. There is merely
> Fatigue, pain, great confusion, sometimes recovery.[5]

Now for the first time in his career his prose and his poetry were functioning simultaneously. It was no coincidence that he had begun "The Place of the Gods" as a poem and then transformed it to a short story; such a metamorphosis would have been previously unthinkable in his creative psychology. In the short stories, for an American audience that numbered in the millions, he was a kind of dramatic editorialist; the themes and statements of his fiction were large and bold, and they were read and pondered as editorials were not.

In the poems—not only in "Nightmare at Noon" and "Minor Litany," but also in "Nightmare for Future Reference" and "If This Should Change"[6]—in the poems he enunciated the same set of principles on a sharper, more personal level. The accent differed, but for the first time the voice was the same. "I don't think poetry should put its head in a bag," Benét wrote James Farrell. "I don't think it should be the exclusive possession of an intellectual few. That is my only quarrel with the dogmatist intellectuals. But I would burn no books and suppress no writers."

Always he labored to purge from his own work the shrill bombast which blurred the verse of other American poets who were writing in the same vein. "Perhaps as hard a task as any the poet has," he said in 1940 in one of his reviews, "is to write from immediate emotion and yet write well. He may want, with all his heart, to cry out against injustice, but . . . he is likelier to commit rhetoric than poetry."[7] He did less and less casual hack work each year. The few assignments he accepted —an article for *Stage* on Maxwell Anderson, another on witchcraft for *Esquire,* a radio version of *Much Ado about Nothing* for NBC, an occasional preface[8]—he tried to do without the haste and superficiality of his earlier literary journalism.

In 1938 he was asked to write the Tercentenary Ode commemorating the first meeting of the General Court

341

in the Colony of New Haven. He worked hard on the poem during May and June, attempting as always now to kindle emotion without igniting mere thunder. "I oughtn't to be rhetorical at my age," he noted in his diary. He disliked writing verse to order; the necessary impulse was seldom present, and it was a rupture of his working schedule. He managed, nevertheless, to evoke the three-hundred-year-old fears of colonists who were no more terrified of the future in 1638 than their descendents in 1938.

The known street, the known neighbor, the graves where the kinsfolk lie,
The settled life, the sure ending . . .[9]

Now, too, he received tempting offers to undertake the sort of public life with which MacLeish had identified himself. *Fortune* asked him to accept an editorship; the new president of The University of Rochester urged him to become librarian. Indiana University invited him to accept a chair in American letters; MacLeish suggested that he become Consultant on Poetry at the Library of Congress. He was asked to succeed Henry Canby as editor of the *Saturday Review of Literature*. He declined them all, though each would have meant financial security and reprieve from the endless pressures of a working writer's deadlines. "Still no story," he noted in his diary during this period of growing public luster. "Rental company writing me angry letters." It was pleasant, he said, to know he was worth $15,000 a year on the open market, but despite the rental company he preferred to be his own man.

Each time he got a little ahead with the current bills, each time the *Post* or *Country Gentleman* raised his story price, to $1500, to $1750—and now $2,000 from *Good*

Housekeeping—then each time there were poems to be written, freedom to be savored, young writers to be helped, extravagances to be bought for his family. "Try to work a little," he observed of himself one day. "Odd that when opportunity offers of really making some money, I feel perfectly apathetic, because I have some and am enjoying life."

More particularly, however, he was hoarding his leisure for a major effort. Now for the first time he was firm when Carl Brandt talked to him about one more story when he was already a story ahead. "Sorry," he told Brandt in 1938, "but I'm going to be busy on *Western Star* for the rest of the summer. Will you tell *Good Housekeeping* that." It was a poem for which he had made notes as early as 1928. He talked with George Doran about it in 1930, and told him the theme and the title. In December 1931 he discussed it with Dan Longwell. The next day the excited Longwell sent a memorandum to the other Doubleday editors. "He wants to be finished with it in about six months," Longwell reported to his associates. In 1934, when Benét transferred to Farrar and Rinehart, he signed a contract for this same new poem, with the same title. And now, in the last years of the 1930's, the project was essentially no further ahead than it had been when Don Longwell, in 1931, had anticipated receiving the manuscript in six months.

Western Star was thus the principal casualty of the long years of hack work and literary journalism and national leadership in the cause of American letters. More and more it became for him a responsibility to meet, a commitment to face, a burden to assume. In his letters he sometimes likened it to a bird around his neck, a chain around his leg. In his diary he marked off his birthdays by the progress or lack of it which the past

343

year had brought to the poem. He was embarrassed when the young poets asked him how his new long one was coming along; he was humiliated when they stopped asking at all.

"Must have ½ *Western Star* completed by 40," he wrote a little desperately in his diary in 1937, on his thirty-ninth birthday. He was fearfully conscious that time was running out. "It has suddenly come upon us [all]," he wrote Margaret Widdemer in 1937, "that the works may blow up."

The scope of *Western Star*, both in his mind and in eventual execution, dilated from year to year. His original conception was to tell the story of America from the landing of Columbus in the fifteenth century through the driving of the golden spike for the Central Pacific Railroad in the nineteenth. He explained to George Doran in 1930 that his sense of America was of two majestic and continuing phases, the preservation of the Union and the continual, restless movement of its people. He had dealt with the first in *John Brown's Body;* the second would be the theme of *Western Star*.

Dan Longwell, after talking to Benét in 1931, envisioned a twinhood of American epic. Longwell described the projected relationship as one in which *John Brown's Body* was "the *Iliad* of our country, [*Western Star*] being the *Odyssey*." Later in the 1930's Benét visualized for a time a structure that encompassed western migration as far back as the eleventh century. Thus in 1938 and 1939 he wrote two ballads which set the moment of the march westward in medieval Normandy and Marco Polo's Venice. "The Ballad of the Duke's Mercy" and "The Ballad of Marco Polo," each published in the *Atlantic Monthly* in 1939, had obvious connections with the central plan of *Western Star*.[10] The sons of the Norman poacher in the first ballad were destined for the English invasion of 1066; the Norman was thus a progenitor of Dickie Heron, the principal founder of the fictional American family who were planned as the main characters of *Western Star*.

These peripheries of the march west were abandoned to time and Benét's final conviction that the poem should contain no more than ten books. The role he had originally designed for Columbus, which would have included several scenes and a soliloquy from jail, shrank similarly to half a dozen lines in the final stanza of the prelude. But if the scope was reduced during the 1930's, the theme remained constant both in his mind and in those sections which he completed and which were finally published in 1943. He never lost his clear sense of the westward march. The songs and lyrics of the opening scenes were full of its imminence.

There was a wind over England, and it blew.
(Have you heard the news of Virginia?)
A west wind blowing, the wind of a western star,
To gather men's lives like pollen and cast them forth,
Blowing in hedge and highway and seaport town,
Whirling dead leaf and living, but always blowing,
A salt wind, a sea wind, a wind from the world's end,
From the coasts that have new, wild names, from the
    huge unknown.

What he fixed on by 1937, when he at last began to work in sustained earnest on *Western Star*, was a frontier history of America from the first Atlantic settlements until the closing of the open land at the end of the nineteenth century. "My greatest task," he said in 1939, "will be to catch the moving panorama of fron-

345

tier life from the point of view of the frontier instead of from the East."[11] The published sections of 1943 indicated how imaginatively he had evoked that point of view, both in the full-dimensioned portraits of such historical figures as John Smith and the well-drawn fictional characterizations of Dickie Heron and Sir Gilbert Hay.

The annual theft of his time and energy by magazine fiction had been accompanied by a professional bounty which displayed itself to full advantage in *Western Star*. The latter's fictional characters were in every way superior to those of *John Brown's Body*. They were more fresh, more individual, less stock, with no caricatures such as Jack Ellyat. All of them—knights, younger sons, Puritans, merchants, secretaries—were vigorous and plausible. The difference between *John Brown's Body* and *Western Star* was also, of course, nothing more than the difference between youth and maturity. A decade of pain and compromise and fulfilled responsibility had consolidated in Benét a wisdom and serenity which were no more than potentials in 1926 and 1927.

Now, too, his involvement in the contemporary political and social issues gave *Western Star* an immediacy which could not have been present in *John Brown's Body*. He had sufficient confidence in his voice so that he did not hesitate to make asides to the reader. "And we would all have done better," he wrote of the Jamestown failures, "—no doubt of that."

We would not have squatted down in a fever-marsh
Just as the mosquitos bred and the heat began.
(The Pilgrims did not—and yet the Pilgrims died.)
We would have known which Indians were friendly.
(Let's hope we know as much of the Martians.)

346

We'd not have quarreled and wrangled—with a crew
Made of ex-soldiers, fledgling aviators,
Truckdrivers, furniture-salesmen, drugstore-clerks,
Machinists, workmen, a radio-announcer
And a sprinkling of nice clean boys from Yale or Harvard.
We'd have known the Martian birds and the Martian
    beasts
And how to hunt them and trap them. We'd have known
The ways of the Martian climate and all the ropes.
In fact, we would have done wonders.

It was this capacity to dramatize the past, gained in large part through the decade of historical fiction, which was *Western Star's* great strength. It more than compensated for the absence of the high lyric bursts and poetic fever of *John Brown's Body*. Nor were these totally missing from *Western Star;* they existed in the courtship of Dickie Heron and in the rousing "Jack of the Feather." The depth of authenticity, both of people and events and terrain, was unmistakeable. The burden of research to which he assigned himself was prodigious; he undertook to master a century and a half of complicated local and national history.

During the summers of 1937 and 1938, therefore, and again in 1940, he rented Henry Canby's house in eastern Connecticut, despite his fondness for Rhode Island. "I have to be near a good reference library," he explained to Brandt. Each week he drove the twenty miles from Killingworth to New Haven to get books from the Yale Library. His cousin Andrew Jones rode in with him one day; years later he remembered the excitement which Benét's arrival caused. "Everyone came out to see Benét the poet." Once again, however, as with *John Brown's Body*, he was working in advance of most scholarship.

347

Professional historians had tracked Frederick Jackson Turner into the West, but so far most of their labor was in the form of unsynthesized monographs.

"If anybody in the world had written even a competent and connected history of the Western frontier from say 1745 to 1815," Benét wrote the Yale Librarian, "I would feel better. As it is, I continue to take notes in order to form judgments which will probably be wrong when formed."

He spent the entire summer of 1937 reading material on the Virginia and Massachusetts settlements. "Work on Pilgrims," he noted in his diary. "Really a wonderful story." He had no patience with the version of the settlers which he called "Mencken's stock Puritan," but for him there was nevertheless a sharp distinction between Puritan and Pilgrim. "I can like the Pilgrims," he told Andrew Jones, "but it is dam hard for me to like the Massachusetts Bay crowd."

The American past was alive for him now, with his new sensitivity to the present, as it had never previously been. Even the wooded country around Killingworth, largely unsettled, was reminiscent of the period about which he was writing. He employed some of the fruit of this research in his lectures. Wallace Stegner remembered years later his own excitement when he heard Benét talk at Iowa about the use of western material in fiction and poetry. Benét was characteristically diffident about his own capacity. "I wish prominent historians wouldn't contradict each other as much as they do," he told Brandt during the summer of 1938. "How's a poor poet to know which is right."

Brandt, once he grasped the seriousness of purpose with which Benét was now approaching *Western Star*, was a pillar of strength. He worked even harder than before to get top prices for each new story. He went back over the stories which had been rejected years before; he triumphantly telegraphed Benét each time he sold an editor a manuscript the latter had turned down five or six years earlier. Brandt schemed endlessly for ways in which *Western Star* itself could be made partially self-supporting. He arranged with *Esquire* that they should publish a fragment of it—a hundred or a hundred and fifty lines, he told Benét—at two dollars per line. He talked so persuasively of the poem to the *Saturday Evening Post* that its editors, not celebrated for their sponsorship of American verse, were almost ready to schedule it sight unseen.

Benét was grateful to the agent for his good intentions, but he firmly rejected each careful strategy. He did not like to speculate on unfinished work; he was also unwilling to exploit his buyer or his audience. He continued to purchase the time for *Western Star* with the exhausting short stories. In the midsummer of 1938 he began Book Two, and he worked on it straight through October. "Feel encouraged," he noted in his diary.

He wrote a lively progress report to Carl Brandt: "Conditions are rather unsettled here at Jamestown, but with God's will we yet hope to plan a nation." He and Rosemary saw a good deal of Christopher LaFarge and his wife that winter in New York. Benét and LaFarge read aloud from the long poems they were both writing, with the ladies as audience. LaFarge approved the sections Benét had completed, which he later declared to be superior to what was published in 1943. Benét was heartened by the austere New England approval.

He was painfully aware that the American material which had once been almost his monopoly was now being embraced enthusiastically by most of his contemporaries. "A lot of the boys are now fiddling around with some of the material I want to cover," he had written Douglas Moore as early as 1934, "and I want to get in ahead of them and stake out my claim." Now, several years later, that kind of understandable urgency was even more pressing. "God knows what it will look like," he told Paul Engle after the hard summer's work of 1938, "but it pleased me to get back to it."

His conception of the final plan became a frontier panorama that would extend from the first English colonies to the death of Sitting Bull. In 1939, after six weeks of movie work on a best-selling novel called *Miss Bishop*, he was able to support a long stretch of concentration on *Western Star*. All through that autumn and winter, and on into January 1940 he worked on it, some days in the New York Public Library, other days in the new house they had rented on East 68th Street. He worried most, LaFarge remembered, about repeating himself. "He was always changing, rejecting, revising."

In part this was his determination to make *Western Star* the very best work of which he was capable. In part, too, it was the poignant uncertainty of a gifted craftsman whose confidence was damaged; he had used too many tools competently to be absolutely self-assured any longer with the one tool wherein his major talent had lain. In 1937, when he launched this first sustained work on *Western Star*, he was doubtful of his capacity. He uneasily wrote Engle that he was going "to try and see if I can do a long job again." Always, in addition to the fixed burdens of short stories and Yale Poets and Rivers of America, of Academy affairs and reviews and reports for Farrar and Rinehart, there were major intrusions which he felt he could not resist.

He spent valuable weeks working on a musical comedy

350

idea with LaFarge and Dick Myers. It was called *You've Got to Be Rich,* a gay burlesque of the Manhattan upper classes; Benét wrote a number of charming songs for it. Several producers were interested, but nothing came of it; he had obliged two friends, but he had also lost additional working time. A far more productive collaboration of this same period was the one with Douglas Moore. In 1937 they did *The Headless Horseman,* a short operetta based on Irving's "The Legend of Sleepy Hollow." It was produced first at the Bronxville High School, by whom Moore had originally been asked to compose it; shortly afterward it was nationally broadcast by NBC, and later it was published for professional use.

Then in 1938 Moore asked him to write a longer libretto for an American opera. Benét, who was by now weary of the efforts of other writers to dramatize "The Devil and Daniel Webster," suggested the latter. They talked to the indifferent Metropolitan about a production. "Useless trying to do anything with Met," Benét wrote angrily in his diary. The rebuff from orthodoxy, in addition to his affection for Moore, quickly stimulated a month of hard work on the libretto. "I have been sinfully making a one-act opera," he confessed to Brandt in June 1938, when the agent inquired as to the state of his new short story.

The collaboration with Moore was one of the most pleasant working relationships of Benét's career. "We were both interested in the same kind of American folk-material," Benét said later. "Well, why not try and do something about it—something without the pretensions of grand opera but something which, if we were lucky, could use American speech and American folk-music and do it with sincerity." He made substantial revisions in the story, creating a major role for Jabez' wife, compressing the action from seven years to a few hours and beginning the narrative with the wedding of Jabez and Mary.

He discovered a major advantage in adapting one's own work. "The original author," he explained, "can neither complain or sue." The result was polished and inventive work by both Benét and Moore. "While recognizing the limits of a tradition," Benét explained when he was asked about its relationship to conventional opera, "we have tried to make certain experiments within those limits. For it is only by experimentation that a new thing can grow.[12]

The opera was produced by the new and lively American Lyric Theater, under the direction of John Houseman. It had a superb production, opening at the Martin Beck on May 18, 1939, to an enthusiastic audience and excited notices by the critics. The front office, however, was not equal to the production; the timing was bad and the advertising frugal. "Christ, what a management!" Benét wrote in his diary during rehearsals. "I could make a better one out of plasticine." What would certainly have been a long run had it opened in February was cut to a few performances when the management closed for the summer.

The life of the opera continued, however, in wartime productions by USO troupes and then as the annual feature of the Old Sturbridge Festival in Massachusetts. "As a theatrical production," said Brooks Atkinson in a review that was characteristic of the response, *"The Devil and Daniel Webster* represents some of the finest and most painstaking work of the season."[13] It was a critical endorsement which encouraged Benét's confidence in native material as he returned to *Western Star*. "Hope to finish poem this year," he had written in his diary on the first day of 1939. The spring dissolved in rehearsals for the opera, but by the end of the year he had worked enough on the poem so that he was again delinquent with his current short story.

"I have spent the last 2½ months taking notes for *Western Star*," he explained to Brandt the day after Christmas, "which really will have to get finished before I have a long white beard." He returned briefly to it in the summers of 1940 and 1941, but the bulk of what was published in 1943 had been finished by the end of 1939. Now the headlines in the morning paper, and the news broadcasts to which he listened every hour, and half the night, were joined to the other intruders on his working schedule. "Every time I try to go back to my long poem," he told Brandt in October 1941, "I think why the hell write about the early history of Pennsylvania with the world blowing up. And yet, work ought to be done."

Always *Western Star* was at the back of his mind, as it had been since 1928, but he worked no more on it. In 1941 he put the manuscript in a safe deposit vault, a symbolic gesture of his commitment to propaganda for the duration. Henry Canby telephoned one day to say he'd found a scenario of the poem in the stone studio at Killingworth where Benét had worked during the summers of 1937, 1938, and 1940. "Tear it up," Benét instructed him. Time had at last run out on him. Now he felt that such energy as he could spare from making a living belonged to whatever services the government asked of him.

17. Casualty

News from Manila very bad. Hardly know what to expect of 1942—but God preserve the United States!

BENÉT, whose previous indifference to politics had prepared him poorly for the events of the early 1930's, was more ready than most of his countrymen for the crises with which that decade ended and the new one began. During each successive year of the 1930's he became increasingly better informed about national and international realities. The range of his friendships now extended far beyond the conventional literary ones of his young manhood.

He saw a good deal—both through his relationships with MacLeish and Barry and as a result of his own public and social status—of those responsible members of big business and Wall Street and the judiciary who were clustering around the New Deal, men like Robert Lovett and Forrestal and Judge Learned Hand and Thomas Finletter. He talked to Willkie a number of times, at the Century Club and on committees and at small dinners. He had known Walter Millis and Charles Merz, of the *Tribune* and *Times,* since the days at Yale.

Each year he heard from his Uncle Larry, when the munitions executive returned to the United States, a first-hand account of official European thinking; his uncle predicted the various stages of Allied and Axis maneuver with cool and pessimistic accuracy. Benét's own friendships among European refugees were wide and intimate. He had followed the Spanish Civil War with understanding and despair, knowing it to be a tragic prelude and linked personally to it through his nephew's enlistment in the International Brigade. By the time the United States went to war in December 1941 he had been active for months, writing material for both private and governmental agencies and sitting with almost every anti-fascist committee in New York. "He was one of those persons whom we called self-starters," said an official of the Writers War Board, "who were so busy already with war writing that he needed no assignments from us."[1]

When the young Providence poet, Winfield Scott, interviewed him for the *Evening Bulletin* in 1939, he found Benét already preoccupied with the situation of the writer in wartime. Benét felt a professional obligation which he discharged primarily through his leadership in the American Academy of Arts and Letters. He insisted continually that the Academy and the Institute must maintain and extend their grants and loans for those artists whose work or markets were threatened by the times. There were American writers of all ages, he pointed out to the Institute membership, whose work was of great importance to the future of letters and yet who didn't fit into the immediate pattern of the war effort.

"Not every artist can write propaganda, for instance," Benét declared. "Longfellow did—Melville didn't. It would be silly to ask for a propaganda novel from Jane Austen—and William Blake's comments on the great crisis of his time, the French Revolution, concern them-selves with a revolution that may have occurred in his own mind but certainly never occurred in France. And yet, Heaven knows, if art and letters are to go on, we need the Jane Austens, the Melvilles and the Blakes. That is part of our duty, part of our responsibility as members of this Institute." [2]

So far as his own obligations were concerned, he was never in doubt. "We Benéts," he explained to a colleague who marveled at his new patience with Algonquin com-mittee meetings, "are an Army family." Along with the rest of his generation he remembered vividly the distaste he had once felt for the patriotic bombast of older American writers during the first World War. He was realistically aware that few of their reputations had ever recovered from the official uses to which they put them-selves in 1918. He resolved the dilemma in one of the best of his wartime short stories. "After the last war," says a character in "The Prodigal Children," which was published in the *Saturday Evening Post* in December 1942, "the one thing I swore I'd never write was propa-ganda. But this one is for our skins, and the chips are down." [3]

When James Farrell became alarmed at what seemed to him the attempts of men like MacLeish and Van Wyck Brooks to "politicalize" literature, he quoted Milton to Benét on the dangers of artistic tyranny. Benét coun-tered with another line from Milton, reminding Farrell that the Englishman had also said, "I cannot praise a fugitive and cloistered virtue." Benét was similarly un-impressed by the majestic professional isolation which Hemingway assumed at the beginning of World War II. "A writer's job is to tell the truth," Hemingway wrote in 1942. "If, during a war, conditions are such that a writer cannot publish the truth because its publication would do harm to the State he should write and not publish." [4] Benét answered Hemingway with direct rebuttal.

"I don't happen to agree with Hemingway's thesis. If you don't believe in what you write, that's something else. If you do believe in what you write and yet write badly, sloppily, untruthfully, that's your fault. . . . If what I am writing today as propaganda will hurt my eventual reputation as a writer—very well, then let it. Maybe, later on, some of the things I have written will make me squirm—OK, I have squirmed before. Anyhow, I can't just sit on my integrity as a writer, like a hen on a china egg, for the duration. And maybe even if I did, nothing could hatch." [5]

As early as the summer of 1941, when he was asked to comment on papers which had been read at a widely publicized meeting of the Conference on Science, Philosophy, and Religion, Benét stated his position clearly. His sense of a writer's obligation was far more than a matter of instinctive patriotism; he did not assume it suddenly on December 7, 1941. It was part of a reasoned and professional creed. "If the artist believes," Benét wrote the director of the Conference, "I think he should state his belief. It will never be earlier. For neither his freedom of speech nor his liberty of action will automatically preserve themselves."

As always, his principles were a rational mixture in which the basic ideals were bolstered by hard-headed realism. "The issue," Benét declared, "is between life and a certain chance to do your work and get it done—and death and no chance to get it done." He had no patience, on the other hand, with the widely held axiom that the writing of propaganda required little more than the glib fluency of a copywriter. "Great artists can write great

357

propaganda," he declared. "They can point a moral. But the belief must be inside—you cannot hand it to them like a tablet of benzedrine." He was similarly impatient with the ponderous approach which confused well-meaning solemnity with effective propaganda. He criticized bluntly the language of the final statement which was released by the Conference.

"It is not first-class language," Benét told Louis Finkelstein, the distinguished head of the Conference. "I know how difficult it is to draw up such a statement. The ideas are there all right—they repay careful study. But they are presented, in the main, without force or fire —in the pithless, indeterminate style that disfigures so much of American scholarship. If men are drawing up a new declaration of independence—a declaration of the independence of man's spirit—they should do it with at least as much care for the sound and sense and bite of English words as Jefferson gave to his own Declaration. . . . Well, to me, though I agree with the thought, and though I speak with deference, [the statement] is pianola-English. It does not remind me of the great beliefs men have held dear—it reminds me of nothing so much as of a little book gotten out by the disciples of James Joyce and called *An Exagmination and Incamination of the Factification of Work In Progress.* Can't important ideas be stated so they stir the mind? They have been, in the past." [6]

Benét's own willingness to volunteer his talents for propaganda was limitless and conscientious. The committee chairmen and their executive secretaries quickly discovered that he would do responsible and thoughtful work for impossible deadlines. He undertook, at the sacrifice of his own work and income and well-being, assignments that were sometimes trivial, sometimes momentous, occasionally inane, always difficult and wearing. At various times between 1940 and 1943 he wrote an inscription for a marker to be erected on East River Drive, acted as narrator on a Victory Front radio program, discussed a new magazine called *Transatlantic* for English readers, aided in a Books-across-the-Sea enterprise, served on the nominating committee for the Civil Liberties Union, met a number of times with Rex Stout and the Writers War Board, helped make the selections for an album of Whitman's poetry, and wrote a greeting to be sent from the American publishing industry to its English counterpart. "If I have to do any more of these pious things," he noted in his diary, "I might as well be ordained." He continued to do them.

He spoke at a meeting to raise money for France Forever, wrote an article for Russian War Relief, advised the Theatre Guild on their plans for a patriotic venture, met with Citizens for Victory, collaborated with Douglas Moore on a documentary film called *Power and the Land* for the REA, lunched with the Atlantic Panel, attended air-raid meetings, wrote a long critique of official Army lectures, did an article on Daniel Webster for the Treasury Department, sat on a literary committee for the USO, gave radio readings of his poetry, revised a pledge for all nations originally written by Dorothy Thompson, was asked absurdly to write "a new Marseillaise" for the federal government, and wrote a pledge of allegiance to be taken by all Civilian Defense workers. "I seem to be becoming the Wendell Willkie of poetry," he wrote Brandt in June 1941, "not entirely a happy thought." Occasionally there were requests so preposterous that he had to say no.

"I agree there ought to be a poem written about Pearl Harbor," he replied patiently to a suggestion from Carl

Brandt, in this case concerning a magazine commission for which he would for once have been paid, "but that is just one of those things I can't do." There were, however, few things he wasn't willing to do if any valid argument existed for their relationship with the war effort. "This whole winter and spring has gone by like a runaway colt," he told Engle in June 1941. "I don't know what I have done with it—I seem to have done very little and yet I have been working all the time at one job or another."

The paradox was understandable. Many of the jobs were the kind for which there could be no immediately visible results; others were simply the lost, intangible hours of long committees. Even the writing itself was of a peculiarly perishable kind, for the bulk of his war work was in the form of radio scripts. Most of them were free verse dramas, to be produced in a single broadcast. Even when they were rebroadcast again and again, as so many of them were, there was none of the permanence of a book or even a Broadway run. Others were speeches to be delivered by some public personality; his own sense of identification with the words could never be as intimate as with a poem or a short story.

The first of these major addresses was characteristic of most of them in its scope and its success. It was written at the request of the Council for Democracy, to be read by Raymond Massey on the day after the Presidential election of 1940. The Council hoped that some large national statement might heal the dividing wounds of a bitter campaign. Benét worked three full days on the speech. On the evening of November 6, as he sat in his study writing yet another script—this one about Canadian-American relations and called "The Undefended Border"—he switched to the Carnegie Hall rally. The first speakers were dull and there was no announcement of Massey; Benét turned off the program. "Guess they couldn't get him or something," he speculated in his diary without bitterness, though he had spent three days on a script which apparently wasn't going to be used.

The Council had, however, engaged Massey, and he did read the speech, which Benét had entitled "We Stand United." The results were more electrifying than even the Council had hoped. It was covered by the national press as a major news story. Only Benét kept a sense of proportion. "Front page of *Times*," he noted in his diary the next day, "talks about my 'Lincoln-like words.' Well, well. Get radiotherapy." [7]

The national success of the speech inaugurated a major part of Benét's propaganda, consolidating the relationship between himself and the Council for Democracy. Most of his scripts during 1941 and 1942 were commissioned by the Council, a private agency organized on the principle that there should be at least one national group devoted solely to the cause of democracy and broad enough to unite all loyal Americans. During those two years the Council, though it had several counterparts, was by far the most imaginative and adult of the propaganda ventures. The America United Rally which sought to heal the Roosevelt-Willkie ruptures was characteristic of the Council's useful and workable projects. Benét was their principal writer, pleased to be able to work with the freedom they allowed him and fortunate in the excellent casts and productions they provided.

The Council's officers and executive committees were an admirable cross-section of the American professions, including as they did men like Raymond Gram Swing, Ernest Angell, C. D. Jackson, Lyman Bryson, Cass Canfield, Farrar, Walter Millis, and George Shuster. C. D.

Jackson, on loan to the organization from his job with Henry Luce—the latter was one of the Council's principal financiers—was its most energetic official during the early months. "A holding company was needed," Jackson said later, "to coordinate and to raise funds. It wasn't so much activist as educational." Its intention and organization were ideally suited to Benét. It was flexible and literate, operated during its first eighteen months by men who were willing to speculate on fresh material. There was a minimum of bureaucratic sluggishness and ad agency tinsel. "Benét," said Carl Friedrich, the Harvard professor of government who was an active executive of the Council for some time, "was, of all the really distinguished literary people who helped with the Council, undoubtedly the most genuinely unselfish contributor to the cause. He also lacked all exhibitionism, and just worked." [8]

It was Jackson, however, who most fully sensed and exploited Benét's gifts. Theirs was an incongruous alliance, Jackson a trusted assistant of Luce, Benét disliking intensely many of the principles on which *Time* operated. A genuine harmony nevertheless developed between the two men. Benét respected Jackson's organizational skill and resolve; Jackson was awed not only by Benét's creative energy but also by his capacity to understand and respond to all levels of American experience. "I never knew a man who could get along so instinctively with all kinds of people," said Jackson, himself a formidable mixer.

It was typical both of their personal relationship and of the informal organization of the Council that when Jackson decided the Council should do a Fourth of July broadcast in 1941 he went directly to Benét without consulting his fellow officers. Jackson brought with him on that occasion nothing but the desire to have a program and the pledge that he would guarantee a national hook-up and a good production. They talked for about an hour. "Benét was appalled at the six-week deadline," Jackson remembered later, "but he said he'd try it."

Benét went to work on June 3. He decided to call the script "Listen to the People." He worked every day, afternoon and evening, for eight days. He finished retyping the final draft at 11 o'clock on the night of the eighth day. He had lunch with Jackson the next day and Jackson read the script while they ate. He said it was fine, wonderful. He was delighted and impressed. Benét was less sure. "It should require the talent of a Milton," he wrote in his diary, "and I am not a Milton. However, somebody ought to say something."

Jackson arranged for an NBC broadcast with Henry Hull and Howard Lindsay as the principal voices; CBS, normally less timid than NBC, had thought the script inflammatory. *Life*, Jackson now told Benét, was extremely anxious to publish the poem in its July 7th issue. If this were done, however, the revisions would have to be made in far less time than Benét had planned. "Don't see how I can do it," Benét wrote in his diary. "But suppose I can." He worked until 2 A.M., then went downtown to the *Life* offices the next morning and cut another sixty lines.

Half an hour before the broadcast the final rehearsal showed them running two minutes too long. Benét cut the script once more and "Listen to the People" went on the air at 4:15, just before an address by President Roosevelt. The timing of the broadcast, as well as the enormous circulation of *Life*, meant that Benét was heard by more Americans than any other serious writer in the history of the United States.[9] The response was extraordinary. Letters and telegrams came to him, and to *Life* and NBC, from every part of the nation. "Your poem thrilled me," Arthur Train wrote him. "It is superb and inspiring and will have a tremendous effect throughout the nation. Congratulations!" It was, Van Wyck Brooks assured him, "a fine poem."

Benét, however, was back at his desk the next day in Stonington, Connecticut, where he and Rosemary had at last bought the home they had wanted since 1929. Now, in a workroom on the third floor from which he could see both the ocean and the planes from the nearby Navy station, he tried to catch up on all the lost income of the past months. "No money, and owe more than in a long time."

In the mail, to be sure, there came a check from *Life* for $500, for "Listen to the People." Benét endorsed the check and sent it to the USO. He would accept no payment whatsoever for any of his writing that was connected with the war. When he could not avoid the payment, as in this case, he consistently turned the money over to either the Army Fund or the USO. He instructed Brandt that all his English royalties were to be given to the Spitfire Fund for the duration.

"I couldn't do anything else," he told the agent, whose awed reaction was to dig out of the files a story that had been rejected in 1934, retitle it himself, and sell it to the *American Magazine* for $1500. Of the nineteen stories which Benét published between 1940 and early 1943, in fact, four had been written some years before.[10] They were bought now, appropriately, by the very magazines for which they had originally been intended. Thus, incongruously, at a time when his new short stories were being cited as classics, he was simultaneously appearing in *Redbook* and *Harper's Bazaar* and the *American* with these culls from what Brandt called the B-file.

Several of his new stories, on the other hand—"The Captives" and "The Minister's Books" in particular— were effectively constructed from the frontier research he was doing for *Western Star*. Others, like "The Great Swinglefield Derby" and "The Angel Was a Yankee," were hasty and inferior fragments of Americana. A small group of these final stories of his career, however, were among his major achievements. In them he somehow matched, despite the full-time obligations of his war work, the noble themes and expert craft of "Into Egypt" and "The Blood of the Martyrs." Such a story was "Freedom's a Hard-Bought Thing," published in the *Saturday Evening Post* in May 1940. Like everything he was writing now, it brought the same extraordinary flood of letters; descendents of Negroes who had escaped on the underground, and relatives of those who operated it, wrote to thank him for it. The grandson of a slave wrote to describe how the bells in his grandfather's collar had been packed with mud as he dodged his pursuers. Once again, as so often in the past, Benét was given the O. Henry Memorial Award for the best American short story of the year.

He had less and less time, however, for new work that required the concentration of such major short stories of this period as "The Bishop's Beggar," "A Judgment in the Mountains," "The Prodigal Children," and "Freedom's a Hard-Bought Thing." He was kept financially solvent only by Brandt's tireless ingenuity, his own dogged and profitable labor during 1941 on a skillful movie version of "The Devil and Daniel Webster"— Hollywood provided the title, *All That Money Can Buy*

—and the unexpected bonanza of a new two-volume collection of his poetry and fiction which was chosen as a Book-of-the-Month Club selection in 1942. "Absolutely no money," he noted in his diary, "so borrow $1000 from B&B. Then JF phones to say I will get $3000 from BofM for advance on collected works."

The *Selected Works* was heavily subscribed by the book club members, in large part as a result of his new status as America's most widely heard poetic voice. He continued to get these improbable riches from work which had in most cases been written years before. "Stan [Rinehart] stuns me," he noted in 1942, "by saying B of M has paid further on set and I will get about $6000 more." He insisted on omitting some of the material which Basil Davenport, its editor, had chosen, including five short stories and some verse from *Heavens and Earth*. He also argued against Farrar and Rinehart's tendency to make the volumes overelaborate. "My only other criticism," he wrote Farrar, "is on the hand-lettered 'Benét' on the title-page, which seems to me unnecessarily fussy."

On the whole, however, he was comforted by the quality of what he had written in the past, republished as it was in the midst of his wartime propaganda. "I am pleased and impressed by having this sort of edition," he told Farrar, "and, thinking of my latter end, feel I probably don't deserve it." He was amused by the grudging respect which the critics gave the two volumes when they were published in June 1942. "The boys are always surprised that in spite of the fact that I am read, I show craftsmanship. If I had blown up like Bromfield then they could have written an article on how I used to have promise. But I haven't blown up."

And yet as he read the galleys of *Selected Works* he

also felt a profound melancholy. He had done most of this work in the twenty-three fruitful years between his seventeenth and fortieth birthdays. Now he was forty-three and the conviction was growing within him that his major work was done. "Will I ever do good work again?" he wondered in the diary. He doubted it more and more. *Western Star* was still unfinished. His time and energy were monopolized by the radio scripts for the Council for Democracy. His health was bad and clearly growing worse; he felt dreadful most of the time now, and he had difficulty sleeping without pills.

"He was the unhealthiest looking man I ever saw," said C. D. Jackson years later, thinking of the months in 1941 and 1942 of his association with Benét. When Edgar Mowrer called on Benét in the fall of 1942, to ask him to write a short history of the United States for the OWI, the newspaperman was appalled by his condition. "He seemed in bad health and feeble in body." Then, as always, Benét summoned strength from some reservoir of purpose. "The impression of feebleness disappeared once he began to talk," Mowrer recalled, "and I was amazed by the vivacity with which he discussed matters of world politics and the world situation about which I felt myself well informed." [11]

Privately, however, Benét knew the reservoir was not limitless. He made a new will in 1941, and when Bob McClure came East in 1942 he sensed a tranquillity in Benét which seemed to him to indicate that the poet was living from day to day in serene expectation. He took a Sunday off from propaganda in the fall of 1942 and spent the day with Philip Barry in East Hampton. They sat on the porch and somehow their talk drifted to epitaphs. "I know what yours should be," said Barry. "Even Stephen." Benét said he liked that. Barry developed it further.

"Even Stephen? *He* must go? Even Stephen. Even so."
Benét grinned. "I like that too," he told Barry, "but it's
sort of scarey."

As always he was philosophical and ironic about his
distress. "I am old, I am arthritic," he wrote Emerson
Tuttle at Yale, apologizing for a lecture invitation he
could not accept, "I am a ruined tower, like Wilkins
Micawber." There were times when he could not be in-
wardly tranquil, though he could still be philosophical.
"Get dummy for collected edition," he wrote in his diary.
"A very handsome tombstone."

Despite his weariness Benét sought no easing of his
propaganda load. "His health was all shot," said Wallace
Stegner, who met him in Cambridge that winter, "he was
gnarled and bent with arthritis. I was so upset at the
change in him that I literally lost my way driving into
South Station and almost made him miss the Owl." Tom
Chubb, who had known him well for twenty-five years,
passed him on the street one day in 1942 without recognizing him; Norman Rosten saw him on Madison Avenue, stooped and bent "as an old man." He himself was
equally shocked at the condition of some of his contemporaries. "Edna Millay looks deathly ill," he wrote in his
diary, "and it makes my heart turn over to see her. God,
what ruins we come to!" In 1942 and 1943, nevertheless,
he undertook assignments even more extensive than any
he had done during the previous two years.

In January 1942 he was persuaded by Norman Corwin
to write a script for a major official program called *This
Is War*. He worked on it all through the second half of
February, doing the preliminary research between calls
from Washington and the War Department and then
writing the script in long four- and five-hour stretches

from mid-afternoon to early evening. "Very hard sort of thing to do without being completely phony. However— we'll see." It was characteristic of both his sensibility and his intelligence that, at a time when the American military experts were forecasting a technological war, he celebrated the role of the infantryman. He finished the script at the end of the month; Corwin, the most experienced and prominent of the radio playwrights, told him it was by far the best in the series.

Benét spent most of the next week attending rehearsals and cutting lines. "Radio," he noted in his diary, "is an ungrateful medium." The show was a great success, but Benét scarcely had time to return to his own work before Farrar and Jackson made him an even more exacting proposition. They persuaded him to do a six-weeks program under the title *Dear Adolf*.[12] All during April and May he sat in on conferences about the show and read the material which the Council's staff had been collecting. He decided to call the first script "Letter from a Farmer," and to follow that pattern in each of its five successors. He talked to Glenway Wescott's brother, who owned a thousand acres in New Jersey, and he continued reading agricultural journals and the Council's correspondence from farmers all over the country.

He finished the first script in early June, in a drive of concentration that lasted for two straight days without interruption. "Rosemary thinks it's good. Work so hard I sleep badly. Feeling kind of strung up." The series was given the desirable time of five o'clock on Sunday afternoons. The reception to it and its five successors, on which he spent June and July, was more enthusiastic than to anything he had previously done for radio.

The actors—Massey, Helen Hayes, Cagney, Melvyn Douglas, William Holden, Joseph Schildkraut—were all major performers, and the praise for Benét's scripts was unanimous. The various Letters in the rest of the series— from a businessman, a housewife, a soldier, a worker, a foreign-born citizen—were enlivened by a sharp literacy and technical proficiency which filled experienced radio writers like Corwin and MacLeish and Norman Rosten with admiration. "We'll choke you with wheat and corn, Adolf," says the Farmer, "we'll drown you in New York State milk." Here and there a critic was suddenly aware that Benét was making literary history.

"Mr. Benét could not have chosen a better time or a greater subject for his first regular radio series," said John K. Hutchens in the New York *Times,* "and it would seem that some of his colleagues among the first-rank writers might follow his lead—the 'names' who wrote so passionately a little while ago, and should not be silent now . . . if they have their doubts about [radio]'s value as an artistic medium, let them ponder on the success with which Mr. Benét, long established as a poet and short story writer before he turned to radio, adjusted himself to a new field. Not all of them are so well equipped as he, lacking his poet's gift of the sharp, exact word and the singing phrase. But they might have a try at it." [13]

Benét himself was now more assured about the medium in general, and aroused by possibilities he was beginning to grasp more clearly. A young man from the Council, Marshall Schulman, remembered the workmanlike manner in which Benét revised a script while he waited to rush it down to the studio. "It was extraordinary to me," Schulman said later, "how calm and businesslike he was, even under the extreme pressure of time under which we were working at that moment." Benét did not hesitate to attempt some fantasy; he made a jeep talk, and got away with it, on one of the scripts. "I am getting a little more on to these things," he conceded as he worked on the third of the *Dear Adolf* shows. Even *Time*, who had rarely given him a good notice in the past, was crisply approving. "The most engaging of U.S. fight-talk programs, NBC's *Dear Adolf*," they said in early August, "bows off the air this Sunday after six successful broadcasts. Unlike many another morale program, it is quitting before the thread shows through the tires." [14]

Now, however, Benét encountered the basic mind of radio. Pressure was put on him—not by the Council—to continue the series in the autumn. Network officials talked winningly to him about all the other Letters he could write; there could be, an executive assured him solemnly, a Letter from a Mechanic, a Letter from an Aviator, a Letter from a Nurse. Like so many of the people he had known in Hollywood, the extent of their professional creativity was to take somebody else's good thing and run it into the ground. The pressure grew more painful when one of the Council's employees confided pleadingly to Benét that NBC had promised him a good job if he could persuade the poet to resume the series.

None of this was calculated to make an ill man more healthy. Such peace of mind as still remained was additionally disturbed when his doctor first forbade him to fly to England, on an officially approved assignment, and then told him flatly that under no circumstances was he even to consider accepting the major's commission which the Army now offered him. Benét visited Washington, once to talk to Lord Halifax about Anglo-American relations, and once to appear at an exhibition of his work in the Library of Congress—"the most well attended in the

371

entire series," he was told—and he and Rosemary and the children had a pleasant month at Stonington in the late summer of 1942.

In the fall, however, he resumed the radio work. He did a Thanksgiving program, and a script for Massey to use on Lincoln's Birthday; and for a Christmas production by the Lunts he wrote the highly successful "A Child Is Born," which would become in later years an annual classic of radio and television.[15] He went to interminable meetings of the Council for Democracy, much disturbed that its success and prestige were making it increasingly conservative. His "Prayer" was read by President Roosevelt at United Nations ceremonies. For the *Post* he wrote one of the declarations in a series on the Four Freedoms. He accepted a commission from the Lunts for an Easter script—though here again, as always, the fee would go to the USO—and in the early winter of 1943 he wrote *America*, a 40,000-word chronicle of the United States, for the Office of War Information.

This history was published in 1944, in almost every language in use by twentieth-century man. Thousands of copies were distributed throughout Europe and Asia. In Hungary it was the first book printed after the liberation. Stephen Vincent Benét never knew how far his last published words traveled, nor how much his sense of America meant to the newly freed citizens of Europe. He died at his home in New York, on 68th Street, on March 13, 1943. He was forty-four years old.

A heart attack on February 18 had put him in the hospital for a week, and when he'd returned home the doctor had confined him to the second floor. By the first week of March, however, he felt much better. "Symptoms imaginary," he scoffed in the diary as he noted that he'd had a cardiogram that day. He began to take brief walks, and he finished up *America* and started sketching out the Easter show for the Lunts. His working title was *The Watchers by the Stone*. On March 9 he filled out his income tax for the previous year. "Discover to my horror I will have to pay about $8000, when I haven't got it. Well, well. Drink some claret Kipper [LaFarge] brought —very good."

On the night of March 12 they had a pleasant evening together. Only Tommy, away at Exeter, was missing. Stephanie had come home from Swarthmore for the week end. They played some records and talked a while before going to bed. He woke up about 3 o'clock, without warning, and Rosemary held him in her arms while he shuddered through several minutes of agonizing pain, and then he died. The funeral was on March 15. There were editorials in most of the nation's newspapers, and a telegram from the White House. "Grief is an agony," Rosemary wrote in his diary on March 16, under the final entries in his own hand, "but, alas, you don't die of it." The next day was the twenty-second anniversary of their engagement. "My real life," she wrote, "began and ended at this time of year."

The last lines he himself wrote in the diary were concerned not with his own welfare but with that of all Americans. "FDR sends social-security plan to Congress," he wrote on March 11, "which immediately raises a storm of hate from the inept and the reactionary." He had himself provided, however, for the welfare of his own dependents. He had maintained all during those difficult years the quarterly payments which had so haunted him during the early 1930's. When his estate was appraised in 1944, its gross value included $57,432 worth of life insurance.

The *Saturday Review of Literature* began planning a memorial issue which was published on March 27; there was not enough space for all the testimonials from his peers. *Western Star* was published in July—"the work," wrote Bernard DeVoto, thinking back to *John Brown's Body*, "of an older, more seasoned, more subtle and profound mind, and of an older, less exuberant, more disciplined poet." Once again, as fifteen years before, he reached a national audience and received national honors; *Western Star* was distributed by the Book-of-the-Month Club and awarded a Pulitzer Prize. In May the National Institute of Arts and Letters gave him its Gold Medal for literature; several members recalled that in January, when they voted to make the award to him, someone had protested that he was too young. Someone else telephoned a friend in Stonington to tell him Steve was dead. "Oh, no!" the small-town operator interrupted, her voice formal and shocked as she broke in on the conversation. "Is Mr. Benét dead? That will be a great loss to all of us."

Notes

THE Stephen Vincent Benét manuscripts and correspondence, unless otherwise noted, are in the Yale Collection of American Literature. A good bibliography, though it does not list his poetry, and omits several of his early short stories, is Gladys L. Maddocks, "Stephen Vincent Benét: A Bibliography," *Bulletin of Bibliography and Dramatic Index, 20* (September 1951, April 1952).

The documentation that follows, in order to keep these notes at a manageable length, is somewhat arbitrary. Footnoting of correspondence has been kept to a minimum, particularly when the date and recipient of the correspondence are apparent from the text. No documentation has been provided for the references to entries in Benét's diaries, since they are unpublished and unavailable for general use. Interviews and correspondence between the author and associates of Benét are as a rule cited only on their initial appearance in the notes. The following abbreviations and short titles are used throughout:

W. R. Benét, "Steve,"	William Rose Benét, "My Brother Steve," *SRL, 24* (November 15, 1941).
Bacon, *Semi-Centennial*	Leonard Bacon, *Semi-Centennial,* New York, 1939.
Digest	*Reader's Digest, 37* (October 1940).
CAF	Charles A. Fenton.
(int.)	Material obtained through author's interview.
SEP	*Saturday Evening Post.*

"Sixth Man"	SVB, "The Sixth Man," in *Breaking into Print*, ed. Elmer Adler (New York, 1937). Reprinted from *Colophon, 15* (October 1933), [45]–[48].
SRL	*Saturday Review of Literature.*
SVB	Stephen Vincent Benét.
YLM	*Yale Literary Magazine.*

Benét's published works, which are in general cited by title alone, are as follows:

Five Men and Pompey (Boston, 1915)
The Drug Shop (New Haven, 1917)
Young Adventure (New Haven, 1918)
Heavens and Earth (New York, 1920)
The Beginning of Wisdom (New York, 1921)
Young People's Pride (New York, 1922)
The Ballad of William Sycamore (New York, 1923)
King David (New York, 1923)
Jean Huguenot (New York, 1923)
Tiger Joy (New York, 1925)
Spanish Bayonet (New York, 1926)
John Brown's Body (New York, 1928)
The Barefoot Saint (New York, 1929)
The Litter of the Rose Leaves (New York, 1930)
Ballads and Poems (New York, 1931)
A Book of Americans (New York, 1933)
James Shore's Daughter (New York, 1934)
Burning City (New York, 1936)
The Devil and Daniel Webster (New York, 1937)
Thirteen O'Clock (New York, 1937)
Johnny Pye and the Fool-Killer (New York, 1938)
Tales before Midnight (New York, 1939)
The Ballad of the Duke's Mercy (New York, 1939)
Nightmare at Noon (New York, 1940)
Tuesday, November 5, 1940 (New York, 1940)
Dear Adolf (New York, 1942)
A Child Is Born (Boston, 1942)
Selected Works (New York, 1942)
They Burned the Books (New York, 1942)
Western Star (New York, 1943)
America (New York, 1945)
We Stand United (New York, 1945)
The Last Circle (New York, 1946)

CHAPTER 1. *The Colonel's House*

The research on Benét's boyhood and adolescence, described in Chapters 1 and 2, was made easier and more accurate by the assistance of a number of generous people, including Mrs. Leonard Bacon, Donald S. Bridgman, James Brunkhurst, William L. Brunkhurst, Bishop Charles C. J. Carpenter, Mrs. Julia Shaler Harper, Eleanor B. Hays, Miss Robert Kinkead, Mrs. Charles M. McCrary, Kathleen Norris, Mrs. Winthrop Osterhout, Archibald B. Ragan, Montgomery Ridgely, and Mrs. Walter E. Young.

1. SVB, "The Most Unforgettable Character I've Met," *Digest*, p. 113.

2. Bacon, *Semi-Centennial*, p. 116. Bacon, who graduated from Yale in 1909, two classes behind William Rose Benét, was teaching English at the University of California in 1910. Bacon's most intimate friendships within the Benét family were with William and Laura, his contemporaries. He and Stephen saw a good deal of each other during the 1930's, however, when Benét and his family spent a part of almost every summer in Peace Dale, R.I. Once or twice they rented Bacon's home there while the latter was abroad. Bacon dedicated *Semi-Centennial*, his autobiography, to the youngest Benét, referring to Stephen as "one who has given encouragement to a fellow poet." Bacon received a Pulitzer Prize for poetry in 1941. He died in 1954.

3. *Digest*, p. 113.

4. John Farrar, "For the Record," in *Stephen Vincent Benét* (New York, 1943), p. 20. The quotation is from a reader report by Benét on a manuscript which had been submitted to the publishing house of Farrar and Rinehart, Inc., in 1940. For more on the long friendship and professional association between Benét and Farrar, see later chapters. SVB, "The Giant's House," *Elks' Magazine*, 7 (June 1928), 20.

5. SVB to Douglas Moore, [February] 1934. This letter is owned by Mr. Moore, whose work as a distinguished composer of American music often paralleled Benét's prose and poetic at-

titudes toward native material. Moore knew Benét slightly at Yale, in 1915, and increasingly during subsequent years in Paris and New York. They became not only intimate friends but congenial and effective collaborators. See esp. Chapters 5, 7, above.

6. SVB to Carl Brandt, March 6, 1940. In this letter to his literary agent, who died in 1957, Benét was outlining the article about his father which was later published in the *Reader's Digest* as "The Most Unforgettable Character I've Met." See note 1 above.

7. *Digest,* p. 114.

8. Bacon, *Semi-Centennial,* pp. 116–17.

9. SVB, "The Magic of Poetry and the Poet's Art," *Compton's Pictured Encyclopedia* (Chicago, 1936), Vol. 11.

10. SVB to Carl Brandt, March 6, 1940. *Digest,* p. 113.

11. *Digest,* p. 113.

12. Bacon, *Semi-Centennial,* p. 116.

13. SVB and Rosemary Benét, "J. P. Marquand: A Really Expert Writer," *New York Herald Tribune Books,* 9 (March 16, 1941), 5. Colonel Benét's autobiography, which he had planned during his years on active service, was never either published or, indeed, completed, though it was several hundred pages long in typescript. Laurence Benét, who spent his own retirement in genealogical research on the Benét ancestry, had several copies of his brother's candid and lively manuscript typed and circulated within the family. The manuscript was one of Stephen's most prized possessions. In his own diary he noted on several different occasions that he had once again read the autobiography with pleasure. It is now in the Yale Collection of American Literature.

14. SVB, "Going Back to School," *YLM,* 82 (June 1917), 322. Reprinted, *Young Adventure,* p. 38; *Ballads and Poems,* pp. 146–7.

15. SVB, "Portrait of a Boy," *Century Magazine, 93* (January 1917), 345. Reprinted, *Young Adventure,* p. 87; *Ballads and Poems,* pp. 125-6.

16. *Wilson Billboard* (April 15, 1938). This was an interview with Benét in the undergraduate newspaper at Wilson College.

CHAPTER 2. *Georgia*

1. SVB to Carl Brandt, January [3] 1932. Benét was writing to his agent about some exasperating editorial objections the *SEP* had made to a short story called "The Yankee Fox." The story was eventually published in *Woman's Home Companion, 60* (June 1933), 12.

2. SVB to Pauli Murray, [July] 1941. This letter is owned by Miss Murray. She began sending poems and short stories to Benét in 1939, having been encouraged to begin writing, she told him, by statements he had made about the role of the Negro artist in America. Benét discussed a number of her manuscripts with Miss Murray, both by letter and at his home in New York, in 1940 and 1941.

3. SVB, "The Giant's House," *Elks' Magazine, 7* (June 1928), 26,

4. SVB to Margaret Mitchell, [July] 1936. The correspondence between Benét and Miss Mitchell was occasioned by the latter's gratitude to Benét for a review of *Gone with the Wind.* The letter is owned by Miss Mitchell's estate.

5. SVB, "Flem Snopes and His Kin," *SRL, 21* (April 6, 1940), 7.

6. SVB to Alice Lee Myers, [February] 1932. This letter is owned by Mrs. Myers. The friendship between Stephen Benét and Mr. and Mrs. Richard Myers was a long and intimate one which began in Paris in 1920. See Chapter 5, above.

7. William L. Brunkhurst to CAF (int.), January 10, 1955.

8. William L. Brunkhurst, "Information Concerning Life of Stephen Vincent Benét," January 8, 1955. An unpublished manuscript.

9. SVB to Margaret Mitchell, [July] 1936.

10. W. R. Benét, "Steve," p. 4. A briefer version of this article was published in *SRL, 26* (March 27, 1943), 5–7, and a more complete one in William Rose Benét and John Farrar, *Stephen Vincent Benét* (New York, 1943), pp. 1–11.

11. "Sixth Man," p. 26.

12. Ibid., p. 25.

13. W. R. Benét, "Steve," p. 4.

14. Farrar, "For the Record," p. 20.

15. "Sixth Man," p. 22.

16. W. R. Benét, "Steve," p. 4.

17. SVB to Alice Lee Myers, [February] 1932.

18. SVB to Paul Engle, October 4, 1935. Benét's correspondence with Engle is in the Lockwood Memorial Library at the University of Buffalo. For a description of the relationship between Benét and Engle see Chapters 11, 13, above.

19. SVB to Basil Davenport, [August] 1933. This letter is owned by Mr. Davenport, the New York editor who was a friend of Benét from the mid-1920's until the latter's death in 1943. Davenport edited Benét's *Selected Works*.

20. W. R. Benét, "Steve," p. 4. Bertha Runkle, *The Helmet of Navarre*, New York, 1901.

21. SVB, "Soldier with Burgoyne," *SRL, 23* (November 2, 1940), 5.

22. SVB to Rosemary Benét, [June] 1922.

23. SVB to Robert McClure, October 7, 1942. This letter is owned by Mr. McClure, a friend of Benét's from undergraduate days at Yale, who was in 1942 writing the first of his several novels. McClure is now editor and publisher of the Santa Monica (Cal.) *Evening Outlook.*

24. SVB to "Tom Graham," [August] 1912. Benét presented this copy of Lewis' first novel to the Yale University Library in 1941, and apologized for its worn pages. "You will not find the book in 'mint' condition," he wrote Chauncey B. Tinker, "I read and reread it."

25. SVB, "Winged Man," *New Republic, 4* (August 7, 1915), 20. Reprinted in *Young Adventure,* pp. 79–81; *Ballads and Poems,* 52–4.

26. "Sixth Man," p. 24.

27. James Walker Benét to Odus Creamer Horney, July 18, 1915.

28. "Sixth Man," p. 27.

29. *The Oxford Anthology of American Literature,* ed. William Rose Benét and Norman Holmes Pearson, 2 (New York, 1939), 1523.

30. James Walker Benét to Odus Creamer Horney, July 18, 1915.

CHAPTER 3. *Bright College Years*

Their generous willingness to talk and correspond about the period discussed in Chapters 3 and 4 indebted me to N. F. Austin, the late Shreve C. Badger, Sherman Baldwin, Professor Blanche B. Boyer, William S. Braithwaite, Francis W. Bronson, the late Donald M. Campbell, the late Rodney Chase, Thomas Caldecot

3. BRIGHT COLLEGE YEARS

Chubb, Elliot E. Cohen, the late Thomas R. Coward, Wilbur L. Cross, Jr., William C. DeVane, William Douglas, Samuel S. Duryee, Norman Fitts, Maxwell E. Foster, Hamilton Hadley, Henry Hallowell, Roswell G. Ham, Sr., Harry G. Hayes, Allan V. Heely, Mrs. Ellwood Hendrick, C. Vincent Henry, Jr., Cyril Hume, Thayer Jaccaci, Raymond Jenkins, Sherman Kent, Gilbert Knipmeyer, Chester J. LaRoche, Carleton A. Leavenworth, W. Sargent Lewis, Wilmarth S. Lewis, Claude Lloyd, Carl L. Lokke, Irving W. Lyon, Ronald C. Marsh, Herbert R. Mooney, Benjamin C. Nangle, Robert P. Pflieger, Robert Redfield, Mrs. Edward Bliss Reed, Guy H. Richards, Barclay Robinson, Carl Purington Rollins, Malcolm Ross, Lawrence F. Rossiter, Henry L. Savage, Hartley Simpson, Samuel C. Slaymaker, David H. Stevens, Mary Curry Tresidder, Wheeler Williams, and Dean K. Worcester.

1. The entire dedication was as follows: "This Book Is Dedicated To STEPHEN VINCENT BENÉT our most distinguished classmate for whom we all had great affection, profound respect and admiration." *A Twenty-Five Year Record: Class of 1919, Yale College* (New Haven, 1946), [3].

2. *The Letters of William James,* ed. Henry James (Boston, 1920), 2, 202.

3. SVB to Egbert S. Oliver, [January] 1935; letter in possession of Professor Oliver, Oregon State College. In 1935 Oliver was an instructor in English at Willamette University and engaged on a project to measure the role of undergraduate training in writing as reflected in the experience of a number of contemporary American writers. He summarized his very useful material and conclusions in "Can Creative Writing Be Taught?" *English Journal,* 26 (January 1937), 39–47.

4. Van Wyck Brooks, *Scenes and Portraits* (Dutton, 1954), p. 97.

5. SVB, "American Names," in *Ballads and Poems,* p. 3.

6. Allan V. Heely to CAF, April 21, 1954. Mr. Heely, a member of the faculty at Phillips Andover Academy from 1924 through 1934, has been headmaster of the Lawrenceville School since 1934. At Yale he was a fellow member with

382

Benét of a number of clubs and organizations, including the *Record,* Canterbury Pilgrims, Pundits, Elizabethan Club, and Alpha Delta Phi.

7. *YLM, 81* (1915–16): "Three Days Ride" (October), 13; "The City Revisited" (November), 42; "The General Public" (December), 90; "Portfolio" (January), 147; "Atheist's Tragedy" (February), 171; "Poor Devil" (February), 190; "The Breaking Point" (March), 199; "1814" (April), 236; "Working It Out" [short story] (April), 237; "The Ballad of John Faa" (April), 251; "A Ballad of Aegispotamos" (May), 271; "Lonely Burial" (May), 293.

8. Dean K. Worcester to CAF, June 3, 1954. Worcester, like Benét, belonged to the Canterbury Pilgrims, the Elizabethan Club, and Wolf's Head.

9. Culbreth Sudler to CAF, April 17, 1954. Mr. Sudler, Class of 1920, knew Benét through the *Record,* of which Sudler became managing editor in 1918.

10. Archibald MacLeish to CAF (int.), July 26, 1954.

11. Culbreth Sudler to CAF, April 17, 1954.

12. SVB, "The Quality of Courage," *Chimaera, 1* (May 1916), 12; "A Vision of Revolution," *Chimaera, 1* (July 1916), 48; "Portrait of a Boy," *Century Magazine, 93* (January 1917), 345; "Rain after a Vaudeville Show," *Seven Arts, 1* (January 1917), 238; "Roads and Hills," *Seven Arts, 1* (January 1917), 62.

13. SVB, "The Hemp," *Century Magazine, 91* (January 1916), 342.

14. Irving Whitney Lyon to CAF, April 28, 1954. Mr. Lyon, Class of 1919, was much interested in writing as an undergraduate.

15. *The Crack-Up,* ed. Edmund Wilson (New York, 1945), p. 248. Malcolm Cowley to CAF, October 7, 1957.

16. SVB to Shreve Badger, [March] 1943. Badger shared member-

ship with Benét in the Vorpal Blades and Wolf's Head. They corresponded frequently after graduation. Badger died in 1956.

17. SVB, "Ballade of the Summer Girl," *Yale Record, 44* (April 12, 1916), 517.

18. Effingham Evarts to CAF (int.), July 7, 1954. Evarts, a member with Benét of the Elizabethan Club and Wolf's Head, was one of his two or three closest friends at Yale.

19. These lines are from "The Tapiad," one of a number of unpublished satiric poems about Yale which Benét wrote in 1917 for the volume projected by the Vorpal Blades and intended to appear under the ironic title *The Songs of Dear Old Yale.*

20. Culbreth Sudler to CAF, April 17, 1954.

CHAPTER 4. *War*

1. SVB, "The Difficult Way," *YLM, 83* (November 1917), [65].

2. SVB, "Everyone Falls for the Blonde," *Yale Record, 45* (April 12, 1917), 464.

3. SVB, "Scholastic Work Is Still the Most Important Thing at Yale," *Yale Record, 46* (December 14, 1917), 55.

4. SVB, "Canned Salmon," *Everybody's Magazine, 52* (March 1925), 30–6.

5. SVB, "Flood-Tide," *Yale Review, 10* (October 1920), 141–2. Though the poem was not published until 1920, "it was written," according to William Rose Benét, "while he was still at Yale." *Poems for Youth,* ed. William Rose Benét (Dutton, 1925), p. 495.

6. SVB, "The Campus—Spring," *YLM, 82* (April 1917), 204–5. Reprinted as "Campus Sonnets," *Young Adventure,* pp. 48–51.

7. SVB, "The Difficult Way," *YLM, 83* (October 1917), [65].

8. SVB, "Portrait of a Young Love," *New Republic, 15* (June 15, 1918), 208. Reprinted as "Portrait of Young Love," *Heavens and Earth,* p. 86; *Ballads and Poems,* p. 134. SVB, "Queen's Gambit Declined," *Contemporary Verse, 6* (September 1918), 43. Benét never reprinted "Queen's Gambit Declined," a kind of elegant version of his light verse for the *Record.* SVB, "Come Back!" *Youth: Poetry of Today, 1* (December 1918), 28. Reprinted, *Heavens and Earth,* pp. 60–1. SVB, "Lost Lights," *The Poets of the Future,* ed. Henry T. Schnittkind (Boston, 1918), 81–2. Reprinted, *Heavens and Earth,* pp. 58–9.

9. SVB, ["Romeo and Juliet"], *YLM, 83* (October 1917), 61.

10. Alfred Bellinger to CAF (int.), September 26, 1954. Mr. Bellinger graduated from Yale in 1917 and became a member of the Department of Classics in 1920.

11. Robert Van Gelder, "Mr. Benét's Work in Progress," *New York Times Book Review, 6* (April 21, 1940), 20.

12. Arthur Train, *My Day in Court* (New York, 1939), 350; SVB, "Breaking the Codes," *SRL, 19* (April 1, 1939), 11.

13. Robert Redfield to CAF, June 28, 1956.

14. SVB to Shreve Badger, [December] 1918; SVB, "Behind the Lines in Wartime Richmond," *SRL, 16* (May 15, 1937), 6; SVB, "Men of Destruction," *SRL, 18* (May 21, 1938), [3].

15. SVB, "Skin-Changing," *YLM, 84* (February 1919), [61].

16. SVB, "Expressions Near the End of Winter," *Dial, 66* (March 8, 1918), 248. Reprinted, *Heavens and Earth,* p. 57; *Ballads and Poems,* pp. 173–4. SVB, "Jaufre Rudel Beholds the Lady of Tripoli," *Ainslee's, 43* (May 1919), 62. SVB, "The Trapeze Performer," *Ainslee's, 43* (July 1919), 159.

17. Louis Untermeyer, "New Volumes of Poetry," *Yale Review*, 8 (July 1919), 862; Babette Deutsch, "Realists and Orators," *Bookman, 48* (February 1919), 754; W.S.B., "The Poetry of Young Adventure," Boston *Evening Transcript* (January 22, 1919), p. 9.

18. Charlton M. Lewis to Committee on Fellowships, Graduate School, New Haven, March 5, 1919.

19. SVB, "Devourer of Nations," *S4N, 2* (December 1919), [78]. Reprinted, *Heavens and Earth*, p. 78; *Ballads and Poems*, p. 202.

20. SVB, "Wisdom-Teeth," in *Heavens and Earth*, pp. 69–70.

21. SVB, "Talk," in *Heavens and Earth*, p. 82.

22. SVB, "Lunch-Time along Broadway," *S4N, 9* (July 1920), [1]. Reprinted, *Heavens and Earth*, p. 41; *Ballads and Poems*, pp. 73–4.

23. SVB to Rosemary Carr, [July] 1921.

24. Charlton M. Lewis to Committee on Fellowships, Graduate School, New Haven, March 5, 1919.

25. William C. DeVane to CAF (int.), September 9, 1954.

26. SVB, "The Funeral of John Bixby," *Munsey's, 70* (July 1920), 382–4; SVB, "Summer Thunder," *Smart Set, 63* (September 1920), 79–86.

27. "Notes & Comments," *S4N, 6* (August 1921), [2].

28. Norman Fitts, "Statement of Idea," *S4N, 2* (November 1919), [2].

29. SVB, ["The S4N Society"], *S4N, 1* (November 1919), 7–8.

30. John Carter to CAF (int.), December 2, 1954.

31. SVB, ["The Kingdom of the Mad"], *S4N, 2* (December 1919), [75].

32. Raymond Jenkins to CAF, February 14, 1954.

33. SVB, "The Best Loved Teacher Yale Ever Had," *New York Herald Tribune Books,* 9 (April 16, 1939), 1.

34. SVB, "The Blood of the Martyrs," *SEP, 209* (December 12, 1936), 6.

35. SVB, "Elementals," *Cosmopolitan, 72* (April 1922), 17.

CHAPTER 5. *The Beginning of Wisdom*

For their help in locating the material for Chapters 5-9 I am indebted to E. N. Brandt, Rollo Walter Brown, the Reverend Alan Chalmers, Charles Child, John Dos Passos, Ben Hibbs, Emily Kimbrough, Daniel Longwell, the late Amy Loveman, the Edward MacDowell Association, Inc., Christopher Morley, Burton Rascoe, Robert H. Reed, Belle McDiarmid Richey, Helen Jeannette Smith, and Burton E. Stevenson.

1. SVB to H. Phelps Putnam, August 11, 1920.

2. James Walker Benét to Odus Creamer Horney, March 5, 1921.

3. SVB to Shreve Badger, [August] 1920; SVB to Phelps Putnam, August 11, 1920.

4. SVB, ["The Modern Novel"], *S4N, 3* (January 1920), [5]–[9].

5. H. Phelps Putnam, *Trinc* (New York, 1927), p. 27.

6. SVB to George Abbe, April [4], 1939. For more on the relationship between Benét and George Abbe, poet and novelist, see Chapter 12, below.

7. James Walker Benét to Odus Creamer Horney, March 5, 1921.

5. THE BEGINNING OF WISDOM

8. SVB to Lawrence F. Rossiter, [December] 1929. Rossiter, a classmate of Benét at Yale, was planning a Paris honeymoon.

9. SVB to John Farrar, June 10, 1928.

10. SVB to Rosemary Carr, [August] 1921.

11. "Notes & Comments," *S4N, 13* (November 1920), [2].

12. James Walker Benét to SVB, January 8, 1921.

13. SVB, "Nomenclature," *Literary Digest, 69* (May 21, 1921), 32. Reprinted, *Current Opinion, 71* (August 1921), 242; *Tiger Joy*, pp. 48–9; *Ballads and Poems*, pp. 96–7.

14. Vincent Sheean to CAF, May 13, 1957.

15. SVB, "A Nonsense Song," *Parabalou, 3* (1921), 11; "Song of the Hours," *Parabalou, 3* (1921), 13; "A Sad Song," *Parabalou, 2* (1921), 11–12; "To the Dream," *Parabalou, 3* (1921), 12; "Venus' Song," *Parabalou, 3* (1921), 13–14; "Azrael's Bar," *Bookman, 53* (February 1921), 486; "Epistle to All Friends," *S4N, 16* (March 1921), [2]; "An Immoral Song," *New Republic, 26* (May 11, 1921), 325; "Nomenclature," *Literary Digest, 69* (May 21, 1921), 32; "Difference," *New Republic, 27* (June 15, 1921), 77; "July," *Bookman, 53* (July 1921), 396. With the exception of "Song of the Hours" and "Venus' Song," all these poems were reprinted in *Tiger Joy*. "Epistle to All Friends" was cut to a single stanza—the first —and retitled "Epitaph."

16. SVB to Rosemary Carr, April 7, 1921; SVB to Dean B. Lyman, Jr., [June] 1926; SVB to Rosemary Carr, August 4, 1921. Lyman, a member of the Class of 1918S at Yale, had written an article on Benét's work in the *Yale Alumni Weekly, 35* (June 4, 1926), 1049–50.

17. Rosemary Benét to CAF (int.), August 28, 1954; Carl Brandt to Rosemary Benét, March 15, 1943; SVB to Rosemary Carr, July 26, 1921; Carl Brandt to CAF (int.), January 26, 1955.

18. Thomas Beer, "An Important Attitude," *Literary Review, 3* (September 30, 1922), 64.

19. Thomas Caldecot Chubb, "Young People's Pride," *New York Tribune* (September 10, 1922), p. 7.

20. Elinor Wylie, "Young People's Pride," *New Republic, 32* (October 25, 1922), 229.

21. SVB, "Goobers—à la Française," *Delineator, 101* (August 1922), 5; SVB, "Mad Americans," *Metropolitan Magazine, 54* (January 1922), 12.

CHAPTER 6. *Ballads in Grub Street*

1. SVB to George Abbe, [1935].

2. SVB, "Elementals," *Cosmopolitan, 72* (April 1922), 16; SVB, "Yacobson," *Redbook, 39* (October 1922), 89.

3. *The Barefoot Saint* was finally published by Doubleday, Doran in 1929, in a deluxe edition which embarrassed Benét. See Chapter 10, above.

4. SVB, "The Golden Bessie," *Everybody's Magazine, 48* (June 1923), 3; SVB, "Snake and Hawk," *Ladies' Home Journal, 50* (March 1923), 10; SVB, "The Tiger Smiles," *Redbook, 52* (November 1923), 86.

5. SVB, "Jerry and James and John," *Redbook, 41* (June 1923), 41.

6. SVB, "Beaver!" *Cosmopolitan, 74* (June 1923), 57; SVB, "The Garbageman's Daughter," *Cosmopolitan, 75* (September 1923), 33.

7. SVB, "Sir Willie of the Valley," *Harper's Bazaar, 58* (February 1923), 46.

8. SVB, "Oh, Tricksy April," *New Republic, 30* (April 26, 1922),

256; SVB, "In a Glass of Water before Retiring," *Ladies' Home Journal, 40* (January 1923), 76. Benét included the second poem in both *Tiger Joy,* pp. 58–9, and *Ballads and Poems,* pp. 106–7.

9. SVB, "The Ballad of William Sycamore, 1790–1880," *New Republic, 32* (November 8, 1922), 279. Its audience was further enlarged by its republication a few weeks later in the *Literary Digest, 75* (November 25, 1922), 36, and, the following year, as *The Ballad of William Sycamore,* New York, 1923. The publisher of this limited edition was the same Brick Row Book Shop which issued *The Drug Shop.* Reprinted, *Tiger Joy,* pp. 13–16; *Ballads and Poems,* pp. 5–8. Benét altered its *New Republic* subtitle from "1790–1880" to "1790–1871" in subsequent printings.

10. Jesse Stuart to CAF, April 4, 1957.

11. SVB to John Drinkwater, [March] 1923; *Nation, 116* (May 2, 1923), 520. Drinkwater included "King David" in his *Twentieth Century Poetry* (New York, 1930), pp. 489–97.

12. *Nation, 116* (March 7, 1923), 271; ibid. (May 2, 1923), p. 520.

13. SVB, "For All Blasphemers," in *Tiger Joy,* p. 84.

14. SVB, "King David," *Nation, 116* (February 14, 1923), [177]–9. Also, *King David,* New York, Henry Holt, 1923. Reprinted, *Tiger Joy,* pp. 69–79; *Ballads and Poems,* pp. 83–92. Like "The Ballad of William Sycamore," the poem became a favorite of anthologists.

15. SVB, "X-Ray," *New Republic, 38* (May 21, 1924), 339.

16. SVB, "Dishface," *Redbook, 42* (February 1924), 57; "Uriah's Son," *Redbook, 43* (May 1924), 81; "The Girl Who Walked Home," *Metropolitan Magazine, 59* (July 1924), 34; "The Raveled Sleeve," *Cosmopolitan, 77* (October 1924), 90; "Jolly Roger," *Liberty, 1* (November 1, 1924), 42; "Miranda, the Measles, and Marmaduke," *Redbook, 44* (December 1924), 46.

17. *Redbook, 43* (May 1924), 81.

18. Colonel Benét called his son's attention to the Fitzgerald article in a letter of April 8, 1924. "I wonder if your bard is like his," the Colonel inquired, "a bard that pays interest but that you can't sell. I think it must be a true story."

19. At least six of Benét's columns for *Time* are identifiable, since it was then the magazine's policy to sometimes initial the literary and theatrical comment. Several uninitialed columns during 1923 appear on the basis of style and tone to have been written by Benét. Benét was thoroughly indifferent to the emerging *Time* style; his columns were casual and literary, far more in keeping with the general tone and approach of *Bookman* than with the crisp and knowing idiom which Hadden was devising for *Time*. Benét's initialed columns in *Time* were "Nothing New for Boys," *Time, 1* (May 12, 1923), 14; "Translators," *Time, 1* (May 19, 1923), 14; "Prizes," *Time, 1* (May 28, 1923), 14; "Some Aspects," *Time, 1* (June 4, 1923), 14; "Reciters," *Time, 1* (June 11, 1923), 16; "Literary Pot-Pourri," *Time, 1* (June 25, 1923), 14.

20. SVB, "To See or Not to See," *Bookman, 60* (November 1924), 328.

21. Ibid. (October 1924), p. 210; (December 1924), p. 481.

CHAPTER 7. *The Literary Life*

1. Robert Nathan to CAF (int.), September 14, 1954.

2. SVB to Elizabeth Manwaring, [November] 1931.

3. William Lyon Phelps, "Men now Famous," *Delineator, 117* (September 1930), 94; Garrett D. Byrnes, "Stephen Vincent Benét Says Making Living Writing Poetry Impossible," Providence *Evening Bulletin* (August 27, 1930), p. 17.

4. Norman Rosten to CAF (int.), November 10, 1954; Edward Weismiller to CAF, April 7, 1956.

5. Christopher LaFarge to CAF (int.), October 1, 1954; Mrs. Philip Barry to CAF (int.), August 28, 1954.

6. L. A. G. Strong to SVB, June 6, 1925.

7. *The Oxford Anthology of American Literature,* ed. William Rose Benét and Norman Holmes Pearson (New York, 1939), 2, 1517.

8. SVB, "The Mountain Whippoorwill," *Century Magazine,* 87 (March 1925), [635]–[639]. Reprinted, *Tiger Joy,* pp. 27–34; *Ballads and Poems,* pp. 18–23.

9. SVB, "The Golden Corpse," *SRL, 1* (May 2, 1925), 721–2. Reprinted, *Tiger Joy,* pp. 88–95; *Ballads and Poems,* pp. 119–24.

10. Mark Van Doren, "Tiger Joy," *New York Herald Tribune Books, 5* (September 27, 1925), 4; D. F. G., "Tiger Joy," Boston *Evening Transcript* (October 31, 1925), p. 2; Jessica Nelson North, "A Playful Tiger," *Poetry,* 27 (February 1926), 279.

11. Thomas Beer, "Rake's Progress," *SRL, 2* (April 10, 1926), 699.

12. SVB, "Harrigan's Head," *Everybody's Magazine, 52* (May 1925), 19; "Cigarettes," *Liberty, 2* (June 20, 1925), 14; "Mystery Train," *Liberty, 12* (October 12, 1935), 14.

13. Belle McDiarmid Richey to CAF, December 16, 1954; Esther W. Bates to CAF, December 22, 1954.

14. SVB to Rosemary Benét, June 12, 1925.

15. Rollo Walter Brown to CAF, December 11, 1954.

CHAPTER 8. *Goodly Fellowship*

1. SVB to Phelps Putnam, March 7, 1928.

2. SVB to Rosemary Benét, June 27, 1925.

3. SVB, "Literary Treasure," *Bookman, 63* (December 1925), 47.

4. SVB, "My Favorite Fiction Character," *Bookman, 62* (February 1926), 672; "Bigger and Better Murders," *Bookman, 63* (May 1926), 291; "Defense of Mrs. Anonymous," *Bookman, 64* (October 1926), 168. "My Favorite Fiction Character" was reprinted as a pamphlet in 1938 by the Ysletta Press, and again in *Profile by Gaslight,* ed. Edgar W. Smith (New York, 1944), pp. 154–5.
   SVB, "Out of Focus," *SRL, 2* (May 15, 1926), 786; "High Adventure," *SRL, 2* (June 5, 1926), 838; "Distinctive Work," *SRL, 2* (July 17, 1926), 934.

5. SVB to Phelps Putnam, March 7, 1928.

6. Carl Brandt to CAF (int.), January 26, 1955.

7. Dr. Dana W. Atchley to CAF (int.), September 15, 1954. Both Benét and Marquand were friends as well as patients of Atchley, a Manhattan physician.

8. SVB, "The Odor of Sanctity," *Collier's, 77* (January 23, 1926), 15.

9. SVB, "The Sobbin' Women," *Country Gentleman, 91* (May 1926), 6; "The Shadowy Crown," *Elks' Magazine, 4* (May 1926), 14.

10. Carl Brandt to CAF (int.), January 26, 1955.

11. Robert H. Reed to CAF (int.), February 3, 1955.

12. SVB, "The Lucky Fist," *Collier's, 77* (June 19, 1926), 13.

13. SVB, "Miss Willie Lou and the Swan," *Country Gentleman, 91* (November 1926), 15.

14. "The Sobbin' Women" was the earliest of his magazine fiction which Benét republished in his first collection of stories, *Thirteen O'Clock*. It found an entirely new audience, as so much of Benét's work would do both during his lifetime and afterward, when it was transferred successfully to another medium, in this case a musical film in 1955, *The Seven Brothers*.

    The other stories which Benét wrote during this 1926 period were "Lady Lapith," *Collier's, 77* (May 29, 1926), 16; "Take a Fellow Your Size," *Redbook, 47* (June 1926), 54; "The Language of the Stars," *Liberty, 3* (June 12, 1926), 45; "Blackbeard and Co.—Pirates," *Liberty, 3* (August 21, 1926), 12; "Venus Came Out of the Sea," *New York Masonic Outlook, 3* (January 1927), 137; and "The Amateur of Crime," *American Magazine, 103* (April 1927), 48.

15. SVB, "True Thomas," *Good Housekeeping, 82* (April 1926), 24.

16. SVB, "O'Brien's Choice," *SRL, 20* (July 8, 1939), 5.

17. SVB to Rosemary Benét, May 25, 1925. The story was "Bon Voyage," *College Humor, 13* (March 1928), 62.

18. SVB, "Archimedes' Last Foray," *SRL, 2* (June 19, 1926), 871; "After Attending a Séance," *New Yorker, 2* (July 10, 1926), 24.

CHAPTER 9. *John Brown's Body: One*

1. SVB to Felicia Geffen, [December] 1942. Miss Geffen was assistant to the president of the National Institute of Arts and Letters, of which Benét was then a vice-president. See Chapter 15, above.

2. SVB to Frances Neill Benét, [November] 1926.

3. SVB, "The Color of the American Adventure," *New York Herald Tribune Books, 10* (December 12, 1937), 3.

4. SVB to John Farrar, July 1, 1927.

5. SVB, "The Lost Cause in Literature," *SRL, 21* (November 25, 1939), 6.

6. Helen Jeannette Smith to CAF, April 12, 1957; Burton Stevenson to CAF, March 31, 1957.

7. SVB, "Ship of Democracy," *SRL, 20* (October 14, 1939), 24.

8. SVB, "The Jaw Bone of the Lion," *SRL, 9* (October 29, 1932), 205.

9. Garrett D. Byrnes, "Stephen Vincent Benét Says Making Living Writing Poetry Impossible," Providence *Evening Bulletin* (August 27, 1930), p. 17.

10. Robert McClure to CAF, October 9, 1954.

11. SVB and Rosemary Benét, "John Dos Passos: Evolution of an American," *New York Herald Tribune Books, 9* (September 21, 1941), 6.

12. SVB, "Hands," *World Tomorrow, 10* (July 1927), 304. Reprinted, *Ballads and Poems*, p. 179.

13. Harry Salpeter, "The First Reader," New York *World* (August 16, 1928), 11.

14. SVB, "American Names," *Yale Review, 17* (October 1927), 63–4. Reprinted, *Literary Digest, 95* (October 8, 1927), 36; *Ballads and Poems*, pp. 3–4.

15. SVB, "Invocation," *SRL, 3* (June 11, 1927), 891–2. Reprinted, *The Democratic Tradition in America*, ed. Clayton E. Wheat (New York, 1934), pp. 349–52.

16. M. S. J., "Stephen Vincent Benét Amazed to Find *John Brown's Body* a Best Seller," Philadelphia *Record* (September 1, 1928), 6; SVB to Phelps Putnam, January 20, 1928.

17. SVB, "Two Types of Poetry," *SRL, 4* (December 10, 1927), 425.

18. SVB, "The Lucksmith," *Country Gentleman, 93* (March 1928), 20; "The Giant's House," *Elks' Magazine, 7* (June 1928), 26.

19. SVB, "The Story about the Anteater," *Century Magazine, 116* (October 1928), 751. Benét's feeling for this story is confirmed by the care with which he revised and polished it for republication in 1939 in his second collection of short stories, *Tales before Midnight.*

20. SVB to Carl Brandt, March 6, 1940.

21. SVB, "Candleshine," *Redbook, 51* (September 1928), 46.

22. SVB, "Green Christmas," *Ladies' Home Journal, 45* (December 1928), 10.

23. SVB, "Long Distance," *Ladies' Home Journal, 45* (July 1928), 14; "Fiona and the Unknown Santa Claus," *Ladies' Home Journal, 45* (October 1928), 20. This second story was probably written in June 1926, when Benét mentioned in a letter to his wife that he was writing a Christmas story for *Cosmopolitan.* The latter never published such a story of his. The style and manner of "Fiona and the Unknown Santa Claus" are also more in keeping with his 1926 work. Benét also wrote in France another modern story, "The Wish-Horse," *Delineator, 113* (September 1928), 42, and perhaps the fable *The Litter of the Rose Leaves,* published by Random House in a deluxe edition in 1930.

24. SVB, "Two White Beans," *Country Gentleman, 93* (October 1928), 22.

25. Mrs. C. Frank Reavis to CAF (int.), January 10, 1957.

CHAPTER 10. *John Brown's Body: Two*

For their generous help, and in many cases the loan of Benét correspondence, I am indebted to Eleanor Adlard, Samuel G. Atkinson, Mrs. M. N. Baker, Thomas M. H. Blair, Martha E. Clave, Mrs. John Winchester Dana, Mrs. Stanley Dell, Mrs. Ruth Dotson, Emanuel R. Engel, Harry W. Frost, Jr., Marice F. Gaither, R. M. Gay, Mary Washington Gold, Mary Harris, Miles Hart, Alfred Huger, Burza Jones, William Lybrand, Harriet Lyon, Ralph McGill, W. B. McKenna, Sonice McPherson, H. R. Mooney, Samuel Eliot Morison, Harold A. Mouzon, Leonard Nason, George W. Phinney, Lyda N. Rochmis, C. B. Rollins, Dorothea Baker Shaw, Mrs. Lucy Sheppard, Jewell F. Stevens, William Taylor, Jr., Mrs. Julian W. Tyler, Mrs. Frank Gardner Walter, John N. Ware, and Emily B. Warren.

1. SVB to John Farrar, July 15, 1928.

2. Edna Ferber, *A Peculiar Treasure* (New York, 1939), p. 281.

3. Daniel Longwell to CAF (int.), July 14, 1954.

4. SVB, "High Achievement," *SRL*, 8 (April 2, 1932), [629]. This was a review of Archibald MacLeish's long poem, *Conquistador*.

5. See esp., P. L. Wiley, "The Phaeton Symbol in *John Brown's Body*," *American Literature*, 17 (November 1945), 231–42; Eugene O'Neill, Jr., "*John Brown's Body*: Reappraisal," *SRL*, 32 (August 6, 1949), 34–5; Frederick H. Jackson, "Stephen Vincent Benét and American History," *Historian*, 17 (Autumn 1954), 67–75.

6. Leon Whipple, "Poets American," *Survey*, 61 (November 1, 1928), 168.

7. Herschel Brickell, "A Poetical Best-Seller," *North American Review*, 216 (October 1928), [vi]; Robert Morss Lovett, "The American Conflict," *New Republic*, 61 (August 29, 1928), 51.

8. Allen Tate, "The Irrepressible Conflict," *Nation*, 127 (Septem-

ber 19, 1928), 274; James Boyd, "Gusto and High Desire," *Outlook, 169* (September 5, 1928), 752.

9. SVB to Willian M. Lybrand, [January] 1929.

10. SVB to Emily B. Warren, March 9, 1930.

11. SVB to Sonice McPherson, [January] 1929.

12. Dudley Fitts, "John Brown's Body," *Hound and Horn, 2* (September 1928), 85–6.

13. Ralph McGill to CAF, April 11, 1957.

14. D. S. Freeman to SVB, August 2, 1934; Samuel Eliot Morison to CAF, June 14, 1955; Valentine Mitchell Gammell to CAF (int.), August 17, 1954; C. Frank Reavis to SVB, April 16, 1938; Robert Nathan to SVB, [1936].

15. Vincent Sheean to CAF, May 13, 1957.

16. Frederic S. Cushing to CAF, May 16, 1957. Mr. Cushing was in 1957 assistant director of the college department of Rinehart and Company, successors to Farrar and Rinehart as Benét's publishers. The latter became his publishers in 1934.

17. SVB, "Annotated Edition," *Atlantic Monthly, 172* (October 1943), [55]. Reprinted, *The Last Circle*, pp. 3–4.

18. R. M. Gay to CAF, September 16, 1955.

19. SVB, "The King of the Cats," *Harper's Bazaar, 63* (February 1929), 104. Reprinted, *Thirteen O'Clock*.

CHAPTER 11. *The Wages of Cinema*

1. SVB to William Rose Benét, February 12, 1930.

2. Robert Van Gelder, "Mr. Benét's Work in Progress," *New York Times Book Review, 6* (April 21, 1940), 20.

3. SVB, "Unransomed Saints," *SRL*, 6 (September 28, 1929), 179; "Kentucky Magic," *SRL*, 6 (November 16, 1929), 394; "The Prodigal Guest," *Ladies' Home Journal*, 46 (October 1929), 14; "The Treasure of Vasco Gomez," *Delineator*, 116 (February 1930), 8; "Song," *New Republic*, 60 (September 18, 1929), 123; "Bad Dream," *New Republic*, 60 (October 30, 1929), 294. "The Treasure of Vasco Gomez" was reprinted in *Thirteen O'Clock*. The two poems were reprinted, like so many of Benét's short poems of this period, in *Literary Digest*, 103 (November 23, 1929), 28.

4. Christopher LaFarge to CAF (int.), October 1, 1954.

5. SVB, "Without Benefit of Supervisors," *SRL*, 14 (October 3, 1936), 6.

6. Ibid.; Garrett D. Byrnes, "Stephen Vincent Benét Says Making Living Writing Poetry Impossible," Providence *Evening Bulletin* (August 27, 1930), p. 17.

7. SVB, "A Novel of Character," *SRL*, 6 (May 3, 1930), 1009; "Fantastic Truth," *SRL*, 7 (August 9, 1930), 36; "Little Golightly," *Elks' Magazine*, 8 (May 1930), 20; "The Educated Pig," *Pictorial Review*, 32 (November 1930), 9; "The Curst Kitchen," *Delineator*, 116 (May 1930), 9; "Short History," *Delineator*, 116 (May 1930), 9; "The Island and the Fire," *SRL*, 7 (October 11, 1930), [195]; "Hymn of a Reveler," *Library Journal*, 56 (March 1, 1931), 225. The latter was reprinted, under the title "Hymn of a Reveler to the New York City Librarians," *SRL*, 32 (January 22, 1949), 30.

8. SVB, "Little Golightly," *Elks' Magazine*, 8 (May 1930), 20.

9. Beatrice Kenyon, "The New Poetry," *Outlook*, 157 (April 15, 1931), 536.

10. SVB, "American Honeymoon," *Harper's Bazaar*, 66 (June 1932), 40.

11. SVB, "Days of Sunshine," *Maclean's*, 45 (January 15, 1932), 17.

12. YOUNGER POETS AND OTHER AMERICANS

12. SVB, "A Death in the Country," *Harper's, 144* (March 1932), [427]. When Bob McClure wrote Benét to tell him how much he'd enjoyed "A Death in the Country," Benét replied that it was "a story I've wanted to write for some time. I'm trying to write some better ones occasionally which is a relief." The story was reprinted in *Thirteen O'Clock.*

13. SVB, "An End to Dreams," *Pictorial Review, 33* (February 1932), 7; "The Delphinium Blues," *American Magazine, 113* (March 1932), 30; "A Life at Angelo's," *SEP, 203* (May 2, 1931), 14; "Mr. Penny and the Rhine Maiden," *Delineator, 120* (June 1932), 15; "Glamour," *Delineator, 121* (September 1932), 16; "Serenade," *Delineator, 121* (November 1932), 16. "A Life at Angelo's" was reprinted in *Tales before Midnight;* "Glamour" was reprinted in *Thirteen O'Clock.*

14. SVB, "High Achievement," *SRL, 8* (April 2, 1932), 629; "Our Fathers before Us," *New York Herald Tribune Books, 10* (July 3, 1932), 3; "The Jaw Bone of the Lion," *SRL, 9* (October 29, 1932), 205.

15. Wallace Stegner to CAF, April 13, 1955.

CHAPTER 12. *Younger Poets and Other Americans*

I am indebted to a number of people for their help in connection with Chapter 12, including George Abbe, Frederick B. Adams, Jr., Ben Belitt, Shirley Barker, George W. Corner, George W. Corner, Jr., Eugene Davidson, Norman Donaldson, Paul Engle, Thomas Hornsby Ferril, John Guenther, Helen Gertrude Hicks, John Holmes, Jeremy Ingalls, E. O. James, Frank Merchant, Pauli Murray, Blake Nevius, Norman Rosten, Vrest Orton, Muriel Rukeyser, Winfield T. Scott, Frederick Smith, Margaret Haley Storms, Margaret Walker, and Edward Weismiller.

1. SVB to Robert McClure, March 20, 1933.

2. SVB, "Young Lochinvar," *Pictorial Review, 34* (February 1933), 12.

3. SVB, "The Yankee Fox," *Woman's Home Companion, 60* (June 1933), 12.

4. SVB, "The Bagpipes of Spring," *SEP, 206* (September 16, 1933), 10.

5. SVB, "United Press," *Fortune, 7* (May 1933), 67; "The Enemies," *Delineator, 122* (April 1933), 8; "Too Early Spring," *Delineator, 122* (June 1933), 13; SVB to Paul Engle, [November] 1933. "Too Early Spring" was reprinted in *Tales before Midnight.*

6. Benét was referring to Eleanor and Herbert Farjeon, *Kings and Queens,* New York, 1933.

7. SVB to Eugene Davidson, July [4] 1933. Miss Barker's manuscript was retitled *Dark Hills Under.*

8. Eugene Davidson to CAF (int.), April 12, 1955.

9. Edward Weismiller to CAF, June 14, 1956.

10. Frank Merchant to CAF, June 7, 1955.

11. SVB to Theodora Roosevelt, January 21, 1940.

12. SVB to John Guenther, [August] 1933.

13. Muriel Rukeyser to CAF (int.), May 24, 1957; Margaret Walker to SVB, August 20, 1941.

14. Herschel Brickell, "More American Stories," *North American Review, 238* (July 1934), 94.

15. *Catholic World, 139* (August 1934), 634; Jeremy Ingalls, "James Shore's Daughter," *London Times Literary Supplement, 33* (July 12, 1934), 490; William Plomer, "Fiction," *Spectator, 153* (August 17, 1934), 233; T. S. Matthews, "Rackety Jackets," *New Republic, 79* (May 23, 1934), 51.

1. SVB and Rosemary Benét, "Mary Roberts Rinehart's Bread and Butter," *New York Herald Tribune Books, 9* (October 19, 1941), 7.

2. SVB and Rosemary Benét, "Ernest Hemingway: Byron of Our Day," *New York Herald Tribune Books, 9* (November 3, 1940), 7.

3. SVB to Robert MacAlarney, March 26, 1940; Ellen Barry to CAF (int.), August 28, 1954.

4. SVB, "A Man from Fort Necessity," *SEP, 212* (July 1, 1939), 18.

5. SVB, "Silver Jemmy," *Cosmopolitan, 100* (February 1936), 59.

6. SVB, "Schooner's Class," *Collier's, 101* (June 18, 1938), 14. Reprinted as "Schooner Fairchild's Class" in *Tales before Midnight.*

7. SVB, "Young Lovyer," *Country Gentleman, 104* (February 1934), 8; "The Natural-Born Fool," *Country Gentleman, 104* (August 1934), 10; "The Loves of the Roses," *Country Gentleman, 104* (November 1934), 16; "The Redheaded Woodpecker," *Country Gentleman, 105* (August 1935), 8.

8. SVB, "Witch's Spell," *Delineator, 124* (February 1934), 8; "Dec. 5, 1933," *Redbook, 62* (April 1934), 34; "Lisa and the Far Horizons," *Liberty, 11* (April 7, 1934), 11; "Marrying Town," *Delineator, 125* (September 1934), 8; "Early Morning," *Delineator, 126* (February 1935), 7; "Over the Bumps," *SEP, 207* (March 30, 1935), 10; "The Professor's Punch," *Delineator, 126* (April 1935), 42; "A Story by Angela Poe," *Harper's Bazaar* (July 1935), 38; "We'll Never Be Rich," *Redbook, 65* (July 1935), 38; "The Curfew Tolls," *SEP, 208* (October 5, 1935), 16; "Mystery Train," *Liberty, 12* (October 12, 1935), 14. "The Curfew Tolls" and "A Story by Angela Poe," both of them far superior to the rest of this group, were reprinted in *Thirteen O'Clock.*

9. Philip Blair Rice, "Chronicles in Verse," *Nation, 143* (July 18, 1936), 81; Donald C. Peattie, "A Singing Poet in the Tradition of the Bards," *New York Herald Tribune Books, 7* (June 14, 1936), [1].

10. SVB, ["Muriel Rukeyser"], *Trial Balances,* ed. Ann Winslow (New York, 1935), p. 201.

11. SVB, "The Devil and Daniel Webster," *SEP, 209* (October 24, 1936), 8. Brandt's comments are written in his hand on the note which Benét enclosed with the typescript.

12. Harry Hansen, "Introduction," *O. Henry Memorial Award Prize Stories of 1937* (New York, 1937), p. x.

13. Robert Van Gelder, "Mr. Benét's Work in Progress," *New York Times Book Review, 6* (April 21, 1940), 20.

14. SVB, "The Author Is Pleased," New York *Times* (September 28, 1941), p. 4.

15. SVB, "Daniel Webster and the Sea Serpent," *SEP, 209* (May 22, 1937), 18; "Daniel Webster and the Ides of March," *SEP, 212* (October 28, 1939), 18. The first of these stories was reprinted in *Thirteen O'Clock,* the second in *Tales before Midnight.*

16. Van Gelder.

17. SVB, "The Author Is Pleased."

CHAPTER 14. *Man of Letters*

For their generous help in connection with Benét's work in the various areas covered by this chapter I am indebted to Theodore S. Amussen, George K. Anderson, Arno L. Bader, John J. Baldi, Lucius Beebe, Henry Beston, George Bickford, Seth Bingham, Mrs.

Fredson Bowers, Burke Boyce, Leighton Brewer, James Branch Cabell, Walter S. Campbell, Carl Carmer, Hodding Carter, R. V. Cassill, Hugh J. Chisholm, Jr., Horatio Colony, Reginald L. Cook, Roy W. Cowden, Nathalia Crane, David C. DeJong, Mrs. Esther Dendel, J. Raymond Derby, R. L. DeWilton, Louis Finkelstein, Anne B. Fisher, Robert Fitzgerald, Kimball W. Flaccus, Norman Foerster, Hulbert Footner, John T. Frederick, Lewis Gannett, Richard L. Greene, Alfred J. Hanna, Mrs. Leroy F. Harlow, Walter Hard, Donald D. Jackson, Jonathan H. Kistler, Robert M. Lord, Father John W. Lynch, Harriet Lyon, John H. H. Lyon, Mrs. Robert E. MacAlarney, Louise McNeill, Margaret McVey, George W. Martin, Dale Morgan, David Morton, Frank Luther Mott, Robert Niles, Russell Noyes, Egbert S. Oliver, Seldon Rodman, Edward Shenton, John R. Slater, William Sloane, Chard Powers Smith, Edgar W. Smith, Wallace Stegner, F. B. Streeter, Jesse Stuart, Bennett Weaver, Ann Winslow, Arnold Whitridge, Richardson Wood, and Clyde Zimmerman.

1. Valentine Mitchell Gammell to CAF, December 29, 1956.

2. William Sloane to CAF, February 12, 1957.

3. F. B. Streeter to CAF, January 28, 1955; SVB to Walter Hard, [January] 1943; Stanley Vestal to CAF, January 4, 1955.

4. George Bickford to CAF, January 21, 1957.

5. Mrs. Esther Dendel to CAF, February 6, 1957.

6. J. Raymond Derby to CAF, January 21, 1957.

7. SVB to Mrs. William Vanamee, July 1, 1940. Mrs. Vanamee was assistant to the president of the National Institute of Arts and Letters, by whom Benét had been asked to deliver the annual Blashfield Lecture. See also Chapter 15. Benét's address was subsequently published as "The Power of the Written Word," *Yale Review, 30* (Spring 1941), 522–30.

8. SVB to Florence Locke, January 10, 1935. Miss Locke gave successful recitals of *John Brown's Body* in both the United States and England.

9. R. M. Gay to CAF, September 16, 1955.

10. R. V. Cassill to CAF, May 8, 1957.

11. SVB to Egbert S. Oliver, [January] 1935.

12. SVB to George Abbe, November 2, 1936.

13. Ibid.

14. SVB to Mrs. Mary Winslow, undated; SVB and Rosemary Benét, "C. S. Forester: How to Be a Story Teller," *New York Herald Books, 9* (March 2, 1941), 5.

15. Valentine Mitchell Gammell to CAF (int.), August 27, 1954; SVB and Rosemary Benét, "Robert Nathan: World of His Own," *New York Herald Tribune Books, 9* (May 4, 1941), 6.

16. SVB, "Hard Up for Material," *SRL, 20* (October 14, 1939), 24.

17. SVB, "Advice to Authors," *SRL, 19* (March 11, 1939), 12.

18. SVB, "Georgia Marches Through," *SRL, 14* (July 4, 1936), 6; SVB, "A Family Famous for Over Two Centuries," *New York Herald Tribune Books, 7* (October 6, 1935), 3.

CHAPTER 15. *Academician*

For their generous help I am very much indebted to a number of employees and members of the National Institute of Arts and Letters and the American Academy of Arts and Letters, and particularly to Van Wyck Brooks, Malcolm Cowley, William Adams Delano, James T. Farrell, Felicia Geffen, and Mrs. Hannah Josephson.

405

1. Hamlin Garland, *Companions on the Trail* (Macmillan, 1931), pp. 515, 132.

2. SVB to Felicia Geffen, [December] 1942.

CHAPTER 16. *Western Star*

1. SVB, "Greatness," *SEP, 209* (March 20, 1937), 16; "Daniel Webster and the Sea Serpent," *SEP, 209* (May 22, 1937), 18; "The Place of the Gods," *SEP, 210* (July 31, 1937), 10; "Johnny Pye and the Fool-Killer," *SEP, 210* (September 18, 1937), 10; "The Last of the Legions," *SEP, 210* (November 6, 1937), 18; "A Tooth for Paul Revere," *Atlantic Monthly, 160* (December 1937), 681; "O'Halloran's Luck," *Country Gentleman, 108* (May 1938), 10; "Schooner's Class," *Collier's, 101* (June 18, 1938), 14; "The Die-Hard," *SEP, 211* (September 17, 1938), 10; "Jacob and the Indians," *SEP, 210* (May 14, 1938), 12; "The Cat Named Dempsey," *SEP, 211* (July 30, 1938), 12; "Doc Melhorn and the Pearly Gates," *SEP, 211* (December 24, 1938), 22; "Among Those Present," *SEP, 210* (April 9, 1938), 8; "Into Egypt," *Ladies' Home Journal, 56* (May 1939), 16; "A Man from Fort Necessity," *SEP, 212* (July 1, 1939), 18; "Oh, My Name is William Kidd," *Country Gentleman, 109* (July 1939), 16; "Henry and the Golden Mine," *SEP, 212* (September 23, 1939), 18; "Daniel Webster and the Ides of March," *SEP, 212* (October 28, 1939), 18.

2. Selig Greenberg, "Stephen Vincent Benét, at Pier, Says Short Stories Pay but Poetry Doesn't," Providence *Evening Bulletin* (August 14, 1939), p. 5.

3. SVB to Katherine Manwaring, [October] 1941.

4. Dr. Dana W. Atchley to CAF (int.), September 21, 1954.

5. SVB, "Nightmare at Noon," *New York Times Magazine* (June 23, 1940), p. 7. Reprinted, *Scholastic, 37* (September 16,

1940), 21; *Nightmare at Noon; The Oxford Book of American Verse,* ed. F. O. Matthiessen (New York, 1950), pp. 954–9. SVB, "Minor Litany," *New Yorker, 16* (December 14, 1940), 28.

6. SVB, "Nightmare for Future Reference," *New Yorker, 14* (April 2, 1938), 21; "If This Should Change," *New Yorker, 17* (June 21, 1941), 24.

7. SVB, "Good Water from a Bitter Rock," *New York Herald Tribune Books, 9* (October 13, 1940), 7.

8. SVB, "New Grandeur in Our Theatre," *Stage, 14* (January 1937), 38; SVB, "We Aren't Superstitious," *Esquire, 7* (May 1937), 47. Benét's forewards and prefaces during this period— in addition to those he wrote annually for the Yale Series of Younger Poets—were published in the following volumes: Louise McNeill, *Gauley Mountain,* Harcourt, Brace, 1939; Bertil Malmberg, *Ake and His* World, Farrar and Rinehart, 1940; *Six of Us Talking,* Farrar and Rinehart, 1940; Griffith Bailey Coale, *North Atlantic Patrol,* Farrar and Rinehart, 1942; and Robert Henriques, *The Voice of the Trumpet,* Farrar and Rinehart, 1943.

9. Rollin G. Osterweis, *Three Centuries of New Haven, 1638– 1938* (Yale University Press, 1953), p. 432.

10. SVB, "The Ballad of the Duke's Mercy," *Atlantic Monthly, 163* (February 1939), [169]; "The Ballad of Marco Polo," *Atlantic Monthly, 163* (August 1939), [191]. Also in the hard cover collection *The Ballad of the Duke's Mercy,* 1939.

11. "Stephen Vincent Benét, Noted Author and Poet, Acclaims *The War Years,* Plans New Epic Poem," *Exonian* (December 13, 1939). This was an interview with Benét in the student newspaper at Phillips Exeter Academy.

12. SVB, "Words and Music," *SRL, 20* (May 20, 1939), 10.

13. Brooks Atkinson, "Cheating the Devil to Music," New York *Times* (May 21, 1939), [1].

I am grateful to the following individuals for their help in locating material that related both to the general period and to Benét's work with the various war agencies: Ernest Angell, Dr. Dana W. Atchley, Mrs. James Boyd, Mrs. Griffith B. Coale, Robert B. Craig, Wayne Darrow, William Dieterle, Walter D. Edmonds, Carl J. Friedrich, Brigadier General A. Robert Ginsburgh, John Francis Hagen, Carl Hamilton, Henry Hazlitt, Colonel Robert D. Henriques, Henry Hull, Marian L. Joest, Elliott Kone, Edgar Ansel Mowrer, Kermit O. Overby, Donald Culross Peattie, William B. Phillips, Mrs. Allan Price, Marion L. Ramsay, Vincent Sheean, Rex Stout, Margaret Widdemer, T. Harry Williams, John T. Winterich, and Philip Wylie.

1. Mrs. Alvan L. Barach to CAF, June 13, 1957.

2. SVB to Felicia Geffen, [December] 1942.

3. Marion L. Ramsay to CAF, April 25, 1957; SVB, "The Prodigal Children," *SEP*, *215* (December 19, 1942), 16. Reprinted, *The Last Circle,* p. 191.

4. Ernest Hemingway, introduction to *Men at War* (New York, 1942), p. xv.

5. Edward Weeks, "The Peripatetic Reviewer," *Atlantic Monthly, 173* (January 1944), 121.

6. SVB to Louis Finkelstein, July [28] 1941; *Atlantic Monthly, 173* (September 1944), [24]. These letters are owned by Finkelstein.

7. SVB, "The Undefended Border," in *We Stand United,* p. 119.

8. C. D. Jackson to CAF (int.), August 1, 1956; Carl J. Friedrich to CAF, October 24, 1956.

9. SVB, "Listen to the People," *Life, 11* (July 7, 1941), 90. Reprinted, *Listen to the People,* New York, 1941; *Scholastic, 40* (February 2, 1942), 17; *We Stand United,* p. 135.

10. SVB, "No Visitors," *SEP, 212* (March 16, 1940), 12; "All Around the Town," *Atlantic Monthly, 165* (April 1940), 520; "Freedom's a Hard-Bought Thing," *SEP, 212* (May 18, 1940), 12; "The Great Swinglefield Derby," *Town and Country, 95* (July 1940), 34; "The Angel Was a Yankee," *McCall's, 68* (October 1940), [14]; "This Bright Dream," *Ladies' Home Journal, 57* (December 1940), 16; "The Captives," *Atlantic Monthly, 167* (February 1934), 177; "The Danger of Shadows," *Harper's Bazaar, 75* (May 1941), 66; "Good Picker," *SEP, 213* (May 24, 1941), 12; "The Three Fates," *American Magazine, 132* (November 1941), 26; "William Riley and the Fates," *Atlantic Monthly, 168* (November 1941), 539; "A Gentleman of Fortune," *Redbook, 78* (December 1941), 20; "The Bishop's Beggar," *SEP, 214* (February 14, 1942), 9; "The Gold Dress," *Cosmopolitan, 113* (July 1942), 52; "The Minister's Books," *Atlantic Monthly, 170* (August 1942), 41; "The Land Where There Is No Death," *Redbook, 79* (October 1942), 40; "The Prodigal Children," *SEP, 215* (December 19, 1942), 16; "A Judgment in the Mountains," *Country Gentleman, 113* (January 1943), 10; "As It Was in the Beginning," *SEP, 215* (February 6, 1943), 14.

11. Edgar Ansel Mowrer to CAF, January 2, 1957.

12. SVB, "Dear Adolf," *Life, 13* (July 27, 1942), 74. Reprinted, *Dear Adolf.*

13. John K. Hutchens, "Dear Adolf —," New York *Times* (July 5, 1942), p. 8.

14. Marshall D. Schulman to CAF, August 13, 1956; "Dear Adolf," *Time, 40* (August 3, 1942), 50.

15. SVB, "A Child Is Born," *SRL, 25* (December 26, 1942), 7. This was an abridged version. Reprinted, in full, in *A Child Is Born; We Stand United,* p. 155.

Index

Abbe, George, 387; SVB reads his fiction in MS and makes suggestions about it, 96–7, 308

Academy of American Poets, 220, 333

Adams, Franklin P. (F.P.A.), 56, 74, 259

Adams, Herbert, 320

Adams, James Truslow, 326

Adams, John Wolcott, illustrates SVB's "The Hemp" in *Century*, 56

Adams, Léonie, 330

Agee, James, 263, 330; SVB chooses his *Permit Me Voyage* for Yale Series of Younger Poets, 265

Aiken, Conrad, 42

Ainslee's, 76, 85; SVB's publications in, 385

Alabama, 27

Alberta, University of, *John Brown's Body* required reading at, 220

Aldington, Richard, 42

Alexander, Katherine, replaces Grace George in play by SVB and John Farrar, 138

Algren, Nelson, 330

Allen, Hervey, 147, 277

Alpha Delta Phi. *See* Yale University, Alpha Delta Phi

American Academy of Arts and Letters, 59, 214, 217, 313, 314–32, 349, 355

American Hospital (Paris), 179; SVB's son born there, 180

American Library (Paris), 181; librarians recall SVB working there on *John Brown's Body*, 183–4

American Lyric Theater, produces operetta by SVB and Douglas Moore, 352

American Magazine, 246, 364, 365

Ames, Winthrop, 319

Amherst College, 46; SVB lectures there, 303

Anderson, Maxwell, SVB writes article about, 341, 407

Anderson, Sherwood, 78, 316

Andersonville (Ga.) Prison, SVB explains his *John Brown's Body* description of, 216–17

Andrews, Charles McLean, 58–60, 76, 318; SVB urges award of Academy's Gold Medal to, 319–20

Andrews, Ethel, 60, 67, 135, 144, 189, 231, 281, 282

Andrews, John, 67, 68, 144

Angell, Ernest, 361

Arkansas, 27

Atchley, Dr. Dana W., 393, 406; describes SVB's fortitude, 339

Atkinson, Brooks, reviews operetta by SVB and Douglas Moore, 352

Atlanta University, 307

Atlantic Monthly, 163, 290, 333, 344

Auden, W. H., 261

Augusta (Ga.) Arsenal, 19, 22, 27, 35; SVB dislikes at first, 23; history and description of, 24–5

Austen, Jane, 355–6

Avery Hopwood Awards (University of Michigan), SVB a judge for, 307

Bacon, Leonard, 21, 52, 225, 377; describes Benét home at Benicia (Cal.) Arsenal, 2, 12; his regard for SVB's father, 11, 12; spends part of honeymoon with Benéts at Augusta (Ga.) Arsenal, 35; SVB rents his Peace Dale (R.I.) house, 231, 377; dedicates *Semi-Centennial* to SVB, 377

Bacon, Martha Sherman (Mrs. Leonard), SVB collaborates on wedding ode to her and husband, 35

Badger, Shreve, 74–5, 101, 103, 178, 180, 383–4; SVB describes *The Beginning of Wisdom* to, 96; SVB's long friendship with, 144

Balmer, Edwin, SVB irritated by his editorial suggestions, 286

Bar Harbor (Me.), SVB ushers at wedding there, 97

Barbour, Ralph Henry, 230; SVB reads his fiction during boyhood, 16

Barker, Shirley, 261; *Dark Hills Under,* 401

Barlow, Joel, *Columbiad,* 192

Barney, Danford, 101–2

Barry, Ellen (Mrs. Philip), 101, 144, 224–5, 279, 299; compares SVB to F. Scott Fitzgerald, 146

Barry, Philip, 53, 54, 57, 67, 78, 84, 101, 109, 110, 144, 224–5, 267, 279, 299, 315, 340, 354, 367–8

Battles and Leaders of the Civil War, 24, 182, 191

Baumgarten, Bernice, 40. *See also* Brandt, Carl

Beard, Charles A., 323

Beer, Thomas, 113, 120, 154–5

Bellinger, Alfred R., 13, 72, 385; SVB describes effect of Hollywood to, 240

Benét, Frances Neill (mother), 21, 102, 107, 121–2, 140, 165, 211, 212, 338; characteristics of, 3, 7, 92; SVB's letters to, 6, 9–10, 18, 19, 38, 180, 226, 298, 336–7; SVB's generosity to, 222, 296; death of (*July 8, 1940*), 340

Benét, Col. James Walker (father), 5, 19, 28, 48–9, 66, 67, 93, 98, 102, 107, 108, 121–2, 140, 142, 157, 168, 180, 391; graduates West Point, 1; his tours of duty, 1–2; characteristics, 1–4 *passim,* 9, 21, 31, 39, 78, 92–3, 102; as father, 3, 6, 10, 15, 31, 39, 55, 77; SVB's physical resemblance to, 7; as student of poetry, 10, 11, 30, 49; talks of Civil War to SVB, 10, 23–4; SVB's memoir about, 12, 378; retires, 13, 77–8, 81, 106–7; writes autobiography, 13, 107, 378; attitude toward SVB's early poetry, 38, 42; corresponds with Col. Odus C. Horney, 39, 92–3, 97, 107, 381; influence on SVB, 43, 276; visits SVB at Yale, 72; death of (*March 30, 1928*), 201–3

Benét, James Walker, II (nephew), 355

Benét, Laura (sister), 6, 7, 10, 21, 31, 38, 94, 97, 107, 119, 211, 212, 222, 377; attends Vassar, 3; tutors SVB, 17

Benét, Laura Walker (grandmother), 97–8

Benét, Laurence Vincent (uncle), 5, 6, 8, 18, 39, 49, 98, 101, 102, 187, 270, 354–5; has copies made of Col. Benét's autobiography, 378

Benét, Margaret Cox (Mrs. Laurence Vincent), 102, 103

Benét, Rachel Carr (daughter), 246–7, 260

Benét, Rosemary Carr (wife), 14, 109–10, 113, 117–18, 135, 142, 178, 186, 187, 202, 222, 223, 240, 292, 295–6, 299, 336, 340, 349, 364, 369; meets SVB, 103; effect on SVB's poetry, 103–4; characteristics, 104, 158; described by Vincent Sheean, 104; marriage to SVB, 104, 117–18; SVB's letters to, 108–9, 112, 115–25 *passim*, 138, 139–40, 146–59 *passim*, 165, 176, 177, 214, 222, 223, 234, 235, 239, 252; honeymoon, 117, 121–2; birth of daughter, Stephanie Jane, 137; SVB dedicates *Tiger Joy* to, 152; works for *Vogue*, 164; birth of son, Thomas Carr, 180; writes monthly Letter for *Town and Country*, 191; birth of daughter, Rachel Carr, 246–7; collaborates with SVB on *A Book of Americans*, 255–60; writes "Nancy Hanks," 259–60; collaborates with SVB on

literary profiles for *New York Herald Tribune Books*, 311, 378, 395, 402, 405; admiration for SVB's "Into Egypt," 338; with SVB when he dies, 373

Benét, Stephanie Jane (daughter), 137, 138, 140, 142, 147, 154, 158, 164, 165, 168, 178, 180, 211, 222, 247, 260, 304; characterized by SVB, 226; he writes of her in "Girl Child," 290

Benét, Brig. Gen. Stephen Vincent (grandfather), 1, 4, 5, 7, 8, 203, 217–18; SVB writes poem in memory of, 255

Benét, Stephen Vincent
LIFE: born, *July 22, 1898*, 2; at Benicia (Cal.) Arsenal, 2; attends Hitchcock Military Academy, 15; moves to Augusta (Ga.), 19; enters Summerville Academy, 28; first professional sale of verse, 37; first volume of poetry published, at seventeen, 40; enters Yale, *September 1915*, 52; elected chairman of *Yale Literary Magazine, April 1918*, 63; returns to Yale after World War I, 74; graduates, *June 1919*, 77; works in New York, 78; enrolls Yale Graduate School, 82; receives M.A., 91; sails for France, 97; meets Rosemary Carr, 103; returns to USA, 106; Carl Brandt becomes his literary agent, 109; marries Rosemary Carr, *November 26, 1921*, 117–18; to Europe for honeymoon, 121; birth of daughter, Stephanie Jane, 137; collects verse for *Tiger Joy*, 150; at MacDowell Colony, 158–63; first short-

413

Benét, Stephen Vincent (*cont.*) story sale to *Country Gentleman,* 170–1; applies for a Guggenheim Fellowship, 167; to France with wife and daughter, 177–8; birth of son, Thomas Carr, 180; works on *John Brown's Body,* 180–204; death of father, 201–3; returns to USA for publication of *John Brown's Body,* 211; rejoins family in France, 223; returns to USA with family, 229; Pulitzer Prize for *John Brown's Body,* 229; elected to National Institute of Arts and Letters in *1929,* 314; to Hollywood for *Abraham Lincoln,* 233–40; ill during *1930* and *1931,* 240–4; prepares and publishes *Ballads and Poems,* 243; begins to keep diary, 255, 276; birth of youngest child, Rachel Carr, 246–7; hit hard by depression, 246–52; becomes editor of Yale Series of Younger Poets, 260; writes "The Devil and Daniel Webster," 292–6; has nervous breakdown, 339; poetic energy as World War II approaches, 340–2; works on *Western Star,* 343–53; honorary degree from Yale, 305; elected to American Academy of Arts and Letters in *1938,* 314; quotes Milton on role of writers in time of national crisis, 356; active in Council for Democracy, 360–4; buys Whistler House in Stonington (Conn.), 364; publication of *Selected Works* (2 vols.), 365–6; health becomes worse, 367–8; makes a new will, 367; doctor forbids him to accept army commission, 371; work exhibited at Library of Congress, 371–2; FDR reads his "Prayer" at United Nations ceremonies, 372; will take no money for war writing, 372; writes *America,* 372; dies, 372–4; his last entries in diary, 373; reaction to his death, 373; *Western Star* awarded Pulitzer Prize, 374.

ATTITUDE TOWARD OR RELATIONSHIP WITH: academic world, 81, 89–91, 221, 357; America, 12–27 *passim,* 43, 50, 97, 101, 120, 126, 127–9, 154, 177–8, 197–8, 203, 241, 250, 252, 275, 319, 344–5, 353, 354, 373; army, 7–16 *passim,* 22–3, 69, 169, 197, 356; critics, 32, 80, 96, 114, 127, 128, 148–9, 152–4, 243–4, 259, 271–3, 288, 336, 337, 351–2, 366, 397; expatriation, 50, 87, 97, 98, 119, 120, 126, 186–90, 315; friendship, 50–64 *passim,* 72, 100–1, 106, 113, 114, 144–7, 161, 181, 186–8, 222, 223, 299–300, 331, 354–5, 362, 367–8; health, 200–1, 240–2, 246, 259, 291, 339–40, 367–8, 371, 372–3; Hollywood, 50, 231, 233–40, 241, 245, 250, 273, 274, 287, 295, 316, 349, 365, 371; lecturing, 8, 20, 145, 218, 246, 250–2, 302–6; New York literary life (*see also* New York), 119–20, 122, 187, 223, 229–300; parenthood, 14, 18, 19, 142, 150, 223, 226, 232, 260; politics, 42, 64, 128, 247, 255, 276–89, 303, 319, 320–1, 331, 334–5, 336, 341, 346, 354–5; reading, 16, 28, 31–7 *passim,* 63, 71, 181–4, 226;

reviewing, 26, 166, 194–5, 232, 240, 246, 297, 301, 310–13; Franklin D. Roosevelt, 253, 255, 275–84 *passim*, 320, 373; Shakespeare, 6, 71–2, 157–8, 264, 341; *Time*, 362; World War I (*see* World War I); World War II (*see* World War II); young writers, 22–3, 96–7, 145, 224, 251–2, 260–5, 277–8, 300, 301–2, 306–10, 312–13, 321–2, 327–31, 379.

PROFESSIONAL LIFE: American history, use of, in work, 32, 33, 58, 59, 76, 97, 168–75, 181–5, 195–7, 241, 242, 266, 275, 277–8, 279, 286–7, 292–6, 334, 335, 345–7, 347–8, 349–50, 351–2, 365; finances, 142, 147, 150, 160–7 *passim*, 176, 200–3, 220–7 *passim*, 231, 233, 239, 244–55 *passim*, 264–74 *passim*, 287–98 *passim*, 305, 311, 333–43 *passim*, 364–6 *passim*, 373; literary agent (*see* Brandt, Carl); popular writer, role as, 60–1, 80, 126–9, 148, 190, 211–24 *passim*, 274–6, 295–8, 315, 336, 341, 363, 394; radio, 340, 341, 351, 359–64, 368–72; theater, 85, 134–41, 341, 351–2.

WORKS:

Articles (*see also New York Herald Tribune Books; Time*)—"Bigger and Better Murders," 166; "Daniel Webster," 359; "A Defense of Mrs. Anonymous," 166; "Literary Treasure," 165–6; "The Most Unforgettable Character I've Known," 202; "My Favorite Fiction Character," 166, 393; "New Grandeur in Our Theatre," 341; "The Power of the Written Word," 404; "The United Press," 254; "We Aren't Superstitious," 341.

Movies—*Abraham Lincoln*, 233–40, 242; *All That Money Can Buy* ("The Devil and Daniel Webster"), 366; *Miss Bishop*, 349; *Power and the Land*, 359.

Non-Fiction—*America*, 367, 372.

Novels—*The Bat* (anonymous), 167; *The Beginning of Wisdom*, 16–18 *passim*, 51–2, 53, 58, 84, 85, 91–9 *passim*, 108, 117, 155, 205; *Hotspur* (unfinished), 157–8; *James Shore's Daughter*, 256, 265–73, 274, 287; *Jean Huguenot*, 105–14 *passim*, 151; *The Silver Dollar* (unfinished), 197–8, 200, 201, 207, 228, 256, 272; *Spanish Bayonet*, 142, 154–63, 167, 174, 176, 179, 197–8; *Young People's Pride*, 106, 112–17, 120–1, 122, 156, 266.

Operettas (with Douglas Moore)—*The Devil and Daniel Webster*, 351–2; *The Headless Horseman*, 351.

Plays (with John Farrar) —*Nerves*, 135–41; *That Awful Mrs. Eaton*, 136–41.

Poems—"Abraham Lincoln," 258; "After Attending a Séance," 177–8; "American Names," 50, 190; "Annotated Edition," 221–2; "Archimedes' Last Foray," 177; "Atheist's Tragedy," 383; "Azrael's Bar," 388; "Bad Dream," 232; "Ballad of Aegispotamos," 383; "Ballad of the Duke's Mercy," 344–5; "Ballad of John Faa," 383; "Ballad of Marco Polo," 344–5; "Ballad of William Sycamore," 101, 126–9, 142,

Benét, Stephen Vincent (*cont.*)
148, 150, 156–7, 167, 189,
390; "Ballade of the Sum-
mer Girl," 60; *Ballads and
Poems,* 68, 99, 243–4; *A
Book of Americans,* 255–60,
265, 268; "The Breaking
Point," 383; *Burning City,*
287–92; "Campus Sonnets,"
70; "Carol: New Style," 132;
"The City Revisited," 383;
"Clipper Ships and Cap-
tains," 258; "Come Back!"
385; "Complaint of Body,
the Ass, to Rider, the Soul,"
291; "The Curst Kitchen,"
399; "Daniel Drew," 257–8;
"Devourer of Nations," 79;
"Difference," 388; "Do You
Remember, Springfield?" 287,
290; "The Drug Shop," 56,
57, 76; "Epistle to All
Friends," 388; "Epitaph,"
388; "Everyone Falls for the
Blonde," 65; "Expressions
Near the End of Winter,"
385; *Five Men and Pompey,*
40–3, 49, 56, 57; "Flood-
Tide," 68, 69, 384; "For All
Blasphemers," 131; "For
Those Who Are as Right as
Any," 290; "The General
Public," 383; "Girl Child,"
290; "Going Back to School,"
14–15; "The Golden Corpse,"
149–50, 153; "Grover Cleveland," 258; "Hands," 188–9;
Heavens and Earth, 68, 79–
81, 89, 91, 99, 103, 116–17,
151, 209–10, 366; "The
Hemp," 56, 57, 150; poem
to Brig. Gen. Stephen Vincent Benét ("Here, in the
heart of this remembered
land"), 255; "Hymn of a
Reveler," 241; "If This
Should Change," 341; "An
Immoral Song," 388; "In a
Glass of Water before Re-
tiring," 125, 390; "Invocation," 192–3, 242–3; "The
Island and the Fire," 241,
242–3; "Jaufre Raudel Be-
holds the Lady of Tripoli,"
385; *John Brown's Body,* 8,
41, 43, 101, 127, 131, 148,
158, 167, 175, 179, 180–230,
231, 232, 242–5 *passim,*
250, 266–75 *passim,* 287–92
passim, 304, 340–7 *passim,*
374; "July," 388; "King
David," 101, 129, 142, 148,
150, 156–7, 275, 390; "Ku
Klux" (unpublished), 22;
"Litany for Dictatorships,"
287–90 *passim;* "Lonely
Burial," 383; "Lost Lights,"
385; "Lunch-Time along
Broadway," 81; "Memory,"
290; "Minor Litany," 340,
341; "The Mountain Whip-
poorwill," 148–50, 156–7,
189; "Nancy Hanks" (*see*
Benét, Rosemary); "Night-
mare at Noon," 340, 341;
"Nightmare for Future Reference," 341; "1936," 290;
"Nomenclature," 104; "A
Nonsense Song," 388; "Notes
to Be Left in a Cornerstone,"
290, 291; "Ode to the Austrian Socialists," 291; "Ode
to Walt Whitman," 288;
"Oh, Tricksy April," 126,
389; "Old Man Hopper-
grass," 290; "Peregrine White
and Virginia Dare," 257;
"Poor Devil," 383; "Port-
folio," 383; "Portrait of a
Boy," 16; "Portrait of a
Young Love," 385; "The
Proud Man" (unpublished),
30; "The Quality of Cour-
age," 383; "Queen's Gambit
Declined," 385; "Rain after
a Vaudeville Show," 383;
"The Regret of Dives," 30;
"Reply," 289; "Riddle," 152;

"Roads and Hills," 383; "Robert E. Lee," 258; "A Sad Song," 388; "Scholastic Work Is Still the Most Important Thing at Yale," 66; "Short History," 399; "Short Ode," 290, 291; "Snowfall," 132; "Song," 232; "Song of the Hours," 388; "A Song of the Woods," 35–6; "The Songs of Dear Old Yale" (unpublished), 63, 384; "Sparrow," 288–9, 290; "Talk," 80; "The Tapiad," 63, 384; ("Tapiola"), 278–9; "Tercentenary Ode," 341–2; "Thanks," 289; "Thomas Jefferson," 258–9; "Three Days Ride," 383; *Tiger Joy*, 103, 150–6, 157; "To the Dream," 388; "The Trapeze Performer," 385; "The Twelfth Day" (unpublished), 29; "Venus' Song," 388; ("Wedding Ode to the Leonard Bacons"), 35; *Western Star*, 59, 241–3 *passim*, 274, 333, 343–53, 365, 367, 374; "Western Wagons," 258; "Winged Man," 37–41 *passim;* "Wisdom-Teeth," 79–80; "X-Ray," 132; *Young Adventure*, 72, 76–7, 209, 260.

Prefaces—407.

Radio Scripts—"A Child Is Born," 127, 372; *Dear Adolf*, 369–71; "Listen to the People," 362–4; "This Is War," 368–9; "The Undefended Border," 360; "The Watcher by the Stone," (unfinished), 372–3; "We Stand United," 360–1.

Selected Works (2 vols.)—99, 365–6, 368.

Short Stories—"The Amateur of Crime," 394; "American Honeymoon," 244; "Among Those Present," 334;

"The Angel Was a Yankee," 365; "As It Was in the Beginning," 409; "The Bagpipes of Spring," 254; "The Barefoot Saint," 123, 228–9, 293, 389; "Beaver!" 389; "The Bishop's Beggar," 365; "Blackbeard and Co.—Pirates," 394; "The Blood of the Martyrs," 90, 284–5, 334, 365; "Bon Voyage," 177, 197, 394; "The Butcher's Bill" (unpublished), 30; "By the Waters of Babylon" ("The Place of the Gods"), 335, 336, 340–1; "Candleshine," 203; "Canned Salmon," 68; "The Captives," 365; "A Cat Named Dempsey," 334; "Cigarettes," 392; "The Crime of Professor Sandwich" (unpublished), 245; "The Curfew Tolls," 336; "The Danger of Shadows," 409; "Daniel Webster and the Ides of March," 234, 294–5; "Daniel Webster and the Sea Serpent," 294, 334; "Days of Sunshine," 245; "A Death in the Country," 245–6, 400; "The Delphinium Blues," 400; "Dec. 5, 1933," 402; "The Devil and Daniel Webster," 127, 131, 292–6, 336, 365; "The Die-Hard," 334; "Dishface," 390; "Doc Mellhorn and the Pearly Gates," 334; "Early Morning," 402; "The Educated Pig," 399; "Elementals," 124–5; "An End to Dreams," 400; "The Enemies," 401; "Everybody Was Very Nice," 295; "Fiona and the Unknown Santa Claus," 396; "The Fool-Killer," 195, 196; "Freedom's a Hard-Bought Thing," 365; "The Funeral of John Bixby," 105, 386;

Benét, Stephen Vincent (*cont.*) "The Garbageman's Daughter," 389; "A Gentleman of Fortune," 409; "The Giant's House," 8, 23, 196, 197; "The Girl Who Walked Home," 390; "Glamour," 336; "The Gold Dress," 409; "The Golden Bessie," 124, 133; "Goobers—à la Française," 117; "Good Picker," 409; "The Great Swinglefield Derby," 365; "Greatness," 334–5, 406; "Green Christmas," 203; "Harrigan's Head," 392; "Henry and the Golden Mine," 334; "Into Egypt," 334, 335, 337–9, 365; "Jacob and the Indians," 334; "Jacobson," 389; "Jerry and James and John," 389; "Jolly Roger," 390; "Johnny Pye and the Fool-Killer," 334; "A Judgment in the Mountains," 365; "The King of the Cats," 227–8; "Lady Lapith," 394; "The Land Where There Is No Death," 409; "The Language of the Stars," 394; "The Last of the Legions," 334–5; "Lisa and the Far Horizons," 402; "Little Golightly," 241; "Long Distance," 396; "The Loves of the Roses," 402; "The Lucksmith," 196–7; "The Lucky Fist," 173–4; "Mad Americans," 117; "A Man from Fort Necessity," 282–3, 334; "Manhattan Carol," 286–7; "Marrying Town," 402; "The Minister's Books," 365; "Miranda, the Measles, and Marmaduke," 390; "Miss Willie Lou and the Swan," 174; "Mr. Penny and the Rhine Maidens," 400; "Mystery Train," 392; "The Natural-Born Fool,"

402; "No Visitors," 409; "O'Halloran's Luck," 334; "The Odor of Sanctity," 170; "Oh, My Name Is William Kidd," 334; "Over the Bumps," 402; "The Place of the Gods" (*see* "By the Waters of Babylon"); "The Prodigal Children," 232, 356, 365; "The Professor's Punch," 90; "The Raveled Sleeve," 390; "The Redheaded Woodpecker," 402; "Schooner Fairchild's Class" ("Schooner's Class"), 90, 285, 334, 401; "Serenade," 250, 400; "The Shadowy Crown," 171–2; "Silver Jemmy," 283–4; "Snake and Hawk," 124, 133; "The Sobbin' Women," 172–3, 174, 176, 195–6, 394; "The Story about the Anteater," 202, 396; "A Story by Angela Poe," 402; "Summer Thunder," 105, 386; "Take a Fellow Your Size," 394; *Tales before Midnight*, 335–7, 396, 400–3 *passim; Thirteen O'Clock*, 335–6, 394, 402, 403, 409; "This Bright Dream," 409; "The Tiger Smiles," 389; "Too Early Spring," 401; "A Tooth for Paul Revere," 333, 334; "The Treasure of Vasco Gomez," 229, 232, 399; "True Thomas," 175, 176, 195; "Two White Beans," 202–4; "Uriah's Son," 133, 390; "Venus Came Out of the Sea," 394; "We'll Never Be Rich," 402; "William Riley and the Fates," 409; "Witch's Spell," 402; "Working It Out," 383; "The Yankee Fox," 249, 253–4; "Young Lochinvar," 253, 401; "Young Lovyer," 402

Benét, Teresa Thompson (sister-in-law), 107

Benét, Thomas Carr (son), 211, 222, 223, 247, 260, 272; born in Paris, *September 28, 1926*, 180; characterized by SVB, 226–7; attends Phillips Exeter Academy, 18–19, 373

Benét, William Rose (brother), 3, 5, 7, 10, 38, 42, 49, 52, 72, 85, 102, 119, 136, 152, 161, 167, 178–9, 184–95 *passim*, 201, 202, 222, 224, 225, 229–30, 249, 250, 252, 287, 300, 377; plans to apply West Point, 5; to Yale instead, 5, 39, 43; graduates from Yale, Class of *1907S*, 5; literary and artistic talent, 5–6; begins literary career, 5–6; influence on SVB, 6, 13, 39; works for *Century*, 21, 56, 316; SVB emphasizes poetic debt to, 30, 310; describes father and brother, 31; gives his boyhood books to SVB, 33; sends him books and magazines from New York, 36–7; encourages SVB to submit verse to magazines, 37; arranges publication of his *Five Men and Pompey*, 42; in World War I, 66, 73; marries Elinor Wylie, 98; death of first wife, Teresa Thompson Benét, 107; their children, 107; active in establishing *Saturday Review of Literature*, 149; SVB writes of him in "Hands," 188; praises *John Brown's Body*, 198; death of Elinor Wylie, 225–6; SVB's affection for, 225–6; writes memoir about SVB, 380; identifies date of composition of SVB's "Flood-Tide," 384

Benét-Mercier machine gun, 8

Benicia (Cal.) Arsenal, 10, 14, 21, 35; description of, 2, 12; Benéts regret leaving there, 21–2

Berdan, John M., 47, 57, 62, 136

Berkeley (Cal.), 3, 21

Bethlehem (Pa.) Iron Works, 2

Birth of a Nation, 233

Bishop, John Peale, 58, 120, 187

Bizy (Normandy), Benéts spend summer of *1927* there, 192–3

Blackwood, Algernon, SVB reads, 34

Blake, William, 355–6

Bland, Mrs. Edith (Nesbit), SVB reads her fiction during boyhood, 34

Blast, 86

Bodenheim, Max, 37, 129

Bogart, Humphrey, gets first Broadway notices in play by John Farrar and SVB, 141

Bookman, 76, 105, 119, 315; serializes *The Beginning of Wisdom,* 96; John Farrar editor of, 135; SVB writes monthly drama column for, 138, 139, 140–1; writes articles for, 165–6

Book-of-the-Month-Club, 206–7, 213, 301; and *John Brown's Body,* 210, 211–12; and *Selected Works,* 366; and *Western Star,* 374

Boston (Mass.), 42, 217

Boston *Transcript,* 76, 214

Bottomley, Gordon, 42

Bowdoin College, 46

Boyd, James, 206; reviews *John Brown's Body,* 215

Boyd, Nancy. *See* Millay, Edna St. Vincent, 123

Bradford, Gamaliel, 184

Brady, Alice, 136

419

Brady, William A., 137, 233. *See also* SVB, Plays, *That Awful Mrs. Eaton*

Brady, William A., Jr., 136, 138. *See also* SVB, Plays, *Nerves*

Braithwaite, William S., 71, 76

Brandt, Carl, 109, 134, 138, 142, 148, 179, 187, 195–202 *passim*, 228, 232, 236, 241, 247, 248, 259, 269, 270, 273, 284, 293, 333, 334, 351, 353, 359–60; his admiration for SVB, 109; relationship with SVB, 110–25 *passim*, 156–62, 168, 176–7, 245–6, 249–50, 253, 285, 286–7, 292, 310, 338–9, 343, 348–9, 364–5, 366; visits Benéts in Paris, 191

Brandt, Erd N., 177

Brandt and Brandt. *See* Brandt, Carl

Brandt and Kirkpatrick, 109

Breadloaf Writers' Conference, 211, 305; Farrar active in its formation, 222; SVB lectures there, 222–3, 305

Brick Row Book Shop, 56, 390

Brickell, Herschel, 214, 272

Bridgman, Donald S., 39, 40; SVB's gratitude to, 40

Broch, Hermann, 330

Bromfield, Louis, 226, 366

Brooks, Gwendolyn, 330

Brooks, Van Wyck, 47, 292, 294, 317–18, 331, 364; SVB indebted to his portrait of Webster in *The Flowering of New England*, 292, 294; and National Institute of Arts and Letters, 317, 320, 324, 325, 326; SVB defends, 356

Broom, 86, 315

Broun, Heywood, 279

Brown University, SVB lectures at, 303

Browning, Robert, 153; influence on SVB, 32, 42, 129

Brunkhurst, William L., describes SVB as classmate at Summerville Academy, 29; his unpublished memoir about SVB, 380

Bryant, William Cullen, 220

Bryn Mawr College, 67; SVB lectures there, 303

Bryson, Lyman, 361

Buffalo, University of, SVB's correspondence with Paul Engle deposited at, 380

Burke, Kenneth, 330

Burr, Aaron, SVB uses in short story, 283–4

Butler, Nicholas Murray, 318, 324–6 *passim*. *See also* National Institute of Arts and Letters

Bynner, Witter, 37, 42, 130

Cabell, James Branch, 182; influence on SVB, 95, 113, 123, 228. *Beyond Life, The Certain Hour, From the Hidden Way, Jurgen*, 95

California, 106, 240. *See also* Benicia (Cal.) Arsenal; SVB, LIFE, to Hollywood; San Francisco

California, University of, 3, 21, 22, 47, 377

Calvert correspondence system, SVB studies by, 7, 13

Campbell, Donald M., Jr., 65, 100, 144, 191–2; SVB dedicates "The Golden Corpse" to, 149

Canada, 220; SVB writes "The Undefended Border" about, 360

Canby, Henry Seidel, 47, 49, 82, 88, 112, 126, 165, 191, 194, 312, 317–18, 342; urges SVB to enroll in Yale Graduate School, 81; his writing course at Yale, 83–5, 89, 94; active in establishing the *Saturday Review of Litera-*

420

ture, 149; anxious to see MSS of *John Brown's Body,* 192; writes introduction for college edition of *John Brown's Body,* 219; SVB's debt to, 310; and National Institute of Arts and Letters, 317–26 *passim;* rents Killingworth (Conn.) house to SVB, 347, 353

Canfield, Cass, 361

Cannes (France), SVB and wife visit Barrys there, 224–5

Carlisle (Pa.), 10, 19, 20, 38

Carmer, Carl, co-editor with SVB of Rivers of America series, 298, 305

Carr, Rachel (mother-in-law), 104, 108, 137, 147, 154, 165, 211, 223, 249

Carr, Rosemary. *See* Benét, Rosemary

Carr, Thomas (father-in-law), 165, 211, 223; death of, 249

Carter, Henry, 101, 105, 117; SVB rooms with him and John Carter in New Haven, 81, 83; shares Paris apartment with SVB and Stanley Hawks, 100, 105

Carter, John F., Jr., 67, 73, 81, 89, 100, 101, 184, 222; with SVB at North Haven (Me.) in *1917,* 67–8; SVB rooms with him and Henry Carter in New Haven, 81, 83; contributes to *S4N,* 86

Cassill, R. V., describes importance of SVB to him as writer, 306–7

Castro, Col. Frank, Jr., 317, 327

Cather, Willa, SVB's admiration for *The Professor's House,* 90, 248

Catholic World, criticizes *James Shore's Daughter,* 272–3

Century Club, 281, 317, 321, 325, 354

Century Magazine, 110, 114, 123, 148, 315, 335; WRB works for, 21, 56; publishes "The Hemp" when SVB is seventeen, 56

Chamberlain, John, reviews *James Shore's Daughter,* 272

Chambersburg (Pa.), 20

Channing, Edward, 182

Chaplin, Charles S. (Charlie), 235

Chase, Stuart, 330

Chesterton, G. K., read by SVB, 95, 182; *Magic,* 37

Chicago (Ill.), 108, 122, 125, 130, 147, 176, 223, 240, 249; SVB and Rosemary Carr married in, 104, 117–18

Chicago, University of, 104; SVB lectures there, 303

Chicago *Tribune,* 104

Child, Charles, 186, 291; illustrates *A Book of Americans,* 256–7

Chimaera, 56; SVB's publications in, 383

Chubb, Thomas C., 181, 186, 276, 368; reviews *Young People's Pride,* 113–14

Churchill, Winston, SVB reads his novels, 31

Civil War, 4, 8, 167, 182–7 *passim,* 205, 216, 218, 221; his father talks to SVB about, 10, 23–4; SVB visits terrain of, as boy, 20; reads *Battles and Leaders of Civil War* and *The Rebellion Record* during boyhood, 24; SVB regarded as authority on, by editors, 182

Clark, Eleanor, 330

Clement, Merrill, 62

Coates, Robert, 54

Cohn, Louis H., 338

College Verse, 307

Collier's, 170, 173, 333

Collins, Wilkie, SVB reads, 33

Colum, Padraic, 99

Columbus, Christopher, SVB's use of, in *Western Star*, 344, 345

Compton's Pictured Encyclopedia, SVB writes article on poetry for, 11

Conference on Science, Philosophy, and Religion, SVB comments on its conclusions, 357–8

Connecticut, SVB rents house there, 347, 348, 353; buys a house in, 364

"Conning Tower," 56, 259

Conrad, Joseph, 31, 94–5; SVB reads "Typhoon," 29

Considine, John W., Jr., 237, 239

Constant Nymph, promotion of, by Daniel Longwell, 206

Contemporary Verse, 71, 85, 385

Cook, Albert Stanburrough, 89, 91; SVB takes his graduate course in Theories of Poetry, 83

Corwin, Norman, 330, 368, 369, 370

Cosmopolitan, 117, 122, 123, 124, 138, 171, 296; SVB doubts its editorial judgment of "Silver Jemmy," 284

Coughlin, Rev. Charles E., 284

Council for Democracy, 360–4; its officers, 361–2; its objectives described by C. D. Jackson, 362

Country Gentleman, 174, 176, 195, 196, 200, 204, 249, 275–6, 285–6, 296, 333, 336, 342

Coward, Noel, 217

Coward, Thomas R., 301

Cowley, Malcolm, 330; recalls SVB's collegiate fame, 58

Crane, Hart, 315

Crane, Stephen, during boyhood SVB reads his poetry, 11

Cross, Wilbur L., 68, 82, 83, 88, 91, 94, 176, 316, 320; recommends SVB for Guggenheim Fellowship, 167–8

Culver Military Academy, SVB unwilling that son attend, 18

Cummings, E. E., 315

Damrosch, Walter, 320–31 *passim;* SVB's candidate for president of National Institute of Arts and Letters, 325

Dartmouth College, 46

Davenport, Basil, 265, 301, 380; edits SVB's *Selected Works*, 366

Davidman, Joy, 263

Davidson, Donald, SVB reviews his *The Tall Men*, 194–5

Davidson, Eugene, and Yale Series of Younger Poets, 264, 265

Davidson, John, SVB admires his poetry, 37

Davis, Elmer H., SVB reviews his *Giant Killer*, 312

Davis, Jefferson, 27, 183; Allen Tate praises SVB's portrait of, 214

Day, George Parmly, 261; invites SVB to become editor of Yale Series of Younger Poets, 260

de la Mare, Walter, 99

Deland, Margaret, 33

Delineator, 122, 240, 246, 255; SVB's first sale to, 117

Dell, Floyd, 153; *Moon Calf*, 111

Derby, J. Raymond, praises SVB as lecturer, 304

Deutsch, Babette, 129; reviews *Young Adventure*, 76

DeVane, William C., 84; describes Canby's writing course at Yale, 84, 85

DeVoto, Bernard, compares *Western Star* to *John Brown's Body*, 374

Dial, 76

Diary of a Southern Girl, used by SVB for *John Brown's Body*, 183

Dickens, Charles, 18

Doran, George H., 135, 141, 222, 227; becomes SVB's publisher, 151; SVB discusses *Western Star* with, 343, 344. *See also* George H. Doran Company

Dos Passos, John, 323, 395

Doubleday, Doran and Company, Inc., 209, 212, 219, 223, 241, 256, 270, 301, 343; becomes SVB's publishers after merger with George H. Doran Co., 205–6; SVB's sense of obligation to, 228–9; he shifts to Farrar and Rinehart, Inc., from, 291

Douglas, Melvyn, in SVB's *Dear Adolf*, 369

Douglas, Norman, SVB's admiration for, 95

Douglas, William, in Paris with SVB, 100

Dow, John W., principal of Summerville Academy when SVB attends, 28

Dreiser, Theodore, 314, 323

Drinkwater, John, 62; congratulates SVB for "King David," 130; *Twentieth Century Poetry*, 390

Dumas, Alexandre, SVB reads, 34

Eastman, Max, 37

Eaton, Peggy O'Neale, 136. *See also* SVB, Plays, *That Awful Mrs. Eaton*

Eliot, T. S., 251, 316; *The Waste Land*, 166

Elizabethan Club. *See* Yale University, Elizabethan Club

Elks' Magazine, 176, 196, 241, 275, 296, 336; importance to SVB's work, 171–2

England, 124, 138, 174, 179, 282, 284, 345; SVB visits brother and Elinor Wylie there, 193; he admires English Civil List for artists, 328; gives his English royalties to Spitfire Fund, 364; doctor forbids his wartime plane trip to, 371

Engle, Paul, 251, 255, 259, 278, 280, 306, 340, 360; SVB's importance to, 32, 309; *Worn Earth*, 260; SVB's care with correspondence to, 282; deposits SVB's letters at University of Buffalo, 380

Esquire, plans to publish fragment of *Western Star*, 349

Evarts, Effingham, 144; his friendship with SVB, 384

Everybody's, 68, 127, 334

Farjeon, Eleanor and Herbert, 401; their *Kings and Queens* a model for *A Book of Americans*, 256

Farrar, John C., 61, 72, 76, 84, 96, 109, 113, 119, 120, 141, 144, 151, 183–213 *passim*, 223, 227, 259, 277, 300, 366, 369; first meets SVB at Yale, 49–50, 53; serializes *The Beginning of Wisdom* in *Bookman*, 108; introduces SVB to Carl Brandt, 110; collaborates with SVB on two plays, 135–41; praises *John Brown's Body*, 198–9; his editorial skill with *John Brown's Body*, 206–9; and the Breadloaf Writers' Conference, 222; arranges publication of "The Barefoot

423

Farrar, John C. (*continued*) Saint," 228–9; with Stanley M. Rinehart establishes the firm of Farrar and Rinehart, Inc., 255; SVB's debt to, 310; persuades SVB to allow book publication of short stories, 336; active in Council for Democracy, 361; SVB grateful to, for *Selected Works*, 366; writes tribute to SVB, 377. *See also* Farrar and Rinehart, Inc.

Farrar, Margaret, long friendship with SVB, 339–40

Farrar and Rinehart, Inc., 300, 307, 343, 349, 366; becomes SVB's publisher, 291; SVB co-editor of its Rivers of America series, 298, 301–2, 305; SVB the firm's principal reader, 298, 300–2, 377; becomes Rinehart and Co., 398. *See also* Farrar, John C; Rinehart, Stanley M.

Farrell, James T., 311, 331–2, 341; with SVB, discusses role of writer in wartime, 356

Faulkner, William, 26, 306, 311, 323

Ferber, Edna, 206; *Show Boat*, 184; *A Peculiar Treasure*, 397

Ferguson, Sir Samuel, SVB reads poetry of, 37

Feuchtwanger, Leon, 211

Ficke, Arthur Davison, 42

Finkelstein, Louis, 357–8

Finletter, Thomas K., 354

Fisher, Dorothy Canfield, 207, 208

Fisk University, 307

Fitts, Dudley, 330; compares portions of *John Brown's Body* to *Aeneid*, 217

Fitts, Norman, 100; principal founder of *S4N*, 85–7

Fitzgerald, F. Scott, 54, 57, 78, 153, 187, 188, 316, 391; SVB conscious of *This Side of Paradise* as he writes *The Beginning of Wisdom*, 96; *This Side of Paradise*, 96, 205; "How To Live on $36,000 a Year," 134; Ellen Barry compares SVB to, 146; *Tender Is the Night*, 225, 271

Fletcher, John Gould, 129

Florida, 4, 27, 142, 146

Flowering of New England, and "The Devil and Daniel Webster," 292, 294

Foerster, Norman, SVB's respect for, 251

Fontanne, Lynn. *See* Lunt, Alfred

Forrest, Nathan Bedford, 183, 354

Fortune, 252, 254, 255; SVB offered an editorship of, 342

Four Brothers in Blue, used by SVB in *John Brown's Body* research, 182

Four Seas Company, publishes SVB's *Five Men and Pompey*, 42

France. *See* SVB LIFE, expatriation; SVB, Poetry, *John Brown's Body*

Frank, Glenn, 123; rejects "The Barefoot Saint," 114

Frank, Waldo, at Yale, 52

Frankford (Pa.) Arsenal, 2

Franklin, Jay. *See* Carter, John F., Jr.

Freeman, Douglas Southall, 311; praises accuracy of *John Brown's Body*, 182; *R. E. Lee*, 182; acknowledges debt to *John Brown's Body*, 218

Friedrich, Carl, 362

Frost, Robert, 99, 251, 315; SVB persuades friends to read work of, 149–50

Gammell, Valentine Mitchell, 298–9

Gannett, Lewis, 259; SVB a guest reviewer for, 311

Garland, Hamlin, 314–21 *passim*

Garrett, Oliver, SVB admires his Hollywood work, 238

Gay, R. M., describes SVB at Breadloaf, 223, 305

Geffen, Felicia, 394

George, Grace, 136–8 *passim*

George H. Doran Company, 154, 167, 201; SVB switches to, from Henry Holt and Co., 151; merges with Doubleday and Co., 205–6. *See also* Doran, George H.

Georgia, 27, 255. *See also* Augusta (Ga.) Arsenal

Gettysburg College, SVB lectures at, 303

Glasgow, Ellen, 318

Good Housekeeping, 175, 176; raises SVB's story price to $2,000, 342–3

Grant, Robert, 217

Grant, Ulysses S., 31, 183, 203

Griffith, D. W., 233–40; SVB's admiration for, 234

Groton School, 53

Guedalla, Philip, 184

Guggenheim Fellowship. *See* John Simon Guggenheim Memorial Foundation

Guthrie, Ramon, 86, 100, 191; reads first part of *John Brown's Body* in MS, 191

Hadden, Briton, 48, 84, 135, 391

Hale, Edward Everett, *The Man without a Country*, 297

Hamilton, Clayton, 319

Hampton, Wade, mentioned by SVB in short story, 203

Hand, Judge Learned, 354

Hansen, Harry, 294

Hanway, William, 86

Harding, Warren G., administration of, characterized by SVB, 128

Hardy, Thomas, 153

Harlan, John M. (Associate Justice), 281

Harlan, Mrs. John M. *See* Andrews, Ethel

Harper's, 110, 245–6, 335

Harper's Bazaar, 116, 125, 238, 244, 336, 365; rejects *Jean Huguenot* as serial, 108; buys and publishes *Young People's Pride*, 117, 122

Hart, Albert Bushnell, his *American History Told by Contemporaries* read by SVB during boyhood, 32

Hartman, Lee F., 245

Harvard *Advocate*, 58

Harvard University, 45, 47, 54, 101, 217, 242, 303

Hawks, Stanley, rents apartment in Paris with SVB and Henry Carter, 100

Hay, John, his life of Lincoln used by SVB, 182

Hayes, Helen, in SVB's *Dear Adolf*, 369

Hazard, Pierre (Tom), 240

Hecht, Ben, 153, 274

Heely, Allan V., 382–3; describes SVB at Yale, 51

Hemingway, Ernest, 187, 188, 323, 402; *The Sun Also Rises*, 184; SVB disagrees with, on role of writers during war, 356–7

Hendrick, Grace, 67, 68; effect on SVB's poetry, 79

Hendrick, Mrs. Ellwood, 67

Henry Holt and Company, 91, 94, 96–100 *passim*, 209–10; SVB writes them about Cabell's novels, 95; strong poetry list, 99; SVB switches to George H. Doran Co., 151

Hergesheimer, Joseph, 155

Hibbs, Ben, 172, 195, 249, 285–6; responsiveness to SVB's American folk stories, 171

Highlands (N.C.), 27, 148

Hill School, 53

History of the Great American Fortunes, SVB uses, in research for *James Shore's Daughter,* 222

Hitchcock Military Academy, 20, 22, 24, 27, 34, 39, 42; SVB attends, 15–19

Holden, William, in SVB's *Dear Adolf,* 369

Hollywood. See SVB, ATTITUDE TOWARD, Hollywood

Holmes, Oliver Wendell, 220

Holmes, Oliver Wendell (Justice), 217–18

Hopkins, Harry, 285

Horney, Col. Odus C., SVB's father corresponds with, 39, 92–3, 97, 106–7, 381

Hotchkiss School, 53

Hound and Horn, 217

House of Books, Ltd. See Cohn, Louis H.

Houseman, John, directs operetta by SVB and Douglas Moore, 352

Howard, Sidney, 144, 236, 315; urges SVB to show his short stories to Carl Brandt, 109–10

Howard University, 307

Howells, William Dean, 298, 332

Hoyt's Agency, employs SVB as copywriter, 78–87 *passim*

Hull, Henry, in SVB's *Dear Adolf,* 363

Hungary, SVB's *America* first book published there after liberation, 372

Huntington, Anna Hyatt, 316

Huntington, Archer M., 316, 321–7 *passim*

Huntington, Collis P., 316

Hutchens, John K., praises SVB's wartime radio scripts, 370

Huxley, Aldous, *Crome Yellow,* 122

Iliad, 344; SVB likens Civil War general to heroes of, 216

Indiana, 28

Indiana University, offers professorship to SVB, 342

Ingersoll, Ralph M., 254

Informer, SVB's admiration for, 238

Irving, Washington, 127, 274, 286; "The Devil and Tom Walker," 294; SVB adapts "The Legend of Sleepy Hollow" as operetta, 351

Iowa, State University of, 280, 303, 306; SVB as guest lecturer at, 251–2

Iowa State College, 303, 304

Jackson, Andrew, 136, 139. *See also* SVB, Plays, *That Awful Mrs. Eaton*

Jackson, C. D., 361–3, 367, 369; relationship with SVB, 362–3

James, William, compares Yale and Harvard, 45

Jefferson, Thomas, 198, 358; SVB's poem about, 258–9; SVB likens Roosevelt to, in short story, 283–4

John Simon Guggenheim Memorial Foundation, 167, 181, 204, 245, 321, 328; SVB awarded Fellowship, 176; Fellowship renewed for six months, 194; SVB's sense of debt to, 194

Johnson, Robert Underwood, 314, 316, 318, 321

Johnson, Samuel, 56

Johnston, Mary, SVB reads

historical novels of, during boyhood, 31

Jones, Andrew D. T. (cousin), 270, 305, 347, 348

Jones, Frederick S., 49–50, 53, 82, 83

Jones, John Beauchamp, SVB uses *A Rebel War Clerk's Diary* in research for *John Brown's Body*, 183

Joyce, James, 329, 358

Keats, John, SVB writes of, in "The Drug Shop," 56–7

Kennedy, Margaret, successful promotion of her *The Constant Nymph* by Daniel Longwell, 206

Killingworth (Conn.), SVB rents summer home at, 347, 348, 353

Kipling, Rudyard, 129; SVB reads, during boyhood, 32; likens his own intention with American folk tales to *Puck of Pook's Hill*, 250

Krutch, Joseph Wood, 323

Ladies' Home Journal, 124, 232, 333, 339; in *1928* pays SVB highest price for a story to that date, 203

LaFarge, Christopher, 234, 349–50, 373; compares SVB and MacLeish, 146; describes SVB's liberalism, 279–80, 281

Lamont, Mrs. Jean, 178, 180, 190, 192–3, 225

Landon, Alfred M., SVB bets against, in *1936* election, 281

Lardner, Ring, 316, 334

Laughton, Charles, and the touring company of *John Brown's Body*, 220

Laurents, Arthur, 330

Lawrence, T. E., admires *John Brown's Body*, 217

Lawrenceville School, 382

Lee, Robert E., 31, 183; Allen Tate praises SVB's portrait of, in *John Brown's Body*, 214; SVB's poem about, in *A Book of Americans*, 258; reviews a history of Lee family, 312

Lenihan, Winifred, in play by John Farrar and SVB, 136, 139

Leonard, William Ellery, competes for *Nation* poetry prize won by SVB, 129

Levin, Harry, 330

Lewis, Alfred Henry, play by SVB and John Farrar based in part on novel by, 136; *Peggy O'Neal*, 136

Lewis, Charlton M., 47, 77, 85; in *1919* estimates SVB's poetic talent and promise, 77

Lewis, Sinclair, 3, 43, 57, 184, 191, 217, 314; *Hike and the Aeroplane*, 34–5, 381; *Elmer Gantry*, 184; *Work of Art*, 270

Liberty, 133, 177, 296, 333

Library of Congress, 342; exhibition of SVB's work at, 371–2

Lie, Jonas, 320

Life, 205; publishes SVB's *Listen to the People*, 363–4

Lincoln, Abraham, 196, 214, 233, 275, 279, 293, 298; SVB's poem about, for *A Book of Americans*, 258; New York *Times* compares SVB's America United Rally speech to words of, 361; SVB writes Lincoln's Birthday radio script, 372. *See also* SVB, Movies, *Abraham Lincoln*

Lindbergh, Charles A., 192, 275

Lindsay, Howard, in radio production of "Listen to the People," 363

Lindsay, Vachel, 36–7, 129, 287, 304; Moon-Poems, 36; "The Congo," 36–7. *See also* SVB, Poetry, "Do You Remember, Springfield?" 289

Lippmann, Walter, 318

Literary Digest, 85, 105

Literary Guild, 207

Literary History of the United States, 128

Literary Review, 107, 122, 149, 214

Locke, Florence, 304, 404

London *Times*, 210, 215

Long, Huey P., SVB likens him to Aaron Burr in short story about Jefferson, 283–4

Long, Ray, 117–25 *passim*

Longfellow, Henry Wadsworth, 127, 215, 220, 293, 355; "Evangeline," 215; "Hiawatha," 215; "Paul Revere's Ride," 293

Longwell, Daniel, 242, 252, 256, 268, 270–3 *passim*, 291; a major factor in the success of John Brown's Body, 205–6, 210, 219; tribute to, by Edna Ferber, 206; SVB discusses *Western Star* with, 343–4; SVB's debt to, 310

Lorimer, George Horace, 116, 285

Lovett, Robert A., 354

Lovett, Robert Morss, reviews *John Brown's Body*, 214

Lowell, Amy, 37

Lowell, James Russell, 127, 220

Lowell, Robert, 330

Luce, Henry, 84, 205, 291, 362

Lunt, Alfred, 340, 372; SVB working on Easter show for, at time of death, 372, 373

Lyman, Dean B., Jr., 388; SVB explains his difficulties with *Jean Huguenot* to, 106

Lyon, Irving W., 383; recalls SVB's poetic fame among Yale classmates, 56

McClure, Robert, 367, 381, 400; letters to, 154, 202, 241, 247, 248, 253, 277; describes nature of SVB's expatriation, 186–8; SVB discusses wealthy Americans with, 266; congratulates SVB on "A Death in the Country," 400

McCullers, Carson, 330

Macdonald, Letitia, SVB uses memoirs of, in *John Brown's Body* research, 183

MacDowell, Mrs. Edward, 160, 162. *See also* MacDowell Colony

MacDowell Colony, 223; SVB a colonist in *1925*, 158–63

MacDowell Fellowships, 322

McGill, Ralph, impact of *John Brown's Body* on, 218

McHugh, Vincent, 330

MacKenna, Kenneth, 136

McKenna, Stephen, 111

Maclean's, 245

MacLeish, Archibald, 48, 52–8 *passim*, 72, 84, 109, 144, 181, 186, 187, 252, 261, 262, 265, 275, 277, 299, 311, 340, 342, 354, 370; LaFarge compares SVB to, 146; SVB praises Frost's work to, 149–50; *Nobodaddy*, 166; *The Pot of Gold*, 166; *Conquistador*, 251, 397; and the National Institute of Arts and Letters, 318, 320; urges SVB to become Consultant on Poetry at the Library of Congress, 342; SVB defends, 356

McMaster, John Bach, 182

Macmillan Company, SVB reads MSS for, 301

McNutt, Paul V., 280

Maddocks, Gladys L., "Stephen Vincent Benét: A Bibliography," 375

Mahon, Agnes (great-aunt), 107, 226

Malory, Sir Thomas, 89

Mangan, James Clarence, SVB reads his poems during boyhood, 37

Marlowe, Christopher, 88; *Tamburlaine the Great*, 85

Marquand, John P., 13, 78, 378, 393; praises SVB's magazine fiction, 169

Marryat, Frederick, SVB reads during boyhood, 31

Masefield, John, 32, 62, 176; recommends SVB for Guggenheim Fellowship, 168

Mason, Lawrence, 47, 55, 62

Massachusetts, 348

Massey, Raymond, 220, 360–1, 369, 372

Masters, Edgar Lee, 195, 315, 330; praises "King David," 130

Matthiessen, F. O., 128, 131, 288

Maule, Harry E., 244

Melville, Herman, 319, 323, 355–6

Mencken, H. L., 86, 316, 323, 348; reviews *The Beginning of Wisdom*, 96

Merchant, Frank, cites SVB's fair-mindedness, 263

Merz, Charles, 354

Metropolitan, 122, 127, 133, 296, 334; SVB's first sale to, 117

Michigan, 218

Michigan, University of, SVB a judge for the Avery Hopwood Awards, 307

Middlebury College, SVB lectures at, 303

Mielziner, Jo, 141

Millay, Edna St. Vincent, 101, 123, 176, 315, 340, 368; recommends SVB for Guggenheim Fellowship, 168;

congratulates him on *John Brown's Body*, 217

Miller, Max, 238

Millis, Walter, 84, 354, 361

Milton, John, 363; SVB quotes, on role of writer, 356

Minneapolis (Minn.), SVB lectures at, 303, 304

Mitchell, Margaret, *Gone with the Wind*, 23, 321, 379

Mitchell, Sidney K., importance of, to SVB at Yale, 58

Moe, Henry Allen, 194; described by SVB, 167

Monroe, Harriet, congratulates SVB for *John Brown's Body*, 217

Moore, Douglas, 100, 106, 126, 138, 144, 161, 181, 186, 222, 299, 340, 377–8; introduces SVB to Richard and Alice Lee Myers in Paris, 101; collaborations with SVB, 350–2, 359

Moore, Emily (Mrs. Douglas), 100, 106, 138, 144, 186, 299

Moore, Marianne, 330

Morison, Samuel Eliot, praises *John Brown's Body*, 182, 218; *The Growth of the American Republic*, 182

Morison, Stanley, 210

Morley, Christopher, 85, 206

Morris, William, 89, 129, 153; SVB describes his "derivation" from, 32; "The Haystack in the Floods," 33

Moses, Robert, 282, 330

Mott, Frank Luther, 303

Mowrer, Edgar A., 367

Moyle, Gilbert, 42

Mumford, Lewis, 315

Munsey's, 105; first magazine to buy SVB's fiction, 85

Murray, Pauli, 296, 309, 379

Myers, Alice Lee (Mrs. Richard), 101, 106, 144, 178, 186, 192, 299

Myers, Gustavus, SVB reads his

Myers, Gustavus (*continued*)
History of the Great American Fortunes as background for *James Shore's Daughter,* 266

Myers, Richard, 101, 106, 109, 144, 186, 192, 249, 250, 299, 351

Napoleon, 297. *See also* SVB, Short Stories, "The Curfew Tolls"

Nathan, Robert, 120, 147, 180, 193, 218, 278–9, 288, 337

Nation, 76; SVB wins poetry prize of, 129–30

National Institute of Arts and Letters, 297, 313, 314–32, 355–6, 394, 404; awards SVB its Gold Medal, 374

Nebraska, 72

Neihardt, John G., SVB's admiration for *The Song of the Indian Wars,* 195

Nesbit, E. *See* Bland, Mrs. Edith (Nesbit)

Neuilly (France), 201, 204–15 *passim,* 223, 225, 233; SVB describes apartment there, 190–1; Benéts rent house in, 194

New Deal, 68, 281, 282, 320, 354. *See also,* SVB, ATTITUDE TOWARD, politics, Franklin D. Roosevelt

New Hampshire, University of, 261

New Haven (Conn.), 347; SVB writes "Tercentenary Ode" for, 341–2

New Jersey, 73, 369

New Masses, SVB angrily compares *Saturday Evening Post* to, 285

New Republic, 56, 71, 105, 126, 132, 152, 214, 232, 273; its publication of "Winged

Man" in *1915* the professional debut of SVB, 37–8

New York City, 47, 49, 53, 76, 97, 107, 119, 120, 136, 159–69 *passim,* 181–90 *passim,* 205, 210, 222, 224, 233, 242, 247, 255, 262, 268, 276, 280, 284, 298, 300, 315, 317, 334, 338; effect on SVB's poetry, 78–83 *passim. See also* SVB, ATTITUDE TOWARD, New York

New York *Evening Post,* 83, 85. *See also Literary Review*

New York *Herald Tribune,* 26, 214, 259, 305, 354; SVB reviews for, 246, 310–13. *See also New York Herald Tribune Books*

New York Herald Tribune Books, 214, 272; publishes literary profiles by SVB and wife, 378, 395, 402, 405

New York *Post,* 273

New York Public Library, 256, 266, 349; SVB's poem about, 399

New York State. *See* Watervliet (N.Y.) Arsenal

New York *Times,* 134, 272, 338, 339, 354, 361, 370; publishes SVB's "Nightmare at Noon," 340

New York Times Book Review, 272

New York *Tribune,* 56

New York University, SVB lectures at, 303

New York *Sun,* 272

New Yorker, 177, 287, 290, 291, 303, 340

Nichols, Dudley, SVB praises his Hollywood work, 238

North American Review, 214, 272

North Carolina, 27, 148

North Haven (Me.), 67–8; SVB uses, in short story, 68

Northampton (Mass.), 85
Noyes, Alfred, 32

O'Brien, Edward J., 169–70, 174, 175–7, 197, 250; SVB's estimate of, 176
O. Henry Memorial Award, 134, 174, 175, 197, 250, 294, 365
Odyssey, Daniel Longwell likens *Western Star* to, 344
Office of War Information, 367; SVB writes *America* for, 372
Ohio State University, 47
Oliver, Egbert S., corresponds with SVB, 382
Ordnance, Department of, 1, 12, 25, 31, 66, 197; improvement of, by SVB's grandfather, 4
Osborn, Paul, and *John Brown's Body*, 220
Osterweis, Rollin G., *Three Centuries of New Haven, 1638–1938*, 407
Outlook, 215

Parabalou, 101, 105; SVB's poetry in, 388
Paris, 87, 91, 100, 109, 117–26 *passim*, 147, 178, 180–230 *passim*, 249, 256, 257, 270, 338, 378, 388; SVB's feeling for, 97–9; reads *Peter Whiffle*, 98; describes city to Phelps Putnam, 100; effect of, on SVB, 101. *See also* SVB, ATTITUDE TOWARD, expatriation
Parker, Dorothy, 334
Parrington, Vernon Louis, 153–4
Payson and Clarke (publishers), William Rose Benét works for, 226
Peace Dale (R.I.), 33, 231–2, 240, 242, 254, 268, 280, 377. *See also* Rhode Island

Peattie, Donald Culross, 288
P.E.N. Club, 191
Pennsylvania, 256, 257, 338. *See also* Carlisle (Pa.)
Pennsylvania, University of, 47
Peterborough (N.H.), 158, 160. *See also* MacDowell Colony
Phelps, William Lyon, 47, 56, 62, 262, 316, 325, 327; congratulates SVB for *John Brown's Body*, 217; describes SVB, 145; SVB's tribute to, 90; defended by SVB, 57
Phi Beta Kappa, 40, 104, 217, 240, 303
Philadelphia (Pa.), SVB considers buying house there, 222
Phillips Andover Academy, 382
Phillips Exeter Academy, 218; SVB lectures there, 303; son attends, 19, 373
Pictorial Review, 116, 156–64 *passim*, 246, 253
Pierce, Frederick E., SVB takes graduate course of, at Yale, 83
Poetry, 76, 86, 153, 217
Poetry Journal, publishes "After Pharsalia," 42
Poetry Society, 119; SVB shares annual award of, with Carl Sandburg, 116–17
Porter, Quincy, 86, 100
Potter, Stephen, death of, 72
Pound, Ezra, 314, 323
Princeton University, 47, 54, 58
Proust, Marcel, SVB reads in French, 184
Providence (R.I.) *Evening Bulletin*, interviews SVB, 335, 391
Pryor, Mrs. Roger A., SVB uses reminiscences of, in *John Brown's Body* research, 183

Pulitzer Prize, 297, 319, 328, 377; to *John Brown's Body*, 229–30; to *Western Star*, 374

Putnam, Phelps, 54, 84, 93, 95, 100, 194; urged by SVB to apply for Guggenheim Fellowship, 176

Pyle, Howard, 35; illustrates SVB's "Snake and Hawk," 124

Reader's Digest, 202

Redbook, 122, 124, 127, 133, 171, 296, 333, 365; SVB questions editorial judgment of, 286–7

Redfield, Robert, describes SVB in *1918*, 74

Reed, Edward Bliss, 217, 227, 261; lends SVB money, 91, 100, 134

Reed, Robert H., 171, 195, 249; recalls *Country Gentleman's* purchase of "The Sobbin' Women," 172

Rhode Island, 33, 218, 241, 257, 261, 267, 281, 284, 333, 347. *See also* Peace Dale (R.I.)

Richmond (Va.), 292

Rinehart, Alan, 212, 256

Rinehart, Mary Roberts, 402; *The Bat*, 167

Rinehart, Stanley M., 151, 167, 176, 256, 366. *See also* Farrar and Rinehart, Inc.

Robin Hood, 13; SVB's boyhood poem about, 35

Robinson, Edwin Arlington, 10, 160–2, 195, 206–7, 210; *Tristram*, 195, 206–7, 210; comments on *John Brown's Body*, 209

Roche, Arthur Somers, 73

Rochester, University of, SVB offered librarianship of, 342

Rock Island (Ill.) Arsenal, 2

Rollins, Carl Purington, 72

Roosevelt, Franklin Delano, 253, 255, 275, 278, 280–1, 320, 331, 360–1, 363, 373; SVB compares abuse of, to contemporary abuse of Lincoln, 279; "Silver Jemmy" a fictional parallel between him and Lincoln, 283–4; reads SVB's "Prayer" at United Nations ceremonies, 372

Roosevelt, Theodore, 5

Roosevelt Medal, awarded to SVB, 265, 269–70

Rossetti, Dante Gabriel, SVB reads during boyhood, 37

Rossiter, Lawrence F., 388; SVB describes Paris to, 98–9

Rosten, Norman, 145, 263, 309, 330, 368, 370

Rukeyser, Muriel, 263, 288, 330; gratitude to SVB, 264; *Theory of Flight*, 264

Runkle, Bertha, SVB reads her *The Helmet of Navarre* during boyhood, 33

Rural Electrification Agency (REA), SVB collaborates with Douglas Moore on documentary film for, 359

Russell Sage College, SVB lectures at, 303

Sacco-Vanzetti case, 187, 192, 276

St. Augustine (Fla.), SVB lectures at, 303

St. Mark's School, 53, 68

St. Nicholas Magazine, 29, 37; awards prize to SVB's "The Regret of Dives," 30; publishes his "A Song of the Woods," 35–6

St. Paul's School, 53

San Francisco (Cal.), 2, 15, 22, 34

San Rafael (Cal.), 18. *See also* Hitchcock Military Academy

Sanborn, Robert Alden, 42
Sandburg, Carl, 99, 182, 311, 318; *Smoke and Steel,* 117
Sandford, Frank Leslie, 206
Saturday Evening Post, 21, 116, 134, 169–71 *passim,* 250, 283, 292–5 *passim,* 315, 333, 334, 342, 349, 356, 365, 372; SVB's first sale to, 246; his relationship with, 253–4, 284–5, 379; rejects SVB's "Into Egypt," 338–9
Saturday Review of Literature, 149, 177, 192, 229, 232, 242, 246; SVB as reviewer for, 26, 166, 310–13; offered editorship of, 342; its Memorial Issue to him, 374. *See also* Maddocks, Gladys L.
Scarsdale (N.Y.), 98–125 *passim*
Schenck, Joseph M., 240
Schildkraut, Joseph, in SVB's *Dear Adolf,* 369
Schlesinger, Arthur M., Jr., 330
Schramm, Wilbur, 306
Schulman, Marshall, 370
Scott, Winfield T., interviews SVB, 355
Scribner's, 110
secession, 86, 315
Sell, Henry, 108, 110, 116; rejects *Jean Huguenot,* buys *Young People's Pride,* 116–17
Semple, Ellen. *See* Barry, Ellen
Senior societies. *See* Yale University, senior societies
Sessions, Roger, 86
Seven Arts, 56; SVB's poems in, 383
S4N, 85–9, 94, 105; origins of name, 86
Shakespeare, William, 6, 71–2, 157–8, 264; *Romeo and Juliet,* 72; *Hamlet,* 264; *Much Ado about Nothing,* 341
Shapiro, Karl, 330

Shaw, Irwin, 330
Sheean, Vincent, 219; describes Rosemary Carr, 104
Shelley, Percy Bysshe, 55, 79; "Prometheus Unbound," 151
Shelley Award, SVB a judge for, 307
Sherman, William T., 26, 27, 203
Shubert, Lee, 135
Shuster, George, 361
Simonds, Bruce, 100
Skull and Bones. *See* Yale University, senior societies
Sloane, William, 300, 301; admiration for SVB, 302
Smart Set, 85, 86
Smith, C. Aubrey, 136
Smith, Lewis Worthington, 42
Smoke, 261, 298–9
Société Hotchkiss et Cie, Laurence V. Benét managing director of, 5
South Carolina, 27
Spalding, Albert, 320
Spanish Civil War, 355
Speyer, Leonora, 129
Stafford, Jean, 330
Stallings, Lawrence, 78, 206; *What Price Glory,* 140
Steele, Wilbur Daniel, 134
Stegner, Wallace, 368; describes SVB as lecturer, 251, 348
Stein, Gertrude, 187
Steinbeck, John, 323
Stevenson, Burton, 130, 395
Stewart, Donald Ogden, 120, 181
Stonington (Conn.), 372, 374; SVB buys house there, 364
Stout, Rex, 359
Stout, Wesley, his editorial objections to "Schooner's Class," 285
Strachey, Lytton, 184
Strong, L. A. G., praises "The Mountain Whippoorwill," 148

433

Stuart, Jesse, and "The Ballad of William Sycamore," 127
Swarthmore College, Stephanie Benét attends, 373
Swing, Raymond Gram, 361
Sudler, Culbreth, 383; his characterization of SVB as undergraduate, 54, 55
Summerville Academy, 28, 29, 38, 43, 53; faculty, 28; principal, 28; academic standards, 28, 38–9; SVB graduates from, 39
Survey, 214

Taft School, 53
Taggard, Genevieve, 129
Tarkington, Booth, 134
Tate, Allen, 129, 330; reviews *John Brown's Body*, 214
Taylor, Deems, 320
Tennyson, Alfred Lord, 56, 89
Texas, 27
Thackeray, William M., 31; *Henry Esmond*, 34, 154
Thomas, Augustus, 319
Thomas, Norman, 247, 276
Thompson, Dorothy, 279, 399
Time, 48, 84, 135; SVB writes column for, 134–5, 391; his attitude toward, 362; praises SVB's *Dear Adolf* radio scripts, 371
Tinker, Chauncey Brewster, 47, 56, 73, 90–1; writes foreword for SVB's *Young Adventure*, 72; congratulates SVB for *John Brown's Body*, 217
Train, Arthur, 73–4, 320–31 *passim*, 364
Transatlantic, 359
transition, 86, 315
Trollope, Anthony, SVB's fondness for work of, 34, 184
Turner, Frederick Jackson, 348
Tuttle, Emerson H., 368
Twain, Mark, 127, 185, 319

United States Military Academy, West Point, 1, 4, 5, 8, 25; SVB hoped to attend, 8, 39; he lectures at, 8, 303; his children baptized there, 8; former chaplain of, conducts committal service at his funeral, 8
Untermeyer, Louis, 42, 76, 165
Untermeyer, Richard, 165

Van Doren, Mark, 153
Van Doren, Irita, 311
Van Vechten, Carl, *Peter Whiffle*, 98
Vanamee, Mrs. William, 317, 325–7 *passim*, 404
Vance, Arthur T., 156, 160
Variety, 237
Vassar College, 3
Vermont, 211
Vetluguin, Valdemar, 286
Villard, Oswald Garrison, his *John Brown, 1800–1859* used by SVB in research, 182
Virginia, 174, 348
Vorpal Blades. *See* Yale University, Vorpal Blades

Walker, Margaret, 263; her gratitude to SVB, 264
Wallace, Edgar, SVB's search for his fiction, 184
Walpole, Hugh, 111
Wanamaker Book Fair, 119
Warren, Charles, 326
Warren, Emily B., writes SVB about portrait of her father in *John Brown's Body*, 216
Warren, Gen. G. K., 216
Washington, D.C., 2, 4, 280, 368, 371; SVB serves there during World War I, 73–4
Washington, George, 275–6; SVB's short story about, 282–3
Watervliet (N.Y.) Arsenal, 1, 81, 91, 92, 105

Wavell, Field Marshal Sir Archibald P., quotes from *John Brown's Body*, 220

Weaver, John V. A., 120

Webster, Daniel, 293, 294–5, 360. *See also* SVB, Short Stories, "The Devil and Daniel Webster"

Weeks, Edward, and "Litany for Dictatorships," 290

Weismiller, Edward, describes SVB, 145; his sense of obligation to SVB, 262–3; *The Deer Come Down*, 262

Wellesley College, SVB lectures at, 246, 303

Wells, H. G., 34

Welty, Eudora, 330

Wescott, Glenway, 369

West Point. *See* United States Military Academy, West Point

Whipple, Leon, 214

Whitman, Walt, 208, 215, 288, 289, 319, 359. *See also* SVB, Poems, "Ode to Walt Whitman"

Widdemer, Margaret, 344

Wilder, Thornton, 54, 57, 84

Williams, Tennessee, 330

Williams College, 46; SVB lectures there, 303

Willkie, Wendell, 354, 360–1; SVB ironically likens himself to, 359

Wilson, Edmund, 58

Wilson College, 303; SVB interviewed at, 379

Wiman, Dwight D., 136

Wirz, Henry, SVB explains his characterization of, in *John Brown's Body*, 216–17

Wolf's Head. *See* Yale University, senior societies

Wolfe, Thomas, 311, 323

Woman Wrapped in Silence, SVB predicts success of, 301

Woman's Home Companion, 253, 333

Wood, Clement, 129

Woolley, Monty, 85, 136, 217

Worcester, Dean K., 383

World War I, 37, 64–71 *passim*, 113, 356; SVB rejected for military service, 66, 73; effect of, on his poetry, 69, 78; memorizes eye-chart, 73; honorably discharged, 73; describes his three days in army, 73

World War II, 218–19, 220, 353, 354–74 *passim*

Writers War Board, 355, 359

Wyeth (N.C.), 35; illustrates SVB's "Snake and Hawk," 124

Wylie, Elinor (sister-in-law), 98, 114, 193; death of, 225–6

Yale Alumni Weekly, 388

Yale Book of Student Verse, 1910–1919, SVB a co-editor of, 85

Yale Club of New York, 134

Yale Graduate School, 81, 83, 97, 126; SVB applies for admission to, 77; withdraws application, 81; reapplies, 81–2; enrolls in, *October 1919*, 82–3; curriculum, 83; his reaction to, 88; its encouragement of his talent, 91; awards M.A. to him, 91; awards him traveling fellowship for *1920–21*, 91, 97

Yale Literary Magazine, 14, 51–4 *passim*, 59–63 *passim*, 70, 75, 114; his editorials in, 65, 70–1; reviews *Romeo and Juliet* for, 72; SVB's *1915–16* publications in, 383

Yale Record, 51–4 *passim*, 60–6 *passim*, 82, 85, 103, 383

Yale Review, 68, 76, 82, 85, 190; publishes SVB's "The

435

Yale Review (continued)
    Power of the Written
    Word," 404
Yale Series of Younger Poets,
    72, 260–5, 298, 307, 349,
    407
Yale University, 39, 81, 112–
    14 *passim*, 136, 144, 165,
    181, 234, 266, 316, 347, 348,
    368, 377–84 *passim*, 388;
    WRB enrolls in, and grad-
    uates from Sheffield Scien-
    tific School, Class of *1907S*,
    5; SVB takes entrance exams,
    June 1915, 28; flunks, is
    tutored, passes make-ups, 28,
    38, 39–40, 43, 48; writes
    satiric poems, *The Songs of
    Dear Old Yale*, 63, 384; re-
    ceives B.A., *June 1919*, 76–
    7; lectures at, 303; receives
    honorary degree from, 305.
        Faculty, 45, 47, 54–5, 57–
    64 *passim*, 73, 75, 82, 85, 91,
    217, 261, 310; library, 45,
    63, 381; classmates' tribute
    to SVB, 45, 382; English De-

partment, 46, 47, 53, 57, 82,
    83, 85, 90, 167, 261; literary
    renaissance, 46–8 *passim*, 53–
    4, 60–2, 85–91, 112; Pierson
    Hall, 48–52 *passim;* senior
    societies, 48–55 *passim*, 62,
    63, 75, 383, 384; "Daily
    Themes," 57; Vorpal Blades,
    64, 384; Connecticut Hall,
    69, 74; ROTC, 69, 96; fac-
    ulty estimate of SVB, 77;
    effect of Yale on SVB's
    poetry, 83; Alpha Delta Phi,
    136, 303, 383; Elizabethan
    Club, 383–4.
        See also Yale Graduate
    School; *Yale Literary Maga-
    zine; Yale Record*
Yale University Press, 72, 85,
    209, 260. *See also* Yale Series
    of Younger Poets
Yardley, Herbert A., 73
Yeats, William Butler, 62, 217
Young, Stark, 217
Youth: Poetry of Today, 71;
    SVB's publications in,
    385